Ancient
Gnosticism

Ancient Gnosticism

Traditions and Literature

Birger A. Pearson

Fortress Press
Minneapolis

To Karen, my suzugos *for fifty years*

Library of Congress Cataloging-in-Publication Data

Pearson, Birger Albert.
Ancient Gnosticism : traditions and literature / Birger A. Pearson.
    p. cm.
    Includes index.
    ISBN-13: 978–0–8006–3258–8 (alk. paper)
    ISBN-10: 0–8006–3258–3 (alk. paper)
    1. Gnosticism. I. Title.
BT1390.P37 2007
299'.932—dc22   2006101605

Manufactured in the U.S.A.
11   10   09   4   5   6   7   8   9   10

Contents

Contents

Maps and Illustrations

Preface

THIS BOOK HAS BEEN IN THE MAKING for some forty-five years. I was a student at the Lutheran seminary in Berkeley, California, when the *Gospel of Thomas* was published in 1959 (Leiden: Brill; New York: Harper & Brothers). It was published with the Coptic text and English translation on facing pages. The Coptic alphabet seemed to be familiar (resembling Greek uncial letters), but there were some extra characters. I could see a few Greek words, but the rest was *not* "all Greek to me." Since the *Gospel of Thomas* was an interesting text, and part of a "library" of what promised to be interesting texts, I resolved to study Coptic. So when I began my doctoral studies at Harvard in 1962 I began my study of Coptic with Professor Thomas Lambdin.

Then, during the academic year 1963–64, Professor Gilles Quispel of Utrecht was a visiting professor at Harvard. He gave a lecture course on Gnosticism and also led a small seminar of students who had some knowledge of Coptic. There were four of us, and Quispel led us through the Coptic text of the *Apocryphon of James,* one of the tractates in the "Jung Codex" (Nag Hammadi Codex I,2). Since it was not yet published, we were obliged to hand back our copies of the text when the seminar was over. (That trac-tate was first published in 1968.) I was "hooked."

My doctoral dissertation, "The *pneumatikos-psychikos* Termi-nology in 1 Corinthians: A Study in the Theology of the Corinthian Opponents of Paul and its Relation to Gnosticism," had a chapter devoted to the study of all of the evidence then available on how the Gnostics interpreted Genesis 2:7. The dissertation was defended in April, 1968 (published in 1973), when I was then on the faculty of the Department of Religion at Duke University. (I moved to the University of California at Santa Barbara the following year.) In the Spring of 1968 Professor James M. Robinson visited Duke and recruited Professor Orval Wintermute, Wintermute's student John D. Turner, and myself to become part of a team of scholars constituting the "Coptic Gnostic Library" project, a research project based at the Institute for Antiquity and Christianity at the Claremont Graduate School in Claremont, California. Robinson, a professor at Claremont, was the Institute's director and director of the project. The project's goal was to publish a critical edition and English translation of all of the Coptic codices discovered in 1945 near Nag Hammadi, Egypt. I was given a set of thirty-six black-and-white photographs of the fragments of Nag Hammadi Codex X, and spent part of the summer of 1968 working with others in Claremont on the project. After many years of work, which included visits to the Coptic Museum in Old Cairo where the manuscripts are kept, my edition, *Nag Hammadi Codices IX and X,* was finally published by Brill in 1981. Some years later I edited the last of the sixteen volumes to appear in the "Coptic Gnostic Library" series, *Nag Hammadi Codex VII* (Brill, 1996).

Over the years, most of my research and publication activity has been focused on the study of Gnosticism, Egyptian Christian-ity, and Coptic texts, Gnostic and non-Gnostic. A couple of years ago, Michael West, Editor-in-Chief of Fortress Press (and a former student of mine at UC Santa Barbara), asked me to produce an introductory book on Gnosticism for the press. I agreed, and this book is the result. I want to thank him for that invitation, and for his encouragement during the preparation of this book.

I also want to acknowledge here with thanks the cooperation of others at Fortress Press: Tim Larson, Assistant Managing Editor, who served as copy-editor of the book, and Neil Elliott, Acquisitions Editor, who made some useful suggestions and saw the book through the press. I also want to thank Lisa Karnan, a doctoral candidate at the Claremont Graduate University, for preparing the indices, and Dennis R. MacDonald, Director of the Institute for Antiquity and Christianity at Claremont, for facilitating the preparation of the indices.

Over the years my wife Karen has prodded me to write a book that might be of interest to "ordinary people." I have finally taken her admonition to heart, and sincerely hope that this book will live up to her expectations. I lovingly dedicate this book to her.

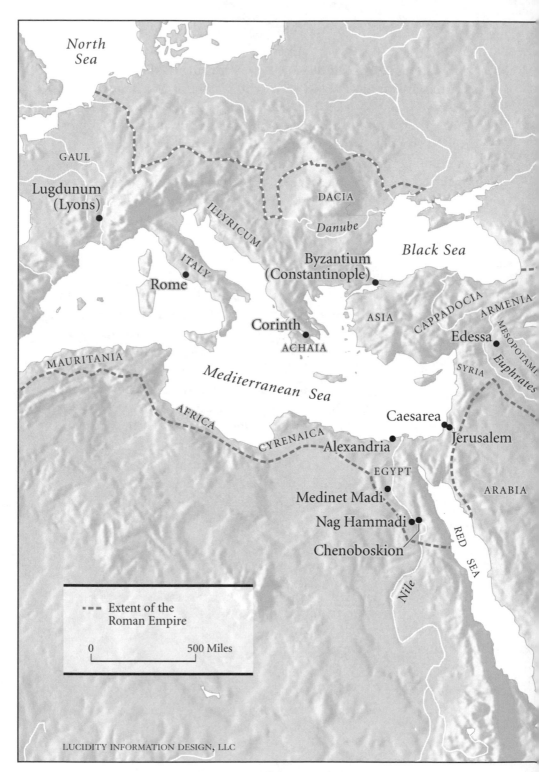

Map of the World of Ancient Gnosticism

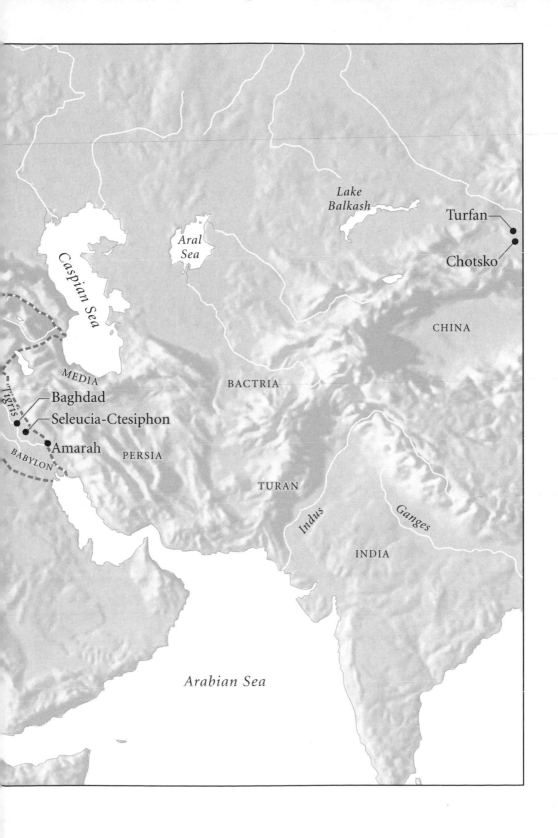

Introduction

WHILE THERE ARE OTHER INTRODUCTORY BOOKS on ancient Gnosticism, there is, to my knowledge, no introductory work that surveys the entirety of the primary literary evidence and introduces the individual texts. This book is intended to provide such an introduction, and it is my hope that it will also provide its readers with the incentive to study the primary texts. The primary sources, after all, are the most essential evidence for the study of ancient Gnosticism.

This book is designed for the nonspecialist reader, and for college and university students engaged in the study of ancient religious history. I hope that it will be found useful as a textbook for courses in ancient Gnosticism. I have not provided any footnotes, something that might prove irritating to scholars, but I do provide at the end some suggestions for further reading.

In the first chapter I discuss the problem of how to define "Gnosticism" and delineate its essential features. It has become fashionable among some scholars today to call into question the utility of the term "Gnosticism" in historical scholarship. So I undertake not only to defend the use of the term in scholarship, but also to define

Gnosticism and delineate the parameters of what sorts of historical evidence can usefully be included in the use of the term.

The word "Gnosticism" is based on the Greek word *gnōstikos* ("gnostic") applied in antiquity to people who claimed a special kind of religious "knowledge" (*gnōsis*), and for whom that knowledge served as the basis of their salvation. I try to define what sort of "knowledge" it is that is the key ingredient in "Gnosticism." The approach that I take to the evidence is that of a critical historian of ancient religions.

The earliest evidence we have for ancient Gnosticism comes from the first century of our era. Since no religion or religious movement takes shape in a vacuum, I discuss something of the cultural and religious environment of the first-century Graeco-Roman world. I argue that ancient Platonism, on the one hand, and ancient Judaism, on the other, provided the most ancient Gnostic teachers and prophets with the ingredients they used in creating a religion of salvation based on gnosis.

I also discuss in that first chapter the sources for our knowledge of Gnosticism. These sources are basically of two kinds: reports about Gnostic teachers and groups written by some of the early church fathers and other opponents of the Gnostics, and primary sources produced by the Gnostics themselves. Our fund of primary sources has grown dramatically with the discovery of Coptic Gnostic manuscripts in Egypt, principally the thirteen papyrus codices discovered in 1945 near Nag Hammadi, Egypt, but others as well. Of the forty-four different tractates in the Nag Hammadi collection, plus those in the Berlin Codex (discussed below), forty of them are introduced in this book. The other six are not "Gnostic" in any sense of the word, and so have been omitted from consideration here. The Coptic texts are all Egyptian translations of writings originally composed in Greek.

Four other Coptic manuscripts discovered in Egypt have Gnostic writings in them. Two of the tractates in the aforementioned Berlin Gnostic Codex are introduced in this book, and late writings from the Bruce and Askew Codices are also briefly discussed. The Codex Tchacos has only recently come to light. It contains two tractates also found in the Nag Hammadi collection, plus two hitherto unknown Gnostic tractates, the much-heralded *Gospel of Judas,* and a very fragmentary writing tentatively called the *Book of Allogenes.*

In chapter 2 I discuss the earliest Gnostic teachers and groups as they are known to us from the writings of St. Irenaeus and other church fathers, from Simon "Magus" to the so-called "Cainites," a sect that actually never existed.

Irenaeus is our earliest witness to a group he refers to as the *gnōstikē haerēsis,* which can either be translated "Gnostic school of thought," or "Gnostic heresy." The ideas found in his description of their teachings are related to those of groups other church fathers refer to as "Sethians" (after the name of the third son of Adam in the Bible). It turns out that a large number of Coptic texts attest to the same basic set of traditions as those described by the church fathers. So, in chapter 3, I discuss "Sethian" or "Classic" Gnosticism, with introductions to fourteen Gnostic tractates. "Sethian" or "Classic" Gnosticism is one of the two most important manifestations of ancient Gnosticism. Its influences can also be seen in a number of other Gnostic writings whose sectarian affiliations are unclear.

As already noted, it is posited in this book that Gnosticism originated in a Jewish environment. The earliest attested mythological systems of "Sethian" or "Classic" Gnosticism are made up of innovative reinterpretations of biblical and Jewish traditions, especially Jewish traditions of biblical interpretation. Chapter 4 is devoted to studies of Gnostic biblical interpretation, focusing particularly on Gnostic reinterpretations of the early chapters of Genesis, and of Jewish interpretations of the biblical texts.

Basilides, who taught in Alexandria in the early second century, utilized Gnostic traditions in devising his own version of Christianity. He was the very first early Christian teacher to write commentaries on texts that would eventually become part of the New Testament canon. He and his son and pupil Isidore are discussed in chapter 5.

The greatest ancient Christian Gnostic of all, Valentinus, was a prominent teacher, first in Alexandria and then in Rome. His teachings and those of his followers are discussed in chapter 6, which also includes introductions to seven Valentinian tractates from the Nag Hammadi collection. Next to "Sethian" or "Classic" Gnosticism, Valentinian Gnosticism is the other of the two most important manifestations of ancient Gnosticism.

The early third-century church father Hippolytus of Rome provides unique information on several groups of Gnostics who advocated systems of mythology that posited three principles. These are discussed in chapter 7. Also included is a three-principle text preserved in Coptic that is part of the Nag Hammadi collection.

The Nag Hammadi codices include a large number of Gnostic writings preserved in Coptic whose sectarian affiliations are unclear. Fourteen of them are introduced in chapter 8, plus one from the Berlin Gnostic Codex, and the writings of the Bruce and Askew Codices.

One of the first tractates of the Nag Hammadi collection to be published was the *Gospel of Thomas*. It is also the Nag Hammadi text that has elicited the most attention on the part of scholars and the general public. While I do not consider the *Gospel of Thomas* to be a "Gnostic" writing, according to the definition I advance in chapter 1, I include it in this book, in chapter 9, along with related texts that represent what I call "Thomas Christianity." That variety of Christianity, which emphasizes self-knowledge, was at home in Syria from the second century on. Another Nag Hammadi tractate representing Thomas Christianity is also introduced in chapter 9.

Hermetism is another religious current that emphasized self-knowledge as the basis for salvation. This religion arose in Alexandria, Egypt, probably in the first century CE. It features the Egyptian god Thoth in Greek guise as "Thrice-Greatest Hermes," who gives revelatory instruction to his "son" and other pupils. Hermetism is the subject of chapter 10. There I introduce two of the Greek Hermetic texts, and three Hermetic texts in the Nag Hammadi collection.

In the form of Manichaeism Gnosticism became a world religion. Founded by the prophet Mani in the third century, his religion was spread by his followers throughout the Roman Empire, and eastward as far as China, where it survived into the seventeenth century. In chapter 11 I discuss the life and writings of Mani, the religious system that he created, and the history of Manichaeism in the Roman Empire.

In the form of Mandaeism the ancient Gnostic religion has survived into our own times. In chapter 12 I discuss Mandaean literature, Mandaean doctrines, rituals, and ethics, and survey the history of Mandaeism from the first century up to the present.

In a brief Epilogue I reprise the highlights of the previous chapters and then say something about the persistence of Gnosticism, illustrated by various Gnostic churches and societies that have sprung up in our time. At the end of the book there are suggestions for further reading, and indices.

When I quote from ancient sources in the course of the book, I usually use standard translations, sometimes in modified form. Occasionally I will use a translation of my own.

The following works are cited in abbreviated form for readings from primary sources:

Foerster 1, cited in chapters 2, 3, 5, 6, 7, 9, and 10. Werner Foerster, ed., R. McL. Wilson, trans., *Gnosis: A Selection of Gnostic Texts*, vol. 1: *Patristic Evidence*. Oxford: Clarendon Press, 1972.

Foerster 2, cited in chapter 12. Foerster, *Gnosis*, vol. 2: *Coptic and Mandaean Sources*. Oxford: Clarendon Press, 1974.

Layton, cited in chapters 3, 5, 6, 8, 9, and 10. Bentley Layton, *The Gnostic Scriptures: A New Translation with Annotations and Introductions*. Garden City, NY: Doubleday & Co., 1987.

NH Library, cited in chapters 3, 6, 7, 8, 9, and 10. James M. Robinson and Richard Smith, eds., *The Nag Hammadi Library in English*, 3rd revised edition. San Francisco: Harper & Row, 1988.

MacDermot, *Bruce Codex*, cited in chapters 3 and 8. Carl Schmidt, ed., and Violet MacDermot, trans., *The Books of Jeu and the Untitled Text in the Bruce Codex*. Leiden: E. J. Brill, 1978.

MacDermot, *Pistis Sophia,* cited in chapter 8. Carl Schmidt, ed., and Violet MacDermot, trans., *Pistis Sophia.* Leiden: E. J. Brill, 1978.

Gardner-Lieu, cited in chapter 11. Iain Gardner and Samuel N. C. Lieu, eds., *Manichaean Texts from the Roman Empire.* Cambridge: Cambridge University Press, 2004.

Writings from the Nag Hammadi Codices are cited by codex, treatise, page, and line number. Thus a reference to NHC VII,5:118, 12–13 cites the Fifth treatise in that codex (Three Steles of Seth), page 118, lines 12–13.

Unfortunately, the two volumes edited by Werner Foerster and translated from the German by R. McL. Wilson are out of print. They are presumably available in most college, university, or seminary libraries. An updated version is certainly a desideratum.

A completely new one-volume translation of the tractates in the Nag Hammadi Codices, plus those in the Berlin Gnostic Codex and the Codex Tchacos, appeared in 2007: *The Nag Hammadi Scriptures: The International Edition,* edited by Marvin W. Meyer; San Francisco: HarperSanFrancisco. This new translation reflects the latest results of the three major projects at work on the Nag Hammadi texts since they began to be published: The Coptic Gnostic Library project of the Institute for Antiquity and Christianity at the Claremont Graduate University in Claremont, California; the Berliner Arbeitskreis für Koptisch-Gnostische Schriften based at Humboldt Universität in Berlin, Germany; and the Bibliothèque copte de Nag Hammadi, based at the Université Laval in Québec City, Canada. Since I have participated in the preparation of this new translation I now have page proofs of the entire volume. So I have been able "in the last minute" to include citations from that work, with pagination, in chapters 3, 6, 7, 8, 9, and 10 of this book, abbreviated as *NH Scriptures.*

1. What is Gnosticism?

Avoid the godless chatter and contradictions of what is falsely called knowledge, for by professing it some have missed the mark as regards the faith.

THIS IS THE PARTING ADMONITION of a Christian leader of the early second century, writing in the name of the apostle Paul to his disciple Timothy (1 Timothy 6:20b-21, RSV). The writer is warning his readers (hearers) against a version of the Christian religion that presents itself as "knowledge" (*gnōsis*), involving teachings meant either to complement or to replace the essential doctrines of the Christian faith. The writer warns that embrace of such teachings will lead to "miss[ing] the mark," by which he means essentially apostasy from the true Christian faith.

Later in the same century St. Irenaeus, bishop of Lyons in Gaul (modern France), writing around the year 185, adopts "Paul's" terminology ("falsely called knowledge") to describe a number of Christian heresies that he thinks pose a danger to the catholic faith. His five-volume work, entitled *Refutation and Overthrow of Falsely Called Knowledge* (usually abbreviated as *Against Heresies*), provides in its first volume more or less detailed presentations of the doctrines of the heretics known to him. He then refutes these doctrines in the remaining four volumes, countering them with his interpretation of the catholic faith based on the church's creed and the teachings of the Lord and his apostles.

Most of the heretics and heresies attacked by the good bishop as "falsely called knowledge" fall into a category of teaching usually referred to nowadays as *Gnosticism*. I say usually because there has arisen in recent times objections on the part of some scholars to the use of the term *Gnosticism* in scholarly discourse. It is argued, correctly, that *Gnosticism* is a term that was not in use in ancient times. It is also argued, again correctly, that the term *Gnosticism* has been used in so many different ways that it has led to a good deal of confusion as to what the term is supposed to mean. Nevertheless, I think there is some utility in retaining the term, as the title of this book indicates. In that case, what is needed is some clarity as to how the term is to be defined, and what kinds of doctrines and practices should be included in the category *Gnosticism*.

1. Gnosis and Gnosticism: Problems of Definition

As already noted, the term *Gnosticism* has been used in a wide variety of ways. So when I use it in this book, I need to clarify what I mean by the term, and what I think it should mean in historical scholarship. My own stance in this discussion is that of a historian of ancient Mediterranean and Greco-Roman religions, whose task it is to describe and interpret various religious trends as they appeared in the Greco-Roman world of the first centuries CE. Many of the various religions that were practiced by people in that period of time are easy enough to define. For example, a good deal is known about the worship of the Egyptian goddess Isis, not only in Egypt but in

The question here is this: Can we speak about Gnosticism as a religion comparable to Mithraism, or Judaism, or Christianity? And if so, how are we to define it in such a way as to do justice to the numerous sources at our disposal?

the larger Greco-Roman world. The same can be said for Mithraism, widely practiced by members of the Roman military. Judaism, too, as practiced in its homeland and in the Diaspora, is a
well-known phenomenon in the his-
tory of Greco-Roman religions, as
is Christianity in its various manifestations. The question here is this:
Can we speak about Gnosticism as
a religion comparable to Mithraism,
or Judaism, or Christianity? And if
so, how are we to define it in such a
way as to do justice to the numerous
sources at our disposal?

*But when Irenaeus used the
term "the Gnostic heresy"
(Against Heresies 1.11.1),
he was using a term that
can also be taken in a neutral sense, for the Greek
word* haerēsis *simply means
"school of thought."*

First of all, let's take a look at the term *Gnosticism*. It was first
coined in the seventeenth century by an Englishman named Henry
More, who used it in an expository work on the seven letters of
the book of Revelation. He used the term *Gnosticisme* to describe
the heresy in Thyatira (Revelation 2:18-29), in the same sense
that a contemporary of his, Henry Hammond, used the expression "the Gnostick-heresie." The latter term comes out of the
writings of St. Irenaeus. *Gnosticism* is a term made up by adding
the suffix *-ism* to the adjective *gnostic* (Greek *gnōstikos*), meaning
"knowing" or "knowledgeable." It is clear that Henry More used
the term *Gnosticism* in a pejorative way, with allegorical application to seventeenth-century Christian interdenominational polemics.
But when Irenaeus used the term "the Gnostic heresy" (*Against
Heresies* 1.11.1), he was using a term that can also be taken in a
neutral sense, for the Greek word *haerēsis* simply means "school
of thought." Indeed, Irenaeus was referring to a specific school of
thought, a group of people "who call themselves *Gnōstikoi*" (that
is Gnostics, knowledgeable ones, *Against Heresies* 1.25.6). Use of
the term *Gnosticism* in reference to the beliefs and practices of this
particular group is not necessarily pejorative at all, even if the term
was originally used that way in English. And it might be added that
the suffix *-ism* (in Greek, *-ismos*) was used by Jews and Christians
in antiquity to refer to their own religions. The earliest examples

are *Ioudaismos* in 2 Maccabees 2:21; 8:1; 14:38 (first century BCE) and *Christianismos* in Ignatius, *Magnesians* 10.1,3; *Philadelphians* 6.1; *Romans* 3.3 (second century CE). (The English word *Christianity* reflects the Latin suffix *–itas* equivalent to the Greek *–ismos*).

The Greek adjective *gnōstikos* was first coined by Plato to refer to a kind of science (*Statesman* 258e) and gained currency in philosophical circles. The appropriation of this term by people who applied it to themselves was a significant innovation, and this usage is noted by both Christian and pagan writers from the second century on. Central to this usage, as can be seen in the root of the adjective, is the claim to a special kind of knowledge (*gnōsis*). Irenaeus observed this, as can be seen from his use of the phrase "falsely called knowledge" to apply to the heretics he was combating.

So, for our purposes in this book, it is essential for us to know what kind of knowledge it was to which the Gnostics laid claim in terms of myth, ritual, beliefs, and practices. Irenaeus is especially helpful in this regard, for he supplies the starting point with a direct testimony (*Against Heresies* 1.29) about the "Gnostic *haeresis*" consisting of a lengthy quotation from one of its books. Thanks to the Nag Hammadi discovery we now know that this excerpt is closely related to part of one of the Coptic texts called the *Apocryphon (Secret Book) of John,* now extant in four Coptic manuscripts. Study of this material reveals that this book is of central importance for our knowledge of the ancient "Gnostic school of thought" known to Irenaeus. It is, therefore, of central importance for our understanding of what can legitimately be called ancient Gnosticism.

Can the term Gnosticism be applied more widely to other kinds of material beside the *Apocryphon of John*? As it turns out, there are a number of other texts we now have that are very closely related, in terms of myth and ritual, to the *Apocryphon of John,* thirteen of them included in the Nag Hammadi Library. These texts, taken together, constitute what scholars refer to as Sethian or Classic Gnosticism. (They will be taken up in chapter 3.) In addition, a number of other sources can be seen to be closely related, in terms of their emphasis on gnosis and their mythology, to Classic or

Sethian Gnosticism, including systems described by Irenaeus under the catch-all phrase "falsely-called knowledge."

Here an objection might be raised: As can be seen by its title, the *Apocryphon of John* is a Christian writing, featuring a revelation given by Jesus to his disciple John. Why, then, not refer to such a text, and others like it, as reflective of a variety of Christianity, rather than examples of a separate category of religion called Gnosticism? Why not just follow Irenaeus and other early Christian heresiologists (heresy hunters) in viewing Gnosticism as a Christian heresy, rather than a distinct religious tradition originally independent of Christianity? That, indeed, is the position advocated by many historians of Christianity.

However, when one takes a closer look at the *Apocryphon of John,* one can see that the basic myth contained in it has no Christian features in it at all. What makes it a Christian work is the frame story and questions by John interpolated into the text by a Christian editor. In other words, an original Gnostic myth has been Christianized editorially with the addition of the frame story and the dialogue features in a process whereby Jesus becomes the revealer of the mythological gnosis given in the core of the text. Another example of the same thing is found in two other Nag Hammadi texts, *Eugnostos the Blessed* (NHC III,3; V,1, and *Sophia* (*Wisdom*) *of Jesus Christ* (NHC III,4; BG,3). (These will be discussed in chapter 8.) Comparative study of the basic myth in the *Apocryphon of John* reveals that it is made up of an innovative reinterpretation of biblical and Jewish traditions. So it is more likely that Gnosticism arose out of a Jewish milieu, and only subsequently came into contact with Christianity, than that it arose from within early Christianity. If one wants to use the term heresy in this connection, one can argue that both Christianity and Gnosticism arose as Jewish heresies.

Moreover, a historian of religions will look farther afield and consider available material that has no Christian connections at all, material that can be categorized as Gnostic in terms of its content. I have in mind here the religion of the Mandaeans (discussed in chapter 12). The Mandaean material shows very interesting points of comparison with Classic Gnostic writings, but the only connection it has at all with the Christian tradition is hostility. The Mandaeans of today constitute a still-living remnant of ancient Gnosticism.

What, then, are the essential features of what can legitimately be called Gnosticism, from the standpoint of the history of religions?

2. Gnosticism: Its Essential Features

As has already been noted, knowledge (gnosis) is of central importance in Gnosticism; indeed, it is a prerequisite for salvation. But what kind of knowledge are we talking about? In Gnosticism saving gnosis comes by revelation from a transcendent realm, mediated by a revealer who has come from that realm in order to awaken people to a knowledge of God and a knowledge of the true nature of the human self. In Gnosticism knowledge of God and knowledge of the self are two sides of the same coin, for the true human self is of divine origin, and salvation ultimately involves a return to the divine world from which it came. As for the bearer of revelation, this differs from one Gnostic system to another. In Christian forms of Gnosticism, the revealer is Jesus Christ, but in other forms of Gnosticism other revealers are posited, often mythological beings (for example, Sophia, "Wisdom," in various manifestations), biblical characters (for example, Adam, Seth), or other noted figures from the past (for example, Zoroaster, Zostrianos).

In Gnosticism saving gnosis comes by revelation from a transcendent realm, mediated by a revealer who has come from that realm in order to awaken people to a knowledge of God and a knowledge of the true nature of the human self.

A characteristic feature of Gnosticism is a dualistic way of looking at God, humanity, and the world, involving a radical reinterpretation of earlier traditions. In terms of theology, the Gnostics split the transcendent God of the Bible into two: a super-transcendent supreme God who is utterly alien to the world, and a lower deity who is responsible for creating and governing the world in which we live. This theology is more or less elaborated in various Gnostic systems of thought, for a number of Gnostic systems posit various divine beings inhabiting the divine world, as well as lower demonic beings involved in the creation and governance of the cosmic order. Indeed, in most Gnostic systems the relationship between the higher and lower realms is expressed in terms of a tragic split in the divine world that results in the genesis of the lower beings responsible for the cosmos.

A characteristic feature of Gnosticism is a dualistic way of looking at God, humanity, and the world, involving a radical reinterpretation of earlier traditions.

Human beings, too, are split personalities. The true human self is as alien to the world as is the transcendent God. The inner human self is regarded as an immaterial divine spark imprisoned in a material body. The human body and the lower emotive soul belong to this world, whereas the higher self (the mind or spirit) is consubstantial with the transcendent God from which it originated. Involved in this dualistic anthropology are creative reinterpretations of the creation stories in the book of Genesis.

In terms of cosmology, the spatiotemporal universe in which we live (the cosmos) is regarded by Gnostics as a prison in which the true human self is shackled. Created and governed by the lower creator and his minions, it is the realm of chaos and darkness in the view of most of the ancient Gnostics. However, it must be admitted that this radical dualism is somewhat mitigated in later Gnostic systems. Even so, the cosmos is regularly regarded as a product of creation, and not in any sense eternal.

The main building blocks of Gnostic mythology consist of innovative reinterpretations of biblical and Jewish traditions.

Just as there was a time-before-time when the cosmos did not exist, so also is there a time-after-time when it will no longer exist. The goal of the Gnostic is to be saved from the cosmic prison in which it now exists and to be restored to the realm of light from which the true human self originated. Gnosis provides the means for achieving this and ensuring the passage of the soul after death back to God. Once the process of liberation is completed, that is when all of the elect are redeemed, the material world will either be annihilated or become subject to eternal darkness. Gnostic eschatology is basically a reinterpretation of standard biblical and Jewish eschatology.

One of the chief characteristics of Gnosticism is *mythopoeia*, the construction of elaborate myths through which revealed gnosis is transmitted. In giving expression to their basic beliefs, the Gnostics put into story form their insights into the human predicament and the means of salvation. Mythopoeia was an ongoing activity of many Gnostic teachers, who recorded and elaborated their mythology in revelatory literature (apocalypses, revelation dialogues, etc.). The main themes of Gnostic mythology are *theosophy*, elaborating on the transcendent God and the divine world; *cosmogony*, how the world came into being; *anthropogony*, involving the origin and imprisonment of human beings; and *soteriology*, how the human self can be saved. As will become evident in the following chapters, the main building blocks of Gnostic mythology consist of innovative reinterpretations of biblical and Jewish traditions.

It used to be fashionable among historians of religions to trace the origins of Gnosticism back to Oriental sources (Babylonian or Iranian), but the Coptic sources now available to us as a result of the Nag Hammadi discovery have provided valuable new evidence for tracing these origins, instead, to Jewish sources.

From what has been said so far, it can be seen that a prominent feature of Gnosticism involves innovation and reinterpretation. But reinterpretation of what?

Where did the earliest Gnostic teachers get their views of God, the world, and the human self? What sorts of religious or philosophical traditions did they use in coming up with the basic features of the Gnostic worldview?

Various answers have been given to those questions by scholars over the last couple of centuries of research on Gnosticism. It used to be fashionable among historians of religions to trace the origins of Gnosticism back to Oriental sources (Babylonian or Iranian), but the Coptic sources now available to us as a result of the Nag Hammadi discovery have provided valuable new evidence for tracing these origins, instead, to Jewish sources. It is also evident from the study of the newer material that Platonist philosophy was a decisive factor in the development of the Gnostic worldview.

3. Historical contexts: Platonism and Judaism

Plato of Athens (427–348 BCE) was arguably one of the most brilliant and seminal minds in human history. Around 388 he founded his famous school, the Academy, which had a continuous history until it was shut down by order of the Christian emperor Justinian in 529 CE. Plato's dialogs and letters constitute an enormous legacy that was studied and restudied in antiquity and into the present. The early history of Platonism after Plato is conventionally divided into three eras: the Old Academy, Middle Platonism (early first century BCE to third century CE), and Neo-Platonism, beginning with Plotinus (205–270).

This, of course, is not the place to present an account of Platonist philosophy, but I want to mention some key aspects of Platonism that are clearly reflected in the Gnostic worldview briefly summarized in the preceding discussion. Additional details will be provided in chapters to follow.

An important feature of Platonism is its metaphysical dualism, which involves a distinction between an immaterial world of being and the material world of becoming. Material things of this world are basically copies of eternal, immaterial forms in the realm of being. Late in his life Plato wrote the *Timaeus*, a dialogue containing a myth of creation. In that myth the divine creator, referred to as the *dēmiourgos* ("craftsman"), creates the physical world according to the eternal pattern in the world of immaterial forms. The product of that creation is the best of all possible worlds, given the intractability of the material out of which it was constructed. Plato did not actually believe in a literal beginning of the world of becoming; for him the cosmos is eternal.

A similar kind of dualism can be found in Gnosticism, in that a radical distinction is made between the lower material world and the immaterial divine world above. Some Gnostics even took over the Platonic term for the creator, the *Demiurge*. But for the Gnostics this world is not at all the best of all possible worlds, nor is it eternal. Its creator is a god who is ignorant at best, and even malevolent in some Gnostic systems. Nevertheless, Gnostic dualism is hardly conceivable without Platonist dualism. Gnostic dualism can be seen as a reinterpretation of traditional Platonist dualism.

Reflected in Plato's *Timaeus* is the "New Cosmology" that became current in the Greco-Roman world from the fourth century BCE. Indeed, this was the standard cosmology until the time of Copernicus in the sixteenth century. We take for granted the cosmology that replaced the "New Cosmology" of the ancient world, according to which the earth is one of nine planets (or eight, since Pluto has recently been "demoted") that orbit the sun. The ancients knew of only five planets ("wandering stars"), plus Sun and Moon, all orbiting the earth. According to the older version of the "New Cosmology" reflected in Plato's *Timaeus,* the earth is surrounded by seven spheres occupied by Moon, Sun, Venus, Mercury, Mars, Jupiter, and Saturn. (In a later version the Sun is moved to the fourth place.) Plato looked upon the planets, and the "fixed" stars, as divine beings.

The "New Cosmology" is reflected, too, in the Gnostic sources, but with a crucial difference. For the Gnostics, the planetary spheres and the Zodiacal sphere above them were occupied by demonic beings (archons or rulers) who governed the world below. These demonic beings were also intent upon keeping human spirits imprisoned in this nether world.

Plato's anthropology is also reflected in Gnosticism. Plato posited a distinction between the human soul and the body. He also distinguished the mind (*nous*) from the lower, emotive soul. For Plato and Platonists, the immortal soul is eternal and preexists its entry into a material body. Plato could even view the body as a kind of tomb for the soul. Plato also put forward a doctrine of the transmigration of souls, according to which immortal souls can enter one body after another, and a doctrine of rewards and punishments of the soul after death.

Something similar can be seen in Gnosticism, in that the soul or spirit is separable from the body, and in some Gnostic systems transmigration is presented as a possibility for some souls. But the Platonic body-soul dualism is radically reinterpreted in Gnosticism, which posits a salvation of the soul based on its reception of gnosis and an eternal annihilation of unsaved souls. The human self is also viewed by the Gnostics as consubstantial with the transcendent God, a doctrine not found in Platonism. Indeed, in Plato's dialogues virtually nothing is said of a transcendent deity. The closest thing to such a doctrine is Plato's idea of "the Good," the ultimate principle of the realm of immaterial forms, which is said to be "beyond being." The supreme transcendent God in Gnosticism is also said to be "beyond being."

One interesting feature of Plato's works is his mythopoeia, his creation of various myths as vehicles for the transmission of his philosophical ideas. As we have seen, mythopoeia is a prominent feature of Gnosticism, too. But in Gnosticism the myths are considered to be divine revelation and certainly not vehicles for the transmission of human philosophy.

So, while the Gnostic worldview is dependent in some way upon Platonist philosophy, it can clearly be seen that the Platonist elements have been reinterpreted in a non-Platonic direction, something that third-century Platonist philosophers such as Plotinus and his pupils certainly noticed. Plotinus's critique of the Gnostics known to him are contained in his *Enneads* (especially *Enneads* 2.9, titled "Against the Gnostics").

As we have already noted, the Gnostics laid claim to a special kind of knowledge revealed from on high. This emphasis on divine revelation is certainly not related to Platonism or any other Greek philosophy. The closest analogues to this emphasis on revealed knowledge are to be found in postbiblical Jewish apocalypses (revelations), dating from the third-century BCE into the first-century

CE. One of the most important of these apocalypses is the *First Book of Enoch*, consisting of five main sections dating from the third-century BCE to the first-century CE. In *1 Enoch*, the antediluvian patriarch, who in the Bible is reported to have been taken by God to heaven (Genesis 5:21-24), reveals to his descendants secret knowledge that he has received on his heavenly journey. This special knowledge is reserved for the elect people of God in the end time.

The kind of Judaism that is exemplified in *1 Enoch* and similar Jewish apocalypses is referred to as apocalyptic Judaism. This is the variety of Judaism that is now well-attested in the Dead Sea Scrolls, a library of biblical and Jewish literature belonging to a Jewish sect whose main settlement was located at Khirbet Qumran, beneath the cliffs overlooking the Dead Sea. Indeed, revealed knowledge (Hebrew *da'at*) is an important feature of many of the Qumran writings, and a number of fragments of the original Aramaic version of *1 Enoch* have been found among the Dead Sea Scrolls.

Of course, it must be emphasized that the content of the revealed knowledge in Gnosticism differs considerably from that of the Jewish apocalypses. In the latter, secret knowledge of the workings of God's created order and his plans for his people are presented. The revealed knowledge in Gnosticism, on the other hand, emphasizes knowledge of the divine self and the means whereby the soul can return to its divine origins.

Indeed, a number of the Gnostic writings are called "apocalypses," or can be so defined in terms of their literary genre.

As we have seen, an important constituent of Gnosticism is a metaphysical dualism, somewhat akin to that of Platonism. Dualism is also a feature of apocalyptic Judaism, but in the latter the dualism is more of an ethical dualism involving contrasts between good and evil, light and darkness, and a divine struggle involving God and his angels on the one hand, and the Devil (under various names) and his angels on the other. Even so, it can clearly be seen that Gnosticism has borrowed some of these elements from Jewish apocalypses, for Gnosticism, too, sets up contrasts between light and darkness, good and evil, and so on. However, in Gnosticism the world-creator is often depicted as a demonic being akin to the Devil or one of the evil angels in Jewish apocalyptic literature.

Another feature in common between Gnosticism and apocalyptic Judaism is the production of revelatory literature. Indeed, a number of the Gnostic writings are called "apocalypses," or can be so defined in terms of their literary genre.

Finally, the eschatology that is characteristic of Gnosticism clearly has biblical and Jewish roots. The cosmos as we know it will end, and God's elect will enjoy their eternal salvation. The main difference between Gnostic eschatology and biblical-Jewish eschatology is that the former is focused on the return of the individual soul to its divine origins.

Where does this leave us? Gnosticism is clearly dependent upon aspects of Platonist philosophy. It is also clearly dependent upon aspects of Jewish religion, most notably apocalyptically oriented Judaism. The most plausible way of explaining these dependencies is to posit a Jewish origin for Gnosticism, involving Jews who had imbibed a good deal of Greek philosophy. Philo of Alexandria (first century CE) is probably the best-known example of a Jew who was deeply influenced by Greek philosophy. Indeed, a historian of Middle-Platonism would, as a matter of course, include Philo in his or her survey of the evidence. But Philo was not a Gnostic.

So I shall conclude this discussion by positing that what we call Gnosticism originated among unknown Jews who incorporated aspects of Platonism into their innovative reinterpretations of their ancestral traditions. At least that is, in my view, the most plausible conclusion that can be drawn from the sources available to us.

4. Gnosticism: The Sources

Until the discovery and publication of primary Gnostic sources preserved in Coptic manuscripts from Egypt, the sources for our knowledge of Gnosticism consisted of polemical writings directed against Gnostic teachers and groups by heresy-hunting leaders (fathers) of what was emerging in various areas as the catholic church. We have already mentioned St. Irenaeus, bishop of Lyons, and his five-volume work *Against Heresies*. The earliest heresiological writing was produced in Rome in the mid-second century by Justin Martyr, a native of Shechem/Flavia Neapolis in Samaria (modern Nablus). Unfortunately, that writing, a compilation (*Syntagma*), is now lost, though some scholars think that it may have been used by Irenaeus in parts of the first volume of his work. In his *First Apology*, written between 150 and 155, Justin provides some information on three heretics known to him, Simon (the "magician" mentioned in Acts 8), Menander, and Marcion. The first two of these clearly belong to the history of Gnosticism. Marcion was a Paulinist Christian who was probably influenced by Gnosticism, but his teachings can hardly be considered Gnostic in any real sense. So I have omitted him from consideration in this book.

Another writer based in Rome was Hippolytus, who flourished in the early third century and became a rival bishop of Rome. His *Refutation of all Heresies* is partly indebted to the earlier work of Irenaeus, but contains much additional information, including quotations of original sources of considerable value.

Tertullian of Carthage was one of the earliest Christian writers using the Latin language rather than Greek. He wrote his *Prescription of Heretics* around the year 200. He also wrote separate works against the Valentinians and against Marcion.

Among the Latin writings of Tertullian that have come down to us is a spurious work entitled *Against All Heresies*. This work is thought by many scholars to be based on an early work of Hippolytus, now lost, titled *Syntagma against All Heresies*.

The church fathers already mentioned included a good deal of vituperation in their attacks against heretics. The Alexandrian writers Clement (d. 211–15) and Origen (d. 253/54), on the other hand, made real attempts to understand their opponents. Clement makes a distinction between true and false knowledge, and claims that the true Gnostic (*gnōstikos*) is one whose learning accords with the official doctrines of the church. Both Clement and Origen preserve quotations from Alexandrian Gnostic writers known to them.

In the late fourth century, Epiphanius of Salamis in Cyprus wrote a lengthy compilation of heresies (not all Gnostic) in a work called *Panarion* ("medicine chest") against *Heresies*. He availed himself of the writings of the earlier heresiologists but also included some quotations from primary Gnostic texts known to him. Most scholars do not have a high regard for Epiphanius's writings, for he is not regarded as a reliable writer. However, his work is useful when he quotes his sources verbatim. One of the most unfortunate aspects of his work is that he led the charge against Origen and Origenism. As a result, the greatest theologian of the ancient church was eventually condemned as a heretic (in 553).

> *One of the most important manuscript finds of the twentieth-century consists of thirteen fourth-century papyrus manuscripts discovered by Egyptian peasants in December, 1945, at the base of a cliff in the desert not far from the town of Nag Hammadi in Upper Egypt.*

Later writers also took up their cudgels against heretics (Ephraem of Edessa, Theodoret of Cyrus, Augustine, John of Damascus, and others), but they provide no useful additional information on Gnosticism. An exception to this observation is Augustine, who, as a former Manichaean, provides considerable information on Manichaeism.

Fortunately, we are no longer dependent upon the works of the church's heresiologists for our knowledge of Gnosticism, for the desert sands of Egypt have preserved a large number of works produced by ancient Gnostic writers.

One of the most important manuscript finds of the twentieth-century consists of thirteen fourth-century papyrus manuscripts discovered by Egyptian peasants in December, 1945, at the base of a cliff in the desert not far from the town of Nag Hammadi in Upper Egypt. They are now housed in the Coptic Museum in Old Cairo. They are codices (not scrolls) and inscribed in Coptic, the latest form of the Egyptian language. (The codex is the earliest form of the modern book. The Coptic language uses a modified Greek alphabet and incorporates into its vocabulary a large number of Greek words.) The Nag Hammadi Codices, plus three other Coptic manuscripts,

Fig. 1.1 The author holding a plexiglass plate containing two joined leaves from Nag Hammadi Codex X, pages 1 and 68 from the treatise *Marsanes*. At the Coptic Museum in Cairo, Egypt, in 1980.

constitute the "Coptic Gnostic Library," the title of a series of editions published between 1975 and 1996, comprising sixteen volumes of Coptic texts with English translations.

The three other Coptic manuscripts beside the Nag Hammadi Codices in the aforementioned series are the Berlin Gnostic Codex, discovered in the late nineteenth century but first published in 1955, and the Askew and Bruce Codices first published in 1851 and 1891 respectively. The Berlin Codex is closely related to the Nag Hammadi Codices and contains two tractates also found in the latter. The Bruce and Askew Codices are less important because they contain highly convoluted texts that represent a late stage in the development of Egyptian Christian Gnosticism.

Another Coptic codex has more recently come to light, the Codex Tchacos, named for the art dealer Frieda Tchacos Nussberger, who purchased it in the year 2000. It has also been referred to as the Maecenas Codex, after the foundation in Basel that has taken charge of its restoration. The Codex Tchacos contains two tractates that are also part of the Nag Hammadi collection, plus two hitherto unknown tractates, the *Gospel of Judas* and a highly fragmentary work tentatively titled the *Book of Allogenes*. The critical edition of Codex Tchacos has not yet appeared at this writing, but an English translation of the *Gospel of Judas* has recently been published (April 2006).

Of course, the Nag Hammadi codices are our most important source for the study of Gnosticism. Unfortunately some of the

Fig. 1.2 The author at work on a Nag Hammadi text in the Coptic Museum, Cairo, in 1974.

codices are badly damaged, much of the damage sustained since their discovery. It is reported that the mother of the leader of the group of peasants who found the manuscripts burned some of the papyrus leaves in her bread oven!

The manuscripts remained inaccessible to scholars into the 1950s when the first publications appeared. These early publications include the *Gospel of Thomas*, published in 1959. In 1961 the United Nations Educational, Scientific and Cultural Organization (UNESCO) became involved in plans for publishing a complete facsimile edition consisting of photographic plates. Several hundred photographs were taken and sent to Paris, and these were used by an American team of scholars working under the auspices of the Institute for Antiquity and Christianity in Claremont, California, in a project directed by the Institute's Director, James M. Robinson. In 1970 an international committee of scholars was appointed by UNESCO, with a subcommittee working on the technical problems of identifying and assembling papyrus fragments for definitive photography. The first volumes of the facsimile edition appeared in 1972, and the last of the codices were published in 1977. Also in 1977, the thirteen Nag Hammadi Codices and the Berlin Codex were published together in a one-volume English translation under the title *The Nag Hammadi Library in English*.

The texts in the Nag Hammadi collection number fifty-two, all of them Coptic translations of works originally produced in Greek. Five of these are represented by more than a single copy; the number of different tractates is forty-four. Most, but not all, of the tractates are Gnostic in character, consisting of previously unknown writings. The manuscripts are now thought to have been part of a Christian monastic library. When St. Athanasius, Archbishop of Alexandria, wrote a circular letter in 367 condemning apocryphal and heretical books, monks in a monastery near the find-site presumably hid the books in a jar so they would not be burned or thrown into the Nile.

Several varieties of Gnosticism are represented in the Coptic texts available to us, and the primary material preserved in Coptic will constitute the most important sources for our knowledge of the Gnostic systems treated in the following chapters. Thirty-eight of the Nag Hammadi tractates are treated in this book. The six not treated are the following: *Dialogue of the Savior* (NHC III,5), featuring Jesus in dialogue with his disciples; *Acts of Peter and the Twelve Apostles* (NHC VI,1), containing apocryphal stories about Peter and the Twelve; *Authoritative Teaching* (NHC VI,3), a work of second-century Alexandrian-Christian Platonism; *Plato, Republic 588A–89B* (NHC VI,5), in a fractured Coptic translation; *Teachings of Silvanus* (NHC VII,4), a composite work of Alexandrian-Christian wisdom teachings; and *Sentences of Sextus* (NHC XII,1), a partial Coptic translation of a book of gnomic sayings previously known in its Greek original. Also included in this book are treatments of a tractate from the Berlin Codex, two from the Codex Tchakos, and the writings found in the Bruce and Askew Codices.

Included in this book are treatments of religious systems that are conventionally included in discussions of Gnosticism, that is, Thomas Christianity (chapter 9), Hermetism (chapter 10), Manichaeism (chapter 11), and Mandaeism (chapter 12). The sources for Hermetism, Manichaeism, and Mandaeism will be discussed in the respective chapters devoted to them.

2. Heresiological Reports on Early Gnostic Teachers and Systems

All those who in any way corrupt the truth, and injuriously affect the preaching of the Church, are the disciples and successors of Simon Magus of Samaria.

THESE ARE THE WORDS OF ST. IRENAEUS, bishop of Lyons, in his five-volume treatise written against "falsely called knowledge" (*Against Heresies* 1.27). Irenaeus traces all of the heresies known to him back to this man, a first-century Samaritan teacher and magician whose activities are noted in the New Testament Book of Acts (ch. 8). Who was this man? Can he really have been the earliest Gnostic?

1. Simon Magus (Foerster 1:27–32; 251–60)

In the eighth chapter of the Book of Acts there is an interesting account of the travels of the Hellenist-Christian teacher Philip (compare Acts 6:5) after the dispersion from Jerusalem of the Hellenist wing of the church (Acts 8:1). Philip goes first to a city of Samaria and encounters there a wonder worker named Simon. Simon is referring to himself as "the Great Power of God," and is honored as such by his followers ("that power of God which is called Great," Acts 8:9-10 RSV). As a result of Philip's preaching, many Samaritans are baptized, including Simon. Peter and John come up from Jerusalem and lay hands upon the group, and they receive the Holy Spirit (Acts 8:14-17). Simon offers money to Peter for the power to convey the Holy Spirit with the laying on of hands (8:19). Peter refuses the money and rebukes Simon, who asks Peter to pray for him (8:10-24).

This story is obviously tendentious, but it probably preserves a historical kernel. Before the arrival of the Christian message in Samaria Simon was active there as a wonder worker and prophet. Simon could hardly have become a Christian, and his message had

nothing to do with Christianity. Instead, Simon's activity fits in with other reports of first-century Samaritan sectarianism featuring the activity of messianic pretenders of various stripes. As for the conflict with Peter, other reports situate that conflict in Rome.

Fig. 2.1 The downfall of the archheretic Simon Magus, depicted as a winged demon (the apostle Peter stands at left). Stone relief, Cathédrale St. Lazare, Autun, France. Photo: Foto Marburg / Art Resource, N.Y.

The story of Simon in the book of Acts may have developed in the following way: Out of the religious ferment in Samaria resulting from the introduction of Christianity there, a story emerges among Christians claiming that even the local Samaritan prophet Simon was attracted to the miraculous power exhibited by Philip, a power superior to that of heathen magic. Simon is disgraced in the story. Then the story is reworked, in accordance with the view of apostolic authority held by the author of Acts, according to which the Twelve have the ultimate authority for the spread of Christianity in Samaria. Peter and John are brought into the story to fit that purpose.

> *The historical Simon was a Samaritan prophet who claimed a divine role for himself ("the Great Power of God"). But was he a Gnostic prophet?*

The historical Simon was a Samaritan prophet who claimed a divine role for himself ("the Great Power of God"). But was he a Gnostic prophet? It is certainly possible that some sort of Gnostic myth was involved in Simon's claim, but that is not explicit in the Acts account. What is clear, historically, is that Simon could not have become a Christian. A connection with Gnosticism could lie in the background of the Acts account, but that connection can only be made explicit on the basis of other sources. Fortunately, such sources exist.

Justin Martyr, a native of Samaria who became a Christian teacher in Rome, claims in his *First Apology* (ch. 26) that, after Christ's ascent into heaven, the demons put forward certain men who claimed to be gods. One of these was Simon, native of a Samaritan village named Gitta. During the reign of the emperor Claudius (41–54) Simon was active in Rome and was worshipped there by Samaritans residing in Rome as "First God." He had a female companion named Helen, a former prostitute, who was honored as the divine Simon's "First Thought" (*ennoia*). Justin claims that a statue set up on the Tiber River, inscribed in Latin SIMONI DEO SANCTO ("to the holy god Simon"), was set up in honor of this Simon.

What do we make of this report? Justin's reference to a statue in honor of Simon in Rome is based on a real statue presumably seen by him in Rome but falsely connected to Simon. The statue was actually found on the Tiber Island in 1574, and its inscription reads *Semoni Sanco Deo Fidio,* "to the faithful god Semo Sanco." The statue was dedicated to a Roman deity, Semo Sanco, who is associated in Roman religion with oaths, heaven, and thunder, and seems to be associated somehow with Jupiter (Greek Zeus). The statue's connection with Simon Magus may have originally been concocted by Samaritan followers of Simon residing in Rome.

Justin's account also has other mythological connections. Simon as "First God" has as his female consort "First Thought" (Helen), and if we can extrapolate from a later source (Irenaeus) we can posit a myth according to which "First God" rescues his "First Thought" from prostitution. Involved here would be a typical Gnostic myth. Justin says no more about Simon in his *Apology,* but may have said more in his lost *Syntagma,* a compilation of heresies that may have been used by Irenaeus. Justin's reference to Simon as "First God" also elicits comparison with the divine title reflected in Acts, "The Great Power of God." As for the term "First Thought" in Justin's account, this can be compared with what he says later in the same work (ch. 64) of the goddess Athena as the "First Thought" of Zeus. Involved here is a philosophical allegorizing of Greek mythology: Zeus, "the father of gods and men," is depicted as a divine Mind or Intellect (the highest god in Aristotle's philosophy), producing his "First Thought" as the beginning point of further emanations in the world of generation. "Mind" in Greek is a masculine noun (*nous*), and "thought" is feminine (*ennoia*).

> *Angels and powers are created, and the feminine aspect of God, symbolizing the human soul, is captured by the world-creating powers in the lower material world.*

Additional details are supplied by Irenaeus (*Against Heresies* 1.23.1–4). Irenaeus introduces Simon with reference to the account in the Book of Acts, supplemented by material drawn from Justin (23.1). He then supplies us with a full-blown Gnostic myth (23.2–3), in which Simon and Helen play the key roles. Simon is depicted as the supreme divine Father, Helen as "Mother of all" and Simon's

"Thought." Angels and archangels emanate from them who are responsible for creating and governing the world. Helen (Thought) is captured by these world-governing angels and imprisoned in the lower world. Simon descends to rescue her and other fallen souls. Irenaeus throws in some Christian details that are clearly secondary (for example, Helen as "lost sheep," Matthew 18:19).

The essential Gnostic myth can be reconstructed as follows: There is one supreme power, the Father, who as *Mind* thinking, itself produces a *First Thought,* from which arises duality. A split in the divine world results in the feminine aspect undergoing further emanation, regarded as a progressive devolution. Angels and powers are created, and the feminine aspect of God, symbolizing the human soul, is captured by the world-creating powers in the lower material world. These powers are ignorant of the primal Father. The captive feminine aspect of God is incarnated, for example, as Helen of Troy, and her latest incarnation brings her to a brothel in Tyre, where Simon redeems her. Simon is symbolically taken as the embodiment of the First God who descends for the purpose of rescuing his First Thought. Myth is thus acted out in human life, and Simon and Helen go about saving others in whom the divine spark is scattered. Salvation comes by gnosis, an awakening of the soul to self-awareness as a result of the revelation brought by Simon. Eventually the world will be dissolved, and those redeemed through the knowledge provided by Simon will be liberated from the world-creating powers. What role the biblical Creator played in this system is not clear. He may have been construed as one of the creating angels, as was taught by Saturninus.

Helen as the object of salvation represents the human soul in need of salvation. In the myth she is "First Thought" and "Mother," a figure comparable to the figure of Sophia (Wisdom) in other Gnostic systems, whose fall is ultimately responsible for the creation of the world. Indeed, later accounts refer to Helen as Sophia (Ps.-Clement *Homilies* 2.25) and Prounikos (that is, "whore," Epiphanius, *Panarion* 21.2.5), a Gnostic epithet of Sophia. This Gnostic mytheme reflects an innovative interpretation of the role of Wisdom in the Bible and Jewish tradition, revered as God's assistant in the creation of the world (for example, Proverbs 8). In the Gnostic view, the creation of the material world is a bad thing, the result of a fall of the feminine aspect of God. In the Simonian system, this myth is acted out in the adventures of Simon's consort, Helen.

Simonian mythology is built out of Jewish-Samaritan biblical traditions, allegorical interpretations of Greek mythology, and popular philosophical (Middle-Platonist) interpretations of God as "Mind." The role of the angels in creating the world is a notion that seems to have been circulating in Jewish-Samaritan circles in the first century, and can be read out of the plural pronoun in Genesis 1:26 ("Let *us* make man"). (Second-Temple Judaism and Samaritanism are offshoots of ancient Israelite religion and share many traditions, including the Torah.)

How much of this mythology goes back to the historical Simon? That is a point on which scholars differ. Indeed, some even doubt the existence of Simon's consort Helen. I tend to grant more credibility to our sources than some would allow. I would suggest that some of the details in Irenaeus's account that are lacking in Justin's can be seen to be implicit in the latter, and, in fact, may be based on the lost work of Justin's to which reference has already been made. Justin was a native of Samaria, and could therefore have had access to reliable traditions about Simon. In any case, I see no reason for him to invent a figure like Helen. So I do not hesitate to refer to Simon Magus as the first Gnostic prophet known to us by name.

Irenaeus throws in some Christian elements in his account. For example, he says that Simon claimed to be the one who "appeared among Jews as the Son, descended in Samaria as the Father, and came to other nations in the character of the Holy Spirit" (*Against Heresies* 1.23.1). This information is undoubtedly false, but may be based on later (second-century) Simonian Gnostic traditions arising from an attempt to adapt Simonian teaching to the growing Christian presence. The historical Simon clearly had nothing to do with the Christian religion. As revealer of gnosis, Simon claimed for himself the role attributed to Christ by Christian Gnostics.

Irenaeus rounds out his account with vituperative references to Simonian religious practices. He accuses Simonian "mystery priests" of licentious behavior and the practice of magic. The Simonians are said to worship an image of Simon made to look like Zeus, and one of Helen made to look like Athena. We are entitled to take this kind of information with the proverbial grain of salt.

Other early Christian writers provide additional information about Simon. Of considerable interest is what is reported about Simon's career in two fourth-century novelistic writings attributed to Clement of Rome entitled *Recognitions* and *Homilies*. In the *Homilies* (2.23–24; compare *Recognitions* 2.8) Simon is said to have been one of thirty disciples of John the Baptist, indeed his favorite. Upon the death of John the Baptist, Simon was absent learning magic in Egypt, and another Samaritan disciple named Dositheus assumed the leadership of the group, claiming to be the "Standing One." Upon his return from Egypt Simon wrested the leadership position away from Dositheus. As the result of a miracle, Dositheus was forced to acknowledge Simon as the "Standing One" and then died.

The term *Standing One* is used in Samaritan and Jewish sources to refer to God, and is therefore a title comparable to "the Great Power." Other sources, too (Clement of Alexandria, Hippolytus of Rome), associate that title with Simon Magus. What is of special interest here is the connection made with John the Baptist. As it happens, John the Baptist is a revered figure among the Mandaeans, who also refer to Jesus as a false prophet (see chapter 12). But it is doubtful that any historical connection existed between Simon Magus and John the Baptist. As for Dositheus, other sources refer to him as leader of a Samaritan sect and a messianic pretender. Whether any connection can be seen between Dositheus and early Gnosticism is doubtful, though he does appear as a revealer of gnosis in one of the Nag Hammadi texts, the *Three Steles of Seth* (NHC VII,5) 118,10.

Our sources are consistent in placing Simon in Rome at the time of his death, though the accounts of his death differ and are certainly subject to considerable doubt. Hippolytus (*Refutation of All Heresies* 6.20) reports that Simon came to Rome and encountered Peter there, who repeatedly challenged Simon's teachings. As a demonstration of his power, Simon instructed his disciples to bury him in a trench, announcing that he would rise on the third day. There he has remained until this day.

A more spectacular account is given in the apocryphal *Acts of Peter* (31–32). Simon, performing "false miracles" in Rome is confronted there by Peter. One day Simon announces that, on the following day, he will fly up to heaven to prove that he is truly the "Standing One." On the next day a crowd gathers, and Simon is carried into the air and is flying over the hills and temples of Rome. Peter utters a prayer and Simon falls out of the sky, breaking his legs in three places. The crowd finishes him off by stoning him, and Peter is vindicated.

Did Simon write anything? Hippolytus (*Refutation* 6.9.4–18.7) provides an account of a philosophical commentary on a writing purportedly produced by Simon entitled *Great Revelation* (*Megalē Apophasis*). The commentary contains three actual quotations from this work (at 6.94; 14.4; 18.2–7). The first of these quotations begins as follows: "This is the writing of revelation of the Voice and the Word, deriving from the Thought of the Great Infinite Power" (my translation). We note here the reference to the "Great Power," a self-designation of Simon, and the term "Thought" (*epinoia* equals *ennoia*) associated with Helen.

The commentary is a philosophical work containing allegories based on the Bible and Homer, including all sorts of learned and quasi-learned information. The cause of everything, according to this system, is fire (a Stoic view). The created world is derived from uncreated fire, beginning with six powers or roots: mind and thought, voice and name, reflection and conception. In these roots is contained the whole power of the Infinite as a seventh power, referred to as "the one who stands, who has stood, and who will stand" (*hestōs, stas, stēsomenos*). The name of this seventh power is, of course, derived from a title given to Simon, "Standing One." This infinite power is contained potentially in all humans, but must be fully formed, presumably by gnosis.

But with these speculations we are far removed from the original Simon Magus. We can suppose that the commentary was produced sometime in the second century by someone belonging to a group of people honoring traditions they traced back to Simon. As to the text of the *Great Revelation* on which the commentary is based, from which only the aforementioned quotations are preserved, it would appear that that text is a pseudonymous work attributed to Simon, and not by the Samaritan magus himself.

2. Menander (Foerster 1.32–33)

Our earliest information about this man comes from Justin Martyr (*Apology* 1.26), who refers to him as a disciple of Simon and a fellow Samaritan from a village called Kapparateia. Justin reports that Menander came to the city of Antioch in Syria, where he "deceived many through magic arts," offering immortality to his disciples. Justin adds that there were still adherents of Menander in his own time (mid-second century). Menander himself was presumably active in Antioch during the latter half of the first century.

Irenaeus (*Against Heresies* 1.23.5) refers to Menander as Simon's "successor." According to Irenaeus, who may be basing his information on the aforementioned lost work of Justin, Menander taught that the highest God ("first Power") was unknown, but that he himself had been sent as a savior. We can assume that Menander taught that human salvation was based on the gnosis revealed by him. Part of this gnosis involved the same feminine deity as was taught by Simon (First Thought, *Ennoia*), and the world-creating angels brought forth by her. The gnosis taught by Menander would free human beings from the power of the world-governing angels, who may have included in their number the biblical Creator as was taught later by Saturninus. Menander's mythic gnosis was also tied to a baptismal ritual, which guaranteed the promise of immortality to his followers.

It is to be noted that there is nothing in our accounts that connects Menander with Christianity. In Menander's gnosis, it is Menander himself who functions as the Gnostic savior who reveals the unknown God to his followers. Menander's doctrine of the world-creating angels may have come from Simon or from the same

Samaritan traditions used by Simon. His baptismal ritual, too, presumably derives from Jewish (or Samaritan) practices at home among various groups active in the Jordan valley. As we shall see, repeated baptisms are practiced by the Mandaeans, who trace their origins back to the Jordan valley. It would appear that Menander's baptism was an initiatory act, comparable to the initiatory washing through which people were made members of the community known to us from the Dead Sea Scrolls (Essenes). Of course, repeated ablutions were part of the ritual practices of the Essenes.

Menander was a first-century figure, a contemporary of early Christians active in Antioch. But in the little that is reported about him, there is nothing to suggest that he came into contact with the Antiochene Christians. The earliest Christian Gnostic known to us by name, Saturninus, was also active in Antioch and may have gotten some of his teaching from Menander.

3. Saturninus or Satornilos
(Foerster 1:40–41; Layton, 161–62)

Irenaeus posits a direct line of succession from Simon and Menander to Saturninus, who taught in Antioch, and Basilides, who taught in Alexandria (*Against Heresies* 1.24.1). (Basilides will be treated in chapter 5.) Justin Martyr says nothing about Saturninus in his *Apology*, but may have treated him in his lost *Syntagma*. In his *Dialogue with Trypho* (ch. 35) he mentions groups of heretics who are named after their founders, and includes here a group called "Satornilians," named after their founder Satornilos. Satornilos is the name used in Greek sources for Saturninus and may have been used by Irenaeus himself. The original Greek version of *Against Heresies* is lost; we know it only in a Latin translation. It may be that the Latin translator supplied a more common name (Saturninus, after the god Saturn) for the person known in Greek as Satornilos. We shall follow the Latin translator and refer to him as Saturninus.

With Saturninus we encounter a Christian Gnostic who assigns the role of savior to Christ as the source of saving gnosis. Irenaeus reports that Saturninus, like Menander before him, posited an unknown transcendent Father, and groups of "angels, archangels, powers, and authorities" emanating from him. The world was created by seven angels, one of whom is "the God of the Jews" (1.24.2). The same angels are credited with creating man, copying an image shining from above. The man thus created was unable to stand erect until the

One would expect the God of the Jews to be equated somehow with Satan, as in some other Gnostic systems.

"power above" took pity and sent into him a spark of life. It is this spark that returns to God after death, the body returning to the material elements of which it is composed. This anthropogony is based on an innovative interpretation of the creation stories in Genesis and is closely related to a myth found in Classic or Sethian Gnosticism, best exemplified in the *Apocryphon (Secret Book) of John* (treated in chapter 3).

Saturninus taught a docetic Christology according to which the divine Savior only appeared to be a real human being, a doctrine that is already attested in the Johannine writings of the New Testament (1 John 4:1-3; 2 John 7). Christ is said to have come "for the destruction of the God of the Jews and the salvation of those who believe in him" (*Against Heresies* 1.24.2), that is, those who have in them the spark of life. Slated for destruction, too, are the wicked people molded by the angels who lack the spark of life.

Saturninus embraced an ascetic way of life, condemning marriage and procreation and espousing abstinence from animal food. A confusing role is assigned, in this system, to Satan, who is said to be an (evil) angel who promotes marriage and procreation, on the one hand, but who also opposes "the God of the Jews," on the other. One would expect the God of the Jews to be equated somehow with Satan, as in some other Gnostic systems. Perhaps Irenaeus misunderstood his source.

If we inquire into the timeframe for Saturninus's activity in Antioch, we come up with no reliable information. Sometime in the early second century would be a safe enough guess.

4. Two Asian Heresies:
Nicolaitans and Cerinthus (Foerster 1:35–36)

In the seven letters addressed by the risen Christ in the New Testament book of Revelation to seven churches in Asia Minor, a group of deviant Christians called Nicolaitans (not included in Foerster's anthology) are roundly condemned. The church at Ephesus is praised for hating the "works of the Nicolaitans" (Revelation 2:6, RSV). The church at Pergamum is reproved for tolerating the Nicolaitans, who are said to promote fornication and the eating of food sacrificed to idols (2:20). The church at Thyatira is reproved for tolerating a prophetess called Jezebel, who is also said to be promoting fornication and the eating of sacrificed food (2:20). She is probably a Nicolaitan leader whose teachings are said to include knowledge of "the deep things of Satan" (2:24).

Who were these people? John the Seer does not tell us anything more about them, but almost a century later Irenaeus (*Against Heresies* 1.26.3) informs us that the founder of the group was Nicolaus, the Jewish proselyte from Antioch included among the seven Hellenist leaders in the early days of the Jerusalem church (Acts 6:5). The only information he gives us in Book 1 about the Nicolaitans is what he has read in the book of Revelation, but in Book 3 he refers to them as "an offset of that 'knowledge' falsely so called" according to which the Creator is distinguished from the transcendent Father of the Lord (3.11.1). This may imply that the Nicolaitans were Gnostics of some sort, but we are certainly entitled to doubt that the Nicolaus mentioned in the book of Acts was a Gnostic.

That claim is made, however, by Hippolytus in his *Refutation of All Heresies*. He points out that there are among the Gnostics differences of opinion, but he then singles out Nicolaus as "a cause of the widespread combination of these wicked men." After his appointment by the Apostles, Nicolaus "departed from correct doctrine," and his followers were condemned by John in his Apocalypse (*Refutation* 7.36). But Hippolytus does not seem to have any independent knowledge of Nicolaus or his teachings.

He is apparently extrapolating from what he has read in Irenaeus's work and the book of Revelation.

One of the characteristic features of the Nicolaitans in the heresiological accounts is their sexual promiscuity, read out of the book of Revelation. Most of the patristic writers follow Irenaeus in tracing their alleged practices back to Nicolaus. One exception is Clement of Alexandria, who attempts to distinguish the licentious practices of the Nicolaitans from the "apostolic" Nicolaus himself, who was misunderstood by his followers (*Miscellanies* 3.25–26; compare 2.118). By the time we get to Epiphanius, heresiological fancy takes over completely. In his *Panarion,* Epiphanius traces all sorts of nefarious practices back to Nicolaus (25.1; 26.1).

The various patristic writers who treat the Nicolaitans seem to have little or no direct knowledge of this group. And where Irenaeus got the notion that the Nicolaitans of the book of Revelation were followers of the Nicolaus referred to in the book of Acts is anyone's guess. The heresiological reports regarding the Nicolaitans are best taken with a great deal of skepticism. In any case, there is little or nothing in what is said of them in the book of Revelation that would lead us to think that they were Gnostics of any sort.

The case of Cerinthus is even more complicated, for the reports about him are contradictory. Irenaeus includes in his catalog of heresies a short account of the teachings of this man, who was active somewhere in Asia Minor. According to Irenaeus, Cerinthus taught that the world was not made by the highest God, but by a lower deity who is ignorant of the transcendent God. That idea is certainly typical of Gnosticism. Cerinthus is also said to have taught that Jesus was not born of a virgin but was the human son of Joseph and Mary. This low Christology is at home not in Gnosticism, but in early Jewish Christianity.

A kind of separation Christology is involved in what is attributed to Cerinthus regarding what happened to Jesus after his baptism: the heavenly Christ descended on him in the form of a dove and proclaimed the unknown Father. At the end, the Christ withdrew from the earthly Jesus, who suffered and then rose from the dead. The spiritual Christ, on the other hand, is incapable of suffering. This kind of Christology is found in some Christian Gnostic systems. But Irenaeus may be interpreting in a Gnostic direction an adoptionist Christology according to which Jesus was adopted by God as his son (the Christ) on the occasion of his baptism. That is a view that is at home in Jewish Christianity. In any case, Irenaeus's presentation of Cerinthus's teachings appears to be a hodgepodge of information without much consistency.

Irenaeus later tells a story about how the disciple John went into a bathhouse in Ephesus and quickly left upon seeing Cerinthus there. Rushing out, he warned bystanders of the danger posed to the bathhouse because "the enemy of truth" was in there (*Against Heresies* 3.3.4). Irenaeus provides no further information on the teachings of this "enemy of truth."

A completely different picture of Cerinthus is given in other sources. The fourth-century church historian Eusebius quotes from a treatise written around the end of the second century by a Roman presbyter named Gaius. In this quotation Gaius attributes to Cerinthus a doctrine based on revelations supposedly given by a great apostle according to which there will be an earthly kingdom of Christ that will last a thousand years (*Ecclesiastical History* 3.28.1). This is obviously a reference to the doctrine of the Millennium found in chapter 20 of the book of Revelation, a book obviously rejected by Gaius. Eusebius reports that Dionysius, Bishop of Alexandria (247–264), said the same thing about the Cerinthian heresy (3.28.4–5). According to these accounts Cerinthus was a chiliast, that is, a teacher who took literally, and expanded on, the doctrine of the thousand-year reign of Christ found in Revelation 20 (the Greek word for 1,000 is *chilioi*). Chiliasm was especially prevalent in second-century Asia Minor, and Irenaeus himself, who came to Gaul from Asia Minor, was a chiliast.

These two views of the teachings of Cerinthus are contradictory. The expectation of a kingdom of Christ on earth is incompatible with the Gnostic view of the material creation and bodily existence. It fits better with a type of Jewish Christianity that also teaches a low Christology such as can also be seen reflected in Irenaeus's account.

So we are driven to the conclusion that Cerinthus was not a Gnostic at all, but a chiliast Christian. He was probably active around the turn of the second century.

5. The Carpocratians (Foerster 1:36–40)

Clement of Alexandria devotes the bulk of the third book of his *Miscellanies* to marriage, and discusses the various views of marriage that have been espoused by the heretics. He reports that "the followers of Carpocrates and Epiphanes think that wives should be common property. Through them the worst calumny has become current against the Christian name" (*Miscellanies* 3.5). Referring to pagan accusations of sexual license allegedly practiced by Christians, Clement is suggesting that it is Christian heretics who have provided the basis for the pagan charges. In the discussion that follows Clement concentrates on the teachings of Carpocrates' son Epiphanes, and says nothing of substance about Carpocrates himself except that he promoted sexual license among his followers in Alexandria.

In a letter fragment attributed to Clement allegedly discovered in 1958 by the historian Morton Smith in the Mar Saba monastery in Palestine, Clement, writing to an otherwise unknown person named Theodore, discusses a *Secret Gospel of Mark* in use by the Alexandrian church, and quotes two passages from it. In that letter it is reported that Carpocrates "enslaved" a certain presbyter of the Alexandrian church from whom he got a copy of the *Secret Gospel*. Carpocrates produced his own version of it, interpreting it "according to his blasphemous and carnal doctrine." Clement adds, "from this mixture is drawn off the teaching of the Carpocratians." One line, "naked man with naked man," quoted from the Carpocratian edition of the gospel, would indicate that Carpocratian sexual license included homosexual acts.

Some scholars have long cast doubt on the authenticity of the letter to Theodore, but many prominent scholars have accepted it as genuine. A learned expert on the detection of forgeries, Stephen Carlson, has recently argued that the letter to Theodore is an elaborate hoax perpetrated by the late Columbia historian Morton

Smith on his unsuspecting colleagues. I am fully persuaded by Carlson's arguments.

From the little information that the real Clement provides, it can hardly be concluded that Carpocrates and Epiphanes were Gnostics. In that respect Clement differs from Irenaeus, who introduces his account of the Carpocratians with the statement that "Carpocrates and his disciples say that the world and what is in it was made by angels, who are much inferior to the unbegotten Father" (*Against Heresies* 1.25.1). That is certainly consonant with what we know of Gnostic doctrine. To be sure, Irenaeus does lay stress on the Carpocratians' licentious behavior.

Irenaeus continues his account with what the Carpocratians teach about Jesus. He was born of Joseph, but had a soul that was superior to that of others in that it "remembered" a vision of the unbegotten God. So Jesus received power to escape the world creators. Though reared in the Jewish traditions Jesus "despised them." By following his example, others are able to despise the creator archons and their laws and escape from their grip. This can be done by practicing every kind of deed that the creator archons forbid. Indeed, those who fail to practice all of the forbidden things will be reincarnated until they pay their dues.

> *"When you are with your adversary on the way, take pains to get free of him, lest he deliver you to the judge and the judge to his servant, and cast you into prison. Truly I tell you, you will not come out from there until you have paid the last penny." According to Irenaeus, this saying of Jesus was used by the Carpocratians to justify licentious behavior in order to escape the grip of the archons.*

One of Jesus's sayings is used as a basis for this doctrine: "When you are with your adversary on the way, take pains to get free of him, lest he deliver you to the judge and the judge to his servant, and cast you into prison. Truly I tell you, you will not come out from there until you have paid the last penny" (*Against Heresies* 1.25.4, my translation; compare Matthew 5:25-26 // Luke 12:58-59). The "adversary" in question is one of the angels, appointed to bring the soul to the "Prince" of the world creators, who hands over the soul to another angel who then shuts it up in another body.

Irenaeus may be basing his account on what he has learned of certain Carpocratians resident in Rome. He reports that one of their leaders is a woman named Marcellina, who came to Rome during the bishopric of Anicetus (154–65 CE). He also says that "they call themselves gnostics." As part of their religious paraphernalia they have painted images of Christ and such philosophers as Pythagoras, Plato, and Aristotle (1.25.6).

As for Carpocrates himself, Irenaeus seems to know little or nothing. And we are entitled to question whether Carpocrates posited the split between the transcendent God and the world creators that Irenaeus attributes to his followers. In any case, we see no trace of such a doctrine in what Clement says about him. So we cannot say with any degree of certainty that Carpocrates was a Gnostic, even though some of his followers are later reported to have referred to themselves as Gnostics.

Irenaeus says nothing about Carpocrates' son Epiphanes. All that we know of him is what is reported by Clement (*Miscellanies* 3.5–9), who had at his disposal a treatise of his entitled *On Righteousness*, from which Clement quotes three selections. Epiphanes defines the "righteousness of God" as a "communion with equality." "The Creator and Father of all" makes no distinctions among his creatures but endows them all with equality." Distinctions of "mine" and "thine" have been introduced by human laws, and it follows from this that women should be shared equally by men. Male sexual desire cannot be legislated against because it is "an ordinance of God." The biblical lawgiver (Moses) must have been joking when he decreed that a man should not covet his neighbor's wife (Exodus 20:17).

In introducing the teachings of Epiphanes, Clement reports that his mother was from the Greek island of Cephallenia. His life lasted only seventeen years, and after his death he was honored as a god in the city of Same on Cephallenia. He had received his education from his father, Carpocrates, including special instruction in Plato, and "founded the monadic Gnosis, from which also the sect of the Carpocratians derives" (*Miscellanies* 3.5.3).

How much of this information can be credited as factual is a matter of debate among scholars. If what Clement says about Epiphanes is true, he must have been a very precocious young man. The "monadic Gnosis" referred to by Clement would presumably indicate that Epiphanes and other Carpocratians in Alexandria taught a single divine principle and made no distinction between a transcendent deity and a lower creator. Indeed, Epiphanes refers to God as "the Creator and Father of all," terminology probably derived from Plato (*Timaeus* 28c, referring to the Demiurge). So the Gnostic dualism attributed to the Carpocratians by Irenaeus does not seem to apply to the Carpocratians in Alexandria known to Clement. Either Irenaeus was wrong about what he said or the Carpocratians known to him, people resident in Rome, had adopted Gnostic dualism in the promotion of their teachings and practices.

In any case, the Carpocratians led by Marcellina in Rome were active in the second half of the second century. We should date the activity of Carpocrates in Alexandria to the early second century.

6. Justin the Gnostic (Foerster 1:48–58)

Hippolytus of Rome is our only source of knowledge about a Gnostic named Justin (*Refutation of All Heresies* 5.23–28). Although Hippolytus does not tell us anything about Justin's life, he does describe his system in considerable detail. We are not informed as to the locus of Justin's activity, but a safe assumption is that he was active in Rome sometime in the second century.

Hippolytus begins his account by stating that Justin teaches doctrines contrary to the Scriptures and the oral or written teaching of the evangelists, basing much of his teaching on Greek myths and legends. Justin is said to bind his followers with oaths not to reveal his mysteries to outsiders. He is also reported to have used many books in his teaching activity, the most notable of which is a book called *Baruch*, named after one of the chief characters in it. Hippolytus reports that part of this book is an allegory of a story told by Herodotus about Hercules' encounter with a Scythian woman who bore him three sons (*Persian Wars* 4.8–10). *Baruch* is said to contain the basic essentials of Justin's entire system, and Hippolytus presents a lengthy account of its contents, liberally sprinkled with quotations from the Bible, both Old and New Testaments. Hippolytus either quotes from, or paraphrases, a copy of *Baruch* that he must have had in his possession.

Justin posits three powers, two male and one female. The primal power is called "the Good," and the second male power is the creator of all things named Elohim (Hebrew for "God"). The female power is of "double mind and double body," a young woman down to the groin but a serpent below the groin (thus resembling the Scythian woman described by Herodotus in his story about Hercules). Her name is Eden (Greek *Edem*, probably associated in the myth with Hebrew *'adamah*, "earth"). From a union between Elohim and Eden twenty-four angels are brought forth, twelve paternal angels belonging to Elohim and twelve maternal ones belonging to Eden, allegorically construed as the "Paradise" of Genesis 2:8. These angels are also called "trees"; the third of the paternal angels is Baruch (Hebrew *barukh*, "blessed"), the "tree of life," and the third of the maternal angels is Naas (Hebrew *nahash*, "snake"), the tree of the knowledge of good and evil (Genesis 2:9). The angels of Elohim take earth from the upper part of Eden and make Adam, putting into him the soul (from Eden) and the spirit (from Elohim). Eve is created similarly, and they are commanded to multiply (Genesis 1:28). The marriage of Adam and Eve is construed as imitating the marriage of Elohim and Eden.

Justin posits three powers, two male and one female. The primal power is called "the Good," and the second male power is the creator of all things named Elohim (Hebrew for "God").

Evil arises as a result of Elohim's departure from Eden. Elohim goes up to the heavens, taking his angels with him, and when he comes to the limit of heaven he sees a light better than the one he had created. Elohim enters through a gate and sees the Good, who invites Elohim to sit at his right hand (compare "Sit at my right hand," Psalm 110:1 RSV). Abandoned by Elohim, Eden, through her angels, brings about the evil of adultery and divorce among humans. She gives special power to her third angel Naas to punish the spirit of Elohim in human beings. Naas deceives Eve and commits adultery with her; he also deceives Adam and commits pederasty with him.

Elohim sees this and sends Baruch down for the assistance of his spirit that is in humans. Baruch is sent to Moses, to the prophets, and to Hercules in attempts to help the spirit of Elohim, but is repeatedly thwarted by Naas. Finally, Baruch is sent to Nazareth and there finds Jesus, the twelve-year-old son of Mary and Joseph, tending sheep. Baruch proclaims to Jesus all that has happened and exhorts him to proclaim to people the news about the father Elohim and the Good. Jesus remains faithful to Baruch, proclaiming his message. Naas, failing to seduce Jesus, arranges to have him crucified. Jesus then leaves the earthly body of Eden on the cross and goes up to the Good. Jesus's ascent parallels that of Elohim, and is paradigmatic of the ascent to the Good that awaits those in whom the spirit of Elohim is awakened through gnosis.

In what appears to be a later gloss, the Good is identified with Priapus, a Greek phallic deity associated with fertility (*Refutation* 5.26.32–35). This association seems incongruous, for the Good in Justin's system is utterly transcendent, beyond the world created by Elohim and Eden.

Justin's gnosis also has ritual elements. Hippolytus quotes the oath sworn by his followers, based on the oath said to have been sworn by Elohim: "I swear by him who is above all things, 'the Good,' to preserve these mysteries and to declare them to no one, neither to turn back from 'the Good' to the creation." They then experience a vision of "what eye has not seen and ear has not heard and has not entered into the heart of man" (compare 1 Corinthians 2:9). They also drink from water in which they have been baptized, a practice also attested among the Mandaeans (discussed in chapter 12).

Justin's system is an interesting mix of biblical, Jewish, Christian, and pagan traditions. At the end of his account Hippolytus asserts that, of all the heresies that he has encountered, none is more wicked than that of Justin (*Refutation* 5.27).

7. Ophites and Ophians
(Foerster 1:84–99; Layton, 170–81)

Some of the church fathers refer to a group of Christian Gnostics called Ophites (Greek *ophitai*) because they are said to honor the snake of Genesis 3 (*ophis* in Greek) as a revealer of saving gnosis. Another group of Gnostics have a similar basis for their name, Naassenes (from the Hebrew word for snake, *nahash*). The Naassenes will be taken up later in this book in chapter 7. The author of a pseudonymous treatise of the third century that has come down to us among the writings of Tertullian (Pseudo-Tertullian, *Against All Heresies*) is the first to describe a system of teachings explicitly ascribed to a group called Ophites. He claims that they honor the snake of Genesis 3 for providing the knowledge of good and evil. That snake is said to have been honored by Moses in the desert when he made a bronze snake (Numbers 21), and by Jesus, when he compared himself to Moses's bronze snake (John 3:14). The author adds that the Ophites introduce this snake into their worship services.

A system of doctrine is then presented by Pseudo-Tertullian: from a single "Aeon" several others are emanated. Another being, Yaldabaoth, produces seven angelic sons, who created man. The man remained powerless and wormlike until he was given a life-spark from the primal Aeon, an anthropogony similar to that of Saturninus (discussed above). Yaldabaoth emitted the serpent, who introduced Eve to the tree of knowledge, and thus conferred upon humankind the saving gnosis.

The first part of Pseudo-Tertullian's account appears to be a summary of a Gnostic midrash (biblical exegesis) such as is embedded in the *Testimony of Truth* (NHC IX,3, discussed in chapter 4). A similar midrash is reflected in Hippolytus's account of the Peratics (discussed in chapter 7). The second part of Pseudo-Tertullian's account is an abbreviated summary of a system described in considerable detail by Irenaeus (*Against Heresies* 30). It is to be noted that Irenaeus refers to that group as "other" Gnostics, beside those he refers to in the previous chapter (chapter 29, containing material parallel to part of the *Apocryphon of John* from Nag Hammadi). Irenaeus never refers to any group as Ophites. (His discussion of the Gnostics of *Against Heresies* 29–30 will be taken up later in chapter 3). Suffice it to say here that Irenaeus refers to a succession of seven angels who govern the world: Yaldabaoth, Yao, Sabaoth, Adoneus, Eloeus, Oreus, and Astaphaeus (30.5). These same angels appear in Origen's discussion of a group he calls Ophians. The same angels are said to have been part of the teachings of "the Sethians," according to a fragmentary Alexandrian Christian writing recently published (Gesine Robinson, *Berliner "Koptische Buch,"* plate 128).

Before taking up Origen's Ophians we should make brief mention of Epiphanius's treatment of the Ophites. His account is based on the material in Irenaeus and Pseudo-Tertullian already mentioned, spiced with his usual vituperations. Epiphanius adds an interesting detail: The Ophites keep a real snake in a basket. When it is time for their "mysteries" (that is, their celebration of the Eucharist) the snake crawls onto a table and coils up among the loaves of bread (*Panarion* 37.5.6). This is perhaps nothing more than a fanciful elaboration of the cryptic statement in Pseudo-Tertullian regarding the role of the snake in the Ophite eucharistic service.

Turning now to Origen's Ophians (Greek *ophianoi*), his discussion of them is found in his lengthy refutation of an anti-Christian treatise entitled *True Doctrine*, written by a second-century Alexandrian pagan named Celsus. Celsus's work is known only from the excerpts quoted and refuted by Origen in his apologetic writing, *Against Celsus*. In a discussion of the soul's journey through the seven heavens Celsus describes a "diagram" that he says was used by certain Christians in their "mystery" (*Against Celsus* 6.24–38). Origen says that the diagram in question, which he claims to have seen, was not used by Christians at all but by a group of people who take pride in being called Ophians, after the snake who revealed the knowledge of good and evil (*Against Celsus* 6.28).

The diagram, presumably inscribed on wood, papyrus, or vellum, contained a drawing of ten circles, held together by a single circle referred to as the "soul of the universe," called Leviathan. Leviathan was depicted again on the outer circle as a snake with a tail in its mouth. Seven "archons" (rulers) are named, associated with the gates of the various heavens, and these are the same seven as are named in Irenaeus's account of the other Gnostics. The chief of these archons (Yaldabaoth) is referred to as the "god of the Jews," said to be "accursed" because he cursed the snake that imparted knowledge to the first man. Other items inscribed on the diagram include the trees of knowledge and life, and key words such as love, life, wisdom, and knowledge (*gnōsis*).

The diagram described by Origen is very complicated and is hard to envisage, though some scholars have attempted to reconstruct it with drawings. It had a ritual use, and was presumably meant to promote the soul's safe journey through the planetary spheres to heaven.

Unfortunately, the diagram described by Origen no longer exists. But there are examples of talismans presumably used by Gnostics. Two Gnostic gems in private collections are worth mentioning here. One is an oval pendant of green jasper. On one side a lion-headed deity is carved, with the names "Ialdabaoth" and "Aariel" on either side. On the other side of the pendant are inscribed the names of the same seven archons that are found in the writings of Irenaeus and Origen already discussed (see Fig. 2.2).

The second gem is a pendant of black steatite, showing on one side a circular band with twelve sections, each with a boss in it, presumably meant to represent the Zodiac; the sun, moon, and planets are also represented. The reverse shows Adam and Eve on either side of a tree with a coiled snake. The Hebrew letters *ḥeth* (for *ḥayyiym*, "life") and *daleth* (for *da'at*, "knowledge") also occur (see Fig. 2.3). These two gems probably functioned as amulets, reminding their wearers of the gnosis, revealed by the paradise snake, that enables them to traverse the heavenly spheres and attain true life.

Fig. 2.2 Gnostic gem. Front: a lion-headed deity with the names "Ialdabaoth" and "Ariel"; on the back, the names of seven archons. Green jasper. Illustration by Christa Rubsam copyright © Augsburg Fortress, Publishers.

Were there groups of people who referred to themselves as Ophites or Ophians? Probably not. Nevertheless, one can speak loosely of an Ophite type of gnosis in which the snake of the paradise story in Genesis is honored as revealer of gnosis. Several of the Coptic texts in the Nag Hammadi corpus contain material in which the paradise snake is so featured (to be discussed in chapter 4). This is the sort of material that would inspire the heresiologists to posit an Ophite or Ophian sect. But there is no evidence at all in the Nag Hammadi material to suggest the existence of an Ophite or Ophian sect. The people in question presumably referred to themselves simply as Gnostics.

8. Cainites (Foerster 1:41–43)

Patristic accounts of the Cainites present us with questions analogous to those relating to the Ophites. Indeed, Ophites and Cainites are brought into close relationship with each other by Clement and Origen in Alexandria and Hippolytus in Rome, but these writers provide no accounts of Cainite teachings. Pseudo-Tertullian is the first to describe a system of teachings explicitly associated with the heresy of the Cainites. His discussion of the Cainites follows immediately on his treatment of the Ophites (*Against All Heresies* 2). His account is obviously dependent upon a system of teachings

Fig. 2.3 Gnostic gem. Front: a serpent spirals at the center of the Zodiac. On the back: Adam and Eve flank a tree around which a serpent—considered by Gnostics a revealer of truth—is coiled. Black steatite. Illustration by Christa Rubsam copyright © Augsburg Fortress, Publishers.

earlier described by Irenaeus. Irenaeus does not refer to Cainites at all, but presents a brief discussion of "still other" Gnostics (*Against Heresies* 1.31.1). These others are said to regard Cain as a superior being, along with such other biblical antiheroes as Esau, Korah, and the Sodomites, all of whom were protected by the intervention of Sophia. Judas Iscariot is honored for accomplishing the "mystery of the betrayal," and they use a document called the *Gospel of Judas*. They have other writings that promote the destruction of "Hystera" (the womb), associated with the creation of heaven and earth. They are also said to promote the same kind of libertine sexual behavior as was advocated by Carpocrates.

Epiphanius has a lengthy description of the Cainites (*Panarion* 38.1.1–3.5) that is obviously dependent upon Irenaeus and Pseudo-Tertullian. Epiphanius adds a few extra details: The Cainites honor the wicked and repudiate the good. Cain's superiority to Abel is based on his having been begotten by a higher power. Epiphanius also reports that they use a book called the *Ascension of Paul*, in addition to the *Gospel of Judas*, but nothing is said of its content.

Irenaeus's report of a *Gospel of Judas* in use by the other Gnostics has elicited some scholarly skepticism. Some scholars have suggested that Irenaeus misunderstood his source, and that the gospel in question could be the *Gospel of Thomas*, in which Thomas is called Judas Thomas, the twin brother of Christ in Thomas Christianity (discussed in chapter 9). But Irenaeus's reference to a *Gospel of Judas* now turns out to be correct, for it has turned up as one of the four Gnostic tractates included in the Codex Tchacos.

With the publication of the *Gospel of Judas* we can now see that there never was a Cainite Gnostic sect as such. As in the case of the Ophites, the Cainites are a figment of the heresiologists' imaginations. The Gnostic system reflected in Jesus's private revelations to Judas in the *Gospel of Judas* is that of the Classic or Sethian variety of Gnosticism (see my discussion of the *Gospel of Judas* in chapter 3). As for the figure of Cain, referred to in Irenaeus's account of the "still other" Gnostics (*Against Heresies* 1.31.1), he is usually treated in a negative light in Gnostic primary sources. There is one source, however, the treatise *On the Origin of the World* (NHC II,5), that features Cain as a revealer of gnosis (see my discussion in chapter 4).

As we have seen, the church fathers have provided us with a good deal of information on ancient Gnosticism and its various adherents. We have also seen, however, that their testimonies are not always reliable. For reliable information on ancient Gnosticism, there is no substitute for the primary sources, that is, the writings of the heretics themselves. We now have a plethora of such sources in the Coptic manuscripts preserved over the centuries by the desert sands of Egypt.

3. Sethian or Classic Gnosticism

Seth, the father of the living and unshakable race...

T HIS PHRASE COMES FROM THE INTRODUCTION to a Gnostic text containing a group of three prayers addressed by the heavenly Seth to the three primal beings of a Gnostic divine triad consisting of the invisible unknowable Father, the divine Mother Barbelo, and the Son Adamas, father of the Seth here named (*Three Steles of Seth*, NHC VII,5: 118,12–13). This divine triad is one of a number of features of a Gnostic system that has come to be defined by some scholars as Sethian Gnosticism, so called because of the prominent role played in it by Seth, a Gnostic savior figure. In the passage here quoted, the heavenly Seth is seen as the spiritual progenitor of a race of those who are saved, or destined to be saved, by the gnosis revealed by Seth. The Sethian system defined by modern scholarship is extrapolated from a group of primary texts preserved in Coptic. The use of the term Sethian may also reflect the influence of some of the patristic heresiologists, who included Sethians among the groups of heretics they were polemicizing against.

In what follows in this chapter, I shall briefly discuss, first, the accounts of those heresiologists who spoke of heretics called Sethians. I shall then treat Irenaeus's account of what he calls "a multitude of Gnostics" (*Against Heresies* 1.29.1) and the doctrines taught by them. I shall also treat briefly the Gnostics attacked by Epiphanius for their licentious behavior (*Panarion* 25–26). I shall turn, finally, to the primary texts preserved in Coptic that are thought to reflect that particular variety of Gnosticism conventionally labeled as Sethian or Classic Gnosticism. Some conclusions can then be drawn, based on the evidence discussed.

1. The Church Fathers' Accounts of Sethians
(Foerster 1:293–305; Layton, 185–98)

Hippolytus of Rome is the first of the church fathers to refer to Sethians (*Refutation of All Heresies* 5.19–22). In his description of their system of doctrine he refers to three primal powers, Light, Darkness, and Spirit between them. Seth plays no role at all in this system, except that he is mentioned as one of three sons of Adam (5.20.2). Hippolytus also refers to a treatise of theirs called the *Paraphrase of Seth* in which, he says, the entire Sethian system is set forth (5.22.1). What Hippolytus says of the Sethians is completely different from anything else that is reported of them. Indeed, one must wonder why he would attribute the teachings he describes to people called Sethians. His account of the Sethian system will be taken up later (in chapter 7).

> According to these Sethians, a great archon called Yaldabaoth, together with six other angelic beings, created man.

A completely different account is given in Pseudo-Tertullian (*Against All Heresies* 2.7), describing a system ascribed to people called "Sethoites" (Sethians). In that account Seth plays a prominent role. Cain and Abel are said to have been created by angels, but the heavenly power above, the Mother (Sophia), gave birth to Seth in order to destroy the angels. She brought about the Flood in order to destroy a mixed breed of people of human and angelic ancestry. But Noah's ark contained not only the pure race of Seth but also Ham, a descendent of the angels. So evil continued after the Flood. Later on, Seth appeared on earth as Jesus Christ.

A recently published fragmentary Coptic codex contains a third-century Alexandrian Christian work of a philosophical character (Gesine Robinson, *Berliner "Koptische Buch,"* 2004). It expands on certain biblical themes, including creation, and comments briefly on the teachings of the Sethians. According to these Sethians, a great archon called Yaldabaoth, together with six other angelic beings, created man. The others are enumerated as Sabaoth, Adonaios, Yaoth, Eloaios, Oraios, and Astaphaios (plate 128). The same archons occur in various other Gnostic sources (see, for example, our discussion of the Ophites and the names Yao, Eloeus, and Oreus in chapter 2).

The heresiologist Epiphanius expands on Pseudo-Tertullian's account in his *Panarion* in his description of the heresy of the Sethians (ch. 39). He adds that they regard a certain woman named Horaia as the wife of Seth (39.5.2). (We shall discuss the figure of Horaia [= Norea] in chapter 4.) Epiphanius also speaks of seven books of theirs attributed to Seth, and books called "Strangers" (*Allogeneis*), and revelations attributed to Abraham and Moses (39.5.1).

Epiphanius locates the Sethians in Egypt (39.1.2) and follows his discussion of them with an account of a closely related group he refers to as Archontics (40). He traces the origin of this group to a defrocked priest in Palestine named Peter, and says that this heresy has spread to Armenia (40.1.1–9). Among the books used by them are the *Lesser Harmony*, the *Greater Harmony*, the books of *Strangers* (*Allogeneis*), and books written in the name of Seth (40.2.1–2; 7.4–5). Epiphanius notes that Seth himself is called "the foreigner" (*Allogenēs*, 40.7.1–2), and adds that Seth has seven sons called "foreigners." (The origin of this title is to be found in an interpretation of "another seed" in Genesis 4:25, discussed in chapter 4.)

The teachings of the Archontics include a doctrine of several heavens, the seventh of which is ruled by Sabaoth, the god of the Jews, whose son is the devil. The eighth heaven is the abode of the "radiant Mother" (Sophia). Seth, son of Adam, was caught up to heaven and returned to teach people not to serve the creator of the world but the higher power above. The Archontics are also said to honor prophets named Martiades and Marsianos, who had experienced visionary trips to heaven (40.2.3–7.7). They are also reported to feign abstinence while engaging in sensuality, and to reject baptism and the sacraments of the church (40.2.4–6). Christ only appeared to have a material body, a doctrine that accords with their denial of the physical resurrection (40.8.2; compare 2.5).

Absent from this account is a discussion of the relationship between Seth and Christ. Given the prominent role played by Seth in their system, it is not unreasonable to assume that Epiphanius's Archontics viewed Christ as a manifestation of Seth, as in the Sethian system previously discussed. Their rejection of baptism is surprising, given the prominence of baptismal ritual in the Sethian system extrapolated from the Coptic primary sources by scholars of Gnosticism. But several other Gnostic groups are reported to have rejected water baptism.

2. The Gnostics Described by Irenaeus and Epiphanius (Foerster 1:100–5, 84–93, 41–43; Layton, 163–81, 199–214)

The first book of Irenaeus's treatise *Against Heresies*, in which the tenets of various adherents of "falsely called knowledge" are set forth, is directed mainly against the Valentinian school (treated in chapter 6). That is the variety of Gnosticism with which he is most familiar, based on his own personal acquaintance with Valentinians and their literature (*Against Heresies* 1: Preface). Chapters 1–8 are devoted to the teachings of the school of Ptolemy, one of Valentinus's most prominent pupils. Chapters 9–10 consist of refutation. Chapters 11–21 are devoted to other varieties of Valentinian gnosis, beginning with a brief account of Valentinus himself (1.11.1). Irenaeus stresses the "inconsistency" of the Valentinian heretics because they hold various and contradictory opinions. One important detail in his brief account of Valentinus is that "Valentinus adapted the fundamental principles of the so-called Gnostic school of thought to his own kind of system" (Layton's translation, p. 225). Irenaeus says that he will discuss the Gnostics later. In chapter 22 Irenaeus sets forth what he calls the "rule of truth," from which the heretics have deviated.

Some scholars have translated the text to read "Barbelognostics," and have accordingly invented a Gnostic system they call "Barbelognosis" (for example, Foerster 1:100–120), but the editors of the standard edition of Irenaeus's work have rightly rendered the text "multitudo Gnosticorum [Barbelo] exsurrexit," excising Barbelo as a secondary scribal gloss.

Irenaeus then takes up for discussion other heretics and heresies in chapters 23–28, beginning with Simon Magus and concluding with Tatian. As we have already noted, some of this material may be based on a lost work of Justin Martyr. In chapter 29 Irenaeus returns to the Gnostics, whose teachings Valentinus is said to have adapted: "Apart from those who come from the above-mentioned Simonians, there has arisen a multitude of Gnostics, appearing like mushrooms out of the ground. The principal doctrines held among them we now relate" (1.29.1). Some scholars have translated the text to read "Barbelognostics," and have accordingly invented a Gnostic system they call "Barbelognosis" (for example, Foerster 1:100–120), but the editors of the standard edition of Irenaeus's work have rightly rendered the text *multitudo Gnosticorum [Barbelo] exsurrexit*, excising Barbelo as a secondary scribal gloss. The rest of chapter 29 is devoted to part of a Gnostic myth that is also found in the *Apocryphon (Secret Book) of John*, one of the Nag Hammadi tractates. That myth is introduced by Irenaeus in the following way: "Some of them (*Quidam eorum*, that is, of the Gnostics) postulate. . . ."

Chapter 30 begins, "But others" (*Alii autem,* that is, of the Gnostics), and Irenaeus then describes other mythic traditions of that larger entity called "the Gnostic school of thought." Chapter 31, with which Irenaeus concludes the first book, begins similarly: "But still others" (*Alii autem rursus,* that is, of the Gnostics). Chapter 30 contains material commonly attributed to Ophites, and chapter 31 material attributed to Cainites. As we already noted (in chapter 2), neither an Ophite nor a Cainite sect can be extrapolated from Irenaeus's account. All three chapters deal with that larger entity referred to as "the Gnostics," or "the Gnostic school of thought," an entity that can with good reason be labeled Classic Gnosticism. This larger entity involved people who referred to themselves as Gnostics, that is, people claiming to be in possession of saving gnosis. Unlike his previous discussions of other groups, Irenaeus provides no names of sectarian leaders or founders. So we are completely in the dark as to who it was who founded the Gnostic school of thought.

The earliest named teacher whose system included a myth similar to that of the Gnostics is Saturninus of Antioch. Irenaeus provides a summary of Saturninus's myth (*Against Heresies* 1.24.1–2, discussed in chapter 2). But Saturninus's system is based on older traditions, so he should not be considered as the founder of the Gnostic school of thought.

Whether or not the Gnostic system described by Irenaeus can legitimately be labeled Sethian Gnosticism remains to be decided. In any case, Irenaeus makes no mention at all of Sethians or Sethian Gnostics. At the end of the first book, after his discussion of the Gnostics, he remarks that "those who are of the school of Valentinus derive their origin from such mothers, fathers, and ancestors" (1.31.3), thus confirming what he had said earlier about the source of Valentinus's own system (1.11.1).

Where did Irenaeus get his information about the Gnostics? We do not know, but I would surmise that he had at his disposal texts or summaries of Gnostic traditions obtained from Valentinians that he had met in Lyons and/or in Rome.

The myth paraphrased by Irenaeus in *Against Heresies* 1.29 begins with a theogony, featuring an "unnameable Father" and his "Thought" (Greek *ennoia*) named Barbelo. (The etymology of *Barbelo* is uncertain, but has sometimes been thought to derive from Hebrew: *b'arb'a* + *'el*, "in four" + "god," an allusion to the Tetragrammaton, that is, the divine name YHWH.) Further emanations in the divine world of beings called "aeons" ("eternities") take place, including Christ, four luminaries, and Adamas. From a lower aeon, Sophia (Wisdom), comes an ignorant and arrogant being who is creator of this world. Irenaeus breaks off his account with the vain claim of the lower creator, "I am a jealous God, and beside me there is no one" (compare Exodus 20:5; Isaiah 45:5; 46:9).

As already noted, Irenaeus's report parallels part of the Coptic *Apocryphon of John,* whose myth will be discussed later. What Irenaeus has before him is just an excerpt from a larger whole, but that larger whole is not to be identified as the *Apocryphon of John,* which probably achieved its present form later than the time of Irenaeus.

Irenaeus begins his discussion of the teachings of the other Gnostics (*Against Heresies* 1.30) with a variant theogony, beginning with the "Father of all," also called "First Man"; his "Thought" (Ennoia); "Second Man" or "Son of Man"; the "Holy Spirit," also called "First Woman"; a third male called "Christ"; and the female "Sophia Prunicus" ("Lewd Wisdom"), from whom come the creators and rulers of the lower world. Yaldabaoth is the chief of seven rulers. His name is often interpreted according to an Aramaic etymology as "Child of Chaos." The six other powers are Yao, Sabaoth, Adoneus, Eloeus, Oreus, and Astaphaeus (discussed in our treatment of the Ophites in chapter 2, and now also found in the Alexandrian treatise cited above) who produce other angelic powers. From Yaldabaoth come all the lower world's evils and demonic forces, and he makes the vain claim, "I am Father and God, and above me there is none" (1.30.6; compare Isaiah 45:5).

An anthropogony follows, with Yaldabaoth saying to his fellow powers, "Come, let us make a man in our image" (Genesis

1:26). When Yaldabaoth breathes life into the creature he unwittingly becomes bereft of the trace of light he had received from his mother. The man receives mind, and that is the human element that is ultimately saved. Yaldabaoth then creates a woman called Eve. The Mother (Sophia) contrives to have the Snake transgress the command of Yaldabaoth, and when Adam and Eve eat of the forbidden tree they come to know "the Power which is above all" and separate themselves from those who had made them (1.30.7). They are then expelled from paradise.

Several other references are made to the Snake. He is said to have been "cast down into the world below" because he had worked against his father (Yaldabaoth). The Snake then produced six sons, and they, together with him, are "the seven demons of the world" (1.30.8). The "objectionable Snake" and his sons conceive Cain, who brings death to the world. The Snake has two names, Michael and Samael (1.30.9). Some Gnostics are reported to say that "Sophia herself became the Snake" and "put knowledge in men" (1.30.15).

The children of Adam and Eve include Cain and Abel, Seth, and Seth's sister Norea. A Gnostic biblical history follows, with references to Noah and the flood, the covenant with Abraham, and several prophets, who are said to belong to the seven archons. Yaldabaoth has Moses, Joshua, Amos, and Habakkuk, and the other prophets are distributed among the other six. Prunicus (Sophia) arranges for Yaldabaoth to produce two men, John from the barren Elizabeth, and Jesus from the virgin Mary. Christ comes down from heaven upon Jesus and leaves Jesus at the crucifixion. After the resurrection Jesus remains on earth for eighteen months, teaching mysteries to his disciples. He then ascends to heaven and sits at the right hand of his father Yaldabaoth. There Jesus "enriches himself with holy souls," while his father is reduced. The consummation will come when all of the spirit of light (the totality of Gnostic souls) is gathered into the Aeon of Imperishability (1.30.10–14).

Irenaeus concludes his account of the Gnostics with a discussion of others who honor Cain (1.31.1–2, material already discussed in chapter 2 in the section on Cainites).

Epiphanius discusses "the Gnostics or Borborites" (Greek *borboritai,* from *borboros,* "mud, filth") in chapters 25 and 26 of his *Panarion* in a highly convoluted account in which all sorts of lewd and lascivious acts are attributed to them. He repeatedly traces these Gnostics back to Nicolaus, "one of the seven deacons chosen by the apostles" (25.1.1). (Nicolaus and the Nicolaitans were discussed earlier, in chapter 2.)

> A constant theme in Epiphanius's account is the group's promiscuous sexual behavior. Libertine sexual behavior is coupled with the prohibition of bringing forth children, something that would prevent the parents' salvation.

Epiphanius's account includes some of the same figures as are found in Irenaeus's discussion of the Gnostics: Barbelo, Yaldabaoth, Yao, Eloaios, Adonaios, Seth, Noria (Norea), and others. But hopeless confusion is evident when, for example, Yaldabaoth is said to be the first offspring of Barbelo, or that these Gnostics venerate Yaldabaoth and compose books in his name (25.5.2–5). From Epiphanius's account it is impossible to see reflected any coherent Gnostic system.

A constant theme in Epiphanius's account is the group's promiscuous sexual behavior. Libertine sexual behavior is coupled with the prohibition of bringing forth children, something that would prevent the parents' salvation. Their rituals are reported to involve the consumption of male semen and female menses, referred to as the body and blood of Christ (26.4.4–5.1). Should one of the group's members become pregnant, the fetus is aborted and ritually consumed (26.5.4–6).

It is clear that the Gnostics treated by Epiphanius have little or nothing to do with those treated by Irenaeus. Some scholarly skepticism has rightly been expressed as to the reliability of Epiphanius's account. What gives us pause, however, is that he reports that he had himself encountered this heresy in Egypt, and successfully rejected the advances of some of the group's women. He says that he reported the group to the bishops there and around eighty people were expelled from the city (presumably Alexandria, 26.17.4–9). He also refers by name to several of the books used by the group, and quotes from a *Gospel of Eve* (26.3.1), a book called the *Birth of Mary* (26.12.1–2), and a *Gospel of Philip* (26.13.2). The quotation from the *Gospel of Philip* contains a revelation from the Lord on what an ascending soul should say to various powers in order to complete the ascent successfully. The *Gospel of Philip* here quoted obviously has nothing to do with the Nag Hammadi tractate of the same name (treated in chapter 6).

It is not inconceivable that groups of deviant Christians calling themselves Gnostics such as those described by Epiphanius really existed. What is clear is that such groups fall outside the scope of what can legitimately be called Sethian or Classic Gnosticism. In any case, there is no primary evidence in our Coptic sources for libertine forms of Gnosticism.

3. Sethian Gnostic Writings Preserved in Coptic

The Nag Hammadi library contains several tractates that are clearly related to one another and show various thematic or literary inter-dependencies. A prominent feature of these interrelated texts is the notion of an elect group of people who see themselves as the spiritual seed or race of Seth, son of Adam. Study of these texts has led some scholars to posit a variety of Gnosticism called Sethianism, featuring a distinct system consisting of the following elements: a focus on Seth as a savior figure and spiritual ancestor of the Gnostic elect, a primal divine triad of an ineffable Father, a Mother called Barbelo, and a Son referred to as Autogenes (Ungenerated), sometimes called Adamas; four emanated light beings or luminaries named Harmozel, Oroaiel, Daveithe, and Eleleth and other super-terrestrial beings related to them; a salvation history thought of as three descents of the Savior, or three critical periods marked by flood, fire, and final judgment; and rituals of baptism and ascent.

Eleven of the Nag Hammadi tractates make up the Sethian corpus, plus the "Untitled Text" of the Bruce Codex, and two from the Codex Tchacos. Of course, not all of the specific Sethian markers are present in all of the texts, which in any case are of various genres. Some of them show no Christian influence: *Apocalypse of Adam, Thought of Norea, Three Steles of Seth, Zostrianos, Allogenes,* and *Marsanes.* Of these, the first reflects strong Jewish influence, and the last four strong influences from Middle Platonism. Other tractates show various degrees of Christianization: *Apocryphon of John, Trimorphic Protennoia, Hypostasis of the Archons,* and *Gospel of the Egyptians. Melchizedek* is a text whose Sethian features appear to be later accretions. Christian influence is clearly present in the late "Untitled Text" from the Bruce Codex, and the two tractates of the Codex Tchacos. Clearly the most important of these tractates is the *Apocryphon of John,* which can also be taken as the best example we have of what can also be called Classic Gnostic scripture.

In addition, several of the other Nag Hammadi tractates reflect the influence of the Sethian type of Gnosticism, notably with respect to certain mythological elements. These will be taken up in due course in the following chapters. We begin our discussion of Gnostic Sethianism with the *Apocryphon of John.*

a. *Apocryphon (Secret Book) of John* (NHC II,1: 1,1–32,9 equals IV,1:1,1–49,28; *NH Library,* 104–23; Foerster 1:105–20; Layton, 23–51; *NH Scriptures,* 103–32).

The *Apocryphon of John* (hereafter abbreviated as *Ap. John*) is extant in four copies, three from the Nag Hammadi corpus and one from the Berlin Codex. Two different recensions are reflected in these copies, a longer one (NHC II,1; IV,1) and a shorter one (NHC III,1; BG,2). The versions in Codices III and IV are very fragmentary, and can be ignored for our purposes here. (*NH Library, NH Scripture,* and Layton contain the longer version, and Foerster 1 the shorter one.) In

In terms of literary genre Ap. John is an apocalypse (revelation), containing secrets revealed by the risen Christ to his disciple John, son of Zebedee.

terms of literary genre *Ap. John* is an apocalypse (revelation), containing secrets revealed by the risen Christ to his disciple John, son of Zebedee. Within the apocalyptic frame at the beginning and end

61

of the text there are two main sections, a revelation discourse and a commentary on Genesis 1–7. The commentary has been modified into a dialogue between Jesus and his interlocutor, John. A number of sources are reflected in the document as a whole, and some internal confusion is evident. But its basic structure is clear enough.

The following outline will illustrate the structure and content of *Ap. John,* citing the Coptic text of the longer version (NHC II) and that of the shorter one (BG) in parentheses.

Preamble and apocalyptic frame	1,1–2,26 (19,6–22,17)
I. Revelation discourse	2,26–13,13 (22,17–44,18)
A. Theosophy	
1. Negative theology: the unknown God	2,26–4,10 (22,17–26,6)
2. Divine emanations and heavenly world	4,10–9,24 (26,6–36,15)
B. Cosmogony	
1. Fall of Sophia	9,25–10,23 (36,15–39,4)
2. Cosmic world of darkness	10,23–13,5 (39,4–44,9)
3. Blasphemy of the Demiurge	13,5–13 (44,9–18)
II. Dialogue: soteriology	13,13–31,25 (44,19–75,15)
1. Repentance of Sophia	13,13–14,13 (44,19–47,18)
2. Anthropogony	14,13–21,16 (47,18–55,18)
3. Adam in Paradise	21,16–24,18 (55,18–62,3)
4. Seduction of Eve; Cain and Abel	24,8–34 (62,3–63,12)
5. Seth and his seed	24,35–25,16 (63,12–64,12)
6. Two spirits: classes of humans	25,16–27,30 (64,12–71,2)
7. Production of Fate	27,31–28,32 (71,2–72,12)
8. Noah and the flood	28,32–29,15 (72,12–73,18)
9. Angels and daughters of men	29,16–30,11 (73,18–75,10)
10. Triple descent of Pronoia	30,11–31,25 (75,10–13)
Apocalyptic frame and title	31,25–32,9 (75,14–77,5)

Ap. John contains a basic Gnostic myth that has been Christianized by editorial additions and revisions. A good analogy can
be found in two other Nag Hammadi texts: The non-Christian *Eugnostos the Blessed* (NHC III,3;V,1) has its Christianized version in
the *Sophia of Jesus Christ* (NHC III,4; BG,3). The Christianization
of *Ap. John* can be seen from its literary structure: When we remove
the apocalyptic framework at the beginning and the end, together
with the dialogue features involving ten questions put to Christ
by his interlocutor John, we are left with material in which nothing identifiably Christian remains, except for some easily removed
glosses. The first part, containing the revelation discourse, may
originally have been a separate unit. It is precisely this material that
is parallel to Irenaeus's paraphrase of a text used by the Gnostics
(*Against Heresies* 1.29). The second part, containing the dialogue,
has some thematic parallels to Irenaeus's treatment of the other
Gnostics (*Against Heresies* 1.30). That part consists essentially of
an esoteric commentary on Genesis 1–7, expanded by material on
the destiny of the soul that appears to have been interpolated into
the commentary (item II.6 in our outline). The anthropogony in
the longer version contains material from a "Book of Zoroaster"
(II 19,10) that is absent from the shorter version. The hymn of Pronoia (II.10 in our outline) is also absent from the shorter version.

Christianizing glosses vary in extent from one version to another.
The heavenly aeon Autogenes, the Son in the Sethian divine triad, is
identified with the preexistent Christ
in the first part of the revelation discourse. That identification is made
initially in the shorter version at BG
30,14–17, but it is absent from the
parallel passage in the longer version
(II 6,23–25). Sophia is called "our
sister Sophia" in the shorter version.
The shorter version has Epinoia
(thought, a manifestation of Sophia) teach Adam and Eve knowledge from the forbidden tree; in the longer version it is Christ who

> *The basic Gnostic myth in*
> Ap. John *(citing hereafter
> the version in Codex II)
> begins with a description of
> the primal Father, the invis-
> ible Monad (sole unity)
> who is above and beyond
> everything.*

does this. Such examples could be multiplied, but the basic point is clear: The various versions of *Ap. John,* taken together, show that the Christian elements in it are secondary. The basic text, apart from the Christian additions or revisions, is an early Gnostic text that consists of innovative reinterpretations of biblical and Jewish traditions.

As for the Christianized version that we have, *Ap. John* shows considerable influence from the Gospel of John in the New Testament. Indeed, it can easily be construed as an esoteric continuation of the Gospel of John, featuring postresurrection revelations that continue the post-resurrection material in the Gospel of John (chs. 20–21). Now it is clear who the anonymous "beloved disciple" in the Gospel of John is: He is Jesus' disciple John, son of Zebedee. This reflects the second-century tradition identifying the anonymous author of the Gospel of John as the disciple John. *Ap. John* can thus be taken as a Gnostic second volume of the Gospel of John. I suggest a late second- or early third-century date for the original Greek version of *Ap. John* as we now have it in Coptic translation.

The basic Gnostic myth in *Ap. John* (citing hereafter the version in Codex II) begins with a description of the primal Father, the invisible Monad (sole unity) who is above and beyond everything. I use the word "description" loosely because much of this account consists of a negative theology, with a series of negative adjectives: "invisible," "illimitable," "unsearchable," "immeasurable," "ineffable," "unnameable," and so on. (Part of this passage, II 3,10–35, corresponds almost word-for-word to one found in *Allogenes* XI 62,28–63,23.) Yet, there are positive assertions as well: "light," "life-giving," "grace," and so on. Such assertions prepare us for the divine unfolding that begins with the first of a number of emanations, his "Thought" (Greek *ennoia*), "the first power" (called Barbelo, who is also "Mother-Father," "thrice-male," "the first to come forth"), and so on (4,27–5,11). She becomes the initiator of further emanations granted by the invisible Father: "fore-knowledge," "indestructibility," "eternal life," and "truth." She also becomes the Mother of a divine "son" called Autogenes ("self-begotten"), from whom emanate additional entities, including four luminaries called Harmozel, Oroiel, Davithai, and Eleleth, and the "perfect Man" called Geradamas (or Pigeradamas, also called Adamas. The prefix "ger" may be taken as the Hebrew word for "stranger.") Associated with each of the four luminaries are other aeons (eternal realms, personifications of virtues or positive attributes): Grace, Truth, and Form with Harmozel; Conception (or Reflection, *epinoia*), Perception, and Memory with Oroiel; Understanding, Love, and Idea with Daveithai; Perfection, Peace, and Wisdom (Sophia) with Eleleth.

The perfect Man can clearly be seen as a heavenly projection of Adam. The virginal Spirit (that is, the Father) places him over the first aeon in association with Harmozel. Geradamas then places his own son Seth over the second aeon by the second luminary Oroiel. The "seed of Seth," the "souls of the saints," are placed over the third luminary Daveithe, and the souls of those who come late to repentance are associated with Eleleth. All of these beings are said to "glorify the invisible Spirit" (9,24).

Then comes a tragic break within the heavenly world. Sophia, the youngest of the aeons, desires to bring forth a likeness of herself without the consent of the invisible Spirit and without a consort, and the result is an ugly being called Yaldabaoth. He is the first of the lower archons (rulers), and from him come twelve other archons and seven rulers over the seven heavens (that is, planetary spheres). The chief archon has two other names, Saklas (from Aramaic "fool") and Samael (Hebrew "blind god"). In his foolish arrogance he says, "I am God and there is no other God beside me" (11,19–21; compare Isaiah 45:5; 46:9).

Additional archons are produced, a group of seven powers and 365 angels. Yaldabaoth then organizes the lower spatiotemporal cosmos. Seeing what he has created he says, "I am a jealous God and there is no other God beside me" (Exodus 20:5; Isaiah 45:5, 46:9). The tractate's author remarks sarcastically that Yaldabaoth is ignorantly indicating to the angels that there is another God,

"For if there were no other one, of whom would he be jealous?" (13,12–13). With this vain claim made by Yaldabaoth, a topos that recurs in several other Gnostic texts, we can very clearly see who he really is: He is the biblical Creator of heaven and earth. There is, indeed, another deity above him. But that deity, too, can easily be identified with the Jewish God. So what the Gnostics have done is split the biblical God into two. (This will be elaborated on in the following chapter.)

The myth continues with an extended commentary on key texts in the biblical book of Genesis, with editorial comments explicitly contradicting what Moses said. The Mother (Sophia) "moves" agitatedly to and fro, not "over the waters" as Moses would have it (Genesis 1:2), but in shame and repentance. The invisible Spirit consents to her being elevated to the ninth sphere of heaven "until she has corrected her deficiency" (14,12–13). A voice comes from heaven and rebukes Yaldabaoth: "Man exists and the Son of Man" (14,14–15). A luminous human-formed image appears in the cosmic waters, and Yaldabaoth says to his fellow archons, "Come, let us create a man according to the image of God and according to our likeness, that his image may become a light for us" (15,1–4; compare Genesis 1:26–27). They then create a being of soul-substance that they call Adam, and each of the angels contributes something to his formation. The longer version of *Ap. John* elaborates on this with 365 angels with strange names contributing parts of Adam's body (15,29–19,10, a passage said to be taken from "the Book of Zoroaster").

The longer version has Christ ("I," in dialogue with John) appearing in the form of an eagle on the tree to teach them and awaken them from sleep (23,26–31), recognizable as a Christian gloss. In the shorter version it is Epinoia who appears in the form of an eagle on the tree and teaches knowledge to Adam and Eve (BG, 60,19–61,4), surely a more original feature.

But Adam remains lifeless until the Mother (Sophia) contrives to retrieve the remaining power that she had given to Yaldabaoth by getting him to breathe into Adam life-giving breath. When he does this Adam comes to life (compare Genesis 2:7), but Yaldabaoth becomes bereft of what is left of the spiritual power he had gotten from his mother. Seeing that Adam's intelligence is greater than that of those who had made him, thanks to the spirit breathed into him, they throw him down "into the lowest region of all matter" (20,8–9). A "helper" is sent to Adam, luminous Epinoia (Reflection) hidden in Adam who is also "Life" (Zoe equals Eve). The archons then imprison Adam in a material body of darkness and death.

The archons place Adam in paradise and encourage him to eat of their "tree of life," which is really death, while trying to keep him away from the "tree of knowledge." Yaldabaoth makes another creature in the form of a woman "according to the likeness of the Epinoia which had appeared to him," and part of "the power of the man" is brought into the female creature (22,34–23,4). Adam and Eve taste "the perfect knowledge" from the forbidden tree. The longer version has Christ ("I," in dialogue with John) appearing in the form of an eagle on the tree to teach them and awaken them from sleep (23,26–31), recognizable as a Christian gloss. In the shorter version it is Epinoia who appears in the form of an eagle on the tree and teaches knowledge to Adam and Eve (BG, 60,19–61,4), surely a more original feature.

The chief archon then casts Adam and Eve out of paradise. He seduces Eve and begets in her two sons, bear-faced Elohim and cat-faced Yave. Yave he sets over fire and wind, Elohim over water and earth. Yaldabaoth calls them Cain and Abel. He also plants sexual intercourse into Adam and Eve, inspiring them with his "counterfeit spirit" (24,31).

Adam then begets "the likeness of the Son of Man" and calls him Seth (compare Genesis 4:25), after the heavenly race, and the Mother (Sophia) sends down her spirit, "which is in her likeness and a copy of those who are in the Pleroma" (24,36–25,5). The product of Sophia here is unnamed, but may be seen as an equivalent of Seth's consort-sister Norea, about which more will be said subsequently (ch. 4). It is said that "she will prepare a dwelling place for the aeons which will come down," perhaps a reference to the totality of the Gnostic elect, the seed or race of Seth (25,5–7).

At this point in the text there is an extended discussion of the destiny of human souls. This passage, in the form of a catechism (25,26–27,30), appears to be a secondary interpolation. Those of the "immovable race" (of Seth) on whom the Spirit of life descends will be given eternal life. Ignorant souls, in whom the counterfeit spirit is dominant, will be reincarnated and given another chance. Apostate or unrepentant souls will be subject to eternal punishment. This passage, with its two opposing spirits, is comparable to one in the *Rule of the Congregation,* one of the Dead Sea Scrolls, featuring opposing spirits of light and darkness (1QS III,13–IV,14).

The myth continues with Yaldabaoth bringing fate (Greek *heimarmenē*) and all sorts of evils upon humans, and then deciding to bring about a flood. Noah and others from the immovable race are hidden in a luminous cloud. Yaldabaoth then sends his angels to the "daughters of men" (compare Genesis 6:1-4) and they produce the "counterfeit spirit" by whom the whole creation becomes enslaved until now (27,31–30,11).

The myth in the shorter version of *Ap. John* concludes with a brief reference to the blessed "Mother-Father," that is, Barbelo, who is "rich in mercy," and in whose "seed" she is "taking form" (75,10–13). The longer version has, instead, a concluding hymn featuring a threefold descent of an aspect of Barbelo called Pronoia (Providence). In this hymn Pronoia speaks in the first person, telling of her three descents into the realm of darkness (that is, this world). In her third descent she manages to awaken to gnosis "the one who hears," that is, a representative of the Gnostic elect. The hymn concludes with Pronoia proclaiming her success: "I raised him up and sealed him in the light of the water with five seals, in order that death might not have power over him from this time on" (31,22–25). The "sealing" in water with "five seals" is a baptismal ritual to which reference is made in several other Sethian texts.

Immediately following the hymn, the concluding frame story resumes, with the savior announcing his ascent to John: "I shall go up to the perfect aeon. I have completed everything for you in your hearing" (31,26–28). This juxtaposition of the two "I's" invites us to conclude that the editor of the longer version saw Christ as an incarnation of Pronoia. Indeed, that is what we find in another Sethian tractate, the *Trimorphic Protennoia* (NHC XIII,1), in which Protennoia (First Thought) speaks in the first person of her threefold descent to the world. She announces at the end of her discourse, "I put on Jesus. I bore him from the cursed wood, and established him in the dwelling places of his Father" (50,12–15).

The myth in *Ap. John* is a rather complicated one, and was probably developed from a simpler version. For example, Barbelo is clearly a Sophia (Wisdom) figure. As Ennoia, the Thought of the invisible Father, she is comparable to the mythic Ennoia found in the systems of Simon and Menander. But in *Ap. John* this Sophia figure appears at several levels: Barbelo; the younger aeon Sophia, whose fall results in the creation of the world; the restored Mother Sophia; Epinoia (Reflection), Adam's helper, who also brings gnosis to Adam and Eve; and (in the longer version) Pronoia (Providence), who accomplishes the salvation of the Gnostic elect. It is also to be noted that the various mythic references to Gnostic salvation involve a feminine savior figure: Barbelo, the Mother, Epinoia, and Pronoia. Although Seth is named in the text, both as a heavenly figure and as the son of Adam on earth, he plays no active role in bringing salvation to the elect Gnostics, even if their souls are seen to constitute the totality of the seed of Seth in the heavenly world.

When and where did the Sethian Gnostic myth reflected in *Ap. John* arise? I would provisionally assign it either to Antioch in Syria or to Alexandria in Egypt, sometime in the early second century. *Ap. John* in its Christianized form is probably a product of late second- or early third-century Alexandria.

b. *Apocalypse (Revelation) of Adam* (NHC V,5: 64,1–85,32; *NH Library*, 277–86; Layton, 52–67; *NH Scriptures*, 343–56)

The *Apocalypse (Revelation) of Adam* (hereafter abbreviated as *Apoc. Adam*) is a testamentary revelation given to Adam by three heavenly visitors and mediated by Adam to his son Seth.

Adam tells of the subsequent history of the world and the salvation of the Gnostic elect. In terms of literary genre, *Apoc. Adam* is both an apocalypse and a testament. Both of these genres are widespread in the literature of post-biblical Judaism; indeed, *Apoc. Adam* is the only Gnostic work included in the standard edition of the *Old Testament Pseudepigrapha* (ed. by James Charlesworth). It is a testament in that Adam is depicted as giving final instructions to his son

> *Close parallels have been noted between* Apoc. Adam *and Jewish Adam literature, especially the* Life of Adam and Eve *and the* Apocalypse of Moses.

Seth just before his death "in the seven hundredth year" (64,2–3), that is, seven hundred years after the birth of Seth, when Adam was two-hundred-and-thirty-years-old (according to the Greek version of Genesis 5:3-4; Adam is recorded as living nine hundred thirty years, Genesis 5:5). The biblical prototype of Jewish testamentary literature is the patriarch Jacob's blessings of his sons (Genesis 49).

At the end of the tractate, it is said that the revelations contained in it are inscribed in stone on a high mountain (85,9–11). This detail reflects a first-century Jewish tradition recorded by the Jewish historian Josephus. According to this tradition the progeny of Seth, acting upon a prediction by Adam of the world's destruction by flood and fire, recorded their astrological and other lore on two steles, one of brick to survive fire, and one of stone to survive the flood (*Jewish Antiquities* 1.67–71).

Close parallels have been noted between *Apoc. Adam* and Jewish Adam literature, especially the *Life of Adam and Eve* and the *Apocalypse of Moses*. It is possible that *Apoc. Adam* and the *Life of Adam and Eve* share a common source, that is, an earlier apocalypse of Adam. Of course the Gnostic intentionality evident in *Apoc. Adam* reflects a radical reinterpretation of earlier Jewish traditions.

The following outline will illustrate the structure and content of *Apoc. Adam*, citing the pages and lines of the Coptic text:

In the first part of the tractate, Adam narrates the experiences that he and Eve had after their creation. A comparison with the *Life of Adam and Eve* is instructive: In that text Adam and Eve, banished from paradise, repent of their sins (chs. 1–11). In *Apoc. Adam,* Adam reports that Eve had given him "knowledge of the eternal God," which made both of them like angels, superior to "the god who had created us and the powers with him" (64,12–19). Thus a contrast is immediately set up in the text between the transcendent eternal God and the lower Creator. The latter acts with jealous wrath against Adam and Eve, in a manner reminiscent of the devil in the *Life of Adam and Eve,* who had been banished from heaven for his refusal to worship the newly created Adam (chs. 12–17). The Creator is not given a name here—he is usually just called "God"—but later in the text he is called Sakla (74,3.7), one of the three names applied to the Creator in *Ap. John.* (In *Apoc. Adam* the Aramaic form is reflected, *Sakla*; elsewhere the Greek ending is used, *Saklas.*)

Adam also tells Seth that he has been given "the name of that man who is the seed of the great generation" (65,6–9), clearly a reference to the heavenly Seth referred to in *Ap. John.* While there is no explication of a Gnostic myth in *Apoc. Adam* such as the one in *Ap. John,* one can certainly see traces of such a myth reflected here and there in the text.

The main part of the text, the revelation mediated by Adam, consists essentially of a historical apocalypse in which the salvation of the elect seed of Seth is the main concern. The Gnostic elect are saved from three cataclysms by the intervention of Seth the savior: first the great flood (69,2–73,29; compare Genesis 6–9), then fire and brimstone (73,30–76,7, with allusions to the destruction of Sodom in Genesis 19:24–25), and finally end-time destruction of the reprobate and redemption of the elect seed of Seth (76,8–85,18).

In the first cataclysm, unnamed angels rescue the elect from harm. In the destruction by fire three angelic beings, Abrasax, Sablo, and Gamaliel, rescue the elect. These three occur in other texts of a Sethian stamp. The final redemption is performed by the savior Seth himself, called the "Illuminator of knowledge" (76,9–10).

This final act of redemption is disturbed in the text by what appears to be a lengthy interpolation (77,18–83,4) in which thirteen kingdoms present different erroneous notions of who the Illuminator is. Reflected in this passage are various mythic traditions found in Greco-Roman religious lore. Only the "generation without a king over it" knows him and the gnosis that he brings (82,19–83,4).

This interpolation disturbs a pattern of statements regarding the Illuminator that some scholars have taken as evidence of Christian influence. This pattern is rooted in biblical literature dealing with the suffering and exaltation of a righteous person (for example, Isaiah 52–53; Wisdom 1–6). In *Apoc. Adam* this pattern can be seen as follows:

1. Earthly persecution
   Signs and wonders of the Illuminator   (77,1–3)
   The wrath of "the god of the powers"   (77,4–15)
   Punishment of "the flesh upon whom the   (77,16–18)
      holy spirit came"
2. Exaltation and judgment
   The peoples acknowledge their sin   (83,4–84,3)
   Condemnation of the peoples   (84,4–28)
   Exaltation of the elect   (85,1–18)

This pattern of events dealing with the Gnostic savior corresponds to the salvation history of the seed of Seth: Threatened with destruction by flood and fire, they are rescued by heavenly intervention. In the final catastrophe, a manifestation of Seth suffers with his seed, and final vindication and victory is achieved. This is intelligible without any necessary reference to Jesus Christ or Christianity.

Toward the end of the text, reference is made to three beings, "Micheu and Michar and Mnesimous, who are over the holy baptism and the living water" (84,5–7). These angelic beings appear in other

It represents a very early stage in the development of Sethian Gnosticism, in which a transition from Jewish apocalyptic to Gnosticism is reflected.

Sethian texts in association with baptism. Three others, also found in other Sethian texts, occur at the very end of the text: "the imperishable illuminators, who came from the holy seed: Yesseus, Mazareus, Yessedekeus, the Living Water" (85,30–31). Reflected here is a baptismal ritual presumably practiced by Gnostics of a Sethian orientation. We encountered evidence of Sethian baptism in *Ap. John,* as well, and several other Sethian texts refer to baptism.

A Syrian milieu can be posited for *Apoc. Adam,* but scholars have not been in agreement about its date. Suggestions as to its date range from the first century BCE to the third century CE. Whatever the date of the document, its Jewish roots are clear. Typologically, if not actually, it represents a very early stage in the development of Sethian Gnosticism, in which a transition from Jewish apocalyptic to Gnosticism is reflected.

c. *Trimorphic Protennoia (Three Forms of First Thought)* (NHC XIII,*1*: 35,1–50,24; *NH Library* 511–22; Layton, 86–100; *NH Scriptures,* 715–36)

As already noted, the longer version of *Ap. John* has a hymn in which Pronoia reveals herself in a series of "I am" statements. That hymn may have been used in the composition of the *Trimorphic Protennoia (Three Forms of First Thought)* (hereafter abbreviated as *Trim. Prot.*). *Trim. Prot.* is a hymnic text in which Barbelo (named at 38,9) as "First Thought" reveals herself in a series of "I am" statements, and tells of her three descents into "chaos," that is, the lower world. The text itself is divided into three subtractates, each of them telling of a descent of Protennoia, first as "Voice" (35,1–42,3), then as

> The descent of Protennoia as "Logos" reminds us of the prologue to the Gospel of John in the New Testament (1:1-18). Some scholars have argued that the Johannine prologue derives from a myth such as is reflected in Trim. Prot. Others have argued that Trim. Prot. and the Johannine prologue share a common sapiential ("wisdom") background.

"Sound" (42,4–46,4), and finally as articulated "Word" (Logos, 46,5–50,21). The text as it now stands has a complicated structure, with alternating sections of poetic material and prose. It clearly reflects editorial development in stages over time.

Trim. Prot. contains several references to the Gnostic myth in *Ap. John.* These include the divine triad of Father, Mother, and Son (37,22); the four luminaries Harmozel, Oroiael, Daveithai, and Eleleth (38,33–39,5); and the demonic creator and ruler over this chaotic world with the three names Saklas, Samael, and Yaldabaoth (39,21–28), who vainly and arrogantly thinks there is no one above him (43,33–44,2). The Sethian baptismal ritual of five seals also appears, associated with angelic beings found in other Sethian texts (48,7–35, compare 50,9–12). These angels include Micheus, Michar, and Mnesimous (48,19–20), whom we encountered in *Apoc. Adam.*

As already noted, Protennoia in her final descent "puts on Jesus" (50,12), and Christian elements are present throughout the text. The descent of Protennoia as "Logos" reminds us of the prologue to the Gospel of John in the New Testament (1.1-18). Some scholars have argued that the Johannine prologue derives from a myth such as is reflected in *Trim. Prot.* Others have argued that *Trim. Prot.* and the Johannine prologue share a common sapiential ("wisdom") background. Still others see the influence of the Gospel of John in *Trim. Prot.*

It has been argued that *Trim. Prot.* is a Gnostic text that has been secondarily Christianized. Given its complicated structure, this is harder to argue for *Trim. Prot.* than it is for *Ap. John,* where source analysis can more easily be applied. It certainly shares a common milieu with *Ap. John,* and I would tentatively assign it to early third-century Alexandria.

d. *Hypostasis of the Archons (Nature of the Rulers)* (NHC II,4: 86,20–97,23; *NH Library,* 161–69; Layton, 65–76; *NH Scriptures,* 187–98)

The *Hypostasis of the Archons (Nature of the Rulers)* (hereafter abbreviated as *Hyp. Arch.*) is a Christian writing in its present form, but, like *Ap. John,* it reflects an early Gnostic myth of Jewish origin. It shares a good deal of material with *Ap. John*, especially in its first part, and parts of it stand in close relationship with another Nag Hammadi text, *On the Origin of the World* (NHC II,5). The Christian elements in the text are prominent at the beginning of the tractate and at its conclusion. There are also indications in the text as a whole of the use of the New Testament, especially the Pauline and Johannine writings.

The tractate consists of two main parts, preceded by a brief introduction. The introduction sets forth the subject matter of the tractate, the real nature (Greek *hupostasis*) of the authorities or archons, and the great apostle (Paul) is quoted in that connection (Colossians 1:13; Ephesians 6:12). The first main part consists of a commentary on Genesis (86,27–93,13), reflecting considerable material in common with *Ap. John*. The commentary begins with the vain claim of the Creator, Samael ("blind god"), followed by a brief mention of the creation of the world (86,27–87,11) and an extensive treatment of the creation of Adam and Eve (87,11–89,17). The authorities try to rape the spiritual Eve, but she turns into a tree and leaves only a shadowy reflection of herself for them to defile (89,17–31).

Unlike *Ap. John*, the paradise snake is given a positive role in *Hyp. Arch.* The "female spiritual principle" comes into the snake, who gets Eve to eat of the forbidden tree (89,31–91,3). (The role of the paradise snake in Gnostic literature will be discussed in chapter 4.)

In *Hyp. Arch.* Seth is not given a prominent role; instead, his sister Norea takes center stage. At Seth's birth, Eve says, "I have borne another man through God in place of Abel" (91,32–33). Though Adam is the father of Seth, he is born "through God," that is, with God's help. At Norea's birth, Eve says "He [God] has begotten on me a virgin as a help for many generations of humankind" (91,35–92,2). Divine intervention is implied in the way Eve describes Norea. (The figure of Norea will be discussed in chapter 4.) When Samael and the other archons try to seduce her, Norea cries out to God for help, and the angel Eleleth is sent to her, promising to teach her about her "root" (92,27–93,13). That passage functions as a transition to the second main part of the tractate.

With the second part of the tractate, beginning at 93,13, the narrative switches from third person to first, with Norea as the speaker, reporting on an extensive revelation given to her by the "great angel" Eleleth. Eleleth identifies himself as "one of the four luminaries who stand in the presence of the great Invisible Spirit" (93,20–22). It is probable that this part of *Hyp. Arch.* is based on a previously existing text, a putative apocalypse of Norea. In the tractate *On the Origin of the World*, reference is made to "books of Noraia" (II 102,10f.; 24f.), and we recall that Epiphanius refers to a "Book of Noria" used by the Gnostics (*Panarion* 26.1.3).

In his revelation, Eleleth tells of the fall of Sophia and the production of her ugly offspring Samael, also called Yaldabaoth, who is thrown down into Tartaros by a powerful angel (94,4–95,13). The text moves next to an account of the repentance and enthronement of Yaldabaoth's son, Sabaoth, which is an interesting passage that has a parallel in *On the Origin of the World* (II 103,32–106,18). Sabaoth repents and condemns his father Yaldabaoth and his mother, "matter." Sophia and her daughter Zoe snatch him up and put him in charge of the seventh heaven. Up there he has a "four-faced chariot of cherubim" and innumerable ministering angels. Sophia has Zoe sit at his right hand, giving him instruction about the eighth heaven, and the "angel of wrath" is seated at his left hand. This passage (95,13–96,3) is built of themes taken from Jewish traditions featuring the God of Israel, including aspects of an early form of Jewish throne mysticism. In *Hyp. Arch.* the God of Israel is further split into two lower deities: he is not only Yaldabaoth the creator, but as Sabaoth he is given partial rehabilitation.

At the end of his revelation, Eleleth tells Norea that she and her offspring are "from the primeval Father." The authorities cannot touch them because the "Spirit of Truth" is in them. At the end, the "true man" will appear and enable them to "ascend into the limitless light" (96,19–97,9). The "true man" here is probably to be understood as a reference to Christ. The tractate ends with a doxology pronounced by the children of light (97,13–21).

Hyp. Arch. is a text that has been developed from a number of earlier sources and traditions. The original Greek version of what we have now in Coptic translation was probably composed in third-century Alexandria.

e. *Thought of Norea* (NHC IX,2: 27,11–29,5; NH Library, 445–47; NH Scriptures, 607–11)

This little writing of only fifty-two lines of Coptic text is a poetic composition in four parts. It lacks a title in the manuscript; the title employed here is a phrase occurring toward the end of the tractate (29,3). The *Thought of Norea* (hereafter abbreviated as *Norea*) is closely related to *Hyp. Arch.*, which actually provides a setting for the text. In *Hyp. Arch.*, Norea

> *Norea's salvation is paradigmatic of the salvation of all of the elect Gnostics.*

is represented as crying out for help (92,33–93,2), at which point the angel Eleleth intervenes. The first part of *Norea* is a prayer addressed to the divine hierarchy, beginning with the "Father of all" and Ennoia (Barbelo in the Sethian system). The second part of the tractate begins, "It is Norea who cries out to them" (27,21–22); her prayer is heard, and she is assured of being "joined to all of the imperishable ones" (20,11).

The third part of the tractate (28,12–23) portrays Norea's activity within the Pleroma ("Fullness," that is, the heavenly world). In the fourth and final part of the text (28,24–29,5) Norea is assured of divine intercession by "the four holy helpers" (28,27–28), that is, the four "luminaries" of the Sethian system, Harmozel, Oroaiel, Daveithe, and Eleleth.

Norea functions in this tractate as a Sophia figure, herself in need of salvation and assuring salvation for her spiritual progeny. Norea's salvation is paradigmatic of the salvation of all of the elect Gnostics. It is to be noted that there are no Christian features at all in the text.

Norea can provisionally be assigned to late second- or early third-century Egypt.

f. *Gospel of the Egyptians,* or *The Holy Book of the Great Invisible Spirit* (NHC III,*2*: 40,12–44,28; IV,*2*: 55, 20–60,30; III 49,1–69,20; *NH Library* 208–19, Layton, 101–20; *NH Scriptures,* 247–69)

The correct title of this tractate is found at the very end of the version in Codex III: "The Holy Book of the Great Invisible Spirit" (69,18–19; the end of the version in Codex IV is lost). In a preceding colophon, another title is given: "The Egyptian Gospel" (69,6, missing from the version in Codex IV), which the editors of the first edition of the text emended to read "The Gospel of the Egyptians." Since that title for the tractate has been in use for many years, it is retained here (hereafter abbreviated as *Gos. Eg.*). But this work should not be confused with an apocryphal New Testament gospel called *Gospel of the Egyptians,* extant in fragments quoted by Clement of Alexandria.

> *Gos. Eg. is a highly complex text, reflecting editorial development over time.*

In two conclusions to *Gos. Eg.,* it is said that the book was written by "the great Seth" (III 68,1–2.10). He is said to have placed it on a mountain called Charaxio for the benefit of the "holy race of the great savior" (that is, Seth, 68,12–13.21–22). The name *Charaxio* is probably based on a Greek verb meaning "inscribe" (*charattō*). So Charaxio is the high-mountain rock on which the writing is inscribed. We have already encountered this motif, Seth inscribing revelations in stone on a high mountain, in *Apoc. Adam.*

Gos. Eg. is a highly complex text, reflecting editorial development over time. The two extant versions differ somewhat from one another and represent Coptic translations of two different Greek versions. Unfortunately, the text is not complete in either of the versions we have, owing to damage to the manuscripts. Citations of the text here will be given to that version that is extant and/or considered textually superior.

The tractate has three main parts. The first deals with the origin of the heavenly world and the divine beings that populate it (III 40,12–44,28; IV 55,20–60,30; III 49,1–55,16). The second main part is a history of the seed of Seth (III 55,16–64,9). The third is a baptismal liturgy that includes a series of hymns and prayers (III 64,9–67,26).

The first part features the same divine beings as are found in *Ap. John,* beginning with the invisible Spirit, unnamable Father. As in *Ap. John,* he is described in a negative theology. But the heavenly world of *Gos. Eg.* has a much heavier population than that of *Ap. John.* From Autogenes come forth another triad of Father, Mother, and Son, and a being called Doxomedon Domedon (possible etymology: "Lord of the House," "Lord of Glory") portrayed on a heavenly throne to which is attached a boxwood tablet inscribed with the vowels of the Greek alphabet, each twenty-two times (the number of letters in the Hebrew alphabet). Each of the members of the second triad has an ogdoad (eight) associated with it. Other divine entities include "thrice-male child" (Christ), a "male virgin" called Youel, a "child of the child" called Esephech, Pronoia (Providence), the "self-begotten" Logos, and Adamas. From Adamas come the four luminaries with consorts adding up to another ogdoad. Beneath the four luminaries are the ministers, Gamaliel, Gabriel, Samlo, and Abrasax. These, together with consorts, make up another ogdoad. The climax of the series of emanations comes with the appearance of Seth, the father of those who would constitute the "seed of the Great Seth," the Gnostic elect.

This material, dealing with the denizens of the heavenly world, is also interspersed with expressions of praise and blessing. The liturgical activity here attributed to the members of the divine world are probably to be taken as projections of the liturgical activity of a worshipping community of Gnostics.

The second main section of *Gos. Eg.* is dominated by the work of Seth. As son of Adamas, he is one of the lower powers of the world of light. It is through him that the light in the lower world is connected with the supreme God. This section also includes prayers performed by Seth. The first one results in the manifestation of

Plesithea ("nearby goddess"), who is called "mother of lights" and depicted as "a virgin with four breasts" (III 56,4–9). Seth takes his "seed" from her and places it in the aeon of the third luminary, Daveithe (III 56,17–22).

The story of the seed of Seth is interrupted by a cosmogonic section, describing the origin of the creator of the lower world from the lower Sophia. He is called Saklas and has a consort called Nebrouel. They produce a series of angels, including twelve cosmic angels (the Zodiac) whose names are also found in *Ap. John*. There follows the traditional "vain claim" of Saklas, "I am a jealous god, and apart from me nothing has come into being" (58,25–29; compare Exodus 20:5; Isaiah 46:9). This is followed by the traditional rebuke from heaven: "Man exists and the Son of Man" (59,1–4). A feminine being called Metanoia (repentance) appears in order to prepare the way for the ascent of the seed of Seth incarnate in earthly bodies.

The text then returns to the history of the seed of Seth, a history dominated by cataclysms of flood, fire, and end time, as in *Apoc. Adam*. Seth undergoes three "advents" (Greek *parousia*, III 63,5). Seth "puts on" Jesus (64, 1–2) and establishes baptism.

The third main section of *Gos. Eg.* consists of a baptismal liturgy. It begins with the names of heavenly beings who are said to preside over the different parts of the liturgy, beginning with Yesseus Mazareus Yessedekeus, whom we encountered in *Apoc. Adam*. Other beings include Micheus, Michar, and Mnesinous, also found in *Apoc. Adam*; the four luminaries; and others (III 64,9–65,26). It is said that those who are worthy will not "taste death" (III 65,26–66,8).

Prayers are then uttered, with invocations of the various beings associated with baptism. These prayers also include mystical names and series of repeated vowels that were presumably chanted in the liturgy. The liturgy concludes with an expression of confidence of eternal life (III 66,8–68,1).

Reference has already been made to the conclusions of the tractate, where the Great Seth is credited as its author. In the colophon, the scribe offers a prayer and identifies himself as Eugnostos ("well known" or "well knowing") "in the spirit," and gives his "fleshly" name as Concessus. The colophon includes the traditional fish acrostic ICHTHUS, the initial Greek letters of "Jesus Christ, Son of God, Savior" (III 69,6–17).

How Christian is *Gos. Eg.*? References to Christ appear throughout, and Christ is a figure in the heavenly world, as is the case with the Christianized *Ap. John.* But in *Gos. Eg.* it is the great Seth who is the Gnostic savior. To be sure, he "puts on" Jesus in his final appearance. But the question remains: Is the tractate a Christianized version of an earlier text of a non-Christian character? Scholars differ on that point. We do note some points of contact between *Gos. Eg.* and *Apoc. Adam,* which is often (but not always) taken to be a text lacking Christian elements.

In any case, the Greek originals of the Coptic translations of *Gos. Eg.* we now have can provisionally be assigned to third-century Egypt.

g. *Melchizedek* (NHC IX,1: 1,1–27,10; NH Library, 438–44; NH Scriptures 595–605)

The tractate *Melchizedek* is only partially extant, owing to serious damage to the manuscript. Less than half of its content remains. Its superscript title is partially preserved on a small fragment and indicates that the tractate is attributed to the ancient priest of God Most High named in Genesis 14:18. In terms of genre, *Melchizedek* (hereafter abbreviated as *Melch.*) is an apocalypse in which Melchizedek conveys to those who are worthy secret revelations received from heavenly emissaries.

> *The first revelation contains a prophecy of the earthly work of Jesus Christ and the rise of false teachings after his resurrection.*

The tractate is made up of three main parts: a revelation mediated by the angel Gamaliel (1,1–14,15); a liturgy performed by the priest Melchizedek in behalf of his community (14,15–18, bottom); and a revelatory vision mediated to Melchizedek by unnamed heavenly brethren, probably including Gamaliel (18, bottom–27,10).

The first revelation contains a prophecy of the earthly work of Jesus Christ and the rise of false teachings after his resurrection. Gamaliel reveals himself, and tells of his special role in bringing to heaven the "assembly of the children of Seth" (5,17–22). He proceeds to invoke in prayer the divine beings that inhabit the heavenly world, beginning with the primal divine triad in Sethian Gnosticism (5,23–6,22). In a highly damaged section of the text, Gamaliel recounts the history of humanity from Adam until the final battle of the end time.

The second main part of the tractate begins with Melchizedek recounting his reaction to Gamaliel's revelation: He glorifies God the Father, and undertakes a series of ritual actions, including baptism and a series of invocations addressed to the same divine beings previously invoked by Gamaliel.

The third main part of *Melch*. begins with an appearance of heavenly messengers to Melchizedek. Melchizedek experiences a vision that includes the sufferings and resurrection of Jesus Christ (25,1–9). From what remains of page twenty-six, one gets the impression that Melchizedek is equated with Jesus Christ, that is, that the biblical priest will reappear in the future as Jesus Christ and perform the work of salvation. The tractate concludes with a warning to Melchizedek to keep the revelations secret from all but the elect. The heavenly informants then ascend back to heaven.

Melch. is usually included in that group of tractates identified as Sethian Gnostic. But the Sethian features of the text are restricted to the invocations of the Sethian heavenly beings, the aforementioned reference to the children of Seth, and the name of the first revealer, the angel Gamaliel. Predominant in the text are non-Gnostic features drawn from Jewish apocalyptic and the New Testament Epistle to the Hebrews. So I suggest that *Melch*., as we now have it, is a non-Gnostic text that has been "Sethianized" by the addition of Sethian Gnostic interpolations and glosses.

I would assign the Greek original of the Coptic version we have to early third-century Egypt.

h. *Three Steles of Seth* (NHC VII,5: 118,10–127,7; *NH Library*, 396–401; Layton, 149–58; *NH Scriptures*, 523–36)

The title of this work is given at the end. The opening passage reads, "The revelation of Dositheus about the three steles of Seth, the father of the living and unshakable race..." (118,10–13). Nothing more is said of this Dositheus, who does not appear elsewhere in Sethian literature. Some scholars think that this is a reference to the first-century Samaritan sect leader by that name who is associated with Simon Magus in the Pseudo-Clementine writings (discussed in chapter 2).

In terms of literary genre, the *Three Steles of Seth* (hereafter abbreviated as *Steles Seth*) is certainly not an apocalypse in the usual sense, even if the three steles are said to be revealed by Dositheus. The steles themselves are attributed to Seth, and this reflects the tradition already noted of Seth's inscribing lore on stone for the benefit of his progeny. The three steles that make up our tractate consist of hymnic prayers addressed by the heavenly Seth and his progeny to the three members of the Sethian divine triad. The first one (118,24–121,17) is addressed to Geradamas (Adamas), the Son in the triad, here treated as the father of Seth. The second stele (121,18–124,15) is addressed to Barbelo, the Mother, and the third (124,16–126,32) to the preexistent Father. The concluding material consists of liturgical rubrics (instructions) as to how to use the prayers in worship (126,32–127,26).

The most important feature of Steles Seth, *however, is not its Platonist metaphysics but its religious character as a series of prayers used in worship services.*

In terms of content, *Steles Seth* reflects considerable influence from third-century Platonist metaphysics, in which triads and triads-in-unity play a prominent role. For example, Barbelo is treated as a "triple power," emanating from one "non-being" triple power, but also a "monad from a pure monad" (121,30–34). The "non-being" Father is "the existence of them all," "the life of them all," and the "mind" of them all (125,28–32). This triad of existence (*huparksis*), life (*zōē*), and mind (*nous*) is a well-known triad in Neo-Platonic metaphysics. *Steles Seth* is one of four Sethian tractates in the Nag Hammadi corpus whose content reflects heavy influence from third-century Platonist school tradition. The others are *Zostrianos* (VIII,1), *Allogenes* (XI,3), and *Marsanes* (X,1). It is also to be noted that there are no traces of Christian influence in *Steles Seth*.

The most important feature of *Steles Seth*, however, is not its Platonist metaphysics but its religious character as a series of prayers used in worship services. Although the prayers are said to have been composed by Seth, much of the text is put into the first-person plural, and there is a prominent thread of praise and blessing running through the tractate. For example, the concluding part of the third stele reads, "We have blessed you, for we are able. We have been saved, for you have willed always that we all do this" (126,29–32).

From the structure of the tractate, and especially its concluding rubrics, we can see that *Steles Seth* is part of a liturgy associated with a particular ritual, a ritual of ascent. In the concluding rubrics we read,

> For they all bless these individually and together. And afterwards they shall be silent. And just as they were ordained, they ascend. After the silence, they descend from the third. They bless the second; after these the first. The way of ascent is the way of descent. (127,11–21)

The last sentence in this passage is a famous fragment of the sixth-century BCE Greek philosopher Heraclitus (B 60). The prayers are directed to be recited in ascending and descending order: 1-2-3, 3-2-1, with observance of ritual silence between the first and second recitations of the third stele.

Exactly how this ascent was induced is hard to envisage, but that a mystic, cultic practice is involved is clear enough. Perhaps the Gnostic's eventual ascent to heaven is acted out in group ritual, involving a descent into the individual self of each participant. The prayers and invocations in the steles were probably chanted.

Steles Seth can safely be assigned to early third-century Egypt. It has even been suggested that it was composed in Lycopolis, where Plotinus, the founder of Neo-Platonism, was born and reared.

i. *Zostrianos* (NHC VIII, *1*: 1,1–132,9; *NH Library*, 396–430; Layton, 121–40; *NH Scriptures*, 537–83)

The philosopher Porphyry (232/3–circa 305), editor of the works of his teacher Plotinus (205–270), writes in his *Life of Plotinus* (ch. 16),

> There were in his time many Christians and others, and sectarians (*hairetikoi*) who had abandoned the old philosophy (Platonism), men of the schools of Adelphius and Aculinus, who possessed a great many treatises of Alexander the Libyan and Philocomus and Demostratus and Lydus, and produced revelations (*apokalupseis*) by Zoroaster and Zostrianus and Nicotheus and Allogenes and Messus and other people of the kind, deceived themselves and deceiving many, alleging that Plato had not penetrated to the depths of intelligible reality. Plotinus hence often attacked their position in his lectures, and wrote the treatise to which we have given the title "Against the Gnostics" (*Enneads* 2.9); he left it to us to assess what he passed over. Amelius went to forty volumes in writing against the book of Zostrianus. (Armstrong's translation)

We know nothing more of the individuals named, presumably Gnostic teachers. But we now have in Coptic translation two of the revelations or apocalypses listed in this passage: *Zostrianos* and *Allogenes*. In the latter, Allogenes "the stranger" is writing to his son Messos. A "Book of Zoroaster" is quoted in the longer version of *Ap. John,* but we do not know if that is the same book as the one referred to in Porphyry's account. Porphyry goes on to say that he wrote a refutation of that book, and showed that its teachings are not those of the ancient Zoroaster. As for Nicotheus, he is a Gnostic prophet mentioned in the "Untitled Text" of the Bruce Codex, but we don't have an apocalypse attributed to him.

Anyway, it is now evident that the Gnostics known to Plotinus and Porphyry were representatives of Sethian Gnosticism.

Zostrianos is the longest tractate in the Nag Hammadi corpus, comprising 132 pages. Unfortunately, the manuscript is heavily damaged, especially in its middle portion. The opening passage is lost, but Zostrianos is named in line 4 of page 1, and it is evident that he is writing in the first person. He is said to be the son of Iolaos (4,10). According to a late tradition, Zostrianos was grandfather of Zoroaster (Zarathustra), the Iranian prophet.

At the end of the tractate we have its title, "Zostrianos," followed by a cryptogram in Greek, translated as "Oracles of Truth of Zostrianos, God of Truth, Teachings of Zoroaster" (132,6–9). This cryptogram was probably not part of the original version of the tractate.

In terms of genre, *Zostrianos* is an apocalypse, presenting a series of revelations consisting of visions and auditions given to Zostrianos by heavenly beings. It is composed in three parts: Zostrianos's autobiographical prologue (1,1–4,20), a lengthy first-person account of his ascent through the heavens (4,20–129,2), and Zostrianos's descent and mission (129,2–132,5).

In the first part of the tractate, Zostrianos recounts how, while meditating, he is visited by "the angel of knowledge" (unnamed, 3,28–30), who invites Zostrianos to accompany him on an ascent through the heavens. At each level of his visionary ascent Zostrianos is baptized in the names of the beings at that level and is given a revelation by the guide for that particular aeon. The content of the various revelations consists of the names of various heavenly beings and their relationship to one another. So *Zostrianos* can be seen as a detailed description of the heavenly world, populated by beings we have already encountered in other Sethian texts, including the heavenly Seth, and many more besides.

In *Zostrianos* we encounter the Platonizing features we have already seen in *Steles Seth*, for example, "triple power" as an attribute of the Invisible Spirit, and the Neo-Platonic triad of Existence, Life, and Mind (with Knowledge substituted for Mind, 15,4–17), but the system of *Zostrianos* is much more complicated. Other features in common with *Steles Seth* include praises and invocations, and the theme of inscribed revelations: "I (Zostrianos) wrote three wooden tablets and left them as knowledge for those who come after me" (130,1–4). The word used for "wooden tablet" (*puksos*) is the same as that of the tablet we found associated with Doxomedon Domedon in *Gos. Eg.*

Zostrianos's report of his writing down of gnosis is part of the third and final section of *Zostrianos,* featuring his descent back to earth and his subsequent mission. The mission he takes upon himself is "preaching the truth to everyone" (130,8–9). He presumably enjoys some success: "An erring multitude I awakened, saying, 'Know those who are alive and the holy seed of Seth. Do not show disobedience to me. Awaken your divine part to God, and strengthen your sinless elect soul'" (130,14–21).

There are no identifiably Christian elements in *Zostrianos*. The Platonizing elements predominate, but there are also indications of Jewish influence. Zostrianos's experience of being assimilated to "the glories" in each of the levels of heaven he traverses (5,15–20) resembles very much the experience of Enoch in the *Second Book of Enoch,* an apocalypse composed in Greek, probably in first-century Alexandria, depicting the ascent of Enoch to the tenth heaven. Enoch reports that he had "become like one of the glorious ones" (*2 Enoch* 22:10). Another indication of possible influence from *2 Enoch* occurs toward the end of *Zostrianos*. At the conclusion of his visionary experience, Zostrianos is told that he has "heard all these things of which the gods are ignorant and that are undefined for angels" (128,15–18). Enoch is told by God, "not even to my angels have I explained my secrets . . . as I am making them known to you today (*2 Enoch* 24:3).

Another example of possible Jewish influence is the name of one of the revealers in Zostrianos, a female being called Youel, "she who belongs to all the glories" (53,13–14), who accompanies Zostrianos on the rest of his celestial journeys. She is also referred to as "male" and "virginal" (54,14–15). She seems to be a double of Barbelo, the "male virgin." Youel is included among the denizens of the heavenly world in *Gos. Eg.* (III 44,25–27). She is clearly a variant of the angel Yaoel, the "Angel of the Lord" who bears the name of God (compare Exodus 23:20–21). Yaoel means "Yao (YHWH) is God." This angel has a prominent role to play in the first- or second-century *Apocalypse of Abraham,* extant only in Slavonic but probably composed in Hebrew. It is striking that the revelatory angel Youel in Zostrianos is a feminine being. As a double of Barbelo, though, her name has a comparable etymology, if the etymology of the name Barbelo can be construed as "in four, God," the "four" referring to the four Hebrew letters of God's biblical name YHWH (Yahweh). The feminine revealer angel Youel also occurs in a tractate closely related to *Zostrianos, Allogenes* (NHC XI,3).

As already noted, there are no indications of Christian influence in *Zostrianos*. So in that tractate the heavenly savior Seth does not "put on Jesus," as he does in *Gos. Eg.* Does he "put on" Zostrianos? That is to say, can Zostrianos be taken as a kind of avatar of Seth? A good case can be made for that. His call at the beginning of the tractate has "the angel of knowledge" exhorting Zostrianos to "save those who are worthy and empower the elect" (4,16–17). And at the end of the tractate Zostrianos announces to those who will listen, "the kind Father has sent you the savior and given you strength.... Listen, for the time is short" (131,14–20).

As to the time and place of the composition of the tractate's Greek original, I would suggest early third-century Alexandria.

j. *Allogenes (The Stranger)* (NHC XI,3: 45,1–69,20; NH Library, 490–500; Layton, 141–48; NH Scriptures, 771–75)

Codex XI has considerable damage at this point in the manuscript, particularly in the top portions of the papyrus pages, so this tractate is not completely extant. But enough remains for us to get a good impression of its content.

The name "Allogenes" means "another race" or "stranger." It is a Sethian name, based on an interpretation of "another seed" in Genesis 4:25, of which more will be said later (in chapter 4). As we noted in our discussion of Epiphanius's treatment of the (Sethian)

Archontics, Allogenes is an epithet of Seth. The same name is given to Seth's sons, according to the same account (*Panarion* 40.7.1). Moreover, Epiphanius reports that the Sethians and the Archontics make use of books called "Allogenes" (*Panarion* 39.5.1; 40.2.2). The tractate *Allogenes* may have been one of them. It can certainly be identified with the apocalypse of Allogenes cited by Porphyry in his *Life of Plotinus* (ch. 16).

> The name "Allogenes" means "another race" or "stranger." It is a Seth name, based on an interpretation of "another seed" in Genesis 4:25.

The title of the tractate is appended at the end, "Allogenes" (69, 20). In terms of literary genre, Allogenes is an apocalypse, written in the name of Allogenes (Seth) who addresses his son Messos (50,19 et passim). Allogenes is, of course, a pseudonym; we don't know who the real author was. It has been suggested that Messos is actually Moses, but that is unlikely. *Mes(s)os* in Greek means "middle," so the name may simply refer to an anonymous "middleman" whose function is to convey Allogenes' revelations to others.

The tractate consists of two main parts. The first part is a revelation given to Allogenes by the "all glorious" angel Youel (45,1–58,7). This is the same revealer angel we encountered in the tractate *Zostrianos*. The second part reports an ascent of Allogenes that leads to a "primary revelation" of the divine "Unknowable One" (58,8–69,19).

In Youel's revelation in the first part of the tractate, Allogenes is given a description of the heavenly world similar to that of *Zostrianos* and *Steles Seth*. The highest level is the Unknown God or Invisible Spirit. He relates to the lower levels of the heavenly world through a triple power consisting of the Neo-Platonic triad of Existence, Life, and Mind. The second main level is the aeon of Barbelo, consisting of three aspects or hypostases called Kalyptos (hidden), Protophanes (first-appearing), and Autogenes (self-begotten), who is elsewhere identified as the Son in the Sethian divine triad. Other beings are also included in Youel's revelation, and it is clear from its content that *Allogenes* shares many features in common with *Zostrianos* and *Steles Seth,* most notably its use of Platonist school tradition.

At the end of her revelation Youel promises Allogenes that he will receive a final revelation of the preexistent God after a hundred years (56,19–22). Allogenes reports that, after Youel's departure, he devoted himself to preparation and meditation for a hundred years (57,24–31).

In the second part of the tractate Allogenes reports what happened when the hundred years were up. He experienced a visionary or meditative ascent through the intelligible world and the various levels of the heavenly world to the Unknown God above, who can only be described in negative terms. The negative theology occurring here contains a section that is almost word-for-word the same as a passage in *Ap. John: Ap. John* II 3,18–35 equals *Allogenes* 62,28–63,23. But Allogenes pushes this motif even further: The Unknown God is "so unknowable that he exceeds those who excel in unknowability" (63,30–32).

At the end of the tractate Allogenes is commanded to write the revelations he has received in a book and leave it on a mountain (68,16–21). The tractate concludes with a final exhortation to Messos, "These are the things that were disclosed to me, O my son Messos. . . . Proclaim them, O my son Messos, as the seal for all the books of Allogenes" (68,34–69,19). The use of the term *seal* here may indicate that this tractate represents the final and most important volume in a series of books attributed to Allogenes.

Like *Steles Seth* and *Zostrianos, Allogenes* has no Christian elements in it. As to the time and place of the composition of its Greek original, I would assign it to mid-third-century Alexandria.

k. *Marsanes* (NHC X: 1,1–68,18;
NH Library, 460–71; *NH Scriptures,* 629–49)

Codex X is one of the most heavily damaged of the Nag Hammadi manuscripts. Fragments of sixty-eight pages remain, but the codex probably had many more pages than that. (Codex VIII, for example, has one hundred forty pages, one hundred thirty-two of them comprising the tractate *Zostrianos*.) The scribe stopped numbering pages after page five, but enough is left of pages one through ten to put them in order. After that, page numbering is completely conjectural, though the order of pages in the middle portion can be determined by content and destruction patterns. The rest of the pages have been ordered using methods of codicological reconstruction, involving analysis of papyrus fiber continuities from one-half of the codex to the other.

One small fragment contains a partial title, restored to read "Marsanes." In the process of reconstructing the codex for final photography (reflected in the *Facsimile Edition*), this fragment was placed at the end of the codex, on a page numbered sixty-eight. On the basis of the content of pages one through ten, there is good reason to think that Codex X consisted of a single tractate, a writing attributed to a Gnostic prophet named Marsanes. Owing to the condition of the manuscript, much less than half of this writing is extant.

The prophet Marsanes is known from two other sources. He, together with another prophet named Nicotheus (or Nikotheos), is named in the "Untitled Text" of the Bruce Codex (ch. 7). As noted above, Nicotheus is also mentioned in Porphyry's *Life of Plotinus* (ch. 16). In the Bruce Codex, Marsanes and Nicotheus are said to be "great ones" who have seen heavenly verities and revealed them to others. Epiphanius, in his discussion of the Archontics, mentions two prophets honored by them, Martiades and Marsianos, who had been snatched up to the heavens and had come down after three days (*Panarion* 40.7.6). ("Marsianos" and "Marsanes" are two different ways of rendering in Greek a name of Syriac origin.) Visionary ascent is certainly a prominent feature of what remains of the Nag Hammadi tractate *Marsanes*. In this tractate Marsanes gives advanced instruction to a group of his followers who have already been initiated into gnosis. The author of the tractate may be the Gnostic prophet Marsanes himself; alternatively he may be an otherwise unknown teacher who claims to be writing in the name of the prophet Marsanes. *Marsanes* reflects a good deal of the Platonist school tradition that we have seen in *Steles Seth, Zostrianos,* and *Allogenes.*

The first part of the tractate reflects an ascent experience, and includes a discussion of the various levels of reality, associated with thirteen seals. Seals one and two represent the realm of sense perception and bodily existence. Seals three through six represent various levels of soul, individual and cosmic. Seals seven through ten represent the various entities of the Barbelo aeon, the realm of pure being. Seals eleven through thirteen represent the realm of nonbeing, that is, beyond being, comprising the Triple-Powered One, the Invisible Spirit, and the Unknown Silent One. Interestingly, the Invisible Spirit, the primal Father in other Sethian tractates, has one entity beyond him, the Unknown Silent One. In this respect, the metaphysics of Marsanes can be compared with that of Iamblichus of Chalcis (circa 250–325), a Neo-Platonist philosopher who posited an "Ineffable" beyond "the One" in Plotinus's system.

The next best-preserved section of Marsanes is from the middle of the codex (pages 24–42) and contains a discussion of the mystical meaning of the letters of the alphabet and their relation to the human soul and to the names of the gods and angels of the Zodiac and other heavenly spheres. The material at the end of the codex is very fragmentary, but includes indications of visionary experiences and heavenly intermediaries who "spoke like the angels" (63,4), one of whom is Gamaliel (64,19), an angelic being who appears in several other Sethian writings. This part of the tractate also includes references to a baptismal ceremony (55,20; 66,1–5).

The baptismal references put Marsanes in close relationship with those tractates that refer to a Sethian baptismal rite. But there are other possible ritual allusions that invite comparison to the theurgy ("work of the gods") practiced by the aforementioned Iamblichus, involving ritual actions that were thought to assist the human soul in its re-ascent. The classic authority for theurgy is the *Chaldaean Oracles,* a second-century collection of revelatory poetry, which became influential in some Middle- and Neo-Platonist circles. For

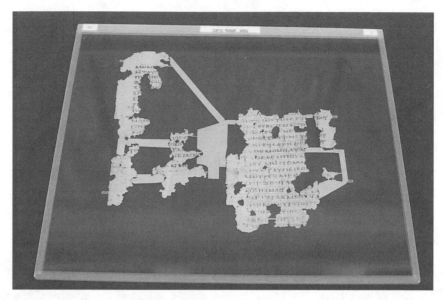

Fig. 3.1 Pages 1 and 68 from the treatise *Marsanes* (Nag Hammadi Codex X). Photo: Birger Pearson.

example, an enigmatic reference in *Marsanes* to "wax images" and "emerald likenesses" (35,1–3) reminds us of Iamblichus's discussion of the use of stones, plants, and so on, in theurgic ritual (*On the Mysteries of Egypt* 5.23).

Marsanes is undoubtedly the latest of the four Platonizing tractates in the Nag Hammadi corpus. Like the other Platonizing tractates, it lacks any Christian elements. I would suggest a mid-third-century date for the composition of its Greek original, or perhaps a little later. Somewhere in Syria is the most likely place for its composition, although Alexandria is not out of the question.

I. The "Untitled Text" in the Bruce Codex (MacDermot, *Bruce Codex*, 226–77).

The beginning and end portions of this tractate are missing; so we don't know what title, if any, was applied to it. It is exceedingly prolix and confusing (if not confused); so it is no wonder that this hodgepodge writing has not attracted much attention since its original publication (Coptic edition, with German translation) in 1892. It contains an elaborate cosmology involving beings known from other Sethian texts, including the heavenly Seth himself, who is invariably referred to as Setheus. There are various levels and entities called "deeps," "fatherhoods," "aeons," "enneads," "decads," "powers," and several "triple-powered entities." Jesus and Christ are also included in it, and there are some quotations from the New Testament.

As already noted, the prophet Marsanes is referred to in this tractate:

> The powers of all the great aeons have given homage to the power that is in Marsanes. They said, "Who is this who has seen these things before his face, that he has thus revealed concerning him?" Nicotheus spoke concerning him; he saw that he was that one. He said, "The Father exists, surpassing every perfection. He has revealed the invisible, triple-powered, perfect one." Each of the perfect men saw him, they spoke of him, giving glory to him, each one in his own way. (ch. 7)

The "power which is in Marsanes" is evidently "the only-begotten one hidden in the Setheus" (ch. 7), presumably construed as the source and inspiration for Marsanes' revelations. It is possible that the author of the "Untitled Text" had access to the Nag Hammadi tractate *Marsanes*.

Toward the end of the text reference is made to the "living water" and "the powers that are over the living water, Michar and Micheu" (ch. 20), figures we have already encountered in other Sethian texts. Whether or not this is a reference to an actual Sethian baptismal ceremony cannot be determined. No other reference to baptism is given in the text.

The prolixity of this tractate leads us to assign it to the very latest stage of Sethian Gnosticism. I would suggest a date sometime in the early fourth century for its composition. Egypt is the most likely place of origin.

m. *Gospel of Judas* (Codex Tchacos 3: 33,1–58,29; *NH Scriptures*, 755–69)

The *Gospel of Judas* is part of a damaged fourth-century Coptic manuscript, the Codex Tchacos, which has been under study and preservation since 2001. A critical edition has not yet been published, but an English translation of the *Gospel of Judas* was published with much fanfare in April, 2006 (R. Kasser, M. Meyer, and G. Wurst, *The Gospel of Judas*, [Washington: National Geographic Society, 2006]. A tentative transcription of the Coptic text of the *Gospel of Judas* is available on the Web site of the National Geographic Society. It is certainly to be identified with the gospel of that title said to have been used among some Gnostics by St. Irenaeus of Lyons (see our discussion of the Cainites in chapter 2, above). It features Jesus in dialogue with his disciples, and privately with Judas, during the week before Passover. Judas is singled out as the only one who is worthy of receiving the mysteries of the kingdom.

Judas is given a revelation by Jesus that begins with the Great Invisible Spirit, Barbelo, and Autogenes (Self-Generated), that is, the primal triad of Father, Mother, and Son typical of Sethian gnosis. Judas is taught about the four luminaries, the heavenly Adamas and Seth, and the incorruptible generation of Seth. The revelation also includes information about the lower world and its rulers, the creation by Saklas and his angels of Adam and Eve, their reception of gnosis, and subsequent generations of people ruled by Saklas (47–55). The mythological system reflected in the *Gospel of Judas* is closely related to that of *Ap. John*.

In the *Gospel of Judas*, the twelve disciples as a group are ridiculed as servants of Saklas, whereas Judas is distinguished from them as "the thirteenth." The text includes a vision that Judas reports to Jesus in which it is prophesied that Judas will be persecuted by "the twelve." Jesus assures him that he will prevail in the end (44–47). Following the lengthy revelation by Jesus, Judas asks Jesus about "those who have been baptized in your name." Jesus replies that they are really offering sacrifices to Saklas. "But you will exceed all of them.

For you will sacrifice the man that clothes me" (56). Judas is told that he will help Jesus' soul escape from his mortal body by handing him over to the authorities, who will crucify the mortal body.

The text concludes abruptly with scribes, lying in wait for Jesus, approaching Judas whom they recognize as Jesus' disciple. "Judas answered them as they wished. And he received some money and handed him over to them" (58). The subscript title, "The Gospel of Judas," occurs on the last line.

In the *Gospel of Judas,* "the twelve" are clearly representative symbolically of the growing ecclesiastical establishment. "The twelve" are worshippers of Saklas. Only the people of the generation of Seth know the true God, and only they will be saved.

Irenaeus wrote his great work *Against Heresies* around 180 CE. I would assign a mid-second-century date to the *Gospel of Judas.* Where it was composed is anyone's guess.

n. *Book of Allogenes* (Codex Tchacos, 4:59–66; *NH Scriptures,* 771–75)

The fourth tractate of the Codex Tchacos has not yet been published. It is reported to be in very damaged condition. No title has been preserved, but the prominence in it of a figure called Allogenes ("Stranger") has led the scholars in charge of its eventual publication to refer to it as the *Book of Allogenes.* However, there is no connection at all (apart from the typical Sethian name) between this tractate and *Allogenes* (NHC XI,3).

I have seen in private circulation four pages of the text. At one point Allogenes, who may actually be identified as Jesus Christ, is in prayer on Mount Tabor, presumably with his disciples. The Devil then comes and tempts him, but Allogenes resists him, saying, "I was called Allogenes because I am from another race." Allogenes is then enveloped in a cloud of light and hears a heavenly voice preparing to offer him "good news."

Nothing more can be said of this tractate until it is finally published. Its inclusion in this chapter of Sethian works would seem to be justified on the basis of the occurrence in it of the name Allogenes.

4. Assessing the Evidence

As we noted in the first part of this chapter, the church fathers who described the tenets of groups of people they called Sethians differ remarkably from one another in their reports. For example, the Sethians of Hippolytus bear no resemblance at all to the Sethians of Pseudo-Tertullian, or those of Epiphanius. It also turns out that the most reliable of the heresiologists discussed, Irenaeus of Lyons, says nothing at all about Sethians. On the other hand, his description of the tenets of the Gnostics, adherents of the Gnostic school of thought, agrees with much of what we have in the primary sources used by scholars to reconstruct a Sethian Gnostic system. For example, the text that he paraphrases in *Against Heresies*

> *The Sethian writings we have reflect a ritual praxis. Two rituals can be seen reflected in them, baptism and a ritual of ascent.*

1.29 is parallel to what we find in the first part of *Ap. John*. And a number of the traditions included in 1.30 have their counterparts in the second part of *Ap. John*. So the evidence surveyed leads us to conclude that the Sethians of the patristic writers did not exist as such. That is to say, there were no groups of people who referred to themselves as "Sethians." On the other hand, there certainly were groups of people who referred to themselves as "Gnostics."

However, we also noted time and again in the primary sources the prominence of Seth, son of Adam, and the seed or race of Seth. This would certainly indicate that there were Gnostics who regarded themselves metaphorically as the spiritual progeny of Seth, thus distinguishing themselves from the rest of humankind.

We also noted in the primary sources that there are many agreements among them such as would lead scholars to posit what might be called a Sethian mythological system. *Ap. John,* found in four different Coptic manuscripts, is clearly the most important source for our knowledge of this system.

On the other hand, there are many differences to be observed among the texts comprising the Sethian corpus. Some of them are clearly Christian texts, featuring Jesus as the revealer of gnosis.

We noted that Jesus is equated with Seth in some of these writings. That Seth "puts on" (or becomes incarnate as) Jesus is also a tradition noted by some of the church fathers in their accounts of the Sethians. Yet, some of the primary texts we discussed have no Christian elements at all. The differences observable among the writings of the Sethian corpus make it very difficult for us to reconstruct any kind of Sethian social history.

Still, the Sethian writings we have reflect a ritual praxis. Two rituals can be seen reflected in them, baptism and a ritual of ascent. *Gos. Eg.* is especially important for its prayers associated with baptism and *Steles Seth* for its prayers associated with the ascent ritual. Sethian ritual praxis certainly involves group activity with a structured religious life. Even so, one can hardly speak of a unified church or sect of Sethian Gnostics. The groups of Gnostics that we can extrapolate from our sources differed greatly from one another. Gnostic teachers obviously had a great deal of freedom to introduce innovations in the myths or rituals embraced by them and their followers.

Even if our sources do not allow us to reconstruct a social history of Sethianism, it is possible to propose in broad outline a history of Sethian or Classic Gnostic traditions. As noted above, *Ap. John,* the most important of the Sethian Gnostic texts, reveals a kind of tradition history, in that it reflects an editorial Christianizing of an originally non-Christian Gnostic myth involving a theogony, cosmogony, anthropogony, and eschatology. This posited myth has features in common with those of Simon Magus and Menander, so it is not unfeasible to posit a first-century origin for it. The use made in it of biblical and Jewish traditions reflects its Jewish origin. Christian Gnosticism is first attested in the early second century, with Saturninus of Antioch. So the incorporation of the figure of Jesus Christ into Sethian Gnostic mythology is a second-century phenomenon. Finally, the third-century Platonizing Sethian texts reflect the incorporation of Middle- and Neo-Platonic school traditions into the Sethian Gnostic tradition. Adherents of this variety of Gnosticism, which lacks any Christian features, attracted the attention of Plotinus and members of his school in

Rome. But different varieties of Christian Gnosticism utilizing Sethian traditions persisted into the fourth century, as attested by Epiphanius and the compiler(s) of the "Untitled Text" of the Bruce Codex.

As we shall see in the following chapters, Sethian Gnostic traditions came to be incorporated into a large number of tractates in the Nag Hammadi collection that are not normally included in the Sethian corpus. And the greatest of all of the second-century Gnostic Christians, Valentinus, based his own mythological system on that of the "Gnostic school of thought," if Irenaeus is to be believed (*Against Heresies* 1.11.1).

4. Gnostic Biblical Interpretation
The Gnostic Genesis

It is not the way Moses wrote and you heard...

THIS PHRASE, TAKEN FROM THE *Apocryphon of John* (II 22,22–23), is illustrative of the ambiguity involved in Gnostic biblical interpretation. It used to be maintained by scholars that Gnosticism, as "the acute Hellenization of Christianity" (Harnack), rejected the Old Testament in favor of the New. But our primary sources have shown conclusively that this is not the case. To be sure, a few Gnostic writers regard the heroes of the Hebrew Bible with scorn, for example, the author of the *Second Treatise of the Great Seth* (NHC VII,2, treated in chapter 8). Others, for example, the author of the *Exegesis on the Soul* (NHC II,6, also treated in chapter 8) cite biblical texts with approval. But the main tendency in Gnosticism is to subject texts of the Hebrew Bible to critical scrutiny and offer interpretations that run counter to the traditional ones. So the author of *Ap. John* can base an elaborate mythology on the opening passages of Genesis and other biblical texts while at the same time suggesting that Moses got it wrong, or didn't understand what he was writing.

In this chapter we shall take a close look at the use made of Genesis and other biblical texts by Gnostic writers in their construction of Gnostic mythology. I shall try to show that the building blocks used in the construction of Gnostic mythology are based on reinterpretations of biblical texts and Jewish traditions of biblical interpretation. It is my contention that the basic Gnostic myth cannot be understood or accounted for at all without taking into account its background in biblical and Jewish writings, Jewish traditions of biblical interpretation, and developments in Jewish theology around the turn of the common era.

> *It is my contention that the basic Gnostic myth cannot be understood or accounted for at all without taking into account its background in biblical and Jewish writings, Jewish traditions of biblical interpretation, and developments in Jewish theology around the turn of the common era.*

In the following discussion we shall concentrate on how Gnostic writers interpret the opening passages of Genesis in the construction of Gnostic myth, attending also to other biblical texts that are introduced in the process of their interpretations of Genesis. We shall also have to look at some tendencies in early Jewish theology that inform the Gnostic innovations.

1. "In the Beginning": The Unknown God

Peoples all over the world have their traditions about the origin of things, how things got to be the way they are. The poet Hesiod gives expression to the views of the ancient Greeks: "Verily at the first Chaos came to be, but next wide-bosomed Earth, the ever-sure foundation of all the deathless ones who hold the peaks of snowy Olympus" (*Theogony* 115–18, Evelyn-White). A similar notion was found among the ancient Mesopotamian cultures: first chaos, then the gods of order. The author of the Gnostic tractate *On the Origin of the World* opens his discourse with a critique of that view: "Seeing that everybody, gods of the world and mankind, says that nothing existed prior to chaos, I in distinction to them shall demonstrate that they are all mistaken" (NHC II,5: 97,24–28).

To be sure, by that time the Greeks had come up with an alternative view: God and the world have always existed, and always will. This was a view put forward by Aristotle and held by Platonist philosophers. Even Plato, whose elaborate story of creation in his *Timaeus* was much studied in antiquity, did not intend his account to be taken literally.

The Bible presents an alternative view: "In the beginning God." This phrase, with which the Bible opens, gives expression to the notion found throughout that God is prior to his creation. From the beginning of the Hebrew scriptures to the end, the one God of Israel is the transcendent Creator. He is transcendent by virtue of his being Creator, and he can be known only in his act of revealing himself. "The LORD is the everlasting God, the Creator of the ends of the earth" (Isaiah 40:28, RSV). The prophet has God say, "I am the LORD, and there is no other; besides me there is no God" (Isaiah 45:5, RSV).

This view of the one transcendent Creator is a hallmark of biblical theology. Jews of the postbiblical period elaborated on this theme in various ways. Philo of Alexandria, a first-century Jewish philosopher profoundly influenced by Platonism, gives expression to this theme in his writings. His treatise *On the Creation* is a commentary on Genesis 1 and 2, but also shows influence from Plato's *Timaeus*. Philo can also use Plato's terms for the Creator, "Father," "Maker," "Demiurge," and other philosophical terms: "Mind (*nous*) of the Universe, transcending virtue, transcending knowledge, transcending the good itself and the beautiful itself" (*On the Creation* 8).

The biblical view of God implies not only his transcendence, but also his unknowability, in that he is known only by self-revelation. This is implied already in Exodus 3:14: "I am who I am" (RSV). The unknowable being of God is developed in Hellenistic Judaism. Note Philo's interpretation of Deuteronomy 32:39, "See now that

I, even I, am he; there is no god besides me" (RSV): "He does not say 'See me,' for it is impossible that the God who IS should be perceived at all by created beings. What he says is, 'See that I am,' that is, behold my subsistence [or existence, *huparksis*]" (*Posterity and Exile of Cain* 168).

The Jewish historian Josephus (late first century) can even use the term "unknown" or "unknowable" (*agnōstos*) for God. He says that Moses represented God as "One, uncreated and immutable to all eternity; in beauty surpassing all mortal thought, made known to us by His power, although what he is essentially is unknown" (*Against Apion* 2.167).

As the biblical view of the transcendence of God developed in postbiblical times, various devices came to be utilized to underscore this transcendence. By the turn of the era the Jews had developed an elaborate angelology and demonology, inherited by Christianity and reinterpreted by the Gnostics. This was not only to underscore the transcendence of God vis-à-vis his creation, but also to remove from him any notion that he is the cause of evil in the world. Evil is attributed not to God but to the devil, demons, or evil angels. For example Sammael in this belief-system is the angel of death and equated with Satan. We have already seen how the same name is used in the *Apocryphon of John* and other Sethian texts in a totally different sense.

> *There is no question at all that Platonism was an important influence on the development of Gnostic dualism and Gnostic notions of God's transcendence. Nevertheless, I would suggest that the Platonic elements in Gnosticism were mediated by Hellenistic (Greek-speaking) Jewish philosophy, such as was espoused by Philo of Alexandria.*

The transcendent God of the Bible comes also to be depicted in mystical terms, according to which God makes himself mystically knowable through his glory (Hebrew *kabod*). This occurs already within the Bible itself. Especially important for this development is the Book of Ezekiel. Ezekiel sees a vision of a throne chariot with four winged "living creatures" (Ezekiel 1:4-25). "And above the firmament over their heads there was the likeness of a throne, in appearance like sapphire, and seated above the likeness of a throne was a likeness as it were of a human form. . . . Such was the appearance of the likeness of the glory of the LORD" (1:26-28 RSV).

These themes, drawn from the Bible and from extrabiblical Jewish literature, form the background for the Gnostics' assertions about the transcendent God and his unknowability.

The revelation discourse in the *Apocryphon of John* begins with the assertion of the oneness and transcendence of God: "The Monad [is a] monarchy with nothing above it. [It is he who exists] as [God] and Father of everything, the [invisible] One who is above [everything]" (II 2,26–30). To be sure, the negative theology that follows can be accounted for without recourse to Judaism, that is, with reference to contemporary Platonist philosophy. And there is no question at all that Platonism was an important influence on the development of Gnostic dualism and Gnostic notions of God's transcendence. Nevertheless, I would suggest that the Platonic elements in Gnosticism were mediated by Hellenistic (Greek-speaking) Jewish philosophy, such as was espoused by Philo of Alexandria. For example, in his treatise *On Dreams* Philo refers to God as "unnamable," "ineffable," and "incomprehensible" (ch. 167). All three of these terms are reflected in the Coptic text of a single passage in the *Apocryphon of John* (BG 24,2–6).

Another key idea in Gnostic theology is that God can be referred to as *Man*, a notion that can be read out of such key passages in the Bible as Genesis 1:26–27 and Ezekiel 1:26–28. This feature can only be accounted for with reference to key texts in the Bible and Jewish traditions.

So it can be concluded that the Gnostic theology of the unknown God is based on biblical and Jewish traditions. But there is one crucial difference: in the biblical and Jewish tradition the one transcendent God is also the Creator of the universe. That is where the Gnostics parted company with their traditional religion. They split the biblical God into two: the transcendent God above the creation, and a lower creator responsible for the world as we now know it. And this split in the deity is read out of key biblical texts that are given an innovative interpretation.

2. "God Created": The Gnostic Demiurge

Unde malum? "Whence comes evil?" This is an important question in the development of human philosophy and theology. By the turn of the era, Jewish writers solved this question by attributing evil to wicked demonic forces who were thought to be temporarily in charge of things until God, in the end, would make all things right. This is a prominent feature of what is referred to as Jewish apocalyptic, reflected in the latest book of the Hebrew Bible, Daniel, and nonbiblical Jewish apocalypses (revelations), the most important of which is the *First Book of Enoch*. *1 Enoch* is divided into five main sections written from around the third century BCE to the first century CE (*1 Enoch* is quoted in the New Testament at Jude 14–15.)

> *The Gnostics saw evil as something inherent in the material creation itself.*

But is the answer to the problem of evil posited in Jewish apocalyptic a satisfactory one? Who created those demonic powers in the first place? The answer given in apocalyptic Judaism is that God created them in the beginning as members of his hosts of angels, but they rebelled against him and fomented evil among people on earth. But then other questions arise. Why would God create angels he presumably knew would rebel against him?

The Gnostics saw evil as something inherent in the material creation itself. Therefore the created order cannot be the product of the transcendent God but must have been created by a lower divine being. And who is this god? The scriptures bear witness to the world creator and his work of creation, but in the Gnostic view this world creator cannot be the same as the all-perfect transcendent God who exists above and beyond a created order that is marred by imperfection and evil.

In our discussion of the *Apocryphon of John* we noted that the chief archon (ruler, the world creator) has three names, Yaldabaoth, Saklas, and Samael (II 11,16–18). The name Yaldabaoth can be interpreted in an Aramaic etymology to mean "child of chaos." Alternatively, the name can be seen as made up of names or epithets of the biblical God: Ya(o) + (e)l + (a)d(onai) + (S)abaoth. The name Sakla(s) means "fool" in Aramaic, and the claim that he makes reminds us of the words of the Psalmist: "The fool says in his heart, there is no God" (Psalm 14:1). Sammael is the name traditionally given to the "angel of death" in Jewish tradition, and Sammael can also be taken as an equivalent of the Devil or Satan. In Gnostic tradition his name is taken to mean "blind god" or "god of the blind" (*Hypostasis of the Archons* 87, 2–3).

The first main part of the *Apocryphon of John*, the revelation discourse, concludes with an account of Yaldabaoth's creation of the world, followed by a claim that he makes to his fellow archons, "I am a jealous God and there is no other God beside me" (II 13,8–9). Yaldabaoth's claim, here made up of a combination of Exodus 20:5 and Isaiah 45:5, is a widespread tradition in Gnostic literature, referred to in scholarship as the "blasphemy of the Demiurge." The most important texts, in addition to this passage in *Ap. John*, are the *Hypostasis of the Archons* 86,27–31; 94,19–23; *On the Origin of the World* II 103,8–13; *Gospel of the Egyptians* III 58,23–29; Irenaeus, *Against Heresies* 1.29.4; 1.30.6; but there are other references and allusions in Gnostic literature that could be cited.

The blasphemy of the Demiurge is traditionally followed by a rebuke from heaven. The entire tradition includes the following elements:

1. Setting (at some point in the story of creation)
2. Introduction
3. The vain claim, based on texts in Isaiah 45–56, sometimes including Exodus 20:5, as in the *Apocryphon of John*.
4. Editorial comment

5. Rebuke by a voice from heaven
6. Disclosure: "Man exists and the Son of Man."

The blasphemy of the Demiurge is immediately followed in the texts by the story of the creation of man. The main point of juxtaposing the creation of man with the Demiurge's vain claim is to underscore the superiority of (Gnostic) humankind vis-à-vis the Creator. We recall the words of Adam to Seth in the *Apocalypse of Adam:* "for we were higher than the god who had created us and the powers with him, whom we did not know" (64,16–19).

The Gnostic tradition of the blasphemy of the Demiurge can also be seen as spun out of reflection on other biblical texts, dealing with the theme of the rebuke of an arrogant ruler. Especially important in this regard are Isaiah 14:12-15, directed against the king of Babylon (Lucifer); and Ezekiel 28:2-8, directed against the king of Tyre. The Lucifer myth of Isaiah 14 (Lucifer, Greek *heōsphoros*, "dawn-bringer") comes later to be used to depict the fall of Satan from heaven in Jewish and Christian tradition.

Thus the biblical Creator has been demoted in Gnostic traditions to an ignorant, blind, arrogant, even demonic being. But we are then confronted with another question: Where did Yaldabaoth come from?

3. Sophia: Virgin, Mother, Whore

The biblical book of Proverbs contains references to Wisdom (Hebrew *Ḥokhmah,* Greek *Sophia*) as a personified being, a hypostatization of one of the attributes of God described in terms reminiscent of ancient Near Eastern myths of a female deity. In Hellenistic Jewish writings Sophia takes on characteristics that invite comparison with the Greco-Egyptian goddess Isis. Here are two quotations from Proverbs that depict various roles played by Wisdom, most important of which is her role in the creation of the world:

3:18-19: "She is a tree of life to those who lay hold of her; those who hold her fast are called happy. The LORD by wisdom [*ḥokhmah*] founded the earth . . ." (RSV).

8:22-30 (Wisdom speaks): "the LORD created me at the beginning of his work, the first of his acts of old. Ages ago I was set up, at the first, before the beginning of the earth. . . . When he marked out the foundations of the earth, then I was beside him, like a master workman" (RSV).

The first clause in Proverbs 8:22 can be translated, both in the Hebrew and the Greek versions, "The LORD created me, the beginning. . . ." This was noticed by later Jewish writers, who were then able to see Wisdom reflected in the text of Genesis: "In the beginning God created," or "In (or by) Wisdom God created," a reading reflected in the *Jerusalem Targum*. (A Targum is an Aramaic translation/paraphrase of the Hebrew Bible.)

The role of Wisdom is expanded in later writings. In Sirach (Ecclesiasticus) 24, Wisdom announces that the Most High sent her forth to make her dwelling in Israel as Torah. In *1 Enoch* 42 it is declared that Wisdom went to dwell among "the children of the people" but found no dwelling place. So she returned to her place in heaven and settled among the angels.

Wisdom's role is expanded in Hellenistic Jewish texts. Here are some passages from the Wisdom of Solomon (composed in Greek, probably in first-century Alexandria):

7:21-22 ("Solomon" is speaking): "I learned both what is secret and what is manifest, for Wisdom [Sophia], the fashioner of all things, taught me."

7:24-26: "For Wisdom is more mobile than any motion; because of her pureness she pervades and penetrates all things. For she is a breath of the power of God, and a pure emanation of the glory of the Almighty; therefore nothing defiled gains entrance into her. For she is a reflection of eternal light, a spotless mirror of the working of God, and an image of his goodness."

9:17 (in a prayer "Solomon" addresses to God): "Who has learned thy counsel, unless thou hast given wisdom and sent thy holy Spirit from on high?"

10:1-4: "Wisdom protected the first-formed father of the world [Adam], when he alone had been created; she delivered him from his transgression, and gave him strength to rule all things. But when an unrighteous man [Cain] departed from her in his anger, he perished because in rage he slew his brother. When the earth was flooded because of him, Wisdom again saved it, steering the righteous man [Noah] by a paltry piece of wood" (all RSV).

Philo of Alexandria has much to say about Sophia (Wisdom), much of it seemingly contradictory. Here is but a small sample from his treatise *On Flight and Finding:*

Sophia is "daughter of God," a "true-born and ever-virgin daughter" (ch. 50). As daughter of God Sophia is "not only masculine but father, sowing and begetting in souls aptness to learn" (52). The Logos has God for his father, and Sophia as his mother, "through whom the universe came into existence" (ch. 110). We note in this passage a Hellenistic Jewish parallel to the Sethian divine triad of Father, Mother, and Son, as well as a reference to Sophia's role in creation.

The Gnostic treatment of Sophia is very complicated, but clearly involves reinterpretations of previously existing Jewish speculations on the figure of Hokhmah-Sophia. One of the features of the Gnostic treatment of Sophia is that they split her into various levels, into higher and lower manifestations. Her highest manifestation is as "First Thought" of the Primal Father. In the Sethian system this is Barbelo, the Mother in the divine triad. But the glory of Wisdom in Jewish terms, that is, her role in the creation of the world, becomes for the Gnostics her shame. Sophia, as mediatrix of creation in her role as mother of the Demiurge, is viewed as a fallen being. On the other hand, as a repentant fallen being she can play a role as mediator of saving gnosis to the elect. As such she is Mother and Life. And it is through her intervention that man receives his spark of life.

As already noted, Sophia at the highest level is Barbelo in the Sethian Gnostic system. In the basic Gnostic myth as found in the *Apocryphon of John,* Sophia, appearing in association with the luminary Eleleth, is also the last of the aeons of the Pleroma (fullness, that is, the heavenly world, II 8,20). It is subsequently stated that Sophia "wanted to bring a likeness out of herself without the consent of the Spirit—he had not approved—and without her consort" (II 9,28–30). As a result, "because of the invincible power which is in her, her thought did not remain idle and something came out of her which was imperfect and different from her appearance, because she had created it without her consort" (II 10,1–5). Instead of "because of the invincible power within her," the shorter version has "because of the lewd element [*prounikon*] within her" (BG 37,10–11). The product of her lewdness is a monstrous being who looked like "a lion-faced serpent" (II 10,9). Sophia gave him the name Yaldabaoth. He, in turn, drawing power from his mother, begot authorities and rulers who, along with Yaldabaoth, produced and govern the lower world.

What is this "lewdness" (*prounikon*) attributed to Sophia? Sophia herself is given the name Prounikos (lewd, lascivious) in a number of Gnostic texts (for example, Irenaeus, *Against Heresies* 1.29.4; 30.3), and this designation refers to her fallen state resulting from her desire to bring forth without the consent of her partner. We can account for this feature of the Sophia myth, her fallenness, by seeing in her a heavenly projection of Eve, whose fall is narrated in Genesis 3. Just as the divine Adamas is a heavenly projection of Adam, so is Sophia a projection of Eve. This can be seen clearly, for example, in a passage in the *Ap. John* where she is referred to as "the Holy Spirit who is called the mother of the living" (II 10,17–18; compare Genesis 3:20). Her fall, too, is a projection of the story of the fall of Eve. Indeed, the production of a child without her consort reflects an extrabiblical Jewish tradition according to which Eve's first child (Cain) was the product of an adulterous union with the angel Sammael. (More will be said about this tradition later in this chapter.)

> The Gnostic treatment of Sophia is very complicated, but clearly involves reinterpretations of previously existing Jewish speculations on the figure of Hokhmah-Sophia.

But Sophia repents, and this repentance is narrated in an interesting twist on Genesis 1:2, which reads in the Greek version, "the

Spirit of God was moving over the water." The Spirit referred to in
Genesis is interpreted as Sophia, and her movement is interpreted
as her repentance: "Then the mother began to move to and fro"
(*Ap. John* II 13,13–14). Genesis 1:2 does not mean what Moses
said. Instead, "when she [Sophia] had seen the wickedness which
had happened, and the theft (of power) which her son had committed, she repented. And she was overcome by forgetfulness in
the darkness of ignorance and she began to be ashamed [and was]
moving about" (II 13,21–26). She is finally taken up to the ninth
sphere, where she will stay "until she has corrected her deficiency"
(II 14,12–13).

The redemptive role of Sophia vis-à-vis Gnostic humankind
is spelled out in the rest of the text of the *Ap. John*. A manifestation of Sophia is sent as Epinoia (Thought): "And he (the Mother-
Father) sent, through his beneficent Spirit and his great mercy, a
helper to Adam, luminous Epinoia which comes out of him, who
is called Life. And she assists the whole creature" (II 20,14–19).
Adam's helper is also Eve, "who comes out of him" (Genesis 2:18,
21-23). Epinoia then comes to be identified with the saving tree of
knowledge (II 22,3–6). Later, the Spirit of Life, also a manifestation of Sophia, comes to raise up humanity and heal (Gnostic)
humankind from its deficiency (II 25,2–16). Sophia also plays a
key role in Gnostic salvation history, saving her "trace of light"
from the Flood (Irenaeus *Against Heresies* 1.30.10), and speaking through the prophets to remind people of the "imperishable
light" (1.30.11). As Pronoia, she descends three times to the chaotic world, and in her third appearance provides for the life-giving
baptism of the "five seals" (*Ap. John* II 30,11–31,25).

The dual role of Sophia—as a fallen being in need of redemption and as a life-giving mother and savior—is underscored in
many Gnostic texts and systems. The myth of the fall of Sophia
resulting in the creation of the world is a key element in the development of Gnosticism from its very beginning. This myth occupies
a central place in the teachings of the earliest attested Gnostics,
Simon Magus and Menander, and, in more developed forms, in the
teachings of the Valentinians and other Christian Gnostics.

4. "Let Us Make Man"

Gnostic traditions concerning the creation of man consist of innovative reinterpretations of the Bible, Jewish traditions of biblical interpretation, and nonbiblical Jewish literature. Postbiblical Judaism is rich in legends and traditions pertaining to Adam and his creation. Many of these traditions developed in order to come to grips with difficult questions posed by the biblical text itself. For example, to whom did God speak when he said, "Let us make man in our image" (Genesis 1:26)? Why are there two accounts of the creation of man (Genesis 1:26-27; 2:7)? What is the nature of the breath of life that God breathed into Adam (Genesis 2:7)? What was Adam like before this inbreathing? What was the role of man in the garden? What is the nature of the helper fit for Adam (Genesis 2:18)? What is implied in Adam's naming all the animals (Genesis 2:20)?

The rabbinic midrashim (biblical commentaries) provide rich resources here, recording the views of the various rabbis on questions raised by the biblical text. The most important one for our purposes is *Genesis Rabbah* (hereafter *Gen. Rab.*), written predominantly in Hebrew but with Aramaic sections as well. It is relatively late, probably composed early in the fifth century, but it is important to note that the rabbis quoted are earlier, and the traditions they cite often go back much earlier. Here are a few examples:

To the question with whom God conversed in Genesis 1:26, Rabbi Joshua ben Levi answers, "with the works of heaven and earth." Rabbi Ammi says, "with his own heart." Rabbi Hanina says, "with the ministering angels" (*Gen. Rab.* 8.2–4). This last answer was very popular, and comes close to the original meaning of the text (God conversing with his heavenly retinue). There is a plethora of traditions involving discussions between God and his angels as to whether he should create man or not. In some traditions the angels play a role in creating man (*Gen. Rab.* 8.5–6).

Philo of Alexandria and other Hellenistic Jewish writers come up with a version of the angels' role in the creation of man that shows influence from Plato's *Timaeus*. "Let us make" shows that God took with him others as fellow workers. God himself created man's mind and reason, but his subordinates are responsible for man's lower faculties that are prone to moral vices (*On the Creation* 75; *The Confusion of Tongues* 168–79). The "Father of all" delegated to his "powers" (angels) the task of fashioning "the mortal portion of our soul" while reserving to himself the creation of the human soul's "sovereign faculty," that is, the mind (*On Flight and Finding* 68–69). In his dialogue *Timaeus*, containing his elaborate myth of creation, Plato has the Demiurge himself create man's immortal soul, while assigning to the lower gods the fashioning of man's body (41a–d). The lower gods of Plato become angels of God in Philo's version of human creation.

That Greek ideas were current even among the Palestinian rabbis is shown, for example, by the comment of Rabbi Jeremiah ben Leazar: "When the Holy One, blessed be He, created Adam, He created him an hermaphrodite [the Greek loan word *androgynos* occurs in the Hebrew text], for it is said, 'Male and female He created them and called their name Adam' (Genesis 5:2, *Gen. Rab.* 8.1). Rabbi Samuel ben Nahman says something similar: "When the LORD created Adam He created him double-faced, then He split him and made him of two backs, one back on this side and one back on the other side" (*Gen. Rab.* 8.1). This doctrine may reflect influence from Psalm 139:5, "Thou dost beset me behind and before." But it also clearly reflects the famous myth of the androgyne put into the mouth of Aristophanes in Plato's *Symposium* (189c–192a).

One popular rabbinic interpretation of Genesis 2:7 is that God created man as a *golem*: "Rabbi Tanhuma in the name of Rabbi Banayah and Rabbi Berekiah in the name of Rabbi Leazar said: 'He created him as a lifeless mass [Heb. *golem*] extending from one end of the world to the other; thus it is written, "Thine eyes did see mine unformed substance"'" (Psalm 139:16 RSV, where "my unformed substance" is the Hebrew word *galmi < golem*, *Gen. Rab.* 8.1). Thus, Adam was a lifeless mass (*golem*) before

God infused in him his soul. Psalm 139, in which the Hebrew word *golem* appears, was regularly put into the mouth of Adam in Jewish tradition.

As to the dual accounts of man's creation in Genesis, Philo regularly distinguishes in Platonic fashion the man created according to the image of God (Genesis 1:27) and the man fashioned in the second account (Genesis 2:7). Referring to the man of Genesis 2:7, Philo says, "there is a vast difference between the man thus formed and the man that came into existence earlier after the image of God: for the man so formed is an object of sense-perception, partaking already of such or such quality, consisting of body and soul, man or woman, by nature mortal; while he that was after the (Divine) image was an idea or type or seal, an object of thought, incorporeal, neither male nor female, by nature incorruptible" (*On the Creation* 134). The man created after God's image is the mind (*nous*), which comes to be infused as a divine breath (or spirit, *pneuma*) into the mortal man. Thus, human beings are both mortal and immortal, "mortal in respect of the body, but in respect of the mind immortal" (135). Philo can even refer to the body as a "tomb" of the soul, whose natural home is in heaven (*Allegorical Interpretation of Genesis* 1.108).

The Old Testament pseudepigrapha (postbiblical writings attributed to biblical characters) provide additional material on Adam and his creation. For example, in the *Testament of Reuben* it is said that seven spirits were given to Adam in creation: life, seeing, hearing, smell, speech, taste, and procreation. With these are commingled seven "spirits of error" resident in the various parts of the body: promiscuity, insatiability, strife, flattery, arrogance, lying, and injustice (chs. 2–3). A similar tradition is found in *2 Enoch* 30.

The *Life of Adam and Eve,* extant in a Latin translation from a Hebrew original probably dating to the first century, contains a passage that is probably the earliest witness to a widespread tradition involving the fall of Satan from heaven. That passage reflects influence from the fall of Lucifer in Isaiah 14:12-15. Satan's fall is related to the creation of Adam. When Adam was created in the image of God the archangel Michael commanded all of the heavenly angels to worship the image of God. The devil and some of his fellow angels refused to worship Adam, so God threw them out of heaven down to earth. Satan's fall from heaven aroused his anger against Adam, and that is the reason he plagues Adam and his descendants with evil temptations (*Life of Adam and Eve* 12–16). As we have already noted, the "God" who created Adam is presented in the *Apocalypse of Adam* as a vengeful being much like Satan in the *Life of Adam and Eve*.

These samples from Jewish traditions relating to Adam provide some of the background for understanding the Gnostic material relating to Adam and his creation. We note, too, that these Jewish traditions are not only found in Greek sources, but in Hebrew and Aramaic ones as well—for example, the initial creation of Adam as a *golem*.

Returning now to the *Apocryphon of John* we note, first, the rebuke that comes from heaven when Yaldabaoth claims to be the only God: "Man exists and the Son of Man" (II 14,13–15). Man in this tradition is the highest God, and he reveals his likeness in a human form in the water (14,23–34). The divine image of Man (Genesis 1:26) is projected down upon the surface of the water of Genesis 1:2. Yaldabaoth then says to the authorities with him, "Come, let us create a man according to the image of God and according to our likeness, that his image may become a light for us" (15,2–5). The light (*phōs*) is that of Genesis 1:3, but we also see here a wordplay involving two Greek words with the same spelling (*phōs*), differentiated only according to the accent used: φῶς means "light," and φώς means "man." The "powers" with Yaldabaoth, unlike the angels assisting God in the Jewish traditions, are demonic beings whose intentions are not good.

What the powers create is a sevenfold psychical body (15,5–23). That passage reminds us of the tradition attested in the *Testament of Reuben* on the body of Adam infused with seven spirits. The result of the powers' creation is a lifeless being, inactive and motionless (19,13–15), reminding us of the rabbinic golem tradition. The earliest example of the Gnostic use of this tradition is found in Irenaeus's report on Saturninus: The angels' creation "could not stand erect because of the powerlessness of the angels, but crept like a worm" until the power on high bestowed on him the "spark of life" (*Against Heresies* 1.24.1). Saturninus's worm may, itself, derive from biblical exegesis, that is, from an interpretation of Psalm 22:7: "I am a worm and not a man" (RSV).

In the version of the inbreathing of Adam's immortal element (Genesis 2:7) found in the *Apocryphon of John*, Yaldabaoth blows into Adam's face "the spirit which is the power of his mother." As a result poor Yaldabaoth loses the last vestige of spiritual power that he had inherited from his mother Sophia: "And the power of the mother went out of Yaldabaoth into the natural body which they had fashioned after the image of the one who exists from the beginning. The body moved and gained strength, and it was luminous" (II 19,28–33).

The powers become jealous of Adam, recognizing his superiority over them, and they throw him down into materiality, encasing him in "the tomb of the newly-formed body." As a result "he became a mortal man" (21,10–12), a reverse interpretation of Genesis 2:7: "and the man became a living soul." After that, "the archons took him and placed him in Paradise" (21,16–18).

It can safely be concluded that the anthropogony found in the *Apocryphon of John* and other Gnostic texts is made up of innovative reinterpretations of the biblical text of Genesis and Jewish traditions relating to Adam and his creation.

5. "The Serpent Was Wiser"

The paradise narrative in Genesis elicited a great deal of interpretive comment in Judaism and early Christianity. It certainly did in Gnosticism as well. The Gnostics developed their ideas on the basis of their own interpretations of the Genesis text, but also used a number of previously existing Jewish traditions and interpretive techniques.

The biblical text itself is the occasion for a number of probing questions. In Genesis 3:1 we read, "The serpent was more subtle [or wiser] than any other wild creature that the LORD God had made" (RSV). What is his role in the story? Who is he really? And how is he related to Eve?

The wisdom of the serpent comes up for comment and interpretation in rabbinic sources. In an Aramaic Targum to Genesis (*Targum Pseudo-Jonathan*), the Aramaic version adds a phrase to the original text of Genesis 3:1 (italicizing the addition): "The serpent was wiser *for evil* than any beast of the field." Rabbi Meir said, "because the wisdom of the serpent was so great, therefore the penalty inflicted upon it proportionate to its wisdom" (*Ecclesiastes Rabbah* 1.18, referring to Genesis 3:1 and 14).

A special relationship between the serpent and Eve is also given notice in rabbinic sources. For example, *Gen. Rab.* 20.11 comments on Genesis 3:20: "The man called his wife's name Hawwah (Eve)": "She was given to him for an advisor [or instructor, *ḥywwyth*], but she played the eavesdropper like the serpent (*ḥywy'*)," and we notice the Aramaic wordplay

> The biblical text itself is the occasion for a number of probing questions.

on *instructor* and *serpent*. In an address to Eve, the commentator says, "The serpent was your serpent, and you are Adam's serpent," noting a wordplay on Aramaic *ḥewyah* (serpent) and *Ḥawwah* (Eve). Obviously these sources regard the roles of the serpent and Eve in negative terms.

In his *Allegorical Interpretation of Genesis*, Philo allegorizes the serpent of Genesis 3 as pleasure (*hēdonē*), which is said to include "a bond of love and desire" under the rule of pleasure. He expands on this with reference to the deadly serpents sent by God in the wilderness (Numbers 21:6) and remarks that the healing for this suffering could only be brought about by "another serpent, opposite in kind to that of Eve, namely the principle of self-mastery." In this connection he brings in the reference to the bronze serpent made by Moses (Numbers 21:9). This bronze serpent brings about not only self-mastery but also wisdom (2.77–81).

We note here an exegetical technique involving the use of a catchword. The serpent in Genesis 3 elicits references to other serpents in scripture. Indeed, Philo later refers to the rod of Moses that became a serpent (Exodus 4:1-4), again allegorizing this serpent as pleasure (*Allegorical Interpretation of Genesis* 2:88). This catchword device is typical of Jewish midrash ("study"), and we shall have occasion to notice the same interpretive device in Gnostic material.

Jewish (and Christian) tradition finally identifies the serpent of Genesis 3 with a manifestation of the devil, or closely associates the serpent with the devil. *Targum Pseudo-Jonathan* on Genesis 3:6 provides an interesting example (with the added material in italics): "And the woman saw *Sammael, the angel of death, and she was afraid, and she knew* that the tree was good for food." According to a rabbinic midrash called *Pirqe de Rabbi Eliezer,* Sammael was originally a great prince in heaven. He descended to earth and rode upon the serpent and deceived Eve (*PRE* 13). Later the same text reports that Sammael actually seduced Eve, and she gave birth to Cain (*PRE* 21). The actual equation of the serpent with the devil is very widespread in Jewish and Christian sources (for example, Revelation 12:9 in the New Testament). Note especially the statement in the Wisdom of Solomon 2:24: "Through the devil's envy death entered the world."

Gnostic interpretation of the serpent of Genesis 3 is varied. Some Gnostics interpreted the serpent in a positive light, that is, as a revealer of gnosis. The so-called Ophite systems reflect this interpretation, and Christian versions of this gnosis even identify the serpent with Christ. Other Gnostic texts take over the traditional Jewish negative valuation of the serpent, even if they interpret it in a different way. In the *Apocryphon of John,* the suggestion that the serpent was the one who taught Adam and Eve to eat of the tree of knowledge is countered with the claim that it was Christ who did so. "The serpent taught them to eat from wickedness of begetting, lust, (and) destruction" (II 22,9–15). This interpretation reminds us of Philo's allegorization of the serpent as pleasure and lust. Both positive and negative serpents occur in Irenaeus's account of the "other" Gnostics (*Against Heresies* 1.30): "Sophia herself became the snake" and "put knowledge in men, and for this reason the serpent was said to be wisest of all" (1.30.15; compare 1.30.7). On the other hand, "the objectionable snake," son of Yaldabaoth, introduced death into the world by inducing Cain to kill his brother Abel (1.30.9).

An especially interesting example of the positive valuation of the serpent of Genesis 3 is a Gnostic midrash on the serpent that is embedded in the text of the *Testimony of Truth* (NHC IX,3: 45,23–49,10), to which parallels can be found in the *Hypostasis of the Archons* (NHC II,4) and the treatise *On the Origin of the World* (NHC II,5).

The first part of this midrash consists of a paraphrase of Genesis. It begins with God's command not to eat of the tree in the midst of Paradise, that is, the tree of the knowledge of good and evil (45,23–31; Genesis 2:17, compare 2:9). It then refers to the serpent's wisdom (45,31–46,2; Genesis 3:1), followed by his success in getting Adam and Eve to eat of the forbidden tree (46,2–15; Genesis 3:2-7). God's stroll in the garden and his questioning of Adam and Eve come next (46,16–47,4; Genesis 3:8-13), followed by God's cursing of the serpent (47,5–6; Genesis 3:14) and the expulsion of Adam from Paradise (47,7–14; Genesis 3:22-23).

In this part of the midrash, the serpent's role as a teacher is underscored. "Who is it who has instructed you?" God asks. Adam refers to the woman and the woman says, "it is the serpent who instructed me." We can see reflected here the Aramaic wordplays we noted in the rabbinic material. The Aramaic word for serpent (*ḥywy'*) is associated with the name Eve (*ḥawah*), and both are related via wordplay to the Aramaic verb *ḥw'* (show, instruct).

Similar interpretations of the roles of Eve and the serpent are found in the *Hypostasis of the Archons* and the treatise *On the Origin of the World*, where the snake is referred to as "the instructor" (*Hyp. Arch.* 89,32–91,7; compare *Orig. World* 113,21–114,4).

Our serpent midrash continues with an extended denunciation of God, who maliciously begrudged Adam's eating of the tree of knowledge. "What sort of a God is this?" our author exclaims (47,14–15). It is interesting that the text consistently refers to God, but the lineaments of the lower creator of Gnostic theology are clearly present.

The midrash then continues with references to other biblical serpents: The rod of Moses (and Aaron) that became a serpent and swallowed the serpents of the Egyptian magicians (48,18–26; Exodus 7:8–12, compare 4:2–4); and the bronze serpent of Numbers 21:9 (48,26–49,7). This juxtaposition of biblical serpents is the same kind of Jewish exegetical catchword technique that we saw in Philo's discussion of the serpent and also involves the same biblical texts.

Of course, the Gnostic version does not regard the eating of the forbidden fig tree as a sin; in our midrash Adam is sinned against by a god who begrudges him both knowledge and life.

The midrash concludes, with reference to the bronze serpent, "For this is Christ; [those who] believed in him [have received life]. Those who did not believe [will die]" (49,7–10). I am inclined to see this as a Christian gloss on a previously existing Gnostic midrash on the serpent in which Christian features were lacking.

Incidentally, this midrash identifies the tree of knowledge as a fig tree. In answer to the question posed by God to Adam, "Where are you?" Adam replies, "[I] have come under the fig tree," and God realizes that Adam has eaten from the forbidden tree (46,20–27). The identification made between the tree under which Adam hid (compare Genesis 3:8) and the fig tree (deduced from Genesis 3:7) reflects a possible use of a legend that appears variously in the *Apocalypse of Moses* and in a saying of Rabbi Jose: "Adam after his sin looked for a tree under which to hide, and none of the trees of Paradise would receive him except the tree whose fruit he had eaten in his sin against God" (*Apoc. Mos.* 20.4–5; *Gen. Rab.* 15.7). Of course, the Gnostic version does not regard the eating of the forbidden fig tree as a sin; in our midrash Adam is sinned against by a god who begrudges him both knowledge and life.

The Gnostic texts on the serpent of Genesis 3 surveyed here indicate that there were Gnostics who regarded that serpent as a revealer of saving gnosis, while concomitantly condemning the God who tried to prevent Adam from eating of the tree of knowledge. Traditions like these came to the attention of the church's heresy hunters, who extrapolated from them a Gnostic sect of Ophites, first attested in Pseudo-Tertullian, *Against All Heresies*. As we noted earlier (in chapter 2) an Ophite sect probably never existed as such. Nevertheless, that kind of gnosis that attributes saving gnosis to the Genesis serpent can be referred to as an Ophite type of Gnostic teaching, even if there were no Gnostics who referred to themselves as "Ophites."

6. Cain, Son of Sammael

The Hebrew text of Genesis 4:1, relating the birth of Cain, presented problems to later interpreters. Eve's statement is quite ambiguous: *qaniti 'ish 'et YHWH,* for it can be taken to read, "I have gotten a man, namely Yahweh," instead of "I have gotten a man with the help of YHWH." Rabbinic interpretation of this passage serves to underscore that the offspring of Eve is not YHWH, nor related to him at all; Cain is, rather, the child of Sammael! Note especially *Targum Pseudo-Jonathan,* Genesis 4:1 (I have marked Aramaic additions to the Hebrew text in italic): "And *Adam was aware that* Eve his wife had conceived *from Sammael the angel, and she became pregnant* and bore Cain, *and he was like those on high, not like those below, and she* said, 'I have acquired a man, *the angel of* the LORD.'"

In the treatise On the Origin of the World *there is a more complicated interpretation of Cain.*

This interpretation is bolstered with reference to Genesis 5:3, where it is said that Adam was the father of a son in his own likeness, that is, Seth. Since this is not said of Cain, Cain must have had a different origin. *Targum Pseudo-Jonathan* Genesis 5:3 reads, "And Adam lived a hundred and thirty years, and begat Seth *who resembled his likeness and his appearance. For before that time,*

Eve had borne Cain who was not from him (Adam) and did not resemble him" (Aramaic additions in italics).

With such possibilities, the Gnostics could have a field day with their treatment of Cain. First of all, they opt for the alternative reading of the text of Genesis that is possible in the Hebrew text by identifying Cain with YHWH. The *Apocryphon of John* has the chief archon Yaldabaoth seducing Eve and begetting on her two sons: Eloim (Elohim) and Yave (Yahweh). "And these he called with the names Cain and Abel with a view to deceive" (II 24,15–26). We note, too, that this passage reflects the tradition of the birth of Cain from Sam(m)ael, which is an alternative name for Yaldabaoth in *Apocryphon of John*. The tradition of the birth of Cain from Sammael is also reflected in the *Hypostasis of the Archons* (91,11–14), where Cain is called "their son," that is, the son of the "authorities." And in the *Apocalypse of Adam* (66,25–28), Adam tells Seth, "Then the god who created us, created a son from himself [and] Eve, [your mother]." While Cain is not explicitly mentioned here, he is certainly the son referred to.

These Gnostic texts reflect a negative evaluation of Cain. However, in the treatise *On the Origin of the World* there is a more complicated interpretation of Cain. Of Eve it is said,

> Her offspring is the creature that is LORD. Afterwards, the authorities called it "Beast," so that it might lead astray their modeled creatures. The interpretation of "the beast" is "the instructor." For it was found to be the wisest of all beings. Now Eve is the first virgin, the one who without a husband bore her first offspring. (113,34–114,5)

This is followed by a poem sung by Eve containing a number of self-predications. The poem ends with the words, "Yet I have borne a man as LORD" (114,14–15).

While Cain is not named in the text, it is clear that this passage reflects the alternative translation of the text of Genesis 4:1 already referred to: "the creature that is LORD" and "a man as LORD." (Coptic *joeis* is Greek *kyrios*, translating Hebrew YHWH.) We also note an identification of Cain with "the beast," a reference to the serpent (Greek *thērion* in Genesis 3:2, "the serpent was the wisest of all the beasts"). The beast or serpent is also called *instructor,* and here we recall the Aramaic wordplays we referred to in our discussion of the serpent. Indeed, there is an additional one here: "Beast" in Aramaic is *ḥywa',* and the verbal root *ḥw'* means "instruct." When we unravel this complicated text we can see here a more positive role attributed to Cain in Gnostic exegesis of Genesis.

7. Seth, the Savior

In the previous chapter we looked at several texts that belong together and reflect a certain kind of Gnosticism that has been labeled Sethian. In a number of those texts, Seth plays a prominent role as a Gnostic savior, that is, as a revealer of gnosis. The Gnostic treatment of Seth, son of Adam, is developed out of the Gnostics' interpretation of the Bible and Jewish traditions pertaining to Seth.

The birth of Seth is narrated in two biblical passages. Genesis 5:3 reads, "When Adam had lived a hundred and thirty years [two hundred thirty in the Greek version], he became the father of a son in his own likeness, after his image, and named him Seth." Genesis 4:25 is especially important in the development of Gnostic traditions pertaining to Seth: "And Adam knew his wife again, and she bore a son and called his name Seth, for she said, 'God has appointed for me another child instead of Abel, for Cain slew him'" (RSV).

In somewhat similar fashion the Gnostics could see in Seth not only the progenitor of their own elect race, but also a symbol of Gnostic salvation itself.

The Hebrew text has a wordplay: "God has appointed for me," where the name Seth (Hebrew *Shet*) is related to the verb *shat,* "set" or "appoint." Another wordplay involves "appointed for me," *shat-li,* and (by metastasis, that is, transposition of letters) the word for "plant," *shatil.* The Gnostics were familiar with such wordplays. For example, the *Gospel of the Egyptians* has the great Seth taking his plant out of Gomorrah and planting it in another place to which he gave the name Sodom (III 60,12–18). We note here the reverse evaluation of the sinful cities of Genesis (18:20—19:29).

In Genesis 4:25, the words translated "another child" read literally "another seed" (Hebrew *zera' 'aher*, Greek *sperma heteron*), a phrase that can imply a different kind of seed. It is this idea that is the basis for the application of the name Allogenes ("stranger," "another race") to Seth. We have encountered a number of examples of this usage already.

Philo of Alexandria comments on Seth as another seed, and sees in him "the seed of human virtue," sown from God. Philo sets up a contrast between the impious "race of Cain" and the lovers of virtue, who are "enrolled under Seth as the head of their race" (*The Posterity and Exile of Cain* 171). Such allegorical treatments of Seth come close to the Gnostic theme of Seth as the progenitor of a special race of Gnostics.

The interpretation of "another seed" in rabbinic literature provides additional comparative material. Note, for example, *Gen. Rab.* on Genesis 4:25: "Rabbi Tanhuma in the name of Samuel Kozit said: (She set her eyes on) that same seed who will arise from an alien place. And who is this? This is the Messianic King." In this passage Seth is a symbol for, and progenitor of, the Messiah. A similar idea occurs in *1 Enoch* 85–90. A salvation history is narrated there, telling of the world from creation to the coming of the Messiah. Seth is presented symbolically as a white bull, the people of Israel as a nation of white bulls, and the Messiah as a white bull. The rest of humanity consists of black oxen. In this text Seth is looked upon as the progenitor of the elect race and ultimately of the Messiah.

In somewhat similar fashion the Gnostics could see in Seth not only the progenitor of their own elect race, but also a symbol of Gnostic salvation itself. We have already noted Josephus's account of Seth's role as an antediluvian revealer and his progeny's record of Sethian lore inscribed on steles of brick and stone (*Antiquities* 1.67–71, discussed in chapter 3).

Such traditions as these are taken over by the Gnostics and given a new twist. A number of examples have already been noted:

1. The birth of Seth: *Apocryphon of John* II 24,34–25,2; *Hypostasis of the Archons* 91,31–33; Irenaeus, *Against Heresies* 1.30.9.
2. Seth as an ideal type; for example, "the great incorruptible Seth, the son of the incorruptible man Adamas" in *Gospel of the Egyptians* III 51,5–22.
3. Seth as father of the Gnostic race: *Apocalypse of Adam* 65,6–9; *Three Steles of Seth* 118,12–13.
4. Seth as recipient and revealer of gnosis. This includes authorship of books, revelations inscribed in stone or wood, and so forth: *Apocalypse of Adam* 64,2–8 et passim; 85,10–11.19–24; *Gospel of the Egyptians* III 68,1–3; *Three Steles of Seth* (passim); *Allogenes* (passim).
5. Seth as savior. This includes his role in revelation already noted. But as savior Seth is thought to appear in human history and is presented as an eschatological figure. Note, for example, the coming of Seth as the "illuminator of knowledge" in *Apocalypse of Adam* 76,8–77,18. The heavenly Seth "puts on" Jesus in the *Gospel of the Egyptians* III 64,1–3. Other human revelers of gnosis can also be seen as avatars of Seth in some fashion: Zostrianos, Marsanes, and others, perhaps as human beings possessed by the heavenly Seth.

The important role played by Seth in Gnostic literature is not confined to the Sethian corpus, for we shall encounter him in other Gnostic contexts as well, including Manichaean and Mandaean writings.

8. Norea: Naughty Girl and Gnostic Heroine

An obvious question posed by the Genesis stories of the first humans is this: Who were the wives of the earliest children of Adam? Attempts to answer this question occur in extrabiblical Jewish material. For example, the opening passage in the *Biblical Antiquities,* a first-century writing originally written in Hebrew and whose Greek version was falsely attributed to Philo, reads, "In the beginning of the world Adam became the father of three sons and one daughter: Cain, Noaba, Abel, and Seth" (1.1). Noaba is probably to be understood as a corruption (through Greek Noema) of Hebrew Na'amah. Na'amah is a biblical name that first occurs in Genesis 4:22. There she is named as the sister of Tubal-cain (several generations after Adam's progeny).

In the *Chronicles of Jerahme'el,* a writing dependent upon Pseudo-Philo, we read, "Adam begat three sons and three daughters, Cain and his twin wife Qalmana, Abel and his twin wife Deborah, and Seth and his twin wife Noba." Noba and Noaba are Na'amah. Whereas in Pseudo-Philo Na'amah is named as Cain's twin wife, in the *Chronicles of Jerahme'el* she is named as Seth's twin wife.

> Comparative study of Jewish legends about Na'amah and Sethian Gnostic traditions concerning Norea reveal that Jewish Na'amah and Gnostic Norea are one and the same.

Na'amah is also the name given to Noah's wife in some Jewish traditions. In *Gen. Rab.,* commenting on Genesis 4:22, it is stated that "Na'amah was Noah's wife; and why was she called Na'amah? Because her deeds were pleasing." This opinion, attributed to Rabbi Abba ben Kohana, is contradicted by the majority of rabbis: "Na'amah was a woman of a different stamp, for the name denotes that she sang to the timbrel in honor of idolatry" (*Gen. Rab.* 23.3).

Later mystical Jewish lore has Na'amah in a sexual liaison with the "sons of God" (angels) whose illicit descent to earth is reported in Genesis 6:2. (More will be said about this in what follows.) In the *Zohar* (I 55a) it is said that she went about stark naked, and seduced the angels Aza and Azael. This late legend is not irrelevant to an analysis of the role of Norea in Gnostic lore.

The Hebrew word *na'amah* means "pleasing" or "lovely." Its Greek equivalent is *hōraia.* In fact, Gnostic sources speak of a heroine called Horaia, who is more commonly referred to as Norea.

The name *Norea* can be seen as a hybrid form: Noema plus Horaia. This name may also reflect Norea's association with light, reflecting influence from Aramaic *nura'* (fire, light). Norea is associated with light in some Gnostic texts (for example, *Hypostasis of the Archons* 96,19–21). Comparative study of the Jewish legends about Na'amah and Sethian Gnostic traditions concerning Norea reveal that Jewish Na'amah and Gnostic Norea are one and the same. But whereas the Jewish stories about Na'amah usually portray her as a naughty girl, the Gnostic lore portrays Norea as a savior figure, a female counterpart to Seth.

One of the Sethian tractates already discussed (in chapter 3), the *Hypostasis of the Archons,* is especially important for what it says about Norea. Immediately after an account of the birth of Seth, the birth of Norea is reported: "Again Eve became pregnant, and she bore [Norea]. And she said, 'He has begotten on [me a] virgin as an assistance [for] many generations of mankind.' She is the virgin whom the forces did not defile" (91,34–37). The juxtaposition of the birth stories of Seth and Norea in *Hypostasis of the Archons* implicitly reflects a Gnostic tradition that is explicitly stated elsewhere, that Horaia (Norea) is the sister-wife of Seth (Epiphanius, *Panarion* 39.5.2). This tradition reflects the Jewish association of Na'amah with Seth, as we have already noted.

Norea's role as an "assistance" (Greek *boētheia*) for mankind recalls that of her mother Eve, a "helper" (*boēthos*) to Adam (Genesis 2:18). It may also reflect an alternative name given to Seth's wife in the *Book of Jubilees,* 'Azura, which means "helper" in Hebrew. Her status as a virgin underscores the inability of the archons to defile her, in contrast to what is recorded of Na'amah and the fallen angels in Jewish traditions, and in contrast to what happened to her mother Eve.

Norea (Orea) later tries to board Noah's ark, and when Noah wouldn't let her, "she blew upon the ark and caused it to be consumed by fire"; so Noah had to rebuild it (92,14–18). The attempt on the part of Norea (there called Noria) to destroy Noah's ark is also recorded by Epiphanius in his account of the teachings of the Gnostics (*Panarion* 26.1.3–6).

The story of Norea in *Hypostasis of the Archons* continues with the archons trying to seduce her, and Norea rebukes them with a curse (92,18–27). She then cries out for help and is rescued by the angel Eleleth. As we noted earlier in our discussion of *Hypostasis of the Archons* (in chapter 3), the second part of that tractate is an apocalypse of Norea, in which she narrates what she has learned from Eleleth. Norea thus functions in the text as a Gnostic savior figure, a revealer of gnosis. As such, she can be seen as a female counterpart to the savior Seth.

Norea appears in Manichaean literature as Horaia, a virgin of light (for example, *Acta Archelai* 9). In Mandaean literature the wife of Noah is called Nuraita (Norea).

9. Cosmic Catastrophes: Fallen Angels, Flood, Fire

The biblical story of the great flood begins with a statement remarking on the great wickedness of mankind, that "every imagination of the thoughts of his heart was only evil continually." As a result "the LORD was sorry that he had made man on the earth" and so resolved to blot out humankind from the face of the earth. Only Noah "found favor in the eyes of the LORD" (Genesis 6:5-8). The story of the flood and Noah's ark then continues (Genesis 6:9—8:19 RSV).

But this story is preceded in Genesis by an enigmatic passage in which it is reported that "the sons of God" were captivated by the beauty of "the daughters of men" and so "they took to wife such of them as they chose." The product of their unions was "the Nephilim," "mighty men that were of old" (Genesis 6:1-4). The sons of God in this story were interpreted as angels in later Jewish tradition, and the Greek version of the Bible translates Hebrew *nepilim* as "giants" (*gigantes*).

This story in Genesis becomes greatly elaborated in later tradition, especially in apocalyptic literature. *1 Enoch* 6–10, 15 is especially important in this regard. In that text a group of angels called "watchers" plan to descend to earth and commit fornication with "daughters of men." They put their plan into action, led by an angel variously called Shemihazah or 'Asa'el. The product of their union is the giants. The angels teach metallurgy and warfare to men, and there is much godlessness upon the earth. 'Asa'el and Shemihazah and the other watchers are eventually punished by angelic agents of God. But the results of the angels' fall are dire for humankind. The spirits that have gone forth from the flesh of the giants are evil spirits who survived the flood and are the cause of much evil among humans on earth. It is said that they will continue in their dirty work until the final day of judgment. This story is a key text in apocalyptic Judaism for explaining the origin of evil in the world.

This story in *1 Enoch* was known to, and utilized by, the author(s) of the *Apocryphon of John*. Of course, it was subjected to reinterpretation in the Gnostic retelling. In the *Apocryphon of John* the angels' descent follows upon the flood rather than preceding it. The chief archon makes a plan with his powers and sends his angels to the daughters of men. They are unsuccessful at first, and create a "counterfeit spirit" to pollute human souls (II 29,16–25). The angels then change their appearance to resemble the women's husbands, and commit fornication with them (29,26–30). They teach people metallurgy and warfare, and lead them astray with many deceptions (29,30–30,2). The result of the angels' actions is that the whole creation becomes enslaved (30,2–11).

The chief archon in the *Apocryphon of John* is, in one respect, a counterpart to Shemihazah in *1 Enoch,* as leader of the angels. In another respect, though, he is counterpart to God, the biblical creator, who is determined to keep his entire creation in slavery.

The flood story itself is featured in a number of Gnostic texts. In the *Apocryphon of John* the chief archon plans to bring a flood upon humankind. Noah is forewarned and he, together with others from the immovable race, hides himself, not in an ark as Moses said, but in a luminous cloud, and is thus saved (28,34–29,15). Noah receives a somewhat different treatment in the *Hypostasis of the Archons*. There, Noah builds his ark in obedience to the command of the chief archon (92,8–14). As we have already noted, Norea

(Orea) burns it down, and Noah is forced to rebuild it (92,14–18). Nothing more is said of the flood in that text. Noah is also the agent of Saklas in the *Apocalypse of Adam* (70,16–73,29).

As we have already noted, Sethian Gnosticism features a three-fold salvation history marked by flood, fire, and final judgment. The *Apocalypse of Adam* and the *Gospel of the Egyptians* are the most important witnesses to this scheme. The notion that the world has suffered destruction by flood and fire is found already in Plato's *Timaeus* (22c), and we have noted the tradition recorded by Josephus of the progeny of Seth recording their lore in inscriptions on stone and brick to survive flood and fire. But there are also Jewish testimonies to a threefold schema of flood, fire, and end time. The "Apocalypse of Weeks" in *1 Enoch* 93.1–17 is a case in point. Human history is divided into ten symbolic "weeks" (of years). The flood takes place in the second week (93,4). Destruction by fire takes place in the sixth week with the burning of the temple (93,8), and the final judgment takes place in the tenth week (93,15), followed by eternal righteousness.

In the Gnostic material, the destruction by fire is usually described with allusions to the destruction of Sodom and Gomorrah by brimstone and fire (Genesis 19:24-28). In the *Apocalypse of Adam,* when the undefiled people of the "imperishable seed" are attacked by Saklas with "fire and sulfur and asphalt," Abrasax, Sablo, and Gamaliel descend to bring them out of the fire and the wrath (75,9–76,8). Of course, the cities of Sodom and Gomorrah are given a positive evaluation in the Gnostic material. They are places associated with the great Seth and his seed (*Gospel of the Egyptians* III 60,9–29).

10. Conclusions

In our survey of the Gnostic Genesis, we have concentrated for the most part on the Sethian or Classic Gnostic materials, with special attention to the biblical and Jewish materials that are reflected in Gnostic mythology. We have noted that the building blocks of the basic Gnostic myth, consisting of theogony, cosmogony, anthropogony, soteriology, and eschatology, consist of innovative reinterpretations of biblical texts, Jewish exegetical traditions, and extrabiblical Jewish sources. The same can be said of other, more subsidiary, examples of Gnostic mythology. Any Christian elements that are to be found in Gnostic mythology are purely secondary, as, for example, the heavenly Seth "putting on" Jesus.

What is said of the transcendent God in Gnostic sources is based on Jewish theology as reflected in sources dated to around the turn of the era. The major departure from that theology is the split of the Jewish God into two, with creation attributed to a lower deity. We can, of course, recognize the biblical creator in the actions of Yaldabaoth-Saklas-Samael, even if he is demonized in the Gnostic sources. This demonization itself reflects the use of Jewish sources relating to the devil and other evil angels. The anthropogony reflects innovative reinterpretations of the two accounts of human creation, Genesis 1:26-27 and Genesis 2:7. The influence of the Platonist dualism of body and soul is clearly present, but is, no doubt, mediated through Hellenistic Jewish sources, best exemplified in the writings of Philo. The Gnostic myth of Sophia's fall and redemption is drawn from biblical and extra-biblical texts relating to Sophia's role in creation and human history, with her fall a projection onto the heavenly plane of Eve and her adventures in Paradise.

Any Christian elements that are to be found in Gnostic mythology are purely secondary, as, for example, the heavenly Seth "putting on" Jesus.

We can conclude from this that Sethian or Classic Gnosticism developed as a result of the efforts of educated Jews interested in making sense of their traditions. They did this, not by rejecting their traditions wholesale, but by applying to them a new hermeneutic, whereby their ancestral traditions were given a radically new meaning. The result was, in effect, the creation of a new religion.

That religion developed originally as a phenomenon completely independent of Christianity, probably by the mid-first century. From the second century on, it took on Christian features with the incorporation into its mythology of the figure of Jesus Christ. This took place as the Christian religion was rapidly expanding in the Greco-Roman world and was in the process of separation from the Judaism out of which it emerged.

Scholars have speculated on the social and historical exigencies that motivated the Gnostic innovation. Different answers have been put forward to the questions involved, owing to the difficulties posed by the nature of our sources. I have set forth some ideas of my own on this issue in some of my earlier writings. Now I prefer to set such questions aside. The evidence is certainly there for the Jewish origin of Gnosticism, even if it does not allow us to answer the question as to why it happened the way it did.

5. Basilides and Basilidian Gnosis

Basilides the heresiarch was living in Alexandria; from him derive the Gnostics.

THIS IS ONE OF THE ITEMS LISTED by the fourth-century church historian and bishop Eusebius in his *Chronicle* for the sixteenth year of Emperor Hadrian's reign (132 CE). This is the only mention in Eusebius's *Chronicle* of Gnostics of any stripe. Basilides is here credited with being the founder of the Gnostic heresy, but that is certainly not correct. Basilides was a Gnostic, but there were certainly Gnostics before him, as the previous chapters in this book attest.

Basilides is credited in our meager sources with being a prolific author. Unfortunately, none of his writings remain, except for a few quotations preserved by the church fathers. The earliest account we have of Basilides' teachings is that of Irenaeus (*Against Heresies* 1.24.3–7), who lumps him together with Saturninus of Antioch as a successor to Simon and Menander, with Saturninus active in Antioch and Basilides in Alexandria (*Against Heresies* 1.24.1). As we shall see, Basilides' teachings are Alexandrian through and through, but it is possible that he also spent some time in Antioch before the date cited by Eusebius. His mythological system has some features in common with that of Saturninus, and a sojourn in Antioch would account for this.

1. The Sources (Foerster 1:74–83; Layton, 417–44)

As already noted, Irenaeus's account is our earliest attestation for Basilides, but his account may be dependent upon Justin's lost *Syntagma* (mid-second century, referred to in chapter 1). Irenaeus presents a summary of Basilides' teachings, adding material on teachings and practices of unnamed followers. A completely different account of Basilides' mythology is presented by Hippolytus in his *Refutation of all Heresies* (7.20–27). Scholars differ as to which account comes closest to the teachings of Basilides himself, and some reject both accounts. I count myself among those who accept Irenaeus's account as generally reliable, at least to the extent that it can be supported with reference to the

> *Basilides is thus the very first Christian author to write commentaries on the gospels and other Christian writings that eventually became part of the canonical New Testament.*

extant fragments of Basilides' writings. Hippolytus's account, on the other hand, reflects a later development of Basilidian gnosis.

We have already noted a number of examples of Gnostic writings that lack Christian features, or writings overlaid by a Christian veneer. With Basilides we encounter a Gnostic whose teachings are Christian to the core. If in other cases we can speak of Christian Gnostics, in Basilides' case we have to do with a Gnostic Christian. Eusebius quotes a second-century writer, Agrippa Castor (whose refutation of Basilides is lost), to the effect that Basilides composed twenty-four volumes on "the Gospel" (*Ecclesiastical History* 4.7.5–8). Basilides is thus the very first Christian author to write commentaries on the gospels and other Christian writings that eventually became part of the canonical New Testament. But little credence can be given to the claim for apostolic succession for Basilides, through Peter via Glaukias (Foerster, fragment 2 of Clement's *Miscellanies,* discussed below).

Our most important source for our knowledge of Basilides' teachings is the *Miscellanies* of Clement of Alexandria. Eight quotations or paraphrases of passages from Basilides' writings have been preserved (Layton fragments A–H), and seven of them are preserved by Clement. One of them is given by Origen (Layton fragment F); another one, given by Hegemonius, is probably inauthentic (Foerster fragment 1). In addition, there are nine other

> *What is interesting about Clement's references to Basilides and his followers is that he is not openly hostile to them.*

fragments that provide material on Isidore or unnamed Basilidians, and all of these are from Clement's *Miscellanies* (Foerster fragments 2, 3, 6, 7, 8, 10, 14, 15). What is interesting about Clement's references to Basilides and his followers is that he is not openly hostile to them. While he disagrees with Basilides and his followers on some points, he can show some tacit agreement with them on others. This makes Clement a very valuable source for our knowledge of Basilides and Basilidian gnosis, since we lack primary evidence owing to the loss of the Basilidian writings themselves.

Other church fathers have reports on Basilides and his followers. The most important of these are Pseudo-Tertullian and Epiphanius, but they depend for the most part on Irenaeus's account, and add little of substance to what is reported by Irenaeus.

2. Basilides' Mythological and Philosophical System

a. Theogony

Irenaeus opens his account of Basilides' teaching by presenting the latter's account of the transcendent divine world. From an unoriginated Father came Mind (*nous*); from Mind, Word (*logos*); from Word, Prudence (*phronesis*); from Prudence, Sophia (wisdom) and Power (*dunamis, Against Heresies* 1.24.3). According to this account Basilides presents as first principles an unengendered Father and a pentad of emanations from him. But we learn from Clement that Basilides actually taught a primal ogdoad, and Clement supplies the names for the last two entities, Righteousness (*dikaiosunē*) and Peace (*eirēnē*, Layton fragment A). Additional evidence that Basilides taught a primal ogdoad comes from one of the Nag Hammadi tractates, the *Testimony of Truth* (NHC IX,3: 56–57). (That tractate is discussed in chapter eight.)

Basilides' ogdoad has no parallel in Saturninus's system, so the question arises as to where he got it. The probable source is to be found in an Alexandrian Jewish Gnostic work that we now have in a Coptic version, *Eugnostos the Blessed* (NHC III,3; V,1, discussed in chapter eight). In the system in *Eugnostos*, the transcendent deity is described as the ineffable unbegotten "Father of the All," who is "all Mind [*nous*], Thought [*ennoia*], Reflection [*enthumēsis*], Prudence [*phronēsis*], Reasoning [*logismos*], and Power [*dunamis*]," to which is added Foreknowledge (*prognōsis*, III 71,14–73,16). We see here in *Eugnostos* an ogdoad of first principles, four of which occur in Basilides' ogdoad. Basilides' own four hypostases are derived from scripture or apostolic writings, and reflect Christianization of a preexisting Gnostic system.

b. Cosmogony and Cosmology

Irenaeus's account continues with the production of "powers, principalities, and angels" from Power and Sophia, and these entities create the first heaven and other angels who produce other heavens adding up to 365 heavens, the number of days in the year (*Against Heresies* 1.24.3). Basilides shares with Saturninus a system of creator-angels, but Saturninus posits seven whereas Basilides counts 365. Where did he get this detail?

We turn again to *Eugnostos*, where we find 360 powers and heavens, associated with the solar year. The author of *Eugnostos* bases his system on the Egyptian year of twelve months of thirty days each (III 84,1–85,7). Basilides does the same thing, but adds the five epagomenal days of the Egyptian calendar, completing the number of days in the solar year. We recall, too, that the longer version of the *Apocryphon of John* has 365 angels contributing to the creation of Adam's psychical body (II 15,23–19,10). Epiphanius attributes a similar doctrine to Basilides: man has 365 members, one assigned to each of 365 angels (*Panarion* 1.24.5). Irenaeus attributes to the followers of Basilides the assignment of strange-sounding names to the 365 angels (*Against Heresies* 1.24.5, recalling the strange names of the angels in *Ap. John*), and this detail may go back to Basilides himself.

The creation of the world is credited to the angels occupying the last heaven in Irenaeus's account. He says that "their chief [*archon*] is the one known as the God of the Jews. Because he wished to subject the other nations to his own men, that is, to the Jews, all the other principalities opposed him and worked against him. For this reason the other nations were alienated from his nation" (*Against Heresies* 1.24.4). Saturninus ascribes the creation of the world to seven creator angels (*Against Heresies* 1.24.1). How many angels are posited by Basilides? Irenaeus's account implies that each of the other "nations" had its own chief, and the traditional number of nations in the world in Jewish lore is seventy-two. We also find seventy-two "powers" in *Eugnostos* (III 83,13–19).

That the creator-angels' chief, or Archon, is the Jewish God is also a doctrine shared with Saturninus (*Against Heresies* 1.24.1). According to Irenaeus, the followers of Basilides refer to him as Abrasax, a name that has the numerical value of 365 (*Against Heresies* 1.24.7). (Greek letters of the alphabet were used as numerals. A + B + R + A + S + A + X = 365). This detail may go back to Basilides himself. As to the world created by the Archon and his helpers, Clement reports that Basilides taught that it is "unique" (*monogenēs*, Layton fragment B), a doctrine that goes back to Plato's *Timaeus* (31 ab).

c. Anthropogony and Anthropology

Saturninus includes in his myth an anthropogony featuring a creation by angels of the first man similar to what we find in the *Apocryphon of John* (*Against Heresies* 1.24.1, compare chapter 4).

Irenaeus provides no anthropogony in his account of Basilides' myth, but one is tempted to think that Basilides' system originally included something on the creation of Adam. Irenaeus does have Basilides agree with Saturninus that salvation is for the soul only, the body being "by nature corruptible" (*Against Heresies* 1.24.5).

A fragment from Basilides' writings preserved by Origen (Layton fragment F, Foerster fragment 5) suggests that he taught a doctrine of reincarnation. Clement also attributes that doctrine to Basilides (Layton fragment F, Foerster fragment 5). Some scholars have cast doubt on these reports, but I see no reason to doubt that a Platonizing theologian like Basilides taught the doctrine of reincarnation, as a number of other Gnostic teachers also did.

On balance, there is good reason to conclude that Clement has misunderstood Basilides in his reports, and that whatever kind of determinism was taught by Basilides was based on the writings of the apostle Paul and other early Christian tradition.

Another matter of dispute in scholarship is Basilides' doctrine of human nature and his classification of some people (that is, Gnostic Christians) as elect, over against the rest of humanity. A dominical saying is cited by Irenaeus as current among the Basilidians: "Few people can know these things—only one in a thousand, and two in ten thousand" (*Against Heresies* 1.24.6; compare *Gospel of Thomas* 23). The question that arises in this connection is the basis for human election. Are some people transcendent or saved by nature, as Clement asserts is taught by Basilides (Layton fragments E and C, Foerster fragments 12 and 11)? Saturninus states explicitly that "two kinds of men had been molded by the angels, the one wicked, the other good" (Irenaeus, *Against Heresies* 1.24.2), but there is nothing to suggest that this doctrine was also espoused by Basilides. On balance, there is good reason to conclude that Clement has misunderstood Basilides in his reports, and that whatever kind of determinism was taught by Basilides was based on the writings of the apostle Paul and other early Christian tradition.

d. Christology and Soteriology

Irenaeus's account of Basilides' teaching about the creator Archon is followed by his teaching about Christ: The "unoriginate and ineffable Father" sent his "first-born Mind (*nous*)" as "the Christ" to "liberate those who believe in him from the power of those who made the world." He appeared on earth as a man and performed miracles. He did not really suffer, but Simon of Cyrene was crucified in his stead while Jesus, laughing, ascended to the one who sent him (*Against Heresies* 1.24.4). Here Irenaeus has undoubtedly misinterpreted his source, which probably taught that it was not the Christ but the corporeal Jesus who was crucified. A similar doctrine is found in the *Second Treatise of the Great Seth* (NHC VII,2, discussed in chapter 8).

What Basilides probably taught was that the divine Mind-Christ descended into the human Jesus and displaced his human soul at the time of his baptism, and, at Jesus's crucifixion, the Mind-Christ ascended to the Father. We know from one of the fragments preserved by Clement that Basilides taught that Jesus did suffer (Layton fragment G, Foerster fragment 4, discussed below). Basilides' Christology thus comports with his anthropology: Salvation is for the soul alone, not the corruptible body.

e. Ethical Theory and Doctrine of Providence

Irenaeus concludes his account of Basilides' teaching by asserting that Basilides taught that the Prophets came into being through the world-creators, and the Law through their Archon. It is a matter of indifference to worry about meat sacrificed to idols, or other kinds of behavior that are also matters of indifference (*Against Heresies* 1.24.5). The implication here is that Basilides rejected the authority of the Old Testament. It is possible that he regarded as a matter of indifference the eating of meat sacrificed to pagan gods. This doctrine of indifference in certain ethical matters reflects Stoic influence, but

While Basilides will not attribute willful sin to Jesus, he does not shrink from ascribing sinfulness to him.

140

his apparent acceptance of the practice of eating meat sacrificed to pagan gods, universally condemned in orthodox circles, could have been based on his reading of 1 Corinthians 8.

Irenaeus goes on to accuse Basilides' followers of sorcery and other superstitious practices, as well as denying their Christian identity in times of persecution (*Against Heresies* 1.24.5–6). This is probably nothing more than baseless polemics.

In a fragment quoted by Clement, Basilides is said to teach that it is the will of God to "love everything," including even punishment for sin (Layton fragment D, Foerster fragment 15). Basilides' views concerning human suffering and its relation to divine providence is best seen in three quotations discussed by Clement from Book 23 of Basilides' *Exegetica* (Layton fragment G; Foerster fragment 4). Basilides asserts in the first quotation that Christian martyrs suffer for undetected sins. In the second he asserts that a child suffers because he has sinfulness in him. Basilides says, "I will say anything rather than call Providence bad." In the third quotation the Lord's suffering is treated. Basilides likens Jesus's suffering to that of a child. While Basilides will not attribute willful sin to Jesus, he does not shrink from ascribing sinfulness to him. This quotation also underscores the reality of Jesus's physical suffering, in contrast to the doctrine attributed to him by Irenaeus. In another fragment Basilides asserts that divine punishment, in the form of suffering, is the consequence of all willful sins (Layton fragment H; Foerster fragment 9).

We can conclude this discussion with the observation that Basilides, under strong influence from Stoic and Platonic philosophy, asserts his faith in the goodness of divine providence and the educational value of human suffering. For Basilides, only God is wholly good.

3. Isidore and Other Basilidians

One of Basilides' pupils was his son, Isidore. Three of Isidore's books are quoted by Clement. In a work titled *On the Grown Soul*, Isidore teaches that the human soul is not unitary but has attachments that cause cravings for evil things. Through reason people can control the compulsions of the attachments (Foerster fragment 7). A similar doctrine is attributed to unnamed people around Basilides (Foerster fragment 6).

In a work titled *Ethics,* Isidore takes up the issue of Christian marriage, and cites Jesus (Matthew 19:10-12) and Paul (1 Corinthians 7:9) in his discussion. Isidore says, "sexual intercourse is natural, but not necessary." He also argues for self-control, even to the point of enduring "a quarrelsome wife" (Foerster fragment 8).

Another book of Isidore's is titled *Expositions of the Prophet Parchor.* Clement quotes briefly from the first and second volumes of that work, which has to do with the superiority of prophecy to philosophy. Socrates is cited as an example of a man who had an attendant spirit (Socrates' famous *daimonion*) and was thus superior to people who "pretend to be philosophers" (Foerster fragment 14). Who Parchor was is not known, but Isidore's exposition must have had to do with some kind of revelatory work attributed to a prophet by that name.

Teachings of unnamed Basilidians are cited by Clement on a number of topics. Faith is defined as "an assent of the soul to something which does not affect the senses" (Foerster fragment 10). The elect are said to have faith as something natural to them (Foerster fragment 13). The authority of Basilides is bolstered by his followers with the claim that he was taught by one Glaukias (otherwise unknown), who is said to have been the "interpreter" of the apostle Peter (Foerster fragment 2).

One of the most interesting of the Basilidian fragments deals with the Christian calendar as it relates to liturgical worship. Clement reports that the Basilidians observe the day of Jesus's baptism, spending the previous night in a vigil of scripture readings. "They say that it happened in the fifteenth year of the emperor Tiberius, on the fifteenth of the month Tybi; others, on the eleventh day of the same month" (Foerster fragment 3). The year assigned to Jesus's baptism is obviously based on Luke 3:1. What is especially interesting is that the eleventh of Tybi is equivalent to January sixth in the Julian calendar. It may also be the case that the observance of Jesus's baptism goes back to Basilides himself. That would make him the originator of what Christians continue to observe on January sixth as the Festival of the Epiphany of our Lord.

As noted at the beginning of this chapter, Hippolytus of Rome presents an account of the teachings of Basilides dramatically different from what we find in Irenaeus and Clement (*Refutation of all Heresies* 7.20–27). According to that rather lengthy account, Basilides posits a nonexistent God who sows a seed containing the cosmos. Everything else emerges out of that world seed. That seed contains a threefold sonship. The first one is light and ascends quickly to God. The second sonship needs the help of the Holy Spirit, but is unable to ascend to the Father. The third sonship remains in the world seed.

There are also two archons, one of the Ogdoad and the other one of the Hebdomad. The archons finally understand that there is a world beyond them. The light from above then descends upon Jesus, son of Mary. His passion is interpreted as the beginning of the separation of things into their proper components. The world will continue to exist until the third sonship, meaning the Gnostic elect, will have been purified and ascend with Christ into the realm above. When the tripartite sonship has been established in the region above, God will bring about a great ignorance over the world, and all desire for the world above will cease.

In Hippolytus's view, Basilides developed this system under the influence of the philosophy of Aristotle, and one can see reflected in the doctrine of the world seed something like Aristotle's theory of actual and potential being. However that may be, it is impossible to attribute Hippolytus's account to Basilides or to any of his early followers. Where Hippolytus got his information is itself a mystery, for we know of no Basilidians active in Rome.

4. Conclusions

Very little is known of Basilides' life and career. An Alexandrian context for his work is certain. There he taught from 132 on, or even earlier, into the reign of Antoninus Pius (138–61, Foerster fragment 5). His teachings reflect an Alexandrian milieu, and I am inclined to think that Basilides was an Alexandrian by birth and education. But there is also a connection to Antioch, according to the information supplied by Irenaeus. We have noted some similarities between Basilides and Saturninus of Antioch, but differences as well. A sojourn in Antioch is likely, and he could have left Alexandria during the Jewish revolt against Roman rule in 115–117, which resulted in the decimation of the Jewish population in Alexandria and elsewhere in Egypt. It could very well be that it was in Antioch where Basilides encountered an early form of Classic Gnosticism such as is reflected in the teachings of Saturninus.

We have also noted the influence of the Alexandrian Jewish Gnostic tractate *Eugnostos,* further discussed in chapter 8. Early Christian writings, including some that would become part of the canonical New Testament, were certainly known to and used by Basilides. Indeed, he was the first to write commentaries on early Christian writings, set down in twenty-four volumes in his *Exegetica,* unfortunately lost. Influence from Stoic and Platonic philosophy, as taught in Alexandrian schools, is certainly evident in his work as well. Basilides can be regarded as the very first Christian philosopher known to us.

Basilides can be regarded as the very first Christian philosopher known to us.

Especially prominent in the early propagation of Basilidian gnosis was Basilides' son Isidore, author of at least three books, as cited by Clement. Basilidian gnosis does not seem to have taken hold outside of Egypt, but in Egypt it spread throughout the country and persisted into the fourth century, as we know from Epiphanius (*Panarion* 24).

6. Valentinus and Valentinian Gnosis

Valentinus adapted the fundamental principles of the so-called Gnostic school of thought to his own kind of system.

Finding the way of a certain old opinion, he marked out a path for himself with the subtlety of a serpent.

WITH THESE WORDS IRENAEUS AND TERTULLIAN seek to account for the origins of the heresy propounded by Valentinus, the greatest of all of the second-century Christian heretics. Irenaeus (*Against Heresies* 1.11.1) claims that Valentinus adapted the system of the Gnostics he will describe in detail later (1.29–31), that is, what we have referred to as Classic or Sethian Gnosticism (discussed in chapter 3). Tertullian (*Against the Valentinians* 4) claims that Valentinus, when he was passed over for the bishopric of Rome, acted in revenge to "exterminate the truth," and did so with the help of "a certain old opinion" that he does not identify. Presumably this "old opinion" can be identified as that of Irenaeus's Gnostics.

The earliest attestations of Valentinus and the Valentinians are found in the writings of Justin Martyr and Irenaeus. According to Irenaeus, Valentinus appeared in Rome sometime before 140 and was active there until about 160. Valentinus presumably came to Rome from Alexandria. He is reported to have been born in the coastal Delta area of Egypt, and educated in Alexandria. He probably began his teaching activity in Alexandria before moving to Rome, though nothing is reported about that. In Rome he organized a community of Christians, a "church" (*ekklēsia*) that was said to comprise a spiritual seed of heavenly origins. For the cultic life of his community he composed psalms and homilies. He also wrote learned doctrinal epistles to some of his contemporaries. According to Epiphanius, Valentinus left Rome and went to Cyprus, where he "departed from the faith" (*Panarion* 31.7.2). A sojourn on Cyprus is not elsewhere attested for Valentinus, and we know nothing about the circumstances of his death. In any case, it can certainly be assumed that Valentinus had developed his gnosis before he left Alexandria for Rome.

> *Valentinus's teachings were very influential and attracted a number of prominent individuals who became teachers in their own right, the most prominent of which were Ptolemy, Heracleon, and Theodotus.*

Clement of Alexandria (*Miscellanies* 7.106) reports that the Valentinians claimed apostolic succession for Valentinus through one Theodas (otherwise unknown), supposedly a disciple of Paul. That is highly unlikely, though the apostle Paul is a very important authority for Valentinus and his followers.

Valentinus's teachings were very influential and attracted a number of prominent individuals who became teachers in their own right, the most prominent of which were Ptolemy, Heracleon, and Theodotus. Already in the second century the movement split into an eastern and a western branch. The eastern branch remained closer to the doctrine of Valentinus himself, while the western branch, probably founded by Ptolemy, developed doctrines that differed from those of the eastern branch in terms of protology (doctrine of primal beings), soteriology, and Christology.

A number of second-century Valentinian teachers are mentioned by the church fathers, some of them known to us only by name since their writings have disappeared. These include Alexander, Secundus, Theotimus, and Florinus of the western branch, and Axionicus of the eastern branch. Florinus was a presbyter of the Roman church until he was finally deposed by Bishop Victor toward the end of the second century. Axionicus of Antioch is reported to have been the only one of Valentinus's disciples to remain faithful to the master's teachings.

Only two Valentinians of the third century are known to us: Ambrose, who was converted to catholic Christianity by Origen in Alexandria and subsequently became the latter's patron, and Candidus, with whom Origen debated in Athens. The Valentinian writings of the Nag Hammadi Codices attest

Valentinus was a prolific writer, but much of his work is irretrievably lost.

to fourth-century Valentinian groups, especially in Egypt. Epiphanius, too (*Panarion* 31.7.1), reports that Valentinian groups existed throughout Egypt in his own time (late fourth century).

Valentinian churches seem to have persisted in succeeding centuries as well, especially in the East. The latest mention of Valentinians in Christian sources is found in an antiheretical canon (no. 95) from a church council called by the Byzantine emperor Justinian II and held in his palace in Constantinople in the year 692.

1. Valentinus's Teachings

Valentinus was a prolific writer, but much of his work is irretrievably lost. Six fragments from lost homilies and epistles are preserved by Clement of Alexandria. Hippolytus preserves a short psalm composed by him and a brief notice of a vision experienced by Valentinus. A complete homily preserved in Coptic, the *Gospel of Truth,* can, with considerable confidence, be attributed to him, though this is disputed. Disputed, too, as to its reliability, is the myth attributed to him by Irenaeus. We begin our discussion with the myth.

a. Valentinus's Myth according to Irenaeus
(Foerster 1:194–95; Layton, 223–27)

Irenaeus devotes the first eight chapters of the first book of *Against Heresies* to a lengthy description of a Valentinian system known to him personally, presumably through contacts in Gaul and Rome. That system (discussed below) is associated with Ptolemy and followers of Ptolemy, and features a protology involving a primal ogdoad of aeons ("eternities"), a decade of other aeons, and a duodecad of still others, adding up to thirty. Sophia is the youngest of these, and her fault leads ultimately to the creation of the material world. Following upon a refutation of the myth (ch. 9) and a disquisition on the unity of the catholic faith in contrast to the inconsistencies and contradictions of the heretics (ch. 10), Irenaeus continues his discussion of the inconsistencies of the Valentinians with a short summary of the teachings of Valentinus himself (11.1), Secundus (11.2), unnamed others (11.3–5), and various followers of Ptolemy (12.1–4). He devotes a lengthy section to a discussion of a Valentinian magician named Marcus and his followers (1.13–21, discussed below).

Irenaeus's report on Valentinus's myth, said to be based on that of the Gnostic sect, begins with a protology involving an original dyad, "Ineffable" and "Silence," from which emanate a second dyad, "Father" and "Truth." There follow "Word" (*Logos*) and "Life," "Man" and "Church." These eight constitute a primal ogdoad. From Logos and Life come ten other powers, and from Man and Church come twelve. One of the latter twelve (obviously Sophia, but unnamed here) "became deficient," and the ultimate result was the creation of the world. Thus, according to Irenaeus, Valentinus himself is the originator of the system of thirty aeons that Irenaeus has already attributed to Ptolemy and his followers.

Some scholars have expressed some doubts as to the accuracy of Irenaeus's report. For one thing, Tertullian (*Against the Valentinians* 4) distinguishes the teachings of Ptolemy, which feature names and numbers of the aeons outside of God, and the doctrine of Valentinus, who is said to have included the aeons within God as "senses" and "emotions." Indeed, something like the latter view is found in the *Gospel of Truth* (discussed below). It can also be seen reflected in Valentinus's psalm (fragment 8, below). A primal ogdoad is attributed to Valentinus by the author of the *Testimony of Truth* (NHC IX,3, discussed in chapter 8).

Irenaeus continues his account with two "Limits" (Greek *horos*), one separating *Bythos* (Depth) from the rest of the *Pleroma* ("Fullness," the heavenly world of aeons), and one separating the fallen Mother (Sophia) from the Pleroma. The utterly transcendent Bythos is either equated with the aforementioned Ineffable, or, which is more likely, Irenaeus had earlier omitted to mention a primal Monad called Bythos, from whom come Ineffable and Silence (Greek *Sigē*). Indeed, just such a doctrine is attributed to Valentinus and other Valentinians by Hippolytus (*Refutation of All Heresies* 6.29.2).

The myth continues with the production of Christ and the Demiurge by the Mother (Sophia), who is also said to have produced a "left-hand ruler," that is, the devil. Christ hastens back to the Pleroma, and eventually sends Jesus as savior. The Holy Spirit is also mentioned as having been produced within the Pleroma by Truth.

Irenaeus breaks off his summary at this point, but we can assume that Valentinus's basic myth included an account of the creation of the world, the creation of human beings, and the way of salvation. These items can, in fact, be detected in fragments from Valentinus's writings (discussed below). Valentinus's version of the Gnostic myth undoubtedly followed the basic outline of the myth found in the *Apocryphon of John,* involving a protological account of the Pleroma, the fall of Sophia, the production of the Gnostic creator and his angels, the creation of the world and of the first humans, the saving work of Jesus, and an eschatology. If, as is likely, Valentinus taught a primal ogdoad of aeons, he may have adapted that of Basilides (discussed in chapter 5) and/or that of *Eugnostos* (discussed in chapter 8). We can also assume that a prominent role was assigned to Jesus, the savior.

b. Fragments from Valentinus's Writings
(Foerster 1:239–43; Layton, 229–49)

Clement of Alexandria presents quotations from three of Valentinus's letters (fragments 1–3) and two of his homilies (fragments 4, 6), as well as one from a writing whose genre is not specified (fragment 5). Hippolytus preserves one of Valentinus's psalms (fragment 8), and gives an account of a vision supposedly experienced by Valentinus (fragment 7). A fourth-century author (Pseudo-Anthimus) mentions a book *On the Three Natures* allegedly written by Valentinus (fragment 9), but this report is clearly spurious. So we are left with a scant seven precious quotations from Valentinus's literary output, to which can probably be added the *Gospel of Truth* (considered next).

Fragment 1 (Layton C), from a letter to an unknown recipient, deals with the creation of Adam by the angels. The creator-angels recoil in fear from Adam as a result of the spiritual seed deposited in him from above, and they realize that he is superior to them. As a result they do away with Adam, presumably by imprisoning him in a material body. Clearly reflected here is an anthropogonic myth much like that of the *Apocryphon of John* (discussed in chapter 3).

Fragment 2 (Layton H), also from a letter to an unknown recipient, features two main themes, the Son (Jesus) as the manifestation of the one good Father, and the human heart compared to an inn that can be inhabited by unclean spirits. The Father, through the Son, graciously attends to the heart and enables whoever has such a heart to be pronounced blessed and enabled to see God (compare Matthew 5:8). There is nothing distinctively Gnostic in this quotation.

Fragment 3 (Layton E), from a letter to Agathopus (otherwise unknown), is about the impact of Jesus's divine nature on his human digestive system. So great was his continence that he thoroughly digested what he ate and drank without discharging any residue.

In fragment 4 (Layton F), from an untitled homily, Valentinus assures his hearers that they are immortal "children of eternal life," able to dissolve death and the world and to overcome all corruption.

Fragment 5 (Layton D) is from a writing whose genre is not identified, but one can easily surmise that it came from an epistle. It has some similarities to fragment 1 in that it deals with creation, but this time with the creation of the cosmos. Valentinus here teaches that the created world is inferior to the model of which it is a copy, a theme that shows some influence from Platonism (*Timaeus* 28c–29c), but is also found in Gnostic mythol-

> So great was his conti-
> nence that he thoroughly
> digested what he ate and
> drank without discharging
> any residue.

ogy (for example, *Apocryphon of John* II 12–13). Another theme in this fragment is the name that adorns an artifact. Indeed, there might be found here an allusion to the illicit appropriation by the world-creating powers of the "names" that belong to the transcendent world (also found in *Apocryphon of John* II 12–13).

Fragment 6 (Layton G) is from a homily entitled *On Friends*. In this passage, which Clement cites with approval, Valentinus teaches that there are things found in ordinary books that are also to be found written "in the church of God," namely words that reflect the "law written in the heart" (compare Romans 2:15). Valentinus here expresses a surprising openness to non-Christian culture.

Fragment 7 (Layton A) is a report by Hippolytus of a visionary experience of Valentinus, who is said to have reported that he saw a newborn baby and inquired of it who it was. The baby replied that he was the Logos (Word). Adding to this account is "some tragic myth," Valentinus intends to develop from this his own sect. The context of Hippolytus's report is a discussion of the teachings of Marcus, who also claimed revelatory visions. The basis for Hippolytus's assertion is impossible to determine.

Fragment 8 (Layton, "Summer Harvest") is the only surviving example of Valentinus's psalmody. A short poem composed in good Greek meter, it is titled "Summer" (Greek *theros*) or "Harvest." The psalmist (presumably Valentinus himself) sings about what he sees and perceives. In the first five lines he sees that everything in the universe depends on spirit, perhaps here understood as Sophia, who is sometimes referred to as the Holy Spirit in Valentinian gnosis. The last two lines deal with the transcendent world: from Depth (Bythos, the primal Father) are born the aeons as fruits, and from a primal womb is born a child. The child can be taken as a reference to Jesus, the preexistent savior.

We see reflected in these precious fragments not only a learned Gnostic teacher, but also a devout Christian pastor of souls, a mystic visionary, and a gifted poet.

c. The *Gospel of Truth* (NHC I,3: 16,31–43,24; XII,2: fragments; *NH Library,* 38–51; Layton, 250–64; *NH Scriptures,* 31–47)

Irenaeus refers to the audacious compositions of the Valentinians, which include a "Gospel of Truth" composed "not long ago" (*Against Heresies* 3.11.9). Irenaeus says that it does not in any respect resemble the gospels of the apostles. Pseudo-Tertullian is more specific. He reports that Valentinus has "a gospel of his own" beside the gospels of the church (*Against All Heresies* 4). While the title of Valentinus's gospel is not given, we can safely assume that it was the "Gospel of Truth" referred to by Irenaeus.

Ancient works were often given titles based upon their opening words, and we can be confident that the treatise preserved in Coptic is the Valentinian "Gospel of Truth" referred to by Irenaeus.

We now have in Coptic an untitled work completely preserved in Nag Hammadi Codex I that is now known as the *Gospel of Truth.* The same work, in another dialect of Coptic, was part of Codex XII, but only fragments remain. The title of this work now universally used is based on its incipit (opening passage), which reads, "The gospel of truth is joy for those who have received from the Father of truth the grace of knowing him." Ancient works were often given titles based upon their opening words, and we can be confident that the treatise preserved in Coptic is the Valentinian "Gospel of Truth" referred to by Irenaeus. That is evident, too, by its content, for it is clearly a Valentinian

Gnostic work, and one that can with confidence be attributed to Valentinus himself, for the style of writing resembles that of the fragments of other works by Valentinus.

The *Gospel of Truth* is not a gospel like those of the canonical New Testament, a fact that was already noticed by Irenaeus and Pseudo-Tertullian. What is interesting is that the term "gospel" in its opening sentence is used in its original Christian sense (that is, as the "good news" about Jesus Christ), and we can compare Paul's use of the term in his letters (for example, Romans 1:1-4; 1 Corinthians 15:1). In terms of genre, the *Gospel of Truth* can be understood as a homily or sermon on the gospel in which the author (Valentinus) expounds on the good news of the Father's love and the salvation that is grounded in the work of his son. The exposition of this gospel is given from a thoroughly Gnostic perspective, but in a very allusive way, with allusions to a Gnostic myth and to numerous New Testament texts. In addition, proto-logical, cosmological, and soteriological themes are often presented in psychological terms.

A basic theme running through the *Gospel of Truth* is that igno-rance is the root of cosmic existence, which is essentially illusory, while knowledge of the Father opens the way of returning to him. Indeed, knowledge itself brings about the dissolution of the material world, understood as "oblivion" and "deficiency": "Since oblivion came into existence because the Father was not known, then if the Father comes to be known, oblivion will not exist from that moment on" (18,7–11). "Since the deficiency came into being because the Father was not known, therefore, when the Father is known, from that moment on the deficiency will no longer exist" (24,28–32).

Following upon an introduction (I 16,31–17,4), it is said that error, arising from ignorance of the Father, congealed like a fog and led to the material creation as a substitute for truth (17,4–18,11). One can see in this passage allusions to the myth of Sophia and the work of the Demiurge. But Jesus brings revelation (18,11–19,27). His teachings brought about his crucifixion, which, however, "became a fruit of the knowledge of the Father." Revelation is then compared to a "living book" containing the names of the elect (19,27–24,9). The effects of revelation (24,9–33,2) include the elimination of deficiencies and unification with the Father.

The process of return to the Father (33,33–36,39) involves a gentle attraction upward. The message about Christ is compared to an anointing with ointment (36,13–39), in a passage that may have ritual allusions. Return to the Father is by the Father's will, through his own Name (36,39–40,23), which is the Son. The goal of the return involves resting in the Father (40,23–43,24). The sermon concludes with this consoling sentence: "His children are perfect and worthy of his name, for he is the Father; it is children of this kind that he loves" (43,20–24).

Since the *Gospel of Truth* is a meditative homily we will not find in it any straightforward exposition of mythological or theological doctrines such as might be found, for example, in a doctrinal epistle. Nevertheless, behind the various allusions to be found in the text there can be detected a basic system. A protology can be seen reflected in such passages as these: "When the totality went about in search for the one from whom they had come forth—and the totality was inside of him, the incomprehensible, inconceivable one who is superior to every thought—ignorance of the Father brought about anguish and terror" (17,4–11). "Since the Father is unengendered, he alone is the one who begot him (the Son) for himself as a name, before he brought forth the aeons, in order that the name of the Father should be over their head as lord" (38,32–38).

The totality in the first passage quoted refers to the aeons within the divine Pleroma, who were in the Father and who came forth from the Father. They were unable to know the Father until he graciously revealed himself through the Son (Jesus), who is the name of the Father. Behind the initial ignorance that brings about anguish we see an allusion to the fall of Sophia. The aeons in the Pleroma can also be understood as prototypes of the elect human seed on earth, whose return to the Pleroma is made possible through the work of the Savior.

The soteriology and Christology of the *Gospel of Truth* is best seen in what is said of the work of the Savior, Jesus. The "book of the living," containing the names of the elect, could only be taken by Jesus, who "was patient in accepting sufferings," knowing that "his death is life for many" (19,34–20,14). Jesus "put on that book" and was "nailed to a tree." "Having stripped himself of the perishable rags, he put on imperishability" (20,24–34). Valentinus thus teaches the reality of Jesus' incarnation, his sufferings, and physical death. Having stripped himself of the physical body, Jesus ascended to the Father. Jesus' own experience for many is paradigmatic of the salvation of the elect seed.

Jesus is also said to have become "a fruit of the knowledge of the Father" by being "nailed to a tree" (18,24–26). The knowledge in question is that which is given to the elect through the grace of the Father: "Those whose names he [the Father] knew in advance were called at the end, so that one who has knowledge is the one whose name the Father has uttered. . . . If one has knowledge, he is from above. If he is called, he hears, he answers, and he turns to him who is calling him, and ascends to him. . . . He who is to have knowledge in this manner knows where he comes from and where he is going" (21,25–22,15). Reflected here is a predestination doctrine somewhat similar to that found in Paul's writings in the New Testament (for example, Romans 8:28-30). The elect are those who in other Valentinian writings are called the "spiritual ones" (*pneumatikoi*). They are the ones who are enabled to receive the knowledge that ensures their return to the Father.

Valentinus's system, reflected in the *Gospel of Truth* and in the other texts treated here, is akin to that of the eastern branch of Valentinianism, as seen in texts yet to be considered.

2. Ptolemy and Western Valentinianism

Hippolytus reports that Valentinian teachings are divided into two main groups, eastern and Italian (western). The latter group is represented by two prominent teachers, Ptolemy and Heracleon (*Refutation of All Heresies* 6.35.5–6). Little or nothing is known of Ptolemy's life. His name may reflect Alexandrian influence, since that is the name used by many of the Hellenistic rulers of Egypt after Alexander the Great. So it is possible that he, like Valentinus, had come to Rome from Alexandria.

Some scholars have suggested that he is to be identified with a Christian teacher of the same name reported by Justin Martyr to have been put to death in Rome under a magistrate named Urbicus (*Apology* 2.2). In any case, the Valentinian Ptolemy can be presumed to have been active in Rome in the mid-second century.

Irenaeus provides a lengthy summary of a myth he attributes to Ptolemy and certain Ptolemaeans (*Against Heresies* 1.1–8). Irenaeus's account appears to have been based on several sources woven together. In addition, part of the basic myth summarized by Irenaeus appears in Clement's excerpts from the Valentinian Theodotus (*Excerpts from Theodotus* 45.2–65.2). Hippolytus, too, presents a summary of the same basic myth, though with some variations (*Refutation of All Heresies* 6.29.2–36.4). Epiphanius provides an excerpt from a Valentinian text that reflects the same myth (*Panarion* 31.5.1–8.3), but with additional material. It should be noted that variation was a prominent feature of the Valentinian school; no canonical version of the basic myth seems to have existed. Of course, we should also allow for some misunderstandings or misrepresentations of Valentinian teachings in the reports of the heresiologists.

In addition to the basic myth attributed to Ptolemy and his followers we have, preserved by Epiphanius, a letter penned by Ptolemy to a prominent Christian woman named Flora. We turn, first, to the western version of the Valentinian myth associated with Ptolemy and his followers.

a. The basic Valentinian Myth Attributed to Ptolemy and His Followers (Foerster 1:123–45; Layton, 276–302; Foerster 1:146–54 [Theodotus], 184–93 [Hippolytus]); 234–38 [Epiphanius])

The myth begins with an elaborate protology. The Forefather, also called Depth (Bythos), and his Thought (Ennoia), also called Silence (Sigē), project Mind (Nous), also called Only-Begotten and Father, and his partner Truth (*Alētheia*). Mind brings forth Word (Logos) and Life (*Zōē*), and from them come Man (*Anthrōpos*) and Church (*Ekklēsia*). These eight comprise the primal Ogdoad (1.1).

These aeons then bring forth others, consisting of pairs. From Word and Life come ten aeons, and from Man and Church twelve. The last of the twelve is Wisdom (Sophia). The primal Forefather was known only to Mind, and remained unknown to the others. The youngest of the aeons, Sophia, in an effort to comprehend the Forefather, experienced passion. Her passion was

Various details of this mythology are said to be indicated allegorically in the gospels and epistles of the New Testament (3.1–6).

restrained by a power called Limit (Horos), by whom Sophia was restored to the Pleroma. Only-Begotten (Nous) brought forth another pair, Christ and the Holy Spirit, who assisted the other aeons in the attainment of rest in the realization of the incomprehensibility of the Forefather. All of them together then produced the "perfect fruit" of the Pleroma, Jesus (the Savior) (1.2–2.6). Various details of this mythology are said to be indicated allegorically in the gospels and epistles of the New Testament (3.1–6).

Outside of the Pleroma the aforementioned passion of Sophia became a lower Sophia called Achamoth (from Hebrew *ḥokmah*, "wisdom"). Christ took pity on her and gave her form, and returned to the Pleroma. Achamoth was unable to enter the Pleroma because of the Limit (Horos) that separates the Pleroma from what is outside. From her came the Demiurge, from whom came the lower heavens and other angelic beings, including the Devil. When the Demiurge had formed the world he made an earthly man, into whom he breathed the psychical man (compare Genesis 2:7), and on the man was put the "coat of skin" (compare Genesis 3:21), that is, the physical body. The spiritual seed was sown into the man by Sophia together with the Demiurge's psychical inbreathing (4.1–5.6).

Thus there are three main substances in the human makeup: the material, which will perish, the psychical, and the spiritual. Human beings are divided into three classes: spiritual people who are spiritual by nature, material or earthly people who will perish, and psychical people who are endowed with free will and can choose good or evil. The spiritual people, who are endowed with the spiritual seed from above, are the (Valentinian) Gnostics, the psychical people are non-Gnostic Christians, and the material people are all others. These are indicated allegorically by the three sons of Adam: Seth (spiritual), Abel (psychical), and Cain (material). The Savior came to perfect the spiritual people through gnosis. He also came to save the "psychicals," and took on a body of psychical substance for that purpose. When the entire seed (of spiritual people) is perfected, that is, through gnosis, the mother Achamoth will receive the Savior as her consort and enter the Pleroma. The spiritual people will divest themselves of their souls and become "intelligent spirits," uniting as brides with the angels of the Savior in the Pleroma. The psychical people will achieve a salvation in the "place of the Middle" together with the Demiurge, and the material people, together with the entire material universe, will be destroyed by fire (6.1–7.5). Details of this mythology are found indicated allegorically in the scriptures (8.1–4). The primal Ogdoad is said to have been taught by the disciple John in the prologue to his Gospel (8.5; compare John 1:1–14).

This myth resembles in outline that of the Gnostic sect discussed by Irenaeus, best represented in the *Apocryphon of John*. It also presumably reflects something of the mythology of Valentinus. It is, however, more complicated in terms of the various mythological personages mentioned in it. Especially notable is the doubling of Sophia: the higher Sophia restored to the Pleroma, and the lower one, Achamoth. The salvation brought to mankind by the Savior is meant especially for the psychical people, that is, members of the catholic church. And the body of the Savior is psychical, whereas Valentinus himself taught a real incarnation, that is, a body of flesh, as we saw in our discussion of the *Gospel of Truth*.

Part of the same basic myth is reflected in Clement's *Excerpts from Theodotus* (discussed below), beginning with the account of the coming of the Savior to Sophia (Achamoth in Irenaeus's account). The relevant passage in the *Excerpts from Theodotus*

(43,2–65,2) is not attributable to Theodotus himself but represents a Valentinian source also used by Irenaeus. There are some differences in details, and the scripture references are more numerous.

Hippolytus's version of the myth shows even greater divergences. His version of the protology begins with an unbegotten Father existing alone as a Monad. The Dyad made up of Mind (Nous) and Truth is counted to make up the primal Ogdoad. Sophia's fault lies in her wishing to produce offspring by herself, thus emulating the Father. There is a doubling of Sophia here, too, but the Sophia outside is not called Achamoth. The Demiurge is associated with fire, and is called "foolish." He is regarded as the sole author of the Old Testament scriptures, and the body of the Savior derives from him. Jesus is said to have been created by the Most High, Demiurge, and the Holy Spirit, Sophia (compare Luke 1:35) as a heavenly Logos (Word) proceeding from the Ogdoad and born through Mary to rectify the products of the passion of Sophia, that is, the material world.

Heresy number thirty-one (of eighty) in Epiphanius's *Panarion* is entitled, "Against Valentinians, Also Called Gnostics." In his highly confused account he includes what he claims to be a verbatim excerpt from a Valentinian writing. Formally, the text is a revelatory epistle, and it opens with the following greeting (there is a gap in the text): "In the presence of the intelligent, the psychicals, the fleshly, the worldings, the Greatness < . . . > incorruptible mind greets the incorruptible ones. I make known to you unknown and unspeakable transcendent mysteries" (*Panarion* 31.5.1–2). What follows is a protology partially based on the myth already discussed, but with additional details, such as a second ogdoad. The excerpt concludes with twenty-nine *nomina barbara* (unintelligible names), beginning with *Ampsiou* and concluding with *Masemon* (*Panarion* 31.6.10). Since Epiphanius interprets these as esoteric names of the thirty aeons (compare 31.2.8), one name must be missing.

The writing excerpted by Epiphanius was evidently composed by a Valentinian teacher, probably located in Egypt, who drew together various Valentinian traditions into a new synthesis. One interesting detail is that the primal "Self-Engendered" (Bythos) is said to have initially contained all of the "entireties" (the aeons) within himself (*Panarion* 31.5.3), a doctrine attributable to Valentinus himself, as we have already noted. While some scholars used to think that this writing is an early product of the Valentinian school, it must be concluded, on the contrary, that it is a comparatively late hodgepodge.

> *Flora, otherwise unknown, must have been a prominent Christian woman whom Ptolemy was evidently interested in converting to his own version of Christianity.*

Later in the same section of the *Panarion*, Epiphanius provides a verbatim excerpt from the first part of Book 1 of Irenaeus's *Against Heresies*, including the Ptolemaean myth already discussed (*Panarion* 31.9.1–32.9, *Against Heresies* 1.Preface–11.1). Epiphanius thus provides us with the original Greek version of that part of Irenaeus's great work, which is otherwise extant only in a Latin translation.

b. Ptolemy's *Letter to Flora*
(Foerster 1:154–61; Layton, 306–15)

Epiphanius devotes a separate section of his *Panarion* to Ptolemaeans and includes in his discussion a verbatim quotation of a letter written by Ptolemy to a "dear sister" named Flora (*Panarion* 33.3.1–7.10). Flora, otherwise unknown, must have been a prominent Christian woman whom Ptolemy was evidently interested in converting to his own version of Christianity. The subject of the letter, which is really a doctrinal treatise, is the Law of Moses contained in the Old Testament Pentateuch, and how it should properly be interpreted.

Ptolemy begins by refuting two opposing views, that the Law was established by God the Father or that it was established by the Devil. Instead, the Pentateuch is of multiple authorship, human and divine, as can be seen from the teachings of the Savior. God's legislation forbids divorce (Matthew 19:6-8) whereas Moses allowed a man to divorce his wife (Deuteronomy 24:1). Some parts of the Law are also attributable to the legislation of the elders.

The divine part of the Law consists of three parts: legislation that is "pure," but imperfect, such as the decalogue, which the Savior came to fulfill. The second part is mixed with injustice, such as the law of retaliation ("an eye for an eye," Leviticus 24:20), which the Savior came to annul. The third part is symbolic, involving rituals that have been annulled by the Savior as to their physical performance but which should be interpreted allegorically as referring to heavenly realities.

> *This God is a God of justice, whereas the ungenerated Father, revealed by the Savior, is incorruptible, whose essence is pure light. The Demiurge is only an inferior image of the transcendent Father.*

As to the identity of the God who established the divine parts of the Law, he is to be understood as the Demiurge, the Creator of the world, who stands midway between God the transcendent Father and the Devil. This God is a God of justice, whereas the ungenerated Father, revealed by the Savior, is incorruptible, whose essence is pure light. The Demiurge is only an inferior image of the transcendent Father.

Ptolemy concludes his letter with an expression of hope that Flora will become worthy of further instruction, which would presumably lead to her initiation into the Valentinian church.

3. Heracleon (Foerster 1:162–83)

Heracleon was regarded by Clement of Alexandria as "the most celebrated member of the Valentinian school" (*Miscellanies* 4.71, introducing fragment 50). Hardly anything is known of his life. As we have already noted, Hippolytus associated him and Ptolemy with the Italian (western) school of Valentinian gnosis. This would presumably imply that he was active at some time in Rome. But he is known to us only through fragments of his writings preserved by the Alexandrians Clement and Origen. Those fragments reflect the kind of philological scholarship that was characteristic of Alexandrian culture. And the fact that his writings seem only to have been known in Alexandria would indicate that he was active in Alexandria at some point. I would suggest that he was an Alexandrian who spent some time in Rome as a Valentinian teacher and then returned to Alexandria.

Forty-eight fragments from a commentary by him on the Gospel of John are preserved in Origen's own commentary on the Fourth Gospel (which Origen regarded as the first in importance). A single thirteenth-century manuscript preserves books 1, 2, 6, 10, 13, 19, 20, 28, and 32 (ending with John 13:33) of Origen's multivolume work, written over many years. Quotations from, or references to, Heracleon's commentary appear in books 2, 6, 10, 13, 19, and 20. In addition, the Byzantine scholar Photius cites Heracleon's interpretation of John 1:17 as proving the inferiority of the Mosaic Law (fragment 51).

In his commentary Origen is generally critical of Heracleon's approach. Yet, he does not hesitate to express his agreement with a few of Heracleon's interpretations. In any case, it is clear that Origen regarded Heracleon's commentary as a very important work of Christian scholarship.

Clement quotes from a lengthy comment by Heracleon on Luke 12:8 (fragment 50), which may have come from a commentary on Luke. He also cites a report by Heracleon that some (presumably Gnostics, not including himself) brand with fire the ears of people who are being baptized (fragment 49). A similar practice is attributed to the Carpocratians by Irenaeus (*Against Heresies* 1.25.6). Heracleon's commentary on John, and perhaps one on Luke, can be dated to a time between 160 and 180.

In what follows, I shall comment on some of Heracleon's most noteworthy interpretations of passages in the Gospel of John. Fragments 1–3 focus on the Johannine Prologue (1:1–18). Heracleon interprets John 1:3 to mean that "all things" do not refer to the pleromatic aeons but to the material cosmos, in contrast to Ptolemy's interpretation of the same passage in the basic myth discussed above (Irenaeus, *Against Heresies* 1.8.5). Heracleon says that the Logos "provided the Demiurge with the cause for creating the world."

The figure of John the Baptist (in John 1:19-28) is taken up in fragments 4–6. John symbolizes the "voice in the wilderness" (John

1:23). John's expression of inferiority (John 1:26-27) is attributed to the Demiurge, symbolized by John.

In Heracleon's interpretation of John 1:29 (fragment 10), "lamb of God" refers to the body (of Christ), and "who takes away the sin of the world" refers to him who is in the body, that is, the Savior.

Heracleon interprets "Capernaum" in John 2:12 to mean the material world (fragment 11; compare fragment 40), into which the Savior descended (went down). His going up to Jerusalem (John 2:13) symbolizes the Savior's ascent to the "psychical place" (fragment 12), symbolized by Jerusalem.

The pericope on the cleansing of the Temple (John 2:13-22) is the focus of fragments 12–16. The Passover of the Jews referred to in John 2:13 is taken as symbolizing "the passion of the Savior in the world." The Temple is taken as a symbol of the Church, with the Holy of Holies symbolizing the community of the spiritual people. The number forty-six in John 2:20 is given an allegorical meaning, with *six* referring to matter, that is, the material body, and *forty*, the "uncombined Tetrad" ($1 + 2 + 3 + 4 = 10 \times 4 = 40$), referring to the spiritual seed included in the "inbreathing" (compare Genesis 2:7).

In fragments 17–39 Heracleon takes Jesus's encounter with the Samaritan woman in John 4:4-42 as an allegory of the salvation of the spirituals. The Samaritan woman represents the spiritual elect whom the Savior saves from her ignorance. She is able to respond immediately because of the spiritual seed she has within her. She represents the spiritual people who are enabled to worship God "in spirit and in truth" (John 4:23) because they are akin to the Father. "This mountain" (John 4:20, referring to Gerizim in Samaria) symbolizes the Devil and his world, and Jerusalem represents the Creator whom "the Jews" (psychical Christians) worship. The spiritual people, on the other hand, worship the Father of truth.

The story of the healing of the royal officer's son that immediately follows the story of the Samaritan woman in John (4:46-53) is given extensive treatment in fragment 40. Heracleon interprets this story as an allegory of the salvation of the psychical people, that is, those who lack the spiritual seed. The royal officer (*basilikos*, v. 46) symbolizes the Demiurge. His son symbolizes the people of the psychical nature who are in a state of sin and need the Savior's healing. Heracleon makes it clear that not all of the psychicals achieve salvation; those who reject the salvation effected by the Savior are ultimately destroyed. As for the Demiurge, he believes in the power of the Savior to save those "who are akin to him." We recall that the basic Valentinian myth provides for a partial salvation for the Demiurge.

Jesus's exchange with the Jews in John 8:21-59 is the focus of fragments 41–48. Heracleon teaches that those who are in a state of sin cannot come to imperishability. When Jesus refers to some of his audience as children of the Devil (John 8:43), this means that some people by nature are "of the substance of the Devil," in contrast to the psychicals or the spirituals. But the people addressed in verse 44 "have become children of the Devil, though they were not such by nature." The psychical people can elect their own perdition by acting according to the Devil's desires.

In fragment 49, preserved by Clement, Heracleon refers to some Gnostics' practice of branding, as noted above. In fragment 50, on Luke 12:8, Heracleon discusses what Jesus means to confess him. Confession is of two kinds, confession made in faith and conduct, and that made with the mouth. Both are required, and a person who has made confession in conduct will also make confession by mouth before the authorities when the situation requires it, even if it leads to martyrdom. Heracleon notes that the text of Luke 12:8 reads, literally, "confess in me" (a Semitism). He remarks, "those who are not in him deny him." It should be noted that Clement is quoting Heracleon here with approval.

It is clear from the extant fragments that Heracleon was a gifted exegete and a Christian teacher of high moral and ethical standards. To be sure, his Gnostic orientation is also clear from his

> *It is clear from the extant fragments that Heracleon was a gifted exegete and a Christian teacher of high moral and ethical standards.*

interpretation of the gospel texts, at least of the Gospel of John. There is no explicit elaboration of the basic Gnostic myth in the fragments, even though the myth is alluded to here and there. This would indicate that Heracleon intended his commentary to be read not only by Valentinian Gnostics but also by the wider membership of the church, the majority of whom were psychicals. Heracleon evidently believed that the emerging catholic community included people in whom had been sown the spiritual seed. All they lacked was gnosis. In that sense Heracleon's intention in writing his commentary can be compared to Ptolemy's intention as expressed in his letter to Flora.

4. Theodotus (Foerster 1:222–33)

Among the writings of Clement of Alexandria that have come down to us is a notebook of his entitled "Excerpts from the works of Theodotus and the so-called Oriental teaching at the time of Valentinus," usually known as the *Excerpts from* (or *of*) *Theodotus*. Clement's notebook contains excerpts from the writings of Theodotus, from other Valentinian sources, and critical or speculative comments of his own interspersed here and there. It also contains material from a source also used by Irenaeus in his account of the Ptolemaean (western) Valentinian myth (43,2–65,2, discussed above). Material attributable to Theodotus is found in chapters 1–3, 17, 21–26, 29–30, 32–41, and 66–86 (end). Apart from Clement's notebook, nothing else is known of Theodotus. We can assume that he was a pupil of Valentinus and active in Alexandria.

What Clement presents as the teachings of Theodotus is extremely disjointed. No coherent account of Theodotus's system can be seen in the material presented, but a basic Valentinian myth lies in the background and is reflected here and there. In terms of protology, an original pair of aeons is posited, Depth (Bathos, Bythos) or Father, and Silence (Sigē), from whom are emanated the other aeons (unnamed) of the Pleroma (chapter 29). The unity of the Pleroma is said to depend on the principle of the union of pairs (*suzugia*, 32), with each of the aeons having its own consort (*suzugos*).

Sophia plays a prominent role in this system. She is to be identified as "the aeon that desired to grasp that which is beyond knowledge," and the "twelfth aeon" whose fall brought about suffering (31). She is the mother of Christ, who left her behind and "entered into the Pleroma" (32). She is also the mother of the Demiurge, an "image" of the one who had left her, Christ, who is himself an "image" (or type) of the Father of all. The Demiurge's ugliness is said to have elicited Sophia's disgust (33). She remains outside of the Pleroma until the end (34). In the Pleroma, Christ pleaded for his mother and Jesus was brought forth "by the good pleasure of the aeons" as a comforter (or "Paraclete") for "the aeon which had transgressed" (23). Sophia plays a role in the creation of Adam's psychical body. But the male or spiritual seed was implanted by the Logos, the Savior. The ultimate salvation of the spiritual seed, that is, entry into the Pleroma, will also include Sophia (34).

It is the mission of the Savior, Jesus, to rescue the spiritual seeds scattered among humankind. Genesis 1:27 ("male and female he created them") is interpreted to refer to "the finest production of Sophia." The male denotes the election, and the female the calling. The male beings are angelic, and the female are the spiritual seed. The females, having become male, unite with the angels and enter the Pleroma (21). What is meant here is that every spiritual person resident on earth (female) has an angelic alter ego or partner (*suzugos*) in heaven (male). They are united upon entry into the Pleroma.

Baptism plays a key role in the salvation of the elect. The "angels of whom we are part" were baptized in a heavenly "baptism for the dead" (1 Corinthians 15:29), that is, for us, "so that we too, possessing the name, may not be held back and prevented by Horos (Limit) and the Cross from entering into the Pleroma." The spiritual people on earth are "baptized in the same name as that in which his angel was baptized before him." The angels' baptism was "through the 'redemption' of the name which came down upon Jesus in the dove and redeemed him" (22).

The Valentinians, in contrast to a number of other Gnostic groups, promoted marriage and procreation. This is given expression in the *Excerpta from Theodotus* in an interpretation of a saying of Jesus (from the *Gospel of the Egyptians*): "When the Savior says to Salome that death reigns as long as women give birth, he is not saying this to make child-bearing reproachful, since it is indispensable for the salvation of those who believe." The Savior is said to be speaking of "the woman above [Sophia], whose passions became creation" (67). What is meant is that the entire elect seed must

The Valentinians, in contrast to a number of other Gnostic groups, promoted marriage and procreation.

undergo earthly existence until all are gathered by the Savior. The elect, as long as they are children of the female only, are weak and "without form. "Having been given form by the Savior, we are the children of the man [husband] and of the bride-chamber" (68). One is "given form" by baptism and gnosis.

The redemptive significance of baptism and gnosis is given expression in a passage that is often quoted as an epitome of Valentinian doctrine, indeed of Gnosticism in general:

> It is not the bath [washing] alone that makes us free, but also the knowledge: Who were we? What have we become? Where were we? Into what place have we been cast? Whither are we hastening? From what are we delivered? What is birth? What is rebirth? (*Excerpts from Theodotus* 78.2)

The answers to these questions were provided in the elaborate mythology that was part of the initiation into the Valentinian church. Part of the answer is provided by Theodotus in the passage that follows: "He to whom the mother gives birth is led into death and into the world. But he to whom Christ gives second birth is translated into Life, into the Ogdoad."

The concluding chapters in the *Excerpts from Theodotus* (81–86, omitted in Foerster) are devoted to a discussion of baptism and two other sacraments, the eucharist and chrism, "the bread and the oil," which are "sanctified by the power of the Name" (82.1). Some scholars assign some of this material to Clement himself.

5. Marcus and the Marcosians
(Foerster 1:198–221)

Irenaeus presents an extensive account of the teachings and practices of a Valentinian "magician" named Marcus and his followers
(*Against Heresies* 1.13.1–21.5). Hippolytus also has a report on
Marcus and the Marcosians (*Refutation of All Heresies* 6.39.1–
54.2, not in Foerster) that is partially dependent on Irenaeus but
has independent information of its own. Later patristic accounts
are dependent upon Irenaeus. Irenaeus bases his account on contacts he made with Marcosians in the Rhone Valley of Gaul where
he lived. He also seems to have had some information from Asia
Minor, where he had lived before moving to Gaul. Hippolytus
bases his account on contacts with Marcosians in Rome in the
early third century. Some of his contacts there were familiar with
Irenaeus's report, and denied the truth of some parts of what Irenaeus had written (*Refutation* 6.42.1).

Not much is known about Marcus. He was evidently active for
a time in Asia Minor, for Irenaeus reports that he had seduced the
wife of a deacon in that region (*Against Heresies* 1.13.5, in a passage omitted in Foerster). He was presumably active in the period
between 160 and 180.

Irenaeus begins his account with reports of magical tricks that
Marcus would perform over cups of eucharistic wine, making the
wine change color and pouring wine from a small cup into a larger
one causing it to overflow (1.13.1–2). Marcus is reported to have
had a great interest in rich women, with whom he would have
sex in a bride chamber after giving them aphrodisiacs (1.13.3–5).
Irenaeus reports that his disciples also "led astray many women"
(1.13.6).

It is probable that such accusations of sexual immorality are
polemical distortions of the truth. It appears that Irenaeus is here
equating what he considers to be heresy with sexual impropriety. It is
notable that Hippolytus does not follow Irenaeus in this respect.

Irenaeus's account of Marcus's system begins in chapter 14.
Marcus presents his teachings as a revelation from the Tetrad in

the Pleroma. What is interesting about Marcus's system is that he interprets a Valentinian myth with the use of numerology and alphabet mysticism. The Valentinian aeons are represented as elements or letters of the alphabet. (The Greek word *stoicheion* can mean "element" or a "letter" of the alphabet.) The primal Father "willed to make utterable that of him which was ineffable and to give form to that which was invisible," and "opened his mouth and sent forth a word which was similar to himself." "He uttered the first word of his name, which was 'beginning' (*Archē*)," a word made up of four letters (Greek ἀρχή). He added additional words that made up a name of thirty letters (equals the thirty aeons of the Pleroma, 1.14.1). From the last of the thirty letters "a sound went forth and produced its own elements, after the image of the other elements," resulting in the arrangement of things here below. The letter itself was received up again, but left an echo here below. This is clearly a reference to the fall of Sophia resulting in the creation of the cosmos, her return to the Pleroma, and the lower Sophia (Achamoth) left below. It is then said that each of the thirty letters contains other letters, "so that the number of the letters extends to infinity" (1.14.2).

Marcus then reports that the pleromatic Tetrad revealed to him the body of Truth, whose members are depicted as letters: Her head is Alpha and Omega, her neck Beta and Psi, and so forth, with her feet as Mu and Nu. (The twenty-four Greek letters are presented in couples beginning with the first letter, Alpha, plus the last, Omega, the second letter, Beta, and the second-to-last letter, Psi, and so forth, concluding with the middle letters [Mu and Nu] 1.14.3). Truth then utters the name Jesus, a "special name" with six letters, Ἰησοῦς 1.14.4).

The twenty-four letters of the Greek alphabet are said to be symbolic of three pleromatic powers. The nine (voiceless) consonants belong to Father and Truth, the eight semivowels to Logos and Life, and the seven vowels to Man and Church (1.14.5). Speculation on the numbers six and seven follows, with references to scripture passages containing those numbers. The seven vowels are said to represent the seven heavens (planetary spheres, 1.14.6–8).

The twenty-four letters are then brought into relation with the first two triads of the Pleroma, and with the unutterable name of the Savior (1.15.1).

The supernatural origin of Jesus is explained with reference to the letters of the alphabet that are used as numbers. The alphabet has eight letters for units (excluding the number 6, ς, which is not included in the alphabet), eight letters for tens (excluding the number 90, φ, which is not included in the alphabet), and eight letters for hundreds (excluding the number 900, ϡ, which is not included in the alphabet). "The number 888 signifies Jesus," that is, the letter numerals in his name add up to 888. Before Jesus appeared people were in ignorance and error, but when he appeared they (that is, the spiritual people) "laid aside their ignorance and passed from death to life." "The Father of all desired to remove ignorance and to abolish death. The abolishing of ignorance was the knowledge of him" (1.15.2).

Jesus is said to have passed through the virgin Mary's womb. At his baptism Christ descended upon him in the form of a dove (1.15.3). Speculating on numbers found in two parables of Jesus, nine drachmas in Luke 15:8 and eleven [sic] sheep in Luke 15:4-6, they arrive at the value of "Amen," that is, 99. The defection of Sophia from the Duodecad is likened to a sheep gone astray, leaving eleven aeons of the original twelve (16.1–2).

The material that follows in Irenaeus's account (from 1.17.1 on) does not appear to refer to the teachings of Marcus himself, but to unnamed Marcosians. Material on the creation by the Demiurge and other biblical traditions includes astrological speculations (1.17) and speculation on the meaning of various biblical passages (l.18–19). It is also reported that they have "an innumerable quantity of apocryphal and spurious writings" (1.20.1), and alter various gospel sayings and stories to suit their own purposes (1.20.2).

The last part of Irenaeus's account (1.21) contains interesting information on Marcosian ritual practices, which probably includes information on rituals practiced by other Valentinians as well. Irenaeus mentions first a ritual called "redemption" (*apolytrōsis*), but then immediately says that "there are as many systems of redemption as there are mystical teachers of this doctrine" (1.21.1). Irenaeus reports that those who have attained gnosis must also "be regenerated" through "redemption." A distinction is made between the psychical baptism of "the visible Jesus" (by John) and the spiritual redemption instituted by "the Christ who descended upon him for perfection." The baptism practiced by psychical Christians is related to the baptism of John for repentance, but the redemption practiced by spiritual Christians (that is, Gnostics) leads to perfection (1.21.2). The redemption ceremony can be construed as a ritual of initiation into the Valentinian community.

As to the ritual actions performed in the redemption, Irenaeus reports on a considerable variety of practices performed by different groups. Some of them "perform a mystic rite" construed as a "spiritual marriage." Others baptize with water with invocations of the "unknown Father" and other divine beings. Others employ "Hebrew words" (probably meaning Aramaic) in their invocations. Irenaeus quotes an unintelligible or garbled phrase beginning with *basema,* to which he gives an obviously incorrect translation (*basema* is Aramaic for "in the name"). Still others invoke the Name that Jesus put on, that is, the name of Christ, and quote another name consisting of mostly unintelligible Semitic-sounding words, beginning with *messia* and ending with *Jesu Nazaria,* to which Irenaeus gives another obviously wrong translation (*messia* or *meshiha* means "anointed" or "Christ" in Aramaic). The initiate gives a response and the bystanders invoke peace upon the congregation. An anointing with oil is included in the ceremony (1.21.3).

In all four of these cases, baptism with water was presumably part of the ceremony. Then Irenaeus refers to another group, some, who reject simple baptism with water and use instead oil and water mixed together and poured on the heads of the initiates. Still others reject visible actions altogether, insisting that "perfect redemption" is knowledge of the "ineffable Greatness" and of the "inner, spiritual man" (1.21.4).

Irenaeus concludes his account with a description of a ritual for the dying practiced by "still others." It is not clear whether he regards this as an alternative version of the redemption sacrament, or as a separate rite that may be construed as a ceremony recalling for the dying a previously performed initiatory ritual of redemption. The ceremony involves pouring of oil and water and the recitation of certain formulae designed to make the inner man of the dying invisible to the cosmic powers as he ascends toward the Pleroma. The body is left behind in the world, and the soul is delivered to the Demiurge (1.21.5).

The ceremony also includes instructions as to what the rising soul should say to the various cosmic powers intent on preventing its ascent. To the lower powers, he is to say, "I am a son of the Father, the preexistent Father." He is to proclaim his alienation from Achamoth and his intent to return to the place of his origin. When he reaches the Demiurge himself, presumably at the level of the seventh heaven, he is to say, "I am a precious vessel, more precious than the female who made you (Achamoth). . . . I know myself and am aware whence I am, and I invoke the incorruptible Sophia, who is in the Father, mother of your mother." Upon completion of the formula, the Demiurge and those around him become confused. Casting away "his chain, the soul," the saved spirit "proceeds to his own" (1.21.5).

A similar set of instructions appears in the *(First) Apocalypse of James* (NHC V,4, discussed below in chapter 8). In that version, it is part of a revelation given by the Lord to his brother James and is put into question and answer form. In order to effect his ascent following his impending death, James is to proclaim his origin to one of three "toll collectors" who "confiscate souls." He will ask him who he is and where he came from. The instructions given to James are virtually the same as those given to the ascending soul in the Valentinian ritual. The Lord tells James that, upon completion of the interrogation, he will ascend to his proper place (32,28–35,25).

It would appear that the ritual for the dying described by Irenaeus was a Valentinian sacrament that was widely used by Valentinian Christians, not only by Marcosians. The instructions given by Jesus to his brother James in the Coptic apocalypse reflect the influence of Valentinian gnosis in the composition of that text.

6. Valentinian Writings Preserved in Coptic

The Nag Hammadi library includes several Valentinian tractates. Of the forty-four separate tractates included among the thirteen codices, seven of them can be identified as Valentinian, in terms of their content. Of the five tractates in Codex I, four of them are Valentinian, and some scholars also identify the other one (*Apocryphon of James*, I,2, discussed in chapter 8) as Valentinian. Codex II has one Valentinian tractate, Codex XI two, and Codex XII fragments of one that is found intact in Codex I.

We have already discussed one of the Valentinian tractates, the *Gospel of Truth* (I,3; XII,2), which we attributed to Valentinus himself. The other ones will be taken up in what follows in the order in which they appear in the manuscripts, except for the *Tripartite Tractate* (NHC I,5), which will be discussed last.

a. *Prayer of the Apostle Paul* (NHC I,1: A,1–B,10; NH Library, 27–28; Layton, 303–05; NH Scriptures, 15–18)

This short prayer, inscribed on both sides of the front flyleaf of the codex, consists of three parts. In the first part (A,1–14) the petitioner addresses the preexistent Father, through Jesus Christ, and prays for his return to the place whence he came. In the second part (A,15–25) he prays for bodily health and spiritual illumination, and invokes the authority of "the evangelist," presumably Paul, the "preacher of the Gospel." In the third part (A,25–B,2) he prays for what no angelic eye has seen, no ruler ears have heard, and what has not entered the human heart (compare 1 Corinthians 2:9). The prayer concludes with a doxology (B,2–5). The title that is appended to the tractate, "prayer of Paul the apostle," is given in Greek, the original language of the prayer as a whole.

This short prayer, written by the scribe into the front flyleaf of the codex after the rest of the manuscript had been completed, may be an excerpt from a larger work now lost. Its Valentinian character has been deduced from the occurrence in it of the term "psychic God" (the Demiurge, A,31) and its presence in a codex that is predominantly Valentinian. Its phraseology is indebted to the biblical Psalms and the epistles of Paul, who was, for the Valentinians, their chief apostolic authority.

The prayer was probably composed sometime in the late second or early third century. Its place of origin is uncertain.

b. *Treatise on the Resurrection* (NHC I,4: 43,25–50,18; *NH Library,* 52–57; Layton, 316–24; *NH Scriptures,* 49–55)

An alternative title given by some scholars to this tractate is "Epistle to Rheginos." It is addressed by an anonymous teacher to a person named Rheginos, who has written to the teacher inquiring about the Christian doctrine of resurrection (43,25–44,12). While the text lacks the customary epistolary salutation, it can be taken as a didactic epistle akin to philosophical epistles common in the early Roman period and, more to the point, to Ptolemy's *Letter to Flora,* or the epistles of Valentinus of which only fragments remain.

Indeed, when the text was first published some enthusiastic scholars attributed this writing to Valentinus himself, a view that has largely been abandoned. Who the author really was cannot be determined, but he was obviously a prominent Valentinian teacher. Rheginos was probably an ordinary Christian interested in the teacher's opinions about the resurrection. He can be compared to Flora, the recipient of Ptolemy's letter. Indeed, as with Ptolemy, this author promises Rheginos additional instruction should the opportunity arise (50,5–8).

In his exposition of the subject (44,13–46,2), he bases his discussion on the career of Christ during his sojourn on earth, "while he existed in flesh." The Lord was both Son of God and Son of Man, embracing both humanity and divinity simultaneously. As

Son of God he was able to vanquish death and provide for the restoration to the Pleroma of the elect. "The Savior swallowed up death" (compare 1 Corinthians 15:54). Raising himself up he "swallowed the visible by the invisible," providing for us our immortality. "As the Apostle said, 'we suffered with him, and we arose with him,

Could the resurrection actually be an illusion? No, it is the world that is an illusion.

and we went to heaven with him'" (compare Romans 8:17, Ephesians 2:6). Being drawn up to heaven like rays of the sun, we experience "the spiritual resurrection," which "swallows up" the psychical and the fleshly realms.

The author then takes up several problems for which he supplies the answers (46,3–49,9). Is the resurrection philosophically demonstrable? No, it is a matter of faith, and its certitude is based on election. Doesn't the resurrection entail something bodily? No, it pertains to the inner man. Could the resurrection actually be an illusion? No, it is the world that is an illusion.

In a hortatory conclusion (49,9–50,11), the author exhorts Rheginos not to "live in conformity with this flesh." He is assured that if he flees from the "divisions" and "fetters" on earth, he already has the resurrection. Should he need further instruction the author will be happy to provide it.

The author concludes his letter with an expression of peace and grace upon those who are interested in what he has written (50,11–14) and a personal greeting to Rheginos (50,15–17). A title is appended at the end: "the discourse [or 'word'] about the resurrection."

Though no reference to the Valentinian myth is made in this tractate, it is replete with typically Valentinian vocabulary and clearly belongs to the eastern school of the Valentinian tradition. It relies heavily on the Pauline epistles in its argumentation. For the author, Paul is "the Apostle" (45,24).

The original Greek version is probably to be dated toward the end of the second century or the beginning of the third. Its provenience is uncertain, but Alexandria is likely.

c. *Gospel of Philip* (NHC II,3: 51,29–86,19; *NH Library,* 139–60; Layton, 325–53; *NH Scriptures,* 157–86)

The *Gospel of Philip* is not a "gospel" in the traditional sense; that is, it is not at all like the gospels of the New Testament. Nor can it be called a "gospel" because it is focused on the good news of the salvation wrought by the Savior, as with the *Gospel of Truth* (discussed above). Nor is it a collection of Jesus' sayings, as exemplified by the *Gospel of Thomas* (NHC II,2, discussed in chapter 9). The title, *Gospel of Philip,* that is appended to the end of the tractate is obviously secondary and may have been appended to the tractate by the scribe of Codex II because it follows upon the *Gospel of Thomas.* Like the *Gospel of Thomas,* it is a collection of sayings. It is probably attributed to Philip because Philip is the only apostle named in it (73,8).

Although the *Gospel of Philip* contains sayings attributed to Jesus (fifteen of them), it is a collection or anthology of disparate sentences or paragraphs on various subjects, drawn from different sources and reflecting different genres and orientations. It looks like a lightly edited notebook, somewhat comparable to Clement's notebook containing teachings of Theodotus (*Excerpts from Theodotus,* discussed above).

The Valentinian orientation of the compilation is clear, and it may, in fact, contain material composed by Valentinus himself. However, the materials reflect not only Valentinian traditions but also other Gnostic traditions, and non-Gnostic Christian traditions as well. Over a hundred different units or "sayings" can be differentiated. Some scholars have attached numbers to the individual units, with totals from 107 (Layton) to 127 (Schenke). The different totals reflect the fact that it is not always clear where one paragraph ends and another begins. Another difficulty arises from the fact that the manuscript is damaged in some places, with the result that material has been lost. Scholars have sometimes been able to come up with tentative restorations for some of the lacunae, and these are indicated in the editions and translations with square brackets.

Fig. 6.1 The Apostles Thomas and Philip. Though they are not among the "inner circle" (Peter, James, and John) in the Synoptic Gospels, Thomas and Philip play important roles in the "last discourse" in the Gospel according to John, questioning Jesus about his origin and heavenly destination. Thomas, Philip, and other apostles figure prominently in Gnostic writings as well as the recipients of true, saving knowledge (as in the *Gospels of Thomas* and *Philip* in the Nag Hammadi library). Byzantine mosaic. La Martorana, Palermo, Italy. Photo: Scala / Art Resource, N.Y.

Many of the various units in the *Gospel of Philip* consist of enigmatic sayings or proverbs on life in this world, and exhortations to the elect on how to conduct themselves in the world. The meaning of many of these is not at all clear. Here are three examples: "Those who sow in winter reap in summer. The winter is the world, the summer the other aeon. Let us sow in the world that we may reap in the summer" (52,25–28). "Do not despise the lamb, for without it, it is not possible to see the king. No one will be able to go in to the king if he is naked" (58,14–17). "A donkey turning a millstone did a hundred miles walking. When it was loosed it found that it was still at the same place. There are men who make many journeys, but make no progress towards any destination. When evening came upon them, they saw neither city nor village, neither human artifact nor natural phenomenon, power nor angel. In vain have the wretches labored" (63,11–21).

A Gnostic myth on the creation of the world is reflected in one of the sayings. It is said that "the world came about through a mistake." Although its creator wanted to make it imperishable, he could not because he himself was not imperishable. Only sons are imperishable, and able to receive imperishability (75,2–14).

Many of the sayings are devoted to the person and work of Christ. "Christ came to ransom some, to save others, to redeem others." He "voluntarily laid down his life from the very day the world came into being." When the world "fell into the hands of robbers," he saved it, redeeming "the good people in the world as well as the evil" (52,35–53,14). "Before Christ came there was no bread in the world. But when Christ came he brought "bread from heaven" (55,6–14). "Jesus took them all by stealth, for he did not appear as he was, but in the manner in which [they would] be able to see him." He appeared to angels as an angel, to men as a man. When he appeared to his disciples on the mountain (of Transfiguration), he made them great "that they might be able to see him in his greatness" (57,28–58,10).

Jesus's virgin birth is compared to the birth of Adam: "Adam came into being from two virgins: from the spirit and from the virgin earth. Christ was born from a virgin to rectify the fall which occurred in the beginning" (71,16–21).

Jesus's baptism is referred to in a saying that is damaged: "Jesus appeared [. . .] Jordan. . . . He [who was] once [anointed] was anointed anew. He who was redeemed in turn redeemed others" (70,34–71,3).

Three women named Mary are said to have been especially close to Jesus: "There were three who always walked with the lord, Mary his mother and <his> sister and the Magdalene, the one who was called his companion (koinōnos). His sister and his mother and his companion were each a Mary" (59,6–11). (The second Mary is referred to in the text as "her (Mary's) sister," making this one Jesus's aunt. (I have followed those who would emend the text to read "his sister.") Jesus's companion Mary Magdalene is the subject of another saying, where it is said that Jesus loved her more than all of his disciples because she was more receptive to his teachings (63,32–64,9).

As already noted, the *Gospel of Philip* contains fifteen sayings attributed to Jesus. Seven of these are taken from the canonical gospels of Matthew and John. Two of them come from the *Gospel of Thomas* (saying 19 at 64,9–12 and saying 22 at 67,30–37). The others are otherwise unattested. All of the sayings of Jesus are to be understood from a Gnostic perspective.

Many of the sayings in the *Gospel of Philip* are devoted to the Valentinian sacraments. Indeed, some scholars have even suggested that the tractate as a whole is a sacramental catechesis. Five sacramental actions are specified: "The lord [did] everything in a mystery [or "sacrament"], a baptism, a chrism, a eucharist, a redemption, and a bridal

> *This saying probably refers to a five-stage initiation ritual rather than five individual sacraments.*

chamber" (67,27–30). This saying probably refers to a five-stage initiation ritual rather than five individual sacraments. The eucharist, a repeatable sacrament in itself, is a first communion when associated with the initiation ceremonies.

Several sayings refer to baptism alone (61,12–29; 63,25–30; 64,22–31; 72,29–73,1; and 77,7–15), but even in these cases baptism might be taken as referring to the entire initiation. Baptism and chrism are mentioned together in four sayings (57,22–28; 67,2–9; 69,4–14; and 74,12–24). In one it is said that chrism is superior to baptism, "for it is from the word 'chrism' [anointing] that we have been called 'Christians,' not because of the word 'baptism.' And it is because of the chrism that 'the Christ' has his name" (74,12–17). Chrism is referred to in another saying, where it is said that one acquires the name through chrism, and becomes "no longer a Christian but a Christ" (67,19–27).

Redemption and the bridal chamber are brought together with baptism in an allegory on the temple in Jerusalem and its three main "buildings" (69,14–70,4). The "holy" place is baptism; the "holy of the holy" is redemption; and "the holy of the holies" is the bridal chamber. "Baptism includes the resurrection [and the] redemption; the redemption takes place in the bridal chamber. But the bridal chamber is in that which is superior to . . ." (what follows is damaged).

The Valentinian five-stage initiation, as reflected in the *Gospel of Philip,* includes immersion in water, chrismation with holy oil, and the initiate's first communion. Redemption and bridal chamber are not separate ritual actions, but are to be construed as aspects of, or effects of, the baptism and chrismation with oil. Implied in the terminology is the assurance of salvation after death: redemption from the body and its trammels, and final unification with one's "angel" in the Pleroma.

Some scholars have construed the "bridal chamber" to refer to marriage as a sacrament, and/or to some sort of carnal activity in a ritual called "bridal chamber," but that does not seem to be indicated in the text. Nevertheless, the *Gospel of Philip* does refer to ordinary marriage and sexuality in several passages. Especially striking is the following one: "Great is the mystery of marriage! For [without] it the world would [not exist]" (64,31–32). Thus, a positive evaluation is given of marriage and procreation, and this is typical of the Valentinian tradition as we know it from other sources.

> *A positive evaluation is given of marriage and procreation, and this is typical of the Valentinian tradition as we know it from other sources.*

Even so, a distinction is made between a "marriage of defilement" and the "undefiled marriage" (82,5–6). The former is a marriage in which intercourse is controlled by sexual desire. In the latter, marriage as practiced by Valentinian Christians, intercourse is controlled by pure thoughts. Undefiled marriage is "a true mystery," "not fleshly but pure. It belongs not to desire but to the will" (82,5–8). The married couple should direct their thoughts to God so that the child they conceive will be spiritual. "Now you who lie together with the son of God, love not the world, but love the Lord, in order that those you will bring forth may not resemble the world, but may resemble the Lord" (78,20–24).

The *Gospel of Philip* was probably put together sometime in the late second century, or, perhaps more likely, the first part of the third. Greek is certainly the original language of the tractate, but references to Syriac words in the text (63,21–23; 56,7–9) reflect a bilingual environment such as one would find in Syria, either Antioch or farther east in Edessa.

d. *Interpretation of Knowledge* (XI,1: 1,1–21,35; *NH Library*, 472–80; *NH Scriptures*, 651–62)

Codex XI is one of the most heavily damaged of the Nag Hammadi codices. As many as twenty-five lines are missing from the tops of pages one through eighteen, and the tops of pages nineteen through twenty-one are only partially preserved. Damage has also occurred in the bottom portions of the pages. Nevertheless, from what is preserved one can get a basic idea of the tractate's content.

The title, "The Interpretation of Knowledge," is given at the end. It also occurred on page one, for inkblotting preserved on the front flyleaf of the codex provides evidence of it. The *Interpretation of Knowledge* contains Gnostic interpretations of early Christian traditions as contained in the New Testament gospels and the Pauline epistles. Its genre is that of a homily, probably prepared in the first instance for oral delivery in a congregational setting. While its Valentinian orientation has been questioned by some scholars, there is no reason to doubt that it is the work of a Valentinian teacher of the eastern school of Valentinian gnosis.

A major problem facing the congregation to whom the homily is initially directed is divisions and quarreling in the community. The first eight pages are heavily damaged. The first two pages evidently deal with issues of faith and unbelief. The Savior and a virginal consort (Sophia?) are discussed in the next two pages. Page five contains an interpretation of the parable of the sower (Matthew 13:1–9), and page six contains an interpretation of the parable of the good Samaritan (Luke 10:29-37). Pages seven and eight are too heavily damaged to discuss. Pages nine through eleven contain material on the teachings of the church's "teacher of immortality" (9,19), that is, the Savior, who confronted an unknown "arrogant teacher" (9,20). The saving work of Christ is discussed on pages twelve through fourteen. The problems of disunity in the church are taken up with interpretations of the Pauline epistles in the remaining material (pp. 15–21). The tractate closes with a word of encouragement: "If we surmount every sin, we shall receive the crown of victory, even as our Head was glorified by the Father" (21,31–34).

Nothing is known of the author of this tractate. It is clear that he was a learned exegete of the scriptures and used his teaching authority pastorally in addressing the needs of his community. Where and when he was active cannot be determined, but late second-century Alexandria is a good guess.

e. *A Valentinian Exposition* (NHC XI,2: 22,1–39,39 plus liturgical appendices: 40,1–44,37; *NH Library,* 481–89; *NH Scriptures,* 663–77)

This tractate lacks a title in the manuscript; so a title has been assigned to it by its first translators, based on its content. Up to sixteen lines are missing from the tops of each of the pages, and what remains of the pages reflect considerable damage. Even so, it is possible to see that the tractate is an exposition of Valentinian mythology, consisting of protology, the fall of Sophia, the creation of the world and humankind, and the ultimate return of Sophia into the Pleroma, together with the spiritual seed. As such, it contains much material in common with the accounts of Valentinian mythology given by Irenaeus, Hippolytus, Clement, and Epiphanius. It also contains references to different points of view held by different Valentinian teachers.

A Valentinian Exposition was evidently composed as a text used for catechetical instruction of neophytes preparing for initiation into the Valentinian church. The main tractate ends on line thirty-nine of page thirty-nine and is marked off with decoration in the manuscript. What follows on pages forty through forty-four consists of five liturgical appendices, each of them also delineated by decorations in the manuscript. These appendices are now conventionally titled "On the Anointing" (40,1–29), "On Baptism A" (40,30–41,38), "On Baptism B" (42,1–43,19), "On the Eucharist

A" (43,20–38), and "On the Eucharist B" (44,1–37). This material provides for further instruction to neophytes, preparing them for liturgical rites that will be part of their initiation.

The first part of the tractate deals with the unfolding of the Pleroma, beginning with the primal Father, a Monad dwelling alone in silence, and his Son, Mind (*nous*). Limit (*horos*) establishes boundaries for the aeons in the Pleroma. From the primal Tetrad are projected Word, Life, Man, and Church. The Decad (ten aeons) is projected from Word and Life, the Duodecad (twelve aeons) from Man and Church (22,1–30,38f.).

Not much is left of page thirty-one, but the Sophia myth begins on that page. The fall of Sophia and the saving role of Jesus are the focus of the next main section of the tractate (31,34–34,38). Jesus and Sophia play a key role in the creation of the world and humankind by the Demiurge (35,10–37,38f.).

Page 38 has material featuring interpretations of the opening chapters of Genesis involving Adam and the Devil (Genesis 2–3), Cain and Abel (Genesis 4), the fall of the angels (Genesis 6:1-4), and the flood (Genesis 6:5-17). Page 39 focuses on the restoration of Sophia to the Pleroma, together with the spiritual seed (39,10–39).

The liturgical appendices are unfortunately fragmentary, owing to damage to the manuscript. The first one, "On the Anointing," is a prayer to the Father to send his son, Jesus Christ, to anoint us, and concludes with a doxology. Its position, that is, before the material on baptism, may indicate that the anointing in question is a prebaptismal anointing, otherwise unattested in other Valentinian ritual sources. The second one, "On Baptism A," refers to a "first baptism," that of John for the remission of sins. "On Baptism B" is too fragmentary to be intelligible, but evidently refers to the state of those who ascend into the Pleroma. "On Eucharist A" and "On Eucharist B" are prayers associated with the sacrament of the eucharist.

Nothing is known of the author of this tractate. A late second-century date is probable. Where it was written cannot be determined, but Alexandria in Egypt is a good guess.

f. *Tripartite Tractate* (NHC I,5: 51,1–138,27; *NH Library,* 58–103; *NH Scriptures,* 77–101)

The *Tripartite Tractate* is the only completely preserved systematic treatise of Valentinian gnosis that has come down to us. It is a very lengthy treatise of eighty-eight pages—in the Nag Hammadi corpus only *Zostrianos* (VIII,*1*) is longer—and presents the entire mythological story of pleromatic origins, divine devolution leading to creation, and ultimate reintegration into the divine Pleroma. The text is divided by scribal decoration in the manuscript into three parts. Since no title is given to this treatise in the manuscript, its first editors called it *Tractatus Tripartitus,* or in English, *Tripartite Tractate.* The three main segments correspond to three major acts in the mythological drama. Part I (51,1–104,3) has an account of the primal Father and his aeons. Part II (104,4–108,12) deals with the creation of humanity and Adam's fall. Part III (108,13–138,27) presents the Savior's incarnation and human responses to his coming, culminating in the final restoration.

The language of the text is turgid and often difficult to understand. The difficulties may be accounted for by supposing that the Coptic translator had an imperfect understanding of the Greek prototype.

The first main part of the tractate is divisible into nine units. The first (51,1–57,8) deals with the Father, a "single one" who is wholly ineffable. We note the absence of Silence (*sigē*), the father's consort in some other Valentinian systems. This section contains an elaborate negative theology, such as we have seen in other Gnostic tractates. The second (57,8–59,38) describes two other preexistent entities, named the Son and the Church, who are said to come forth from the Father. The *Tripartite Tractate* thus differs from other Valentinian systems in positing a primal triad, instead of a tetrad. The third (60,1–67,37) describes the Church, which is then said to subsist in "innumerable aeons," who "were

The Tripartite Tractate *is the only completely preserved systematic treatise of Valentinian gnosis that has come down to us.*

forever in the thought of the Father," that is, existing potentially. The fourth (67,38–74,18) notes that these aeons, in turn, produce further emanations by giving glory to the Father. These are not, as in other Valentinian systems, construed as masculine and feminine pairs (syzygies), but are all "properties and powers of the Father." Three levels of aeons in the Pleroma are thus posited.

The fifth (74,18–80,11), which relates the transition from the transcendent Pleroma to the world outside, is marked by the activity of the Logos (Word), an aeon who attempted "to grasp the incomprehensibility" of the Father. What is especially notable in this tractate is that the role played by Sophia in all of the other Valentinian systems known to us is here assigned to the Logos. It is stressed that the Logos's intent was good, even if the results were not—that is, they were the production of deficient beings. It is also stressed that he acted "not without the will of the Father." It has plausibly been suggested that the role of the Logos in this tractate (that is, his role in the creation of the world) is based on Heracleon's exegesis of the Johannine prologue (in fragment 1 of his commentary, discussed above).

In the sixth (80.11–85,15), it is said that the Logos "converted himself to the good." From his conversion, the psychical order of things result while the material order is the result of his defective begetting. The seventh (85,15–90,13) states that, following his conversion, the Logos is split into two. His better self enters the Pleroma and intercedes for "the one who is defective." The pleromatic aeons bring forth the Savior, who is the Father's "beloved Son." In the eighth (90,14–95,38), as a result of the revelation given to the lower Logos by the Savior, "his pleroma" comes into being and stands above the psychical and material orders produced by the Logos. His pleroma is an image of the transcendent Pleroma, and has the name "the Church," that is, the church in the lower world. In the ninth (95,38–104,3), the Logos then establishes the "organization" (*oikonomia*) of the world outside of the Pleroma, appointing archons with various responsibilities. The chief archon is the Demiurge, whom the Logos uses to "work on the things below."

The second part of the tractate is devoted to an interpretation of Genesis 1–3, from the creation of Adam to the fall from Paradise (104,4—108,12). The creation of Adam involves the work of the Logos, who supplies the spiritual part of Adam's soul; the Demiurge, who supplies the psychical part; and "those of the left," that is, the lower archons, who supply the material (*hylikos*) part. All of humankind is understood to have all three parts. Later on, it is taught that there are three types of human beings (118,14—122,12), but that tripartition is not based on different types of souls, but on responses to the Savior's coming. This second section concludes with the observation that death rules as a result of the transgression of the first man, but this, too, comes about in accordance with the Father's will.

The third part of the tractate begins with a discussion of three different theologies, or revelations of truth. "Those on the left," that is, Greeks and barbarians, have a material apprehension of the deity and the world. A second type of apprehension of the truth is that of the Hebrew prophets, who belong to the psychical order of the world ruled by the Demiurge. They proclaimed the coming of the Savior, but did not know who he is (108,13—114,30). The third type of revelation results from the incarnation of the Savior, who let himself be born and suffer and die for those he intended to save. It is also said that others descended with him to share in the Savior's work of salvation. These others can be taken to constitute the spiritual Church on earth (114,31—118,14).

As a result of the Savior's coming, humankind "came to be in three essential types, the spiritual, the psychical, and the material." The elect spirituals respond to the Savior immediately; those who hesitate are the "psychicals" who need further instruction, and those who "shun" the light are revealed to be material. The "psychical race" can choose either good or evil and have a hope of salvation (118,14—122,12).

The process of restoration is then taken up, with a distinction made between the "election" (the spirituals) and the "calling" (the psychicals). The election is given a place within the bridal chamber, while the calling remains outside, like "those who rejoice at the bride chamber." But then, in the end, "all the members of the Church are in a single place and receive the restoration at one time . . . namely, the restoration into the Pleroma" (122,12—129,34). We can understand this to mean that, in

> *The* Tripartite Tractate *presents a revisionist version of the Valentinian system.*

contrast to what is taught in some other Valentinian systems, both the psychicals and the spirituals will enter into the Pleroma at the end. The final redemption is said to be grounded in baptism in the names of Father, Son, and Holy Spirit. This would imply an acceptance of baptism as practiced in the psychical church.

The salvation of the "calling" is given further attention in what follows. In the final restoration, all distinctions among members of the Church will cease, and while the material ones will be given over to destruction, those who are saved will rejoice in "the bridal chamber which is the love of God the Father" (129,34—138,19). The text concludes with a doxology to the Father and the Savior through the Holy Spirit (138,20–27).

The *Tripartite Tractate* presents a revisionist version of the Valentinian system. The differences between it and other Valentinian sources have been noted, and these can be accounted for with the suggestion that its author had taken into account ecclesiastical criticisms of Valentinian doctrines and was attempting to make his treatise more compatible with the doctrines of a growing orthodox establishment.

We know nothing of the author of the *Tripartite Tractate*. In earlier scholarship, it was suggested that it could be attributed to Heracleon. We have noted the possibility that its doctrine of the Logos might reflect Heracleon's influence, but the tractate reflects a stage of Valentinian thought that would place it in the third century. While some scholars have placed the *Tripartite Tractate* in the western school of Valentinianism, more recent scholarship has associated it with the eastern school. As to where the treatise was written, Alexandria is likely.

7. Conclusions

Of all the heretics known to Irenaeus of Lyons, the good bishop regarded the Valentinians as the most dangerous to the church. His concerns about them were well founded, for by his time the movement founded by Valentinus had already spread from one end of the Mediterranean to the other and into the interior regions of Europe and Asia Minor. From what little is preserved of the work of Valentinus himself, we can easily see that he was a brilliant teacher, a poet, a mystic, and a pastor of souls. He was able to adapt an originally non-Christian Gnostic system of thought to a new version of Christian theology and practice, one that attracted a substantial number of converts.

Already during the second century the Valentinian movement split into two basic schools of thought, western and eastern. The eastern variety seems to have remained closer to the teachings of Valentinus himself. The western variety is marked by innovations that can be attributed to his pupil Ptolemy. The main differences can be seen in terms of protology, Christology, and soteriology. The thirty

> *From what little is preserved of the work of Valentinus himself, we can easily see that he was a brilliant teacher, a poet, a mystic, and a pastor of souls.*

named aeons are a feature of western Valentinianism, as well as the doubling of Sophia. The reality of Jesus Christ's incarnation is maintained by Valentinus and the eastern school, whereas the western school attributes a psychical body to the earthly Jesus. Teachers of the western school, too, posit only a partial salvation for the psychical people, who remain outside of the Pleroma at the end. In general, they seem to have had a more rigid anthropology involving the three "races," spiritual, psychical, and material.

That having been said, it should be added that there is evidence of intra-Valentinian discussions and debates, and Valentinian teachers often disagreed with one another on various points in terms of doctrine and practice. As has been noted, there was never any canonical version of the basic Valentinian myth. Valentinians also had their differences in terms of ritual practices.

It should also be remembered that the Valentinians did not refer to themselves as members of a school. Rather, they saw themselves as members of a church (*ekklēsia*). Worship services were a prominent aspect of the life of Valentinian communities, and we are told that Valentinus himself composed hymns for use in their worship life. In the preceding discussion we have noted the importance of the five-stage initiation ceremony and the repeatable sacrament of the eucharist. Some Valentinians may also have had a special rite of redemption for the dying.

Of the sources discussed above, the primary ones preserved in Coptic represent, for the most part, the eastern school of Valentinianism. It should also be said that the sources discussed above do not exhaust our evidence for Valentinianism, for Valentinian influence can be seen in other writings as well. One example of this has already been noted, the Valentinian instructions to the dying that are part of the *First Apocalypse of James*. And we shall encounter additional evidence of Valentinian influence in the Coptic sources yet to be discussed (in chapter 8).

As already indicated, the last mention of Valentinians in ancient Christian sources dates from the year 692, the Trullan Synod convened by Justinian II. But that's not the end of their story, for even now in our own times, Gnostic Christians use Valentinian materials in their worship life (as will be noted in the Epilogue).

7. Three-Principle Systems

Whoever says that the universe proceeds from one principle is mistaken; whoever says that it is from three principles speaks the truth, and will give the demonstration of all things.

THIS STATEMENT COMES FROM A Gnostic writing attributed by Hippolytus to a group he calls "Naassenes" (*Refutation of All Heresies* 5.8.1). That group is one of several Gnostic groups treated in Book 5 of his *Refutation* that posited three principles instead of one as the root cause of all things. Hippolytus's discussion of these groups is found in a large section of his great work that deals with groups and teachers not attested elsewhere in the heresiological literature.

Hippolytus does not begin his treatment of the heresies until Book 5. Since his main aim was to show that the heretics derived their doctrines from pagan sources, he devoted the first four volumes to aspects of pagan (Greek) culture. The first book dealt with the Greek philosophies and their systems, the second and third dealt with Greek cults and mysteries, and the fourth with astrology and magic. Books 2 and 3, and part of Book 4, are lost. Various Gnostic teachers and groups are dealt with in Books 5–8.

The Naassenes are the first Gnostic group treated by Hippolytus (*Refutation of all Heresies* 5.6.3–11.1). Next come two other three-principle groups, the Peratics and the Sethians. Two three-principle systems are treated in Book 8, that of the Docetists and that of Monoimos the Arabian. These two systems will be treated before that of the Sethians, for the latter shows a striking resemblance to that of the *Paraphrase of Shem* (NHC VII,*1*), treated last in this chapter.

1. The Naassenes (Foerster 1:261–82)

The main part of Hippolytus's account of the Naassenes consists of excerpts from, and paraphrases of, a quasilearned Gnostic commentary on two hymns to Attis, the emasculated young god of the cult of the Great Mother, Cybele (5.7.2–9.9). The commentary is frequently referred to in scholarship as the "Naassene Sermon." The two hymns to Attis are given at the end (5.9.8–9). The sermon is preceded by introductory comments on the Naassenes by Hippolytus (5.6.3–7.1) and is followed by additional information on them (5.9.10–11.1).

> Since Hippolytus says that the people of this group are called Naassenes, and call themselves Gnostics, we have the right to suspect that Naassene is a name invented by Hippolytus himself.

In his introductory comments Hippolytus says he will "begin with those who have had the effrontery to praise the serpent, who was the cause of temptation" (that is, the serpent of Genesis 3). They are called *Naassenes,* a name based on the Hebrew word for "serpent" (*nahash*), and they call themselves Gnostics. In the "Naassene Sermon" proper, no attention is paid to the serpent at all. Since Hippolytus says that the people of this group are called Naassenes, and call themselves Gnostics, we have the right to suspect that *Naassene* is a name invented by Hippolytus himself. In any case, Hippolytus's Naassenes are not related in any way to the Ophites or Ophians referred to by other heresiologists (discussed above in chapter 2).

Hippolytus says that these people "reverence beyond all others Man and the Son of Man. Now this Man is bisexual and is called by them Adamas" (5.6.4–5). Adamas (or Anthropos, "Human") can be identified with the second of the three basic principles enunciated in the Naassene Sermon: "Pre-existent," "Self-existent," and "outpoured Chaos" (5.7.9). The first two of these can be compared to the two male figures in the Sethian Gnostic triad, Father ("Man," "Invisible Spirit," and so forth) and Son ("Son of Man," "Autogenes" or "Self-begotten," and so forth). But in contrast to its place in the classic Sethian system, the material world ("outpoured Chaos") is not derivative but is coexistent with the other two principles.

> An exasperated Hippolytus remarks, "So they ramble on, adapting everything that was said or done by anyone to their own theory, saying that everything is spiritual" (5.9.7).

Hippolytus then reports that one part of Adamas is "intellectual" (*noeros*, which is spiritual), another part "psychical," and a third part "earthy" (*choikos*, from the noun *chous*, "dust," in Genesis 2:7). All three parts of Adamas "descended together into one man, Jesus who was born of Mary." There are also three classes of people, "angelic," which is spiritual; "psychical"; and "earthy," which is material. They are also referred to as "chosen," "called," and "enslaved" (5.6.6–7). Valentinian Gnostic influence is probable at this point. Hippolytus says that he is providing here information based on discourses said to have been given by "James the Lord's brother" to "Mariamne" (Mary Magdalene, 5.7.1).

What follows next is Hippolytus's discussion of the aforementioned "Naassene Sermon." Hippolytus says that the basis of the Naassene system is the man Adamas. The Naassenes claim that he is the subject of the question, "His generation, who shall declare it?" (Isaiah 53:8). The whole of the commentary that follows equates the young god of the Attis hymns with Adamas. In the hymns, Attis is said to be called by various names by different peoples: The Assyrians call him Adonis, the Egyptians Osiris, the Greeks the crescent moon, the Samothracians Adamas, and so forth.

The author of the commentary expands on such equations with extended disconnected references to the mythical lore of various peoples and with quotations from Greek poets, biblical writings, writings from the New Testament, apocryphal gospels, and traditions relating to the Eleusinian and other mysteries. The author is also familiar with other Gnostic writings, such as the Simonian *Great Revelation* (discussed above in chapter 2, quoted at 5.9.5). An exasperated Hippolytus remarks, "So they ramble on, adapting everything that was said or done by anyone to their own theory, saying that everything is spiritual" (5.9.7).

At points in the text, Adamas is brought into relation with human souls on earth. For example, comparing Adamas to the god Hermes, "the sender of souls," it is said that he causes the descent of human souls to earth, and aids them in their ascent. Human souls descended from Adamas on high into this "moulded figure of clay" (compare Genesis 2:7) to serve the Demiurge, Esaldaeus (a garbled rendition of *'El Shaddai,* one of the names for God in the Bible; the key text is Exodus 6:3). Esaldaeus is said to be "fourth in number," which probably means that, as the Demiurge, he brought order to the third principle, Chaos (5.7.30–31). Adamas, as Christ, awakens sleeping souls and gives them light (5.7.33).

The "Naassene Sermon" is the work of a widely read individual, presumably meant as esoteric instruction for a Gnostic community. We are left in the dark as to the nature of this community, its structure, rituals, and so forth. That celibacy was enjoined among its members is evident from what is said of the "bisexual" nature of Adamas. The castration of the god Attis is taken to refer to removal of "the earthly parts of the creation" and ascent to "the eternal substance above." "So, in accordance with this thought of theirs, the intercourse of woman with man is in their teaching shown to be most wicked and prohibited" (5.7.13–15).

After quoting the two Attis hymns, Hippolytus remarks that the Naassenes "attend the so-called mysteries of the Great Mother, thinking that through those sacred actions they will best understand the universal mystery" (5.9.10). He also repeats his assertion that they venerate the serpent and are thus called Naassenes (5.10.11).

That these Gnostics were also Christians is surely indicated by the content of a psalm said to have been composed by them.

The psalm opens with a reference to the three principles: "The universal law of the All was the First-born Mind (*nous*), / The second one after the First-born was the outpoured Chaos; / while the Soul received the third rank, with the duty to fulfil the law." The soul is then portrayed in the psalm as a captive, wandering in a labyrinth with no exit. Then Jesus prays to his Father in behalf of the soul, and asks to be sent down to help her "to escape the bitter Chaos." I quote the concluding lines of this beautiful psalm (in Marcovich's translation):

> For that reason send me, Father.
> Bearing the seals I will descend;
> I will pass through all the Aeons;
> I will reveal all the mysteries
> and show the forms of the gods:
> I will transmit the secrets of the holy way,
> calling them Gnosis.

A late second- or early third-century date can be assigned to the Naassene teachings described by Hippolytus. He presumably got his sources in Rome.

2. The Peratics (Foerster 1:283–92)

We noted that the connection made between the Naassenes and the biblical serpent was tenuous at best, but such a connection can be seen in what Hippolytus tells us of the Peratic sect (*Refutation of All Heresies* 5.12.1–17.13). The first mention of Peratics was made before Hippolytus by Clement of Alexandria. In Book 7 of his *Miscellanies* Clement refers to various heresies that have arisen since apostolic times. Some groups are named for their founders, some for their teaching, some for their actions, some for revered figures, and so forth. In this context Clement says, "Some take their designation from a place, as the Peratics" (*Miscellanies* 7.108). Hippolytus reports, instead, that the Peratics apply that name to themselves because they derive it from the Greek verb *perao*, "pass through" or "traverse." He cites their claim that they are the only ones who can "pass through" (and thus escape from) destruction (5.16.1).

Clement's geographical derivation is more likely because the name of one of the group's founders is Euphrates "the Peratic" (5.13.9). The region "on the other side of" (Greek *peran*) the Euphrates river was a designation for Mesopotamia in ancient times. One can thus surmise that Euphrates' original home was somewhere in Mesopotamia. The name given to the group founded by him would thus reflect that connection.

We know nothing of the person named by Hippolytus as a cofounder of the group, Kelbes of Karystia (a town in Greece). As for Euphrates, he is named by Origen as a teacher among the Ophian Gnostics (*Against Celsus* 6.28; compare chapter 2, above). The material on the serpents in Hippolytus's discussion of Peratic doctrine would presumably be attributable to Euphrates.

Hippolytus tells us that the Peratics posit a tripartite division of the universe. The first is unoriginate and good, the second is self-originate and good, and the third is originate (5.12.1–3). Christ is "a three-natured man" who came down from

> *The biblical story of the Exodus provides the occasion for an elaborate allegorical discussion focusing on serpents, starting with the ones in the Sinai wilderness that were biting the Israelites (Numbers 21:6).*

unoriginate being to save those who were brought down into this world. This world, the third principle, will ultimately be destroyed (5.12.4–7).

Hippolytus then devotes a good deal of attention to the astrological teachings of the Peratics, and quotes a garbled passage from a book of theirs (5.13.1–15. 5). The Peratics are also said to make an elaborate symbolic connection between water and destruction. They also regard Cronos (Father of Zeus in Greek mythology) as the power that rules over the world of becoming, which is subject to destruction (5.16.l–3). The Red Sea in the biblical story of the Exodus from Egypt is said to embody the "water of destruction" (5.16.4–5).

The biblical story of the Exodus provides the occasion for an elaborate allegorical discussion focusing on serpents, starting with the ones in the Sinai wilderness that were biting the Israelites (Numbers 21:6). Those serpents are identified with the "gods of destruction," stars that subject people to fickle destiny. "Moses showed them the true perfect serpent." That serpent is the rod of Moses that thwarted the serpents of the magicians (5.16.6–8; compare Exodus 7:10-12).

The "universal serpent" is then identified as "the wise word of Eve," the sign marked on Cain (Genesis 4:15), and ultimately Jesus Christ, the "Son of Man" lifted up like the bronze serpent of Moses (John 3:14; 5.16.8–13). Various serpentine constellations are then brought into the discussion (5.16.14–16). Some of this material might be based on a Gnostic serpent midrash such as the one discussed earlier in this book (in chapter 4).

Hippolytus sums up the Peratic system with the observation that the universe, according to the Peratics, is "Father, Son, and matter." "Midway between matter and the Father there sits his Son, the Word, the serpent who is always moving toward the immovable Father and towards the movable matter" (5.17.1–2). The Savior is said to have differentiated between two fathers, the "Father in heaven" (Matthew 7:11) and the "father" who is "a murderer from the beginning" (John 8:44). The latter is "the ruler and artificer of matter" whose work brings corruption and death (5.17.5–7). "No one can be saved apart from the Son, or ascend without him, who is the serpent (5.17.8).

Some correspondences can be noted between the Peratic system and that of the Naassenes. Use of common sources could account for such correspondences. In any case, Hippolytus's Peratic material can be assigned to late second- or early third-century Rome.

3. The Docetists (Foerster 1:306–12)

Docetism is a very ancient Christian heresy, attested already in the New Testament (1 John 4:1-3). The term, derived from the Greek verb *dokein* ("to seem"), is applied to a doctrine of Christ that asserts that Jesus only "seemed" to be a real man of flesh and blood. The term Docetist is first attested in a writing of Bishop Serapion of Antioch (circa 200, quoted in Eusebius, *Ecclesiastical History* 6.12.6), referring to people in the church at Rhossus in Syria who were using the apocryphal *Gospel of Peter* (of which only fragments now remain). Upon reading that gospel, Serapion decided that it had a docetic view of Christ.

The first heresy discussed by Hippolytus in Book 8 of his *Refutation of All Heresies* is that of a group that he labels as "Docetists" (*Dokētai*, 8.8.2–10.11). Hippolytus claims that members of this group "called themselves Docetists," but that can hardly be

> *It is clearly Hippolytus who first applied the label* Docetists *(Dokeitai) to a group of Gnostics, but it is not clear why he did so: the Gnostic group whose doctrines he was attempting to refute did not in fact teach a docetic view of Christ.*

accepted as a fact. The term *Docetist* can hardly be applied to a distinctive sect, for a docetic view of Christ was espoused by a number of different Christian groups. Hippolytus remarks that he will refute people who claim to maintain steadfastness of doctrine and adds that this claim is only a matter of appearance (*to dokein*, 8.8.2). It is clearly Hippolytus who first applied the label "Docetists" (*Dokeitai*) to a group of Gnostics, but it is not clear why he did so: the Gnostic group whose doctrines he was attempting to refute did not in fact teach a docetic view of Christ. Several Gnostic groups did embrace the docetic heresy, but not the one here discussed by Hippolytus. So we remain in the dark as to the real name of the group he is discussing at the beginning of Book 8. We can assume that they called themselves Gnostics.

The Gnostic system described here by Hippolytus begins with the first God likened to the seed of a fig tree, from which sprout three things: the trunk, the leaves, and the fruit. These are the three principles of the universe, called "aeons" and regarded as bisexual. Since they are perfect, and the number ten is the number of perfection, thirty aeons came into being. The joint product of these aeons is the Savior, born of the virgin Mary (5.8.2–9.2).

An infinite number of patterns shone down from above to the chaos below. The third primal aeon produced the firmament and divided light from darkness (Genesis 1:4-7). From an imprint of this aeon there came the "great Archon," the God who "made heaven and earth" (Genesis 1:1). He is a fiery God who made the world "just as Moses describes," and who held in thrall other imprints from the heavenly world, human souls, until the coming of the Savior (5.9.3–10.2).

The Savior willed to come down and save the souls trapped below. He clothed himself with the "outer darkness," that is, human flesh, the product of the Archon. When the Archon condemned his own creation to death, the Savior put off the human body, put on the body that had been imprinted in the water of his baptism, and ascended back to heaven (5.10.3–8).

Many sects contentiously seek after Jesus, and he appears differently to different groups. Those who derive their natures from here below cannot see the forms of the Savior that are above them. Only "we" (that is, the Gnostics) understand Jesus the Savior completely (5.10.9–11).

Hippolytus's account is sprinkled with proof texts from the Old Testament and from the gospels and Paul. The source that he was using was clearly produced by Christian Gnostics. One can see in it influences from other Gnostic groups as well, such as the Valentinians. One can plausibly situate Hippolytus's "Docetists" in early third-century Rome.

4. Monoimus the Arabian
(Foerster 1:246–50)

All we know of Monoimus is found in Book 8 of Hippolytus's *Refutation of All Heresies* (8.12.1–15.2). He is presumably called "the Arabian" because he came from the Roman province of Arabia, but Hippolytus's information would probably have been based on contacts in Rome in the early third century. There certainly must have been more to Monoimus's system than what we read in Hippolytus's truncated account.

Like the Naassenes, Monoimus posits as the first two principles of the universe Man and Son of Man, the first unoriginate and the second "originate and passible." Everything else ultimately derives from the Son of Man (8.12.1–2). Nothing is explicitly said of a third principle, but something like the Naassene doctrine of "outpoured chaos" can plausibly be posited.

A good deal of Monoimus's system revolves around the number ten, a "single stroke" (the Greek let-

> *There is no explicit mention of Jesus Christ, and Monoimus says that no one knows the Son of Man.*

ter Iota, ι used as the number ten). That single stroke contains within itself the other numbers, and these have become "bodily substances." Colossians 2:9 is loosely quoted in this context: "For the whole fullness was pleased to reside in the Son of Man in bodily form" (5.13.2). The Son of Man is construed as "that single Iota, the single stroke, which runs down from above, which is full and which fills all things" (5.13.4).

An interesting feature of Monoimus's teaching is what he says and does not say about the Son of Man. There is no explicit mention of Jesus Christ, and Monoimus says that no one knows the Son of Man. The whole creation, in its ignorance, "pictures him as one born of woman." "Now the splendor of that Son of Man is incomprehensible till now to all men who are misled by thinking of one born of a woman" (5.13.3–4). So in Monoimus's system, at least in what we have of it, there is no savior, and no doctrine of salvation. Indeed, Monoimus would appear to be engaging in a polemic against Christians who confess Christ, "the Son of Man," as a man "born of a woman" (Galatians 4:4).

In his treatment of the creation of the world, Monoimus cites Moses's account of creation in six days, the seventh day producing earth, water, fire, and air, "out of which the world was made from the single stroke" (5.14.1–2). The ten plagues visited upon the Egyptians in the Book of Exodus are "allegories symbolizing the Creation." Reference is later made to the "God of creation," who "rejoices at the transformation which is wrought by the ten blows of the single stroke, which is the rod of Moses" (5.14.3–8).

At the end of his account Hippolytus quotes from a letter that Monoimus had written to a certain Theophrastus: "Cease to seek after God and creation and things like these, and seek after yourself of yourself." As the result of this process "you will find yourself within yourself, being both one and many like that stroke, and will find the outcome of yourself" (5.15.1).

For Monoimus, and for Gnostics in general, salvation is ultimately grounded in knowledge of oneself.

5. The Sethians (Foerster 1:299–305)

Hippolytus's discussion of a group he calls "Sethians" follows upon his treatment of the Peratics in Book 5 (5.19.1–22.1). As has already been noted, his Sethians bear no relation at all to the Sethians treated by other heresiologists (discussed in chapter 3, above). Seth plays no role at all in the Sethian system, but at the end of his account Hippolytus tells us that we can find a complete account of the system in a book entitled the *Paraphrase of Seth* (5.22.1). The title of this book was presumably the basis for his choice of the name Sethians for the group using it. We know nothing further of the book or its contents, or how it got its curious title. (A "paraphrase" is a restatement or, in the case of a written text, a rewriting. A similar problem is posed by the title of the Nag Hammadi tractate treated next in this chapter.)

In this system, three universal principles are posited: Light, Darkness, and Spirit between. Each principle has within it an infinite number of powers. A problem arises when the three principles are intermingled. Light, "like a ray of the sun," is diffused by the Spirit to the Darkness below, which is a "dreadful water." Darkness keeps in its possession the "spark of Light" and the "fragrance of the Spirit" (5.19,1–6).

From the first impact of the three principles there arises heaven and earth, "shaped like a womb having the navel in the middle." In it there came to life multitudes of living creatures, in which were inseminated light and spirit. From the water there arose "a fierce and violent wind which is the cause of all generation." The wind and the water produced swelling waves, which are "the origin of man or of the mind." Mind holds fast the light and the fragrance of the spirit. A tiny spark of light is intermingled with bodies, and it is the concern of Light from above how the mind might be freed from the death of the body, and from the father below, who is the wind that stirred up the waves of the dark water. "For there was a ray coming from above from that perfect light held fast in the dark, dreadful, bitter, filthy water, which is the spirit of light 'rushing' over the water" (compare Genesis 1:2; 5.19.7–17).

The violent rush of wind "sweeps along" like a winged serpent, from which has come the beginning of the generation of all things. Light and spirit are imprisoned in the "womb of disorder, into which the serpent enters." The wind of darkness produces man. In order to undo the bonds in which the mind (of man) is held, the perfect Word (Logos) of the Light above took on the likeness of that beast, the snake, which is the "form of a servant" (Philippians 2:7), and entered into the unclean womb. So the Word "entered a virgin's womb," and then "washed himself and drank the cup of living, springing water, which everyone must drink who is to put off the form of the servant and put on the heavenly apparel" (5.19.18–22).

With this Hippolytus concludes his summary of the Sethian doctrine. The "washing" and the drinking of "living, springing water" may imply a baptismal ritual in which the water was imbibed. This water would, of course, be distinguished from the dreadful water of Darkness.

Hippolytus continues his discussion with various Old Testament texts used by the Sethians as proof for their doctrines (5.20.1–3). He then tells us that the content of their teachings really comes from such Greek theologians as Musaeus, Linus, and Orpheus, and from Homer and other poets (5.20.4–9). He then elaborates on Sethian doctrines of "infusion and mixture," bringing in analogies and illustrations of various sorts that have been put forward in their writings (5.21.1–12). He concludes his discussion with reference to the aforementioned *Paraphrase of Seth,* where he says the entire Sethian system and all their secrets are to be found (5.22.1).

If we assume that there actually was a book entitled *Paraphrase of Seth* used by a particular group of Gnostics and that Hippolytus's account is a summary of some of its contents, we are still confronted with the question posed by its title, since Seth plays no role in what Hippolytus tells us of the "Sethian" system. Perhaps the book in question can be construed as a retelling of a revelation attributed by certain Gnostics to Seth. After all, Seth was regarded by many Gnostics as a revealer of gnosis *par excellence*. Such a book would probably have been composed sometime in the late second or early third century, perhaps in Rome.

6. *Paraphrase of Shem* (NHC VII, 1: 1,1–49,9; NH Library, 339–61; NH Scriptures, 437–71)

The *Paraphrase of Shem* is one of the longest tractates of the Nag Hammadi corpus. It is also one of the most difficult. In terms of content it is unique, for it bears no relationship at all to any other of the Nag Hammadi writings. The difficulties in the text are of several kinds: faulty translations from Greek into Coptic, corruption of the Coptic text in the process of its transmission, confusion caused by interpolations and additions to the text, and (dare we say it?) the incompetence of its author or final editor. Since the version we have in Nag Hammadi Codex VII is the only one in existence, we are obliged to deal with the text as it is.

The title, "The Paraphrase of Shem," occurs at the top of the first page, marked off by decoration. This is not a very good title, for in terms of its genre, the tractate as a whole is an apocalypse. A better title would be "The Apocalypse (Revelation) of Derdekeas to Shem."

The difficulties in the text begin already in the opening lines: "[The] paraphrase which was about the unbegotten Spirit. What Derdekeas revealed to me, Shem. . . ." What does "paraphrase" refer to? Who is Derdekeas? Who is Shem?

It is not at all clear who Shem is, for the name is invariably given in the text as *Sēem* (Coptic ϹΗΕΜ). Scholars have assumed that this is a variant spelling of Shem, son of Noah (usually rendered in Greek and Coptic as CHM). But then what of the statement given at the beginning by Derdekeas to Shem: "you are the first being upon the earth" (1,20–21)? Such a statement would imply that *Sēem* is some sort of primal Adam figure. Scholars usually get around this by taking that statement to refer to Shem, son of Noah, the most important patriarch after the Flood (compare Genesis 9:18).

The name Derdekeas is best understood as based etymologically on an Aramaic word, *drdq'*, which means "male child." It may not be irrelevant here to mention that "thrice-male child" is an epithet of Seth in the *Gospel of the Egyptians* (NHC III 62,2). It may be that Derdekeas is to be understood as a deliberately cryptic, esoteric name for the Gnostic revealer, Seth. We recall now that Hippolytus referred to a book used by people he called Sethians; the book was titled the *Paraphrase of Seth*. The paraphrase in that case is named for the revealer. The *Paraphrase of Shem* is named for the recipient of the revelation presumably given by the same revealer, Seth. What is especially interesting is that the three-principle system said by Hippolytus to be contained in the *Paraphrase of Seth* bears some striking resemblance to that of the *Paraphrase of Shem*. The extent of the parallels and the possible relationship between the two "paraphrases" remain to be discussed.

The Paraphrase of Shem *is one of the longest tractates of the Nag Hammadi corpus. It is also one of the most difficult. In terms of content it is unique, for it bears no relationship at all to any other of the Nag Hammadi writings.*

But first, we should try to determine what "paraphrase" means in the *Paraphrase of Shem*, and how it should be delineated. In addition to the two occurrences of the word already noted, there is a third in this tractate at 32,27: "This is the paraphrase." This sentence is usually taken to introduce material that follows. The paraphrase in question is interpreted as a commentary on a preceding section featuring various esoteric names (31,4–32,5). The supposed commentary is delineated as that portion of the text that contains interpretations of those names (32,28–34,16).

As we have already noted in the previous section of this chapter, the term *paraphrase,* applied to a written text, means rewriting. So the sentence, "this is the paraphrase," is better taken as the conclusion to the material that is introduced at the very beginning of the tractate, "[The] paraphrase which was about the unbegotten Spirit" (1,2–3). Thus, the paraphrase should be understood as a rewriting of a revelation given by Derdekeas to Shem, concluding with final exhortations given to Shem by Derdekeas (32,19–27). What follows after the paraphrase consists of material that has been added secondarily (from 32,28 to the end of the tractate at 49,9). A scribe has then applied the term paraphrase to the tractate as a whole, giving it the title we now have in the manuscript. Something similar might have happened in the case of the *Paraphrase of Seth* cited by Hippolytus.

The tractate as we now have it consists of several sections. After the title and introduction (1,1–6), Shem tells of how his thought left his body and went up to the pinnacle of creation, where he heard the voice of Derdekeas (1,6–17). What follows in the text is an extended revelation addressed to Shem by Derdekeas, with concluding exhortations (1,18–32,27). This revelation coincides with the paraphrase already delineated. Additional revelations are given to Shem, elaborating on the preceding material and concluding with a final exhortation (32,28–41,21). Shem then tells how he awoke from his ecstasy, marveled at what he had heard, and "walked in faith" (41,21–42,11).

There is an abrupt change of person at that point in the text, and we surmise that Derdekeas is speaking again to Shem: "Your faith is upon the earth the whole day" (42,11–12). Derdekeas expounds on the effects of faith (42,11–23), and then proceeds to prophesy what will happen in the future until the consummation (42,24–45,31). Shem goes into ecstasy again and recites an "immortal testimony," addressing it to the beings with esoteric names mentioned earlier in the text (31,4–32,5). After the recitation of the testimony (45,31–47,7) Shem recounts a visionary ascent through heavenly spheres (47,7–32).

The eschatological prophecy of Derdekeas then resumes very abruptly. Nature will be destroyed and the elect will be "in the ineffable light of the unbegotten Spirit without a form" (47,32–48,30). The text concludes with a parting encouraging word addressed by Derdekeas to Shem (48,30–49,9). There is no concluding word from Shem, as might have been expected in a text of this sort.

If this division of the tractate's content is correct, we can delineate four discourses that make up the revelation of Derdekeas in the tractate as a whole: the primary revelation of Derdekeas to Shem, coinciding with the paraphrase (1,18–32,27); a second discourse expanding on the earlier one (32,28–41,21); a third discourse consisting of prophecies of events leading up to the end of the world (42,11–45,31); and a fourth discourse dealing with the final consummation (47,32–49,9).

The major part of the first discourse deals with cosmogony and anthropogony (1,16–24,29), and it is precisely in this section of the text where parallels can be found to the "Sethian" system described by Hippolytus. At the very beginning of his revelation, Derdekeas refers to the three powers existing in the beginning: Light, Darkness, and "Spirit between them" (1,23–28). The intermediate Spirit is said to be the "root" of Shem and his "race," that is, the Gnostics. Bad things happen when these three powers come into contact. Darkness, consisting of "wind in waters" is attracted to the light coming from Spirit and tries to become equal to him. Derdekeas, the son of Light, comes to the aid of Spirit (2,6–4,12). Out of Darkness the water becomes a cloud, and from it a Womb takes shape. Darkness engages in sexual intercourse with the Womb, and the forms of Nature come into being, four "clouds" called Hymen, Afterbirth, Power, and Water (4,12–6,6). The light of Spirit is kept in bondage by Nature (6,6–35), and Derdekeas appears several times to save Spirit. He eventually induces Nature to create heaven and earth (6,35–20,21). The unchastity of Darkness and Nature then produce demonic beings of various sorts (20,21–24,29).

Following the cosmogony there is material alluding to the stories in Genesis of the Flood (Genesis 6:11—7:24), the Tower of

Babel (Genesis 11:1-9), and the destruction of Sodom and Gomorrah (Genesis 18:16—19:25). These stories are interpreted to refer to the demonic persecution of Shem and his race (Gnostics). The Sodomites are interpreted in the text as righteous people to whom Shem bears witness (24,29–29,33).

> *This revelation, needless to say, is full of obscurities, and I must admit that I am in no position to penetrate them.*

A demon named Soldas then arises and subjects the world to an evil baptism with water, and Derdekeas intervenes in behalf of Shem and his race (29,33–31,4). Derdekeas then gives Shem his "testimony" and provides him with esoteric magical names of beings who will help him "pass by this wicked region." Derdekeas will appear in the demon's baptism and counteract it with the "light of faith" and "unquenchable fire." Shem is then exhorted not to have dealings with the "dark body" and any "unclean work." The end of the revelation is marked with the concluding sentence, "This is the paraphrase" (31,4–32,27).

This revelation, needless to say, is full of obscurities, and I must admit that I am in no position to penetrate them. Derdekeas is clearly a savior figure, a son of Light, who descends several times to intervene in behalf of the Spirit and the race of Shem. But who is Soldas, the troublesome demon who introduces water baptism? (He reappears later at 39,31). It has been suggested that he is a Christ figure, but this is extremely unlikely. It is possible, though, that the figure of John the Baptist lurks behind this demon. The name Soldas itself may be a corrupt form of Esaldaios ('El Shaddai), the name for the Demiurge in the Naassene material already discussed.

The *Paraphrase of Shem* is clearly a Gnostic text, but it is curious that the term gnosis ("knowledge") never appears in it. Instead, the term "faith" is used instead, but in a sense equivalent to "knowledge." Might this have occurred under Christian influence? As we saw, the system treated by Hippolytus that was presumably based on a *Paraphrase of Seth,* with its three principles of Light, Darkness, and Spirit, is a Christian system, for it alludes to Christ as the

Logos born of a virgin. But in the material we have thus far treated in the *Paraphrase of Shem,* no explicit Christian features can be detected. The anti-baptismal stance may reflect a polemic against a form of Christianity known to the author or, perhaps, against a baptist sect related somehow to John the Baptist.

As to the possible relationships between the two paraphrases, *Seth* and *Shem,* no literary dependence either way can be posited. It is likely, however, that behind both of them there lay a common text from which each author drew.

The second part of Derdekeas's revelation begins with explanations of the roles of the various beings whose magical names were previously given (32,27–34,16). Derdekeas then assures Shem of the salvation of his race (34,16–36,1) and Derdekeas's own role in that salvation (36,2–24). Returning to the subject of baptism, Derdekeas speaks of people of "erring flesh" who subject themselves to baptism in "harmful waters." Such people are "deceived by many kinds of demons," for in the water of baptism there is only bondage (36,25–38,28). Derdekeas then tells Shem that when his work on earth is completed, he will ascend back to "the root of the Light." Nature will not succeed in snaring him with the aid of the demon Soldas (40,3). Derdekeas continues this part of the revelation with a statement on a woman named Rebouel. She is a woman "blessed among every race of men," but she will be beheaded. Of Rebouel it is said that she is "the support of the power of the demon who will baptize the seed of darkness" (40,4–31). Derdekeas concludes this part of the revelation with final exhortations to Shem, including a commission to speak to people on earth the things that he has learned (40,30–41,20).

This second part of Derdekeas's revelation picks up on themes previously enunciated, such as the "testimony" about the beings who aid in the soul's ascent, the harmful effects of baptism, and the role of the demon Soldas. What is new in this second discourse is the woman Rebouel and her beheading. It is clear that she is associated somehow with Soldas, but who is she? If, indeed, Soldas refers to John the Baptist, who was beheaded (Mark 6:27), could Rebouel be taken as an allegorical reference to John's prophesying, or to prophecy in general that came to an end with John? One Gnostic text actually says that "the head of prophecy was cut off with John" (NHC I,2: *Apocryphon of James* 6,30–31). Obviously, no certainty can be achieved on that point, and other interpretations of the role of Rebouel are possible.

The third part of Derdekeas's revelation begins abruptly at 42,11. Some scholars take this material as a continuation of a speech of Shem, for there is no break in the text indicating a change of speaker. Since the posited speech of Derdekeas begins, "*Your* [2nd person singular] faith..." it is reasonable to see this as referring back to Shem's faith mentioned previously (at 41,25). In the material that follows Derdekeas prophesies what will happen on earth up until the end, when all the forms of Nature will become "a dark lump" (42,11–45,31).

The fourth and final part of Derdekeas's revelation begins just as abruptly as the previous one, without any indication of a change of speaker. Derdekeas elaborates on the events of the end time leading up to the final salvation of the elect (47,32–48,30). The revelation, and the tractate as a whole, concludes with Derdekeas's parting word to Shem (48,30–49,9).

As already noted, the *Paraphrase of Shem* bears little or no resemblance to any of the other Gnostic writings of the Nag Hammadi corpus. We have noted parallels with the *Paraphrase of Seth* used by Hippolytus. Unlike the latter, however, the *Paraphrase of Shem* lacks any Christian features, though some knowledge of Christianity may (or may not!) be reflected in the text.

There are some interesting parallels in the tractate with some features of Manichaeism, such as the strong stance taken against water baptism. (On Manichaeism see chapter 11, below.) Most notable is the use of a technical term found in Manichaean eschatology, the "dark lump" (*bōlos*) into which all the evils of Nature are resolved. The parallels with Manichaean mythology in the tractate can perhaps be attributed to Manichaean influence. Alternatively, one can see in the tractate a kind of religiosity that can be dubbed "Manichaeism before Mani."

The aforementioned connections with Manichaeism point to a Mesopotamian provenance for the *Paraphrase of Shem*. A date early in the third century can be posited for its composition, but if it reflects Manichaean influence it would have to be dated later. It may have been brought to Upper Egypt in the third quarter of the third century, where it was then translated into Coptic.

8. Coptic Gnostic Writings of Uncertain Affiliation

The twelve disciples [were] all sitting together and recalling what the Savior had said to each one of them, whether in secret or openly, and putting it in books. [And I] was writing what was in my book.

THIS QUOTATION COMES FROM THE *Apocryphon of James* (NHC I,2: 2,7–16), a "secret book" attributed to James, brother of Jesus. James is writing to a person whose name is lost in a lacuna, and refers to a book that he has written in Hebrew and sent to him. He then refers to another "secret book" that he had sent "ten months ago." He then proceeds to recount what happened as he was writing his latest book: the Savior suddenly appeared to them.

The writing of books attributed to apostles and other worthy figures from the past is a typical feature of Christian and other forms of Gnosticism. Gnostic teachers also wrote in their own names as well. Much of the ancient Gnostic literature is lost, but the sands of Egypt have preserved numerous writings of works translated into Coptic.

We have in previous chapters treated Gnostic writings representative of the two most important forms of ancient Gnosticism, Sethian or Classic Gnosticism (ch. 3) and Valentinian Gnostic Christianity (ch. 6). But the sixteen codices constituting the "Coptic Gnostic Library" contain a number of other writings that do not easily fit into categories identifiable on the basis of the heresiological reports. These shall be treated in the present chapter.

The writing of books attributed to apostles and other worthy figures from the past is a typical feature of Christian and other forms of Gnosticism.

As we shall see, a number of these tractates reflect sources and influences from the Classic and Valentinian forms of Gnosticism. All but two of these are Christian writings. One of them (NHC VI,2: *Thunder: Perfect Mind*) is very difficult to classify, and the other one seems to be a product of early Jewish Gnosticism (NHC III,3; V,1: *Eugnostos the Blessed*). The latter has undergone a Christianizing expansion (NHC III,4; BG,3: *Sophia of Jesus Christ*) in which Jesus Christ assumes the role of Gnostic revealer. In what follows we shall treat these two together, and then the other ones in the order in which they appear in the Coptic manuscripts.

1. *Eugnostos the Blessed* (NHC III,3: 70,1– 90,12 and V,1: 7,23–9,9) and *Sophia of Jesus Christ* (NHC III,4: 90,1–119,18 and BG,3: 107,1– 111,1 and 118,13–122,9; *NH Library*, 220–43; *NH Scriptures*, 271–96)

Two versions of the tractate *Eugnostos the Blessed* exist, the third tractate of Nag Hammadi Codex III and the first tractate of Codex V. The two versions are quite different from one another, and probably

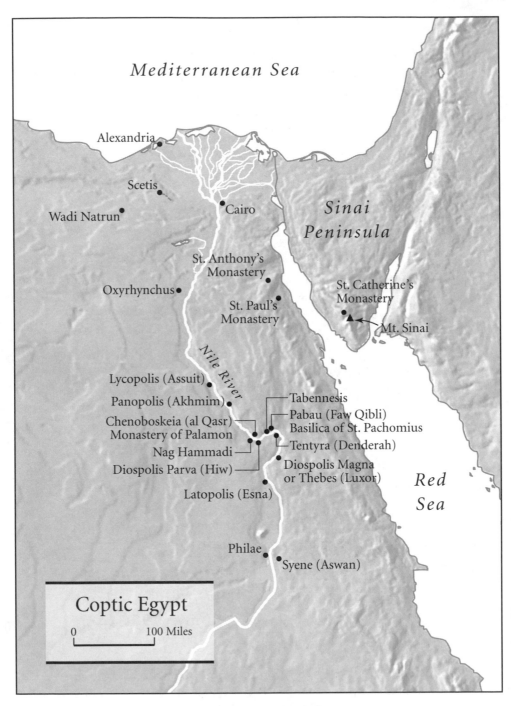

Fig. 8.1 Map of Coptic Egypt. © Lucidity Information Design.

represent independent Coptic translations of a Greek original. The version in Codex III is usually taken to be an earlier version than the one in Codex V. In *The Nag Hammadi Library in English* the version in Codex III is the one chosen for translation, with missing or damaged portions supplemented by the version in Codex V.

The title of the tractate appears in the opening line of the version in Codex III: "Eugnostos, the Blessed, writing to those who are his" (70:1–2). The title is also appended at the end of the version in Codex III. We do not know who Eugnostos was. Eugnostos is probably an assumed name, presumably intended to mean something like "well-knowing" (but the Greek adjective usually has a passive sense, "well-known"). We can compare the colophon at the end of the *Gospel of the Egyptians*. The scribe introduces himself with his spiritual name, Eugnostos, and adds that his "fleshly" name is Concessus (NHC III 69,10–12). As to the epithet "blessed," we can plausibly infer that this is a scribal addition, indicating that the revered author of the tractate is deceased.

In terms of literary genre, the tractate can be defined as a revelatory epistle or letter. The epistolary nature of the text is indicated in the opening salutation, but the tractate lacks an epistolary closing greeting. An interesting feature of its structure is that it adheres closely to rhetorical rules of composition current in antiquity from the time of Aristotle on. The content can easily be divided accordingly into the following components: (1) Introduction (*exordium*), (2) Exposition (*narratio*), (3) Confirmation (*probatio*), and (4) Conclusion (*peroratio*). The subject of the tractate is the true nature of the Divine, presented from a Gnostic perspective. A basic problem addressed is how one can envisage a divine plurality issuing from an original unity.

In the introduction the author states that philosophical attempts to attain the knowledge of God from the ordering of the universe are mistaken. Those who say that the universe is directed by itself, or by providence, or by fate, are all wrong, for in fact "He who Is" is ineffable and unknowable (III 70,1–71,18). A negative theology follows, wherein it is claimed that the transcendent Father is unbegotten, unnamable, unknowable, and so forth. Positively, it is asserted that he is "all mind, thought, reflecting, considering, rationality, and power" (71,18–74,12).

The first part of the Confirmation sets forth as a "principle of knowledge [*gnōsis*]" the distinction between the Lord of the Universe as "Forefather" and his "likeness" as "Self-Father" and "Self-Begetter." Also mentioned is "a multitude of the place over which there is no kingdom," called "children of the unbegotten Father." The latter are presumably the preexistent souls of the Gnostics (74,12–76,12).

Another principle of gnosis follows, with an elaborate discussion of the divine androgynous Man and the denizens of the Pleroma (76,12–90,4). The ineffable light of the Self-grown Father appears as Immortal Androgynous Man. His male name is "perfect Mind," and his female name is "All-wise begettress Sophia." From Immortal Man appear Divinity and Kingdom (76,12–78,2–3), and myriads of angelic beings. Clearly reflected here is an Alexandrian Jewish speculation on God, probably based on the vision of Ezekiel in which the prophet sees the glory of God depicted as a luminous being of human form (Ezekiel 1:26–28). He is the Man in whose image human beings were created, male and female (Genesis 1:27). The aeons, Divinity and Kingdom, are based on Alexandrian Jewish speculation on the principle names of God in the Bible, Elohim (God) and Yahweh (the LORD), two powers representing the creative power of God and the royal power of God respectively.

Additional aeonic beings are generated in the Pleroma, including a multitude of angelic beings called "Assembly [*ekklēsia*] of the Holy Ones," the "Son of Man," a heavenly projection of Adam, and an androgynous light called Savior, whose feminine name is Sophia. From each of twelve androgynous powers are revealed six others adding up to seventy-two, and five additional ones with the total adding up to 360. These beings are brought into relationship with time, the twelve months of the year, and the 360 days of the year. They are also associated with six heavens, seventy-two heavens, and 360 firmaments (78,3–85,9).

Reflected here is speculation on the Egyptian solar year, twelve months of thirty days each. Not included here are the five intercalary or epagomenal days that are part of the Egyptian calendar, resulting in a total of 365 days in the year. This part of the tractate concludes with the following curious statement: "And all these are perfect and good. And in this way the defect of femaleness appeared" (85,5–9). One would expect at this point a discussion of the fall of Sophia that led to the creation of the material world. A similar statement also appears in the same place in the discussion in the parallel passage in *Sophia of Jesus Christ* (BG 107,8–13). But in that tractate "the defect of the female" is mentioned again later (at BG 118,15) in material lacking a parallel in *Eugnostos*. In the latter passage the myth of the creation of the chaotic world by Yaldabaoth follows.

What follows in the second main part of the Confirmation in *Eugnostos* (85,9–90,4) begins with a summary restatement of the preceding material and continues with additional comments on the unfolding of the heavenly world. This section appears to contradict at points what had been stated earlier, and it has been suggested that it is based on a separate source. Named as the first aeon is that of Immortal Man. The second aeon is that of Son of Man, and the third that of "Son of Son of Man who is called Savior" (III 85,9–14, with the addition of V 13,12–13).

> *Assembly is androgynous, the male called* Assembly *and the female* Life, *"that it might be shown that from a female came the life in all the aeons" (85,21–87,9).*

The "Son of Man" can be identified as a heavenly projection of Adam, and the "Son of Son of Man" as a heavenly projection of Seth, son of Adam (Genesis 5:3). What embraces these is the "aeon over which there is no kingdom, the aeon of the Eternal Infinite God" including "the immortals who are in it." That aeon is situated "above the Eighth that appeared in chaos" (85,15–21). It would appear to mark the boundary of the Pleroma, outside of which is the chaotic world whose highest point is the Eighth, that is, the sphere of the fixed stars.

Additional aeons and powers issue from Immortal Man: Unity, Rest, and Assembly. Assembly is androgynous, the male called Assembly and the female Life, "that it might be shown that from a female came the life in all the aeons" (85,21–87,9). One curiosity here is that Assembly is said to be the male name, whereas *ekklēsia* in Greek is feminine. In the background, perhaps, is the Hebrew equivalent, *qahal,* which in Hebrew is masculine.

Additional divine beings are said to have been emanated "for the glory of Immortal Man and Sophia, his consort." These are the types whose likenesses are in "the heavens of chaos and their worlds." Within the Pleroma, "all natures from the Immortal One" reside in light and joy (87,9–90,4).

The author concludes his epistle with the observation that what he has said is enough, "until the one who need not be taught appears among you, and he will speak all these things to you joyously and in pure knowledge" (90,4–11). We are left in the dark as to who this is, but this is made clear by the author of the Christianized expansion, the *Sophia of Jesus Christ.*

Two versions of the *Sophia of Jesus Christ* exist, the fourth tractate of Nag Hammadi Codex III, immediately following *Eugnostos,* and the third tractate of the Berlin Gnostic Codex. The original Greek version is represented by three large fragments of one leaf from a papyrus codex datable to the early fourth century (P. Oxyrhynchus 1081). The two versions have only minor differences from one another, and therefore probably go back to a single Coptic translation. They are also closer to the version of *Eugnostos* in Codex III than the one in Codex V. There is some loss of material in Codex III. In *The Nag Hammadi Library in English,* the version in Codex III is the one chosen for translation, with missing or damaged portions supplemented by the version in the Berlin codex.

> *We are left in the dark as to who "the one who need not be taught" is, but this is made clear by the author of the Christianized expansion, the* Sophia of Jesus Christ.

The title in both versions occurs in the opening line and is also appended at the end. In terms of literary genre it is a revelation dialogue, with Jesus Christ as the revealer and his disciples the interlocutors. The setting is a high mountain in Galilee called "Divination and Joy," where the twelve disciples and seven women are gathered after Jesus's resurrection. They are perplexed about "the underlying reality of the universe and the plan." Suddenly the Savior appears to them resembling "a great angel of light" and greets them with the usual greeting, "Peace be to you." When he sees that the disciples are afraid, he laughs and asks why they are so perplexed and what they are searching for (III 90,1–91,24).

Sophia of Jesus Christ contains thirteen questions put by the disciples, interrupting the text of *Eugnostos*. Sometimes the disciples pose questions as a group, but usually individual disciples are the questioners. Disciples named as questioners are Philip, Matthew, Thomas, Mary (presumably Magdalene), and Bartholomew. Philip speaks first, telling the Savior that they are searching "for the underlying reality of the universe and the plan." The Savior then responds, beginning with the opening passage of *Eugnostos* (92,6).

There are some omissions in the text of material taken from *Eugnostos*. What is more important are the additions found in *Sophia of Jesus Christ*. The first major addition has to do with "all who come into the world." They are like "a drop from the Light," held in bondage by the Demiurge and his robbers. The Savior says that he has awakened them and given them access to the Father (106,24–108,16). The second major addition comes at the end of *Eugnostos*, just before its peroration. That addition contains the myth of the fall of Sophia, the "Mother of the Universe," who wanted to produce offspring without her consort. The result of this "defect of the female" is the "Archbegetter, who is called Yaldabaoth," and the world of chaos below (114,14–25 plus BG 118,14–121,13). This passage clearly reflects the influence of Sethian or Classic Gnostic mythology.

The tractate concludes with final assurances given by the Savior to the disciples of their salvation, based on pure knowledge of the Father, "the God who is above the universe." As children of the Light they have the power to tread under their feet "the Archbegetter" and his angels (BG 121,14–122,9 plus III 117,1–119,8). The Savior then disappears from the disciples, and they go out to preach the "Gospel of God" (119,8–17).

The original Greek version of *Eugnostos the Blessed* has been dated as early as the first century BCE. That is probably too early; a date sometime in the second half of the first century CE is more likely. It shows no obvious Christian influences. The use of Alexandrian Jewish traditions is evident throughout, and it can be regarded as a product of a variety of Jewish Gnosticism that existed in first-century Alexandria. Nothing is known of its author.

The *Sophia of Jesus Christ* can also be assigned to Alexandria and dated to sometime in the second century. Nothing is known of its author.

2. *Apocryphon of James* (NHC I,2: 1,1–16,30; NH Library, 29–37; NH Scriptures, 19–30)

Since no title is given for this tractate in the manuscript, scholars have assigned titles to it on the basis of its content. Since the opening lines have James writing a letter, the tractate's first editors referred to it as "the Apocryphal Epistle of James." But since its main part consists of a revelation contained within a "secret book" (*apokryphon* in Greek, a term used at 1,10 and 1.30–31), the tractate as a whole is now more usually referred to as the *Apocryphon,* or *Secret Book, of James*. The letter enclosing the secret book consists of the opening and closing passages of the tractate (1,1–2,7; 16,12–30).

The name of the recipient of the letter is unfortunately lost. Three letters remain of his name: -ΘΟC (*-thos*). The name of a known second-century heretic active in Asia Minor, Cerinthus (Kerinthos, see chapter 2, above), has been proposed as a possibility, but this is unlikely. So we remain in the dark as to the name of the person purportedly addressed in the letter. The (pseudonymous) writer of the letter is James. Presumably the brother of Jesus is meant (James "the Just," early leader of the Jerusalem church). But he seems to be confused in the text with one of the twelve disciples named James (2,8.15).

At the beginning of the letter James says he has sent a secret book, revealed to him and Peter by the Lord, composed in Hebrew.

He adds that he had earlier sent another secret book revealed to him alone. The content of the first named book, revealed to James and Peter, is then given in what follows.

In terms of its genre, the apocryphon proper is a revelation dialogue, in which Jesus's revelation is punctuated with questions and comments by his disciples, in this case Peter and James. It is introduced with an account of an appearance of the Savior to the disciples "five hundred and fifty days since he had risen from the dead" (2,19–21). Jesus announces that he is going to the place whence he came, and singles out James and Peter for special instructions. The rest of the disciples are left to their own devices (2,23–39).

Jesus's teaching in the *Apocryphon of James* consists of exhortations, parables, beatitudes, pronouncements of woes, and admonitions, all designed to "fill" James and Peter so that they might follow him to heaven. One interesting section is devoted to voluntary martyrdom. Jesus calls upon them to prepare for martyrdom, referring in that context to his own cross (4,22–6,21). Other themes addressed include a rejection of prophecy, whose head was cut off with John (the Baptist, 6,30–31), and the necessity of tending to the Kingdom within, illustrated with parables involving a palm shoot (7,22–35), a grain of wheat (8,20–27), and an ear of grain (13,22–24). The disciples are to be earnest about the word and the kingdom of heaven, which no one can receive unless it is received through knowledge (*gnōsis*, 8,23–27). The Savior assures the disciples that he is telling them all these things "that you may know yourselves" (13:20–22).

Some of the sayings and pronouncements of Jesus in the *Apocryphon of John* are thought to be based on early oral tradition independent of the gospels of the New Testament. That may be so, to some extent, but it is clear that written gospels are also known to the author. For one thing, the disciples are depicted as writing down things they have learned. And specific parables from the gospels are mentioned such as " 'The Shepherds,' and 'The Seed' and 'The Building' and 'the Lamps of the Virgins' and 'the Wage of the Workmen' and 'The Didrachma' and 'The Woman' " (8,6–10: compare John 10:1-15; Matthew 13:24-30; Matthew 7:24-27;

Matthew 25:1-13; Matthew 20:1-16; Matthew 17:24-27; and Luke 15:8-10).

The Savior concludes his admonitions with an assurance of salvation (13,25–14,19), and tells them that he is about to ascend into heaven in a spiritual chariot (14,19–15,5). Jesus then departs, and the two disciples "send (their) hearts upward to heaven." They hear the sound of trumpets and angelic hymns until they are not able any longer to see or hear anything (15,5–28). The other disciples ask them what the Savior had said, and

> *We should remember that not everything written by a Gnostic teacher has to include the complete Gnostic myth.*

they report that he had promised life to them all and revealed to them children who are to come after them. The other disciples are displeased when they hear about those yet to be born. James then sends each one "to another place" and he himself goes up to Jerusalem (15,28–16,11). James then concludes his letter with a final exhortation to the recipient (16,12–30).

The *Apocryphon of James* lacks such typically Gnostic features as the myth of Sophia and the Demiurge. For that reason some scholars have argued that the tractate is not Gnostic at all. Nevertheless, it does emphasize gnosis as the basis for salvation. As for the absence of Sophia and the Demiurge, we should remember that not everything written by a Gnostic teacher has to include the complete Gnostic myth.

Since all of the other tractates in Codex I are representatives of the Valentinian tradition, some scholars have argued that the *Apocryphon of James,* too, is a product of Valentinian Gnostic Christianity. That is a dubious argument, but it is possible to find in it some traces of Valentinian influence. For example, a distinction is made between those "who stand in need of grace" and those who have grace as their own possession (11,13–17). This may reflect the western Valentinian distinction between psychical Christians who receive grace for their use but can also lose it, and spiritual Christians who have grace as their own special possession (Irenaeus, *Against Heresies* 1.6.4).

Another example may be found in the Savior's statement to James, "I have commanded you to follow me, and I have taught you what to say before the archons" (8,33–37). This may reflect influence from the passage in the *(First) Apocalypse of James* (NHC V,3: 32,28–35,25) in which Jesus tells James what to say upon his ascent past the "toll collectors." As we have already noted, that passage reflects formulae from the Valentinian ritual for the dying (Irenaeus, *Against Heresies* 1.21.5, discussed above in chapter 6).

As to the question of the date of the original Greek version of the *Apocryphon of James,* there is a considerable difference of opinion among scholars. Those who argue that the sayings of Jesus in it reflect oral tradition independent of the New Testament gospels tend to date it as early as the first century. Given what has already been said, a date sometime in the second half of the second century is more likely. An Alexandrian provenance is likely, but western Syria is also a possibility.

3. *On the Origin of the World*
(NHC II,5: 97,24–127,17; *NH Library,* 170–89; *NH Scriptures,* 199–221)

The treatise *On the Origin of the World* is completely extant in Nag Hammadi Codex II. It is also represented by a small fragment in Codex XIII and twenty-seven small fragments of another Coptic version now in the British Library (Ms. Or. 4926[1]). The tractate lacks a title in the manuscript, probably owing to a mistake made by the scribe. All six of the other tractates in Codex II have subscript titles. The title of the sixth tractate, the *Exegesis on the Soul,* is given twice, the first time at the place in the manuscript where the title of the fifth tractate should have been. The title of that tractate now in use reflects its theme as reflected in the opening passage.

In broad outline, the tractate as we now have it is organized according to ancient rhetorical conventions, consisting of a prologue (*exordium,* 97,24–98,11), an exposition (*narratio,* 98,11–123,2), a confirmation (*probatio*, 123,2–31), and an extended epilogue (*per-oratio*, 123,31–127,17). In terms of literary genre, however, it is hard to categorize, for it is essentially a compendium of Gnostic ideas taken from a variety of Gnostic sources, and from Jewish apocrypha, Jewish traditions of biblical exegesis, Christian ideas, Greek philosophical concepts, aspects of Greek mythology, magic and astrology, and Egyptian lore. Much of its mythology is based on early Sethian Gnostic literature. Especially notable is the material it shares in common with the *Hypostasis of the Archons* (NHC II,4). It also reflects the influence of Valentinian Gnosticism and Manichaeism. The way the tractate is put together, with apparent glosses and excursuses, leads us to believe that it has grown over time. An earlier work has been expanded with new additions to the text, possibly in several stages.

The tractate's main themes have to do with protology and eschatology. In the prologue, the author states that those who say that nothing existed prior to chaos are wrong, and he says that he will present the truth, that is, that chaos is really a shadow of what existed earlier (97,24–98,11).

The main part of the tractate, the exposition (98,11–123,2), deals mainly with protology, containing an elaborate theogony (98,11–108,2) and an anthropogony that also includes a narrative of the adventures of Adam and Eve in paradise and after their expulsion (108,2–121,35). What is striking, however, is that there is no discussion at all of the primal Father and the various aeons constituting the Pleroma, the heavenly world. Instead, it is said that Pistis Sophia ("Faith Wisdom") exercised her volition and "her will manifested itself as a likeness of heaven." She herself "functioned as a veil dividing humankind from the things above" (98,11–23).

> What is striking, however, is that there is no discussion at all of the primal Father and the various aeons constituting the Pleroma, the heavenly world.

The lack of a discussion of the unfolding of the Pleroma has inspired scholars to look for it elsewhere, in another tractate. That search leads us to a tractate we discussed earlier, *Eugnostos the*

Blessed. As we saw, *Eugnostos* deals exclusively with the primal Father and the aeons emanating from him. Indeed, in comparing the two tractates, it becomes evident that *On the Origin of the World* picks up precisely where *Eugnostos* breaks off. Some similarity of vocabulary between the two tractates, too, leads us to the conclusion that an early version of *On the Origin of the World* was written as a sequel to, or a second volume of, *Eugnostos.*

The unfolding of the lower world of chaos begins with the principle of Jealousy, which came into being in the waters of chaos. From Pistis Sophia comes the creator and ruler of the world of chaos, Yaldabaoth, also called Samael and Ariael. He produces additional archons and the heavens in which they reside. At the consolidation of heaven and earth, with the aid of "Sophia the daughter of Yaldabaoth," he makes his boastful claim, "I am God, and there is no other one that exists apart from me." He is then rebuked by Pistis, who informs him that before him there exists "an immortal man of light" (99,2–103,32). Much of this is familiar from the Sethian mythology we have already studied (in chapter 3), but considerably enlarged with additional material.

Following upon the rebuke of Yaldabaoth, one of his sons, Sabaoth, condemns his father and is exalted to the seventh heaven and there enthroned upon a four-faced chariot, surrounded by heavenly beings who offer him praise. Sophia Zoe, daughter of Pistis, joins him and instructs him about the things in the eighth heaven (103,32–106,19). The enthronement of Sabaoth is also featured in the *Hypostasis of the Archons* (discussed in chapter 3), and one can posit a common source used by the authors of both tractates.

The material on the exaltation of Sabaoth is followed by a section in which other mythological details appear: the engendering of Death and various androgynous beings brought forth by him, the creation by Zoe of seven good androgynous forces, and a resumption of the story of Yaldabaoth's vain claim (106,19–108,2).

The anthropogony that follows begins with Light shining from above with a human likeness in it, called "Adam of Light." He is also referred to as an emissary (probably under Manichaean influence). The archons fashion a body after that image, and Eve-Zoe sends her breath into Adam to enliven him. The story is complicated with the addition of other beings here and there, including Eros; Justice, the creator of Paradise; the tree of gnosis; Psychē ("Soul"), the lover of Eros; an androgynous being called Hermaphroditēs; Eve of Life, whose offspring is "Beast" (the serpent in Paradise); and the "first virgin" Eve, whom the archons try unsuccessfully to rape. This lengthy section concludes with a summary statement about three Adams. The first one (Adam of Light) is spiritual (*pneumatikos*), and appeared on the first day. The second Adam is psychical or "soul-endowed" (*psuchikos*) and appeared on the sixth day. The third Adam is "earthy" (*choikos*), and he appeared on the eighth day (108,2–118,2). These three Adams reflect Gnostic interpretation of the stories of the creation of Adam in Genesis 1:27 and 2:6. The terminology employed also reflects Valentinian influence.

A Gnostic paraphrase of the Paradise story (Genesis 2:8— 3:24) and its aftermath then follows. The seven archons command earthly Adam and Eve not to eat of the tree of gnosis. The "Beast," the "Instructor," wisest of all creatures (Genesis 3:1), gets Adam and Eve to eat from the forbidden tree; so the archons curse them and expel them from Paradise. Adam's original life span of a thousand years is reduced to nine hundred thirty (Genesis 5:5), and that of his posterity to seventy (compare Psalm 90:10). The archons are thrown down to earth where they dwell as evil spirits (118,6– 121,35). Appended to this is a passage reflecting Egyptian lore: the phoenix bird, Egyptian water pots, and two Egyptian bulls interpreted allegorically with reference to three kinds of baptism (122,1–123,2).

The confirmation section (123,2–31) summarizes the effects of the archons on the world, with all people in ignorance "until the appearance of the true man." The epilogue then begins with a discussion of the "angel of knowledge," who is the Savior and the Word (Logos). His coming reveals the four kinds of races: three that belong to the kings of the eighth heaven, and the fourth that is "kingless and perfect" (123,31–125,32). The three kinds of humans previously delineated (probably under Valentinian influence) as spiritual, psychical, and earthy (material) are now superseded by a fourth, a "generation without a king" (compare *Eugnostos* V 5,4–5; III 99,17–19).

The rest of the epilogue is devoted to eschatology. The evil archons and this world of chaos will be destroyed. "The light will withdraw up to its root," together with the kingless elect. "For everyone must go to the place from which he has come. Indeed, by his acts and his knowledge (gnosis) each person will make his nature known" (125,32–127,17).

It is clear that the anonymous author (or final editor) of *On the Origin of the World* was a very learned person, steeped in lore of all kinds. He also does not hesitate to provide documentation for his teachings. He gives us the titles of a number of books that he has consulted, or to which he refers the reader for additional details (all of them unknown to us): "The Archangelic Book of the Prophet Moses" (102,8–9), "The First Book of Noraia" (102,10–11), "The First Account of Oraia" (102,24–25, probably the same as the previous one), "The Book of Solomon" (107,3), "The Configurations of the Fate of Heaven that is Beneath the Twelve" (107,16–17), "The Sacred Book" (110,30; 122,12), and "The Seventh Universe of the Prophet Hieralis" (112,23–24).

On the Origin of the World, as we now have it, is a highly developed tractate that can hardly be dated to a time before the end of the third century. As already noted, however, it may very well be based on an earlier writing, datable to sometime in the second century. It was certainly composed somewhere in Egypt, probably Alexandria.

4. The *Exegesis (Expository Treatise) on the Soul* (NHC II,6: 127,18–137,27; *NH Library,* 190–98; *NH Scriptures,* 223–34)

The *Exegesis on the Soul* is an anonymous treatise meant to lead its readers to a life of chaste otherworldliness. Its main theme is the nature and destiny of the human soul, her descent into a depraved world and the possibility of her repentance and ascent back to heaven. The title is given both at the beginning and at the end of the tractate. The Greek term *exēgēsis,* used in the title, means both "narrative" and "interpretation," and the tractate contains both features. It contains a narrative of the soul's descent and final redemption, and interprets authoritative texts in light of the myth of the soul. The narrative and hortatory elements are illustrated with extensive quotations from the Bible, both Old and New Testaments, and from Homer.

The opening passage credits "wise men of old" with giving the soul a feminine name (*psuchē* in Greek is a feminine noun). She is "female in her nature as well," and is equipped with a womb (127,19–22).

The narrative consists of two parts. The first part tells us of the soul living alone as an androgynous virgin with her father. But then she falls down into a body and enters a life of prostitution. Finally she "weeps before the father and repents." The father mercifully makes her womb turn inward "from the external domain." When this happens she is baptized and cleansed of her pollution, and she is able to regain her former nature "and turn herself back again" (127,22–132,1).

The details of the first part of the narrative are illustrated with extensive quotations from the prophets Jeremiah, Hosea, and Ezekiel, and from First Corinthians and Ephesians in the Pauline corpus.

The second part of the narrative begins with the soul crying out "like a woman in labor." Since she is female, she cannot beget a child by herself. So the father sends her brother to her, to serve as her bridegroom. They enter the bridal chamber and have spiritual intercourse. She gets from him "the seed that is the life-giving spirit," and brings forth spiritual children. The soul regenerates herself and receives the divine nature from her father so that she can ascend back to the place from where she came. This is a gift of grace, bestowed upon her by her savior (132,1–135,4).

The details of the second narrative are illustrated with quotations from Genesis and Psalms, and it concludes with a quotation from John 6:44.

The last part of the tractate (135,4–137,22) consists of exhortations to repentance, not only with the lips but with one's whole soul. The proper actions of repentance are illustrated with quotations from Matthew, Luke, and Acts in the New Testament, from a Jewish apocryphal writing attributed to Ezekiel, from Isaiah and Psalms in the Old Testament, and from books 1 and 4 of Homer's *Odyssey*. The passages from Homer feature Odysseus longing to return to his village, and Helen longing to return to her husband after being deceived by Aphrodite. The passage from Psalm

The basic narrative in the tractate is based on the myth of the soul's descent and ascent current in Middle Platonism. It also shows influences from Greek romances of the early Roman period, and from Jewish apocryphal works in which women play leading roles.

6 quoted last is applied to Israel calling out to God to be delivered from its oppression in Egypt.

The tractate concludes with the following promise: "If we repent, truly God will heed us, he who is long-suffering and abundantly merciful, to whom is the glory for ever and ever. Amen" (137,22–26).

The basic narrative in the tractate is based on the myth of the soul's descent and ascent current in Middle Platonism. It also shows influences from Greek romances of the early Roman period, and from Jewish apocryphal works in which women play leading roles. Since the New Testament is quoted in it, the tractate can be considered a Christian work. Nevertheless, the Christian features are otherwise not prominent. The quotations from the Bible and Homer may derive from florilegia (collections of quotations), such as were commonly used in school settings.

Since the tractate lacks any clear references to the Gnostic Demiurge, some scholars have argued that it is not a Gnostic work. On the other hand, the adventures of the soul in the tractate probably reflect influences from the Gnostic myth of Sophia. And the references to Helen, with the quotations from Homer, may reflect influence from Simonian Gnosticism. The bridal chamber motif may also reflect Valentinian influence.

The *Exegesis on the Soul* was probably composed in Alexandria, Egypt, sometime in the late second century.

5. Apocalypse (Revelation) of Paul
(NHC V,2: 17,19–24,9; NH Library, 256–59; NH Scriptures, 313–19)

The Apostle Paul, writing to his church in Corinth, tells of a visionary experience that he had had some years earlier, involving an ascent up to Paradise in the "third heaven" (2 Corinthians 12:1–4). Sometime in the fourth century an imaginative Christian wrote an extended account of what Paul had seen in the third heaven. That writing has come down to us with the title the *Apocalypse of Paul,* and is regularly included in collections of New Testament apocryphal writings. The *Apocalypse of Paul* preserved in Coptic in Nag Hammadi Codex V is not that apocalypse, though it bears the same title.

The *Apocalypse of Paul* treated here is known only in the Coptic version that is part of the Nag Hammadi corpus. In this writing, Paul travels all the way up to the tenth heaven. The title is given at the beginning of the tractate and at the end as well. There is some loss of material owing to damage to the manuscript.

Valentinians are reported to have given their own interpretation of Paul's account in 2 Corinthians 12 (Irenaeus, Against Heresies 2.30.7).

The tractate begins with an appearance of the Holy Spirit to Paul in the form of a small child. Paul is on the mountain of Jericho on his way to Jerusalem, and the Holy Spirit engages him in conversation and promises to reveal to him hidden things. Paul is also told that he will meet the twelve apostles, and Paul then sees them greeting him (17,20–19,20). The twelve apostles reappear at various stages of Paul's journey.

The Holy Spirit then snatches Paul up to the third heaven and beyond to the fourth. There he sees angels whipping a soul that is accused of "lawless deeds." The soul is then sent down into

Fig. 8.2 Four Apostles (Bartholomew, Philip, Andrew, Peter). Gnostic
writings often appeared under the
name of the same apostles vener-
ated by the orthodox church. Coptic
fresco, 6th century, from Bawit,
Egypt. Coptic Museum, Cairo. Photo:
Borromeo / Art Resource, N.Y.

another body (19,20–21,22).
The Holy Spirit then brings
Paul to the fifth heaven where
punishing angels are whipping souls and goading them
to judgment (21,22–22,10).
Paul then proceeds to the sixth
heaven. There a toll collector lets Paul into the seventh heaven,
where he sees an old man seated on a brightly shining throne. The
old man grills Paul, asking him where he is going and threaten-
ing to detain him. Paul says that he is going to the place from
where he came, and gives him a certain sign, whereupon the old
man turns his face downward to his creation and his authorities
(22,11–23,28). The old man in the seventh heaven is, of course, the
Gnostic Demiurge.

The tractate ends with a brief account of the rest of Paul's journey. He ascends to the eighth heaven, where he is greeted by the
twelve apostles. They proceed up to the ninth heaven and then the
tenth, where Paul greets his fellow spirits (23,29–24,8).

Nothing is known of the tractate's author, or where he composed his apocalypse. It has been suggested that the author was
a Valentinian Gnostic because Valentinians are reported to have
given their own interpretation of Paul's account in 2 Corinthians
12 (Irenaeus, *Against Heresies* 2.30.7). But there is nothing specifically Valentinian in the tractate's content. As to its date, sometime
in the late second century is plausible, though it could also have
been written sometime later.

6. (First) Apocalypse (Revelation) of James (NHC V,3: 24,10–44,10; NH Library, 260–68; NH Scriptures, 321–30)

The third tractate of Nag Hammadi Codex V has the title "The Apocalypse of James" at its beginning and at the end. The fourth tractate has the same title at its beginning. Scholars now regularly distinguish the two with the addition, in parentheses, of the adjectives *first* and *second*. Unfortunately the *(First) Apocalypse of James* is lacking a considerable amount of material, owing to damage to the manuscript. Another Coptic version of the same tractate is found in another fourth-century codex, Codex Tchacos, tractate 2, but that codex has not yet been published. (It is also reported to have suffered considerable damage, with up to a third of it illegible.)

The *(First) Apocalypse of James* contains revelations given by Jesus to his brother James (Jacob, Hebrew *Ya'aqob*). A dominant theme in it is the necessity of suffering and the promise of the soul's ascent after death. The revelations are given in two parts, the first one two days before Jesus's crucifixion (24,11–30,11; compare 25,7–8). The second revelation is given after Jesus's resurrection (31,2–42,19). The first one begins abruptly, without a setting. The second one is set on a mountain called "Gaugelan" (Golgotha? 30,20–21). James has heard of Jesus's sufferings and is waiting to see him again. Jesus appears to him after several days, and James embraces him (30,13–31,14). There is a narrative conclusion at the end of the tractate (42,20–44,8), but damage to the manuscript has made it largely illegible.

The first revelation is in the form of a revelation dialogue, with seven questions or statements put to Jesus by James. Jesus tells James that he (Jesus) is the "image of Him who Is" (compare Exodus 3:14) and that he will be seized "the day after tomorrow." James, too, will be ceased by the powers, but will be able to cast away "this bond of flesh." The powers are not really armed against James, but against Jesus (24,10–28,4).

The fifth speech by James includes a beautiful poetic passage in which James praises Jesus for coming with knowledge to people in ignorance (28,5–29,3). The Lord then promises to reveal to James his redemption (29,3–12). When James asks Jesus if he will reappear after completing his destiny, Jesus assures him that he will. He bids James farewell and "fulfilled what was fitting" (29,3–30,13).

When Jesus appears to James after the resurrection, James complains that this people should be judged for what they have done to Jesus (30,13–31,14). In the interchange that follows the Lord tells James not to be concerned about that. The Lord praises James as God's servant, rightly called "James the Just." The Lord then warns James that he, too, will undergo suffering (31,14–32,28). Jesus says that he will reveal to James his redemption, and then begins an extensive revelation discourse (32,28–38,11).

> *The Savior predicts the destruction of Jerusalem, and commands James to reveal the secrets he has learned to Addai, who is to write them down "in the tenth year" (36,15–23).*

Jesus's discourse contains instructions to James on what to say to the toll collectors as James's soul is about to ascend to heaven. One of the toll collectors will interrogate James as to who he is and where he is from. James is to tell them that he is a son of the Pre-existent Father. He is to distinguish himself from those who belong to Achamoth, who "brought this race down from the Pre-existent one." He is to appeal to knowledge, that is, Sophia, "who is the mother of Achamoth." Then the toll collectors will fall into confusion, and James will be able to go up to his own place. The Savior predicts the destruction of Jerusalem, and commands James to reveal the secrets he has learned to Addai, who is to write them down "in the tenth year" (36,15–23). Much of the remaining discourse is lost, owing to damage to the manuscript.

The dialogue resumes at 38,12, with James inquiring of Jesus as to the identity of seven women who have been his disciples (38,16–17). The answer is lost in a lacuna, but later four women are named: Salome, Mariam, Martha, and Arsinoe (40,25–26). The names of the others are lost in another lacuna, and much of the remaining dialogue is lost as well (40,27–42,19).

The narrative conclusion begins at 42,20, with James going to rebuke "the twelve, and cast [out] of them contentment [concerning the] way of knowledge" (42,20–24). It is probable that a brief mention was made of James's martyrdom, but there is too much lost to be certain of that.

The *(First) Apocalypse of James* was written for a circle of Christian Gnostics who revered the memory of James, brother of Jesus. James was the head of the Jerusalem church until his martyrdom in A.D. 62, and he is portrayed in the text as superior to the twelve disciples. Valentinian Gnostic influence is evident in the lengthy discourse that Jesus gives to James concerning his redemption. The instructions James receives as to what to say in his ascent reflect the influence of a redemption ritual for the dying practiced by some Valentinians (Irenaeus, *Against Heresies* 1.21.5, discussed in chapter 6). The (western) Valentinian distinction between the upper Sophia and the lower Sophia, Achamoth, is reflected in that ritual and in Jesus's revelation in the *(First) Apocalypse of James*.

The mention of Addai in the text (36,15.22) clearly situates it in a Mesopotamian milieu, for early Syrian Christian tradition credits Addai with involvement in the founding of the church of Edessa in Mesopotamia. Since the text also reflects Valentinian influence, one can date it to a time after the introduction of Valentinian Gnostic Christianity into eastern areas of the church, toward the end of the second century.

7. (Second) Apocalypse (Revelation) of James (NHC V,4: 44,11–63,32; NH Library, 269–78; NH Scriptures, 331–42)

Whereas the *(First) Apocalypse of James* is set in the period prior to the martyrdom of James, the *(Second) Apocalypse of James* describes James's martyrdom and what led up to it. So the scribe of Codex V clearly regarded the two tractates as belonging together.

However, there is a strong probability that the second part of the tractate, the report of the stoning of James (61,1–63,32–end), was an independent account secondarily appended to the discourses of James in the first part of the tractate. There are also insurmountable problems in the text as we have it, for large parts of it are missing, owing to damage to the manuscript.

The title, "The Apocalypse of James," is given in the first two lines of the tractate. But the text itself begins, "This is [the] discourse that James [the] Just spoke in Jerusalem, [which] Mareim wrote down. One of the priests had told it to Theuda, the father of the Just One, since he was a relative of his" (44,13–20). It is strange that Theuda, otherwise unknown, and not Joseph, is identified as the "just one's" father. Equally unknown is the identity of Mareim, the supposed scribe.

The title *apocalypse* is a rather loose designation for the tractate, in terms of literary genre, for the first part of the tractate features a series of discourses. Some of these discourses contain revelations given by James or by Jesus, so the title is not completely off the mark. In any case, the title would apply only to the discourses contained in the first part of the tractate (46,1?–60,26f.) and not at all to the martyrdom with which the tractate concludes.

The setting of James's discourses has him sitting "above the fifth flight of steps, [which] is highly esteemed" (45,23–25). What is meant here, no doubt, is a location in the Jerusalem Temple. Unfortunately, the rest of the setting is lost in lacunae.

The discourses begin somewhere at the top of page forty-six. James is speaking, and he claims to have received "revelation from the Pleroma [of] Imperishability," and to be "rich in knowledge." Unfortunately much of the discourse is lost in lacunae.

It is possible to distinguish five other discourses in the tractate. The second one begins somewhere at the top of page forty-eight. James is reporting a revelatory message given to him by Jesus. It contains a series of "I am" statements in which Jesus identifies himself as the "righteous one," "son of the Father," and so forth. In the third discourse, beginning somewhere at the top of page fifty, James gives an account of an appearance of Jesus earlier in his life. In the fourth discourse, beginning somewhere at the top of page fifty-one, James quotes a discourse given to him by Jesus in which Jesus promises him additional revelations and commissions James to be "an illuminator and a redeemer of those who are mine, and now of those who are yours" (55,17–20). Jesus invites James to stretch out his hands and take hold of him. In a brief fifth discourse (57,12–19) James reports Jesus's disappearance, and his own joy at his new understanding.

> *The Lord has taken them captive and closed their ears to his word. Their house, which they say is God's, will be destroyed.*

The last discourse (57,20–60,26f.) is addressed to James's judges. James tells them that they are ignorant of the transcendent Father, as is the god "who created the heaven and the earth" (the Demiurge). The Lord has taken them captive and closed their ears to his word. Their house, which they say is God's, will be destroyed. Thus, the final discourse of James, now addressed to his judges, ends with a prediction of the destruction of the Temple.

The martyrdom, which was probably taken from a preexistent narrative, reports how James was thrown from the pinnacle of the Temple and stoned. Before his death James offers an extensive prayer to God the Father.

> *The martyrdom story, which lacks any Gnostic features, resembles the account of James's martyrdom given by a second-century Christian writer, Hegesippus (excerpted in Eusebius's Ecclesiastical History 2.23).*

The martyrdom story, which lacks any Gnostic features, resembles the account of James's martyrdom given by a second-century Christian writer, Hegesippus (excerpted in Eusebius's *Ecclesiastical History* 2.23). It also follows traditional Jewish regulations governing capital punishment as described in the rabbinic Mishnah (in tractate *Sanhedrin* 6.6). The first part of the *(Second) Apocalypse of James* containing the discourses is clearly a Gnostic work. The original Greek version of the tractate as we now have it was probably written in Syria sometime in the late second century.

8. *Thunder: Perfect Mind* (NHC VI,2: 13,1–21,32; *NH Library*, 295–303; Layton, 77–85; *NH Scriptures*, 367–78)

Not least among the riddles found in this tractate is its title, which occurs at the beginning. Actually, it is two titles, for "The Thunder" is separated from "Perfect Mind" in the Coptic by a punctuation mark. The tractate itself consists of alternating exhortations and "identity riddles" in the form of poetic "I am" statements, attributed to an unnamed feminine revealer figure. The "I am" statements can be called "riddles" because they are self-contradictory (for example, "I am the whore and the holy one; I am the wife and the virgin," 13,18–20). As to the title, "Perfect Mind" can be accounted for on the basis of one of the speaker's pronouncements, "I am the mind of [. . .]," or "I am the [. . .] mind" (18,9). One can conjecturally restore the lacuna to read "perfect": "I am the [perfect] mind." The word "thunder" does not occur in the tractate itself, but one can take "thunder" in the title as an attribute of the speaker's voice, analogous to the thunderous voice of God in the Bible (for example, Job 37:2–5).

The tractate is reasonably well-preserved, with only a few lacunae in the text resulting from damage to the manuscript. It begins with the speaker proclaiming her origin: "I was sent forth from [the] Power, and I have come to those who reflect upon me." She exhorts her hearers to accept her and not to be ignorant of her (13,2–14). In the first set of "I am" pronouncements (13,15–14,15), she identifies herself as "first" and "last," "honored one" and "scorned one," "whore" and "holy one," "wife" and "virgin," "mother" and "daughter," "barren one" with "many sons," and other opposites of a similar sort.

Two of her pronouncements in this section provide clues as to the speaker's identity. The first one, "It is my husband who begot me" (13,29–30), fits the figure of Eve in the Bible, born from her husband's rib (Genesis 2:21–23). The second one suggests a heavenly projection of Eve: "I am the silence that is incomprehensible and the reflection (*epinoia*) whose remembrance is frequent" (14,9–11). Silence and Epinoia are designations for Barbelo and Sophia in Gnostic mythology, and both should be understood as heavenly projections of Eve. Epinoia is also specifically associated with Eve. In the *Apocryphon of John,* a heavenly Eve comes as a "helper" to Adam, "a luminous reflection (*epinoia*) who comes out of him, who is called 'Life'" (*zōē*; II 20,16–19; compare Genesis 3:21).

The identification of the speaker in *Thunder: Perfect Mind* with Eve-Sophia is made all the more plausible when we compare a passage in the treatise *On the Origin of the World.* Eve is referred to as "the first virgin, the one who without a husband bore her first offspring." She then makes several poetic "I am" pronouncements similar to those in *Thunder: Perfect Mind*: "mother," "wife," "virgin," "midwife," and so forth (II 14,4–15).

In the material that follows in our tractate, six additional exhortation sections alternate with five additional sections of "I am" pronouncements. There are several repetitions that occur in this material. The tractate concludes with an exhortation section in which the speaker urges her hearers to give heed to her pronouncements. People are said to embrace "fleeting pleasures" until they "become sober and go up to their resting place. And they will find me there, and they will live, and they will not die again" (21,29–32).

The aforementioned clues linking the speaker with Barbelo, Sophia, and Eve have led one scholar (Bentley Layton) to include this tractate among those he identifies as Classic Gnostic literature. At least, one can see reflected in it Classic or Sethian Gnostic portrayals of Sophia, even if the myth of the fall of Sophia and the production of the Demiurge is absent from the text.

In sum, *Thunder: Perfect Mind* is a piece of Gnostic literature that is quite unique and difficult to classify. Its author is completely unknown, as is the date of its composition (second century?). As to where it was composed, Egypt is a strong possibility, for at one point in the text the speaker says, "I am the one whose image is great in Egypt" (16,6–7). She thus identifies herself with the Greco-

Egyptian goddess Isis, to whom is credited a number of "I am" pronouncements found in stone inscriptions in various parts of the Greco-Roman world.

9. Concept of Our Great Power
(NHC VI,4: 36,1–48,15; NH Library, 311–17; NH Scriptures, 391–401)

This tractate has three different titles. The one currently used in scholarship occurs at the end: "The Concept (Greek *noēma*) of Our Great Power." Two titles occur at the beginning, "The Perception of Understanding," and in the second line, "The Concept of the Great Power." The two titles are separated by a Coptic punctuation mark. "Great Power" is a designation for the supreme God in this tractate. The aim of the tractate is to foster an "understanding" (one possible translation of Greek *noēma*) of the Great Power.

The tractate poses a number of problems. These include logical and grammatical inconsistencies, unclear use of pronouns, and textual corruptions. It is probably a composite work in which Christian glosses and additions have been added to a non-Christian Gnostic writing. In terms of literary genre, it can loosely be termed an apocalypse, since it features revelations of the nature of the universe and prophecies of what will happen in the future.

> *It is probably a composite work in which Christian glosses and additions have been added to a non-Christian Gnostic writing.*

The tractate opens with an invitation to the readers (or hearers) to come to a knowledge of "our great Power" (36,3–37,5). This is followed by an account of the creation. The Great Power, identified as fire, enters chaos and sets in motion the qualities of which the universe is composed: spirits, soul, and flesh (37,6–38,9). History after the creation is divided into two aeons: the "fleshly aeon" and the "psychical [or 'soul-endowed'] aeon." The fleshly aeon begins with the giants, the offspring of fallen angels (compare Genesis 6:1–4). The Flood takes place as a judgment of them, but Noah and his sons are preserved (38,9–15). The psychical aeon is the current age, into which all sorts of sin and impurity have come. The final conflagration will bring an end to all earthly wickedness (38,16–40,23).

The text is interrupted here with a Christian addition (40,24–43,2), featuring a description of "the man who knows the Great Power," that is, Christ. This section features the ministry of Christ, his victory over death, and the mission of the church. A passage that appears to be a continuation of the non-Christian writing (43,3–11) is then followed by a series of Christian additions. These additions feature prophecies of the troubles that will precede the final consummation (43,11–45,27). They include a war brought about by the archons (43,29–44,10), the career of an anti-Christian "archon of the west," who is the forerunner of the Antichrist (44,13–31), and the reign of the Antichrist (44,31–45,27). It has been suggested that the "archon of the west" is the emperor Julian "the Apostate," who died in 363.

> The judgment process will then come to an end, and the souls of the pure, those who have maintained celibacy, will achieve their rest.

The non-Christian material resumes with a description of the consummation and the final aeon. The universe will be burnt up after the Great Power and the souls who know him withdraw from the earth. The fire will burn for fourteen hundred and sixty-eight years (45,27–46,33). The judgment process will then come to an end, and the souls of the pure, those who have maintained celibacy, will achieve their rest. The souls of the impure will apparently spend eternity in penitence (47,27–48,13).

This tractate lacks any apparent influence from Classic (Sethian) forms of Gnosticism. The Old Testament God is depicted as having been appointed by the Great Power for "service to the fleshly creation" (37,12–23). There is no Sophia figure. Instead, there is a female figure called "Mother of the flame," that is, mother of sexual desire" (40,9–16). The 1,468-year-long conflagration reflects Manichaean influence (compare *Kephalaia*, chapter 24).

It has been shown that the non-Christian parts of the *Concept of Our Great Power* reflect influences from Samaritan traditions as well as Greek philosophy, especially Stoicism. Some similarities have also been noted to Hippolytus's treatment of a Simonian Gnostic commentary on Simon Magus's *Great Revelation* (*Refutation of All Heresies* 6.9.4–18.7, discussed in chapter 2). Indeed, the non-Christian Gnostic writing underlying the tractate may be the product of a revisionist Simonian community. In contrast to other forms of Simonian gnosis, this community rejected sex and marriage.

The non-Christian Gnostic writing was probably composed in Egypt sometime in the early third century. The Christian parts were added later, and if the "archon of the west" is really the emperor Julian, the tractate as we now have it would date from the second half of the fourth century. Nothing is known of its author(s).

10. *Second Treatise (Discourse) of the Great Seth* (NHC VII,2: 49,10–70,12; NH Library, 362–71; NH Scriptures, 473–86)

The title of this tractate is given in Greek at the end, "Second Treatise (*logos*) of the Great Seth." We do not know of any writing referred to as the "First Treatise of the Great Seth," but such a treatise might have existed. Epiphanius speaks of seven books written in the name of Seth (*Panarion* 39.5.1, compare discussion in chapter 3), and it is not impossible that our tractate was one of them. Seth nowhere appears within the tractate itself, which features Jesus Christ as the revealer. But, as has already been observed (in chapter 3), certain Sethian Gnostics saw in Christ a manifestation of the heavenly Seth. The scribe of Codex VII may deliberately have put this tractate in second place, after the *Paraphrase of Shem*, if he understood the revealer in that tractate, Derdekeas, to be a manifestation of Seth (compare discussion in chapter 7).

The *Second Treatise of the Great Seth* is a revelation discourse given by the ascended Christ to his followers. It has some homiletic features, as well as a considerable amount of polemic directed against other Christians who are easily recognizable as members of the growing catholic church. It also has some difficulties, probably resulting from textual corruption or mistranslation of the Greek original.

The main part of the tractate, that is, the material preceded by the Introduction (49,10–50,1) and followed by the Epilogue (69,20–70,10), consists of two sections. In the first section (50,1–57,27) Christ gives a history of redemption, telling the story of his own incarnation and that of his brethren. In the second section (57,27–69,19), he applies the story to the lives of his perfect brethren.

In the Introduction Christ reveals himself as the Son in the divine triad of Father ("perfect Greatness"), Mother ("Truth"), and Son ("Word"). He tells how he was sent down to his earthly spiritual brethren, who had been "made ready" by his sister Sophia. His incarnation in an alien body brought about disturbance among the archons, for he is "a stranger to the regions below" (50,1–52,10). In a lengthy digression on the archons (52,10–55,8) references are made to a double of Sophia called Hope, Yaldabaoth, his repentant son Adonaios, and Yaldabaoth's vain claim.

Though they nailed their man to the cross, that is, Christ's physical body, he himself was "laughing at their ignorance" and ascended back to heaven, where he entered "the new bridal chamber of the heavens" (55,9–57,18).

Christ then returns to the story of his redemptive work. The archons attempt to crucify him, but they fail. Though they nailed their man to the cross, that is, Christ's physical body, he himself was "laughing at their ignorance" and ascended back to heaven, where he entered "the new bridal chamber of the heavens" (55,9–57,18).

The second main section begins with a reference to "three paths" and a "third baptism." There is a considerable lack of clarity in this section, but the reference may be to three different groups whose final destinies are different. The third baptism is probably that of the perfect Gnostics. Christ reveals that the purpose of his descent was for "the destruction of the archons." Christ and his true followers are persecuted down here by ignorant people who "think that they are advancing the name of Christ." They really belong to the archons. But we (Gnostics) are pure, and have the mind of the Father (57,18–60,12).

In an extensive polemic, Christ refers to the world and the archons as "laughingstocks." Included among the laughingstocks are the heroes of the Old Testament, from Adam and the patriarchs to Moses, the prophets, and John the Baptist. Those who are ignorant and blind try to harm Christ and his followers (60,13–65,18). Addressing his perfect brethren, Christ exhorts them not to "become female," and encourages them to remain united in their gnosis because they are "from a single spirit" (65,18–68,24).

After a final attack on his blind opponents, who are said to belong to Yaldabaoth and his archons (68,25–69,19), the tractate ends with a final address to the perfect, concluding with an invitation, "Rest then with me, my fellow spirits and my brethren, forever" (69,20–70,10).

The *Second Treatise of the Great Seth* is not a Sethian or Classic Gnostic tractate, but it does reflect some influences from that variety of Gnosticism and probably Valentinian gnosis as well. Some scholars have associated it with Basilidian gnosis, but that association is based on a misinterpretation of the account of Christ's crucifixion. According to this misinterpretation, Simon of Cyrene is said to have been crucified in Christ's place (55,30–56,13). Irenaeus (falsely) attributed such a doctrine to Basilides (see discussion in chapter 5). In our tractate, the text says that the archons nailed their man, that is, Jesus's human body, to the cross (55,34–35). Basilides taught a similar doctrine, but there is no reason to link him to our tractate.

The tractate reflects a good deal of tension between the perfect addressed in it and other Christians who are blindly persecuting them. This implies a situation in which leaders of a growing catholic church are attempting to root out heresy, something that was happening in Alexandria, Egypt, during the episcopacy of Demetrius (189–232). So we can with considerable confidence assign the composition of our tractate to late second- or early third-century Alexandria. We know nothing of its author, but we can surmise that he was leader of a Gnostic conventicle in Alexandria.

11. *Apocalypse (Revelation) of Peter* (NHC VII,3: 70,13–84,14; *NH Library,* 372–78; *NH Scriptures,* 487–97)

This tractate is to be distinguished from another writing of the same name that is usually included in standard collections of New Testament apocryphal writings. Only fragments remain of the original Greek version of that apocalypse, which was probably composed some time in the second quarter of the second century. It is completely preserved in an Ethiopic version. In it Christ reveals to Peter the fates of the wicked and the righteous after death.

Our Coptic tractate also contains revelations given by Christ to Peter, but from a Gnostic point of view. The title is presented in Greek both at the beginning and at the end of the tractate: "Apocalypse of Peter." In terms of genre, it is a typical apocalypse in which Christ interprets for Peter his visionary experiences and provides extensive revelation. It also has some features in common with the *Second Treatise of the Great Seth,* notably a similar interpretation of the crucifixion and a similar polemic directed against ecclesiastical opponents.

The *Apocalypse of Peter* is divided into five parts: 1. Introduction (70,14–72,4); 2. Peter's first vision (72,4–73,10); 3. Central revelation discourse given by Christ (73,10–81,3); 4. Peter's second vision (81,3–82,16); and 5. Conclusion (82,17–84,13).

In the Introduction, Peter reports that the Savior was sitting in the Temple the day before his crucifixion. He tells Peter that he has chosen him for leadership of "the remnant whom I have summoned to knowledge." Peter is told to "be strong," and is informed that he will be corrected "three times in this night," a reference to Peter's threefold denial (compare Matthew 26:34).

In Peter's first vision, he sees priests and other people rushing toward him and the Savior in a menacing way. The Savior refers to them as "blind," and tells Peter to listen to what they are saying. Peter says to Christ that they are praising him.

People of "those who are outside our number" will name themselves "bishop" and "deacons," claiming that they derive their authority from God. But they are only "dry canals" (71,10–79,31).

The Savior then begins an extensive revelation discourse. He refers to people who will turn away from the truth "in accordance with the will of the father of their error" (presumably the Demiurge). They will adopt false teachings about Christ, and "hold fast to the name of a dead man." Those people are souls who love material things, but immortal souls (the Gnostics) are not like them. They concoct errors and a law against the Savior's pure thoughts, and will continue to do so until "my return" (*parousia*, "advent"). They are a "sisterhood," only an imitation of the true "brotherhood" consisting of Christ's "little ones." People of "those who are outside our number" will name themselves "bishop" and "deacons," claiming that they derive their authority from God. But they are only "dry canals" (71,10–79,31).

This is, of course, an explicit attack against ecclesiastical Christianity and its leadership. The term "dry canals" can be seen as an Egyptian adaptation of the "waterless springs" referred to in 2 Peter 2:17, in a passage attacking false teachers.

When Peter expresses his fear, the Savior reassures him that the attacks against the "little ones" will not continue for long, for "the root of their error will be pulled out." The Savior says that "those who will bring judgment upon themselves are coming," but they cannot touch him (79,32–81,3).

In the account of his second vision Peter reports that he saw the Savior "apparently being seized by them." The Savior replies that the one "into whose hands and feet they are driving the nails is his physical part." The person Peter sees "above the cross, glad and laughing, is the living Jesus." Peter then sees the Savior surrounded by "ineffable light" and "invisible angels" (81,3–82,17).

In the concluding section, the Savior again bids Peter to "be strong." He whom they crucified is a "clay vessel" belonging to Elohim. The real Savior stands joyfully, laughing at their ignorance. Peter is to present these revelations to "those of another race, who are not of this age." The Savior gives a parting promise: "I will be with you so that none of your enemies will prevail over you. Peace be to you! Be strong!" (82,17–84,11). Peter then comes to himself, that is, emerges from his ecstatic trance (84,11–13).

The *Apocalypse of Peter* shows no particular influence from Classic or Sethian Gnosticism. It lacks the typical myth of Sophia and the Demiurge, although the Demiurge is probably meant in the figure of Elohim (82,25). Of the New Testament works used by the author, Matthew and 2 Peter are the most prominent, while there are no references to the Pauline or Johannine literatures. What is surprising, too, is that Peter, who is often downgraded in Gnostic texts, is presented as the leader of the "little ones" constituting the Gnostic elect.

The *Apocalypse of Peter* was probably composed somewhere in Egypt, presumably Alexandria, sometime in the late second century. We know nothing of its author.

12. *Letter of Peter to Philip* (NHC VIII,*2*: 132,10–140,27; *NH Library*, 431–37; *NH Scriptures*, 585–93)

There are two known exemplars of this tractate, the one treated here and one in the Codex Tchacos, a fourth-century Coptic codex that is as yet unpublished. The Nag Hammadi version treated here was probably chosen for inclusion in Codex VIII because it is short enough to fit on the remaining pages of the codex, after the tractate *Zostrianos* had been copied into it (NHC VIII:*1*,1–132,9). The two tractates are not in any way related to one another in terms of their contents.

The title appears in the first two lines of the tractate: "The letter of Peter which he sent to Philip." The text of the short letter then follows (132,9–133,8). What remains of the tractate is not part of the letter. Its literary genre is that of a Gnostic revelation dialogue. So the title of the tractate currently in use is somewhat of a misnomer. Indeed, the letter may have been secondarily added to the beginning of the revelation dialogue.

The putative recipient of the letter, Philip, is probably a composite of two Philips named in the New Testament: Philip the evangelist, who was one of the seven leaders of the Hellenist faction of the early Jerusalem church (Acts 6:5, 8:4–40, 21:8–9), and the apostle Philip, one of Jesus's twelve disciples (Mark 3:18; John 1:43–48, 6:5–7, 12:21–22). He is not named again in the rest of the tractate.

In the letter, Peter writes to Philip, his beloved brother, suggesting a meeting of the apostles for the purpose of organizing their mission. Philip reacts to the letter with joy (133,8–11).

The revelation dialogue begins with Peter's gathering the apostles on the Mount of Olives. They offer up praises to God the Father and to Christ, the "Son of Life." They pray for power to resist those who seek to kill them (133,12–134,9). Jesus Christ then appears to them in a great light. The apostles pose a series of questions. They want to know about "the deficiency of the aeons" and their "pleroma," where they came from and where they are going, and why the "powers" are fighting against them (134,9–135,2).

When the apostles ask him how they are to fight, he replies that they are to go out and preach salvation to the world (137,13–138,3).

Jesus's reply comes in four separate answers. To the first question he tells them that the "deficiency of the aeons" resulted from the disobedience of the mother (Sophia). Her product was the "Arrogant One" (the Demiurge), who produced the cosmos and placed his "powers and authorities" over it (135,8–136,15). He then tells them about how he came down into "their mortal formation" for the salvation of those trapped here below (136,16–

137,4). In his third answer he tells them that they belong to him, and they will become illuminators to mortal humans (137,4–9). In a brief fourth answer, he tells them that they will fight against the powers because the powers do not wish for them to be saved (137,10–13). When the apostles ask him how they are to fight, he replies that they are to go out and preach salvation to the world (137,13–138,3).

The Lord is then taken up to heaven, and the apostles return to Jerusalem, conversing about what they had heard. They go to the Temple and "give instruction in salvation." Peter gives a speech in which he presents an account of the sufferings and resurrection of the Savior. He says that their own sufferings are the result of "the transgression of the mother" (138,3–140,1). After a prayer they are filled with the Holy Spirit and perform healings. They then part to preach the Lord Jesus (140,1–23).

When they come together again Jesus reappears and promises to be with them forever. The apostles then part from one another yet again to preach their message (140,23–27).

While the letter with which our tractate begins contains nothing that can be regarded as Gnostic, the revelation dialogue reflects the influence of Sethian or Classic Gnosticism, especially the myth of Sophia (the mother) and the Demiurge (the Arrogant One). While Jesus is said to have suffered, it is also said that he suffered as one who is "a stranger to this suffering." The sufferings here below are a result of the "transgression of the mother" (139,23).

New Testament writings used by the author include the Gospel of Luke and the Book of Acts, as well as (probably) the Gospel of John. There may also be reflected in the tractate some influences from apocryphal works featuring acts of the apostles that circulated in the church from the second century on. The tractate also reflects a situation in which Christians are subject to persecution.

A late second- or early third-century date can be posited for the *Letter of Peter to Philip*. Its place of origin could be Antioch in Syria, or perhaps Alexandria in Egypt. Nothing is known of its author.

13. *Testimony of Truth* (NHC IX,3: 29,6–74, 30+; *NH Library*, 448–59; *NH Scriptures*, 613–28)

The *Testimony of Truth* is only partially preserved, for damage to the manuscript has resulted in the loss of almost half of the text. The title now in use has been editorially assigned on the basis of a prominent theme in the tractate ("word of truth," 31,8; "true testimony," 45,1). The tractate might have had a title at the end, but the last two pages of the manuscript, containing the end of the tractate, are lost.

The chief concern of the tractate's author is to establish his version of the truth, that is, a radically encratic Gnostic Christianity, versus the heretical opinions of his opponents. His chief opponents are easily recognizable as members of the growing catholic church. Interestingly enough, his opponents also include fellow Gnostics.

> *The true resurrection is self-knowledge (31,22–38,27).*

The *Testimony of Truth* has rhetorical features commonly found in early Christian homilies. Indeed, the first part of it can be seen as a well-constructed homily addressed to fellow members of a Gnostic community (29,6–45,6). The second part (45,6–end), where the manuscript is badly damaged, consists of miscellaneous additions, elaborating on themes already sounded in the first part.

The first part opens with an exordium in which the author appeals to those with spiritual hearing. An attack is made against the Law, summed up in the command to procreate (29,2–30,18). The descent of the Son of Man signals the end of the dominion of the Law (30,18–31,22). An attack is then launched against foolish people willing to suffer martyrdom for their faith, and who believe in a physical resurrection. The true resurrection is self-knowledge (31,22–38,27).

The author then resumes his attack on marriage and procreation. Jesus's virgin birth is taken as a sign that Christians should lead a virginal life. The sawing asunder of Isaiah (compare Hebrews 11:37 and the *Martyrdom of Isaiah*) is interpreted allegorically to signify divisions between those governed by corruptibility and darkness, and those who belong to incorruptibility and light. The archetypal Gnostic renounces the world and will be reintegrated into the realm of imperishability (38,27–44,30). The first part of the tractate concludes with a peroration:

> This, therefore, is the true testimony: When a person comes to know himself and God who is over the truth, that person will be saved and crowned with the unfading crown. (44,30–45,6)

The second part of the tractate opens with a contrast between John the Baptist and Christ (45,6–22). This is followed by an extensive midrash on the biblical snake, which may have been a preexisting source (45,23–49,10; compare discussion in chapter 4).

The material that follows is very fragmentary, but a central theme is the contrast between the "generation of Adam" and the "generation of the Son of Man." In a particularly interesting section, following four pages in the manuscript lacking translatable material, other Gnostics are attacked: the Valentinians, Basilides and Isidore, the Simonians, and others whose names are lost in lacunae. These heretics are attacked for their practices, which include the use of water baptism and the acceptance of marriage and procreation (55,1–58,14f.). The tractate's polemical tone continues in the fragmentary material that remains (61,1–74,30, where the text breaks off).

Particularly striking is his extensive use of Valentinian Gnostic teachings, in spite of the fact that he includes Valentinians among his heretical opponents.

The author's allegorical interpretation of the Bible is based on Alexandrian Jewish and Christian precedents. Particularly striking is his extensive use of Valentinian Gnostic teachings, in spite of the fact that he includes Valentinians among his heretical opponents. The basis for his condemnation of them is their acceptance of marriage and their practice of baptism, but his use of Valentinian traditions might be explained on the theory that he was an ex-Valentinian.

Do we know of any ex-Valentinians who embraced radical encratism? Clement of Alexandria provides information on just such a person in his *Miscellanies* (3,86–95), a man named Julius Cassianus. So it is possible that he was the author of our tractate.

Be that as it may, the *Testimony of Truth* was certainly composed in Alexandria, probably sometime in the late second or early third century.

14. *Hypsiphrone* (NHC XI,4: 69,21–72,33; NH Library, 501–02; NH Scriptures, 701–3)

Hypsiphrone is a short tractate of less than four pages in length, or perhaps an excerpt from a larger tractate, that was inscribed into the last four pages of Codex XI. The title occurs at the beginning, marked with decorations: "*Hupsiph*[*ronē*]." The feminine name Hypsiphrone ("High-Minded") occurs in three other places in the tractate. Unfortunately, the codex is severely damaged, and only four large and two small fragments are preserved of the two leaves constituting those last four pages. The opening sentence has been reconstructed to read: "The book [concerning the things] that were seen [by] Hypsiphrone [revealed] in the place of [her] virginity" (69,22–26).

The tractate would appear to consist for the most part of a first person revelation narrative in which Hypsiphrone relates her coming into the world. Another being is also named in the fragments, Phainops ("Shining-Faced" or "Light-Eyed"), with whom Hypsiphrone is in conversation. At the end of the extant readable material Phainops tells Hypsiprone of a "fount of blood" and a "kindling of fire." So little remains of this tractate that it would be fruitless to speculate further as to its content or meaning.

15. *Gospel of Mary* (BG,1: 7,1–19,5; NH Library, 523–27; NH Scriptures, 737–47)

The *Gospel of Mary* was inscribed into the first nineteen pages of the Berlin Gnostic Codex. Unfortunately the first six pages are

missing, as are pages eleven through fourteen. The nine remaining
pages are largely intact, with only minor loss of text. Two manuscripts of the Greek version are attested by two small papyrus fragments found at Oxyrhynchus in Egypt, both of them dated to the
early third century.

The tractate's title is found at the end: "The Gospel according
to Mariamm (Mary)." Though Mary is not further identified in the
tractate, there is a general consensus that Mary Magdalene is meant.
Mary Magdalene is given a special appearance of the risen Christ in
the Gospel of John (20:11–17). In terms of literary genre the *Gospel
of Mary* can be characterized as a Gnostic revelation dialogue.

At the beginning of the extant text on page seven the Savior is
discussing with his disciples the nature of matter and the passions
that befall the material body. At the end of his discourse he gives
them his peace, telling them that "the Son of Man is within" them.
He commands them to go and preach "the gospel of the Kingdom," and not to constrain anyone with "a law like the lawgiver"
(7,1–9,4).

The disciples begin to grieve, wondering "if they did not spare
him, how will they spare us?" Mary stands up and encourages them
to praise his greatness, "for he has prepared us and made us into
men." With this they take courage and begin to discuss the words
of the Savior (9,5–24). Peter then says to Mary that they realize
that the Savior loved her more than other women, and asks her to
tell them about things he had said to her alone. She then begins to
recount a vision in which the Lord appeared to her and spoke to
her (10,1–22).

After a four-page gap, the text resumes with material featuring Mary discussing the ascent of a soul to heaven through the
various cosmic spheres. Seven vices are personified as powers and
interrogate the soul at the various stages of her ascent. The soul
responds with confidence that she has overcome her ignorance and
will attain to her rest. At that point Mary concludes her account of
what the Savior had told her (15,1–17,9).

Andrew then expresses considerable skepticism about what
she had told them. Peter is even more vehement, asking his fellow

disciples if they thought that the Savior had really spoken with a woman about such things. "Are we to turn around and listen to her? Did he prefer her to us?" (17,10–22).

Mary starts to cry, asking Peter if he thought that she had made all of this up. Levi reproves Peter as a hothead, and acknowledges that the Savior did indeed love her more than them. They should all be ashamed and go out to "preach the gospel, not laying down any other rule or other law beyond what the Savior said" (18,1–21). The tractate ends with the report that they did, indeed, go out to preach (18,21–19,2).

> *Peter is representative of the majority view that women have no place as leaders in the church. Mary is representative of the view that women do, indeed, have a leadership role in the church.*

The position of Mary in the gospel that bears her name is that of a person especially favored by Christ. In a sense, she assumes a role in the text analogous to that of the unnamed beloved disciple in the Gospel of John. In our tractate she is the person responsible for passing on the esoteric teachings of the Savior.

The *Gospel of Mary* also reflects an interesting social situation in the early church revolving around the role of women. Peter is representative of the majority view that women have no place as leaders in the church. Mary is representative of the view that women do, indeed, have a leadership role in the church. Even some men are seen to agree with this view, and Levi functions in the text as such a person. It has been suggested that the *Gospel of Mary* attests to an early leadership role played by the historical Mary Magdalene. But such a suggestion goes beyond our available evidence.

It has been argued that the *Gospel of Mary* is not a Gnostic writing at all. While it does not contain the elaborate mythology we see in many Gnostic writings, there is no reason to doubt that it is a Gnostic writing. It is, of course, a Christian writing, and reflects knowledge of the gospels of the New Testament, and perhaps the *Gospel of Thomas*. Some scholars have also noted influences from Greek philosophy, especially Stoicism.

The *Gospel of Mary* was probably written by the leader of a Gnostic Christian conventicle (perhaps a woman) somewhere in Syria (Antioch) or Egypt (Alexandria). It can plausibly be assigned a date sometime in the second half of the second century.

16. *Pistis Sophia* (the Askew Codex, MacDermot, *Pistis Sophia*)

Pistis Sophia is the title conventionally assigned to the four books contained in the Askew Codex, a fifth-century Coptic codex named for its first owner, A. Askew, who purchased it from a London bookseller in 1772. The manuscript originally contained 178 leaves of parchment, with 354 inscribed pages. Four leaves are now missing.

Pistis Sophia is a late compilation of Gnostic lore assembled from various sources. Books 2 and 3 each conclude with a title in the original hand, "A Part of the Books of the Savior." A later scribe has inserted at the beginning of Book 2 another title, "The Second Book of the Pistis Sophia." The title *Pistis Sophia* is now conventionally given to all four books in the manuscript. However, the fourth book clearly differs in content from the earlier books. Chapter divisions have been assigned to the text by scholars. Book 1 contains chapters 1–62, Book 2 chapters 63–101, Book 3 chapters 102–35, and Book 4 chapters 136–48.

At the beginning of Book 1, it is reported that "after Jesus had risen from the dead he spent eleven years speaking with his disciples." The whole of *Pistis Sophia* contains revelations given by the risen Jesus, mostly on the Mount of Olives, to his disciples, including several women. The disciples pose questions to which the Savior gives extended answers.

Books 1 and 2, through chapter 82, are mainly concerned with the repentance of Pistis Sophia ("Faith Wisdom"), mother of the Gnostic seed. (We have encountered her before in other Gnostic writings.) She is depicted as wandering in darkness, lamenting her fate. Jesus, the power of light, is her savior, who brings her out of chaos. She sings hymns of gratitude, hymns that are interpreted by the disciples with reference to the Sophia story (chapters 1–62). The rest of Book 2 (chapters 83–101) provides details concerning various types of souls, and the origins of passions that destroy the soul.

Book 3 features discourses by Jesus on the disciples' role in preaching gnosis to the world, and details on how souls can escape from the bondage of the archons and attain to the Kingdom of the Light. Sprinkled throughout books 1–3 are extended quotations from the biblical psalms, the apocryphal Odes and Psalms of Solomon, and various New Testament passages.

Book 4 is set on Easter day. The disciples are shown the Zodiac, and receive revelations about the punishment of evil archons. They are promised forgiveness of sins and access to divine mysteries through which they can escape judgment. A complicated ritual is depicted that involves fire, vine branches, wine, and water. Jesus offers a prayer to the Father, which includes magical incantations (ch. 142). He then discourses on the punishments given for various kinds of sins. At the end the disciples are assured of their salvation and go out to preach the "Gospel of the Kingdom" to all the regions of the world (ch. 148).

It has been rightly observed that the books of *Pistis Sophia* belong to a late phase of Gnostic literary composition, and "are not on the highest level of inspiration" (Rudolph). They were probably put together in Egypt sometime in the fourth century. We know nothing about the compiler.

17. *Books of Jeu* (MacDermot, *Bruce Codex*, 1–211)

The two *Books of Jeu* constitute the major portion of the Bruce Codex, named for the person who bought it sometime in the eighteenth century. The other writing in that codex is the "Untitled Text," a Sethian tractate that we have treated briefly elsewhere in this book (in chapter 3). The two main texts in the Bruce Codex are written in different hands, and originally come from different manuscripts. The two codices were bound together into a single codex, which is now housed in the Bodleian Library in Oxford.

The title by which the first text is known does not occur anywhere in the Bruce Codex. It derives from a reference to two "Books of Jeu" in the *Pistis Sophia*. Jesus tells Mary that righteous people "should find the mysteries which are in the Books of Jeu, which I caused Enoch to write in Paradise when I spoke with him from the Tree of Knowledge and the Tree of Life" (*Pistis Sophia*, chapter 134). Since Jeu is the chief deity referred to in the writing that goes by that name, the title *Books of Jeu* is now conventionally used for it. It has been divided into chapters, with Book 1 containing chapters 1–41 and Book 2 chapters 42–52. Parts of the manuscript are missing.

The text consists of initiatory discourses given by "the living Jesus" to his disciples, both male and female. A preamble (chapters 1–4) is followed by descriptions of the emanations that his Father caused Jeu, "the true God," to bring forth to fill the "treasuries of the Light" (5–32). These emanations include different names of Jeu, twenty-eight of them plus others now listed in missing pages. Instructions are given to the disciples on how to enter the sixty treasuries (33–38). Only treasuries 55–60 are named; the other ones are lost in a lacuna in the manuscript.

In answer to questions posed by the disciples regarding these things, Jesus refers to his own emanation (39) and how the disciples will follow him to the place of the true God (40–41). A hymn of praise concludes the first book.

They include Coptic text or magical combinations of letters, often surrounded by circles or squares, or accompanied by other drawings involving circles, crosses, and stars.

Book 2 deals mainly with rituals and formulas required to bring about the ascent of souls into the Treasury of the Light. One of the more interesting sections (45–48) features three baptisms of the disciples by Jesus, with water, fire, and the Holy Spirit. They are accompanied by ritual offerings of bread and wine, and sealing the disciples with seals. Jesus then discusses the "defense" (*apologia*) seal, and other elements associated with each level of the ascent (49–51). More specific instructions, with which the text breaks off (52), feature "defenses" at each of fourteen aeons.

The Books of Jeu include ideographs that are related to the text. Sixty-nine ideographs have been inserted into the single columns of Coptic text. They are referred to with the use of three different terms: "type" (*tupos*), "character" (*charaktēr*), and "seal" (*sphragis*). They include Coptic text or magical combinations of letters, often surrounded by circles or squares, or accompanied by other drawings involving circles, crosses, and stars.

The ideographs can be construed as Gnostic mandalas, meditational aids that enhance the mystical meaning of the rituals described in the text. Some of them may depict graphic symbols actually used in Gnostic ritual. We can compare them with the "Ophite Diagram" described by Origen (discussed in chapter 2).

If the *Books of Jeu* are to be equated with the two "Books of Jeu" mentioned in *Pistis Sophia,* they must have been written a little earlier than *Pistis Sophia.* So a late third-century or early fourth-century date can be plausibly assigned to this writing. It was certainly composed in Egypt. We know nothing of its author.

9. Thomas Christianity

Jesus says, "If those who lead you say to you, 'Look, the kingdom is in the sky,' then the birds of the sky will precede you. If they say to you, 'It is in the sea,' then the fish will precede you. When you come to know yourselves, then you will become known, and you will realize that you are children of the living Father. But if you will not know yourselves, you dwell in poverty, and you are poverty."

Jesus says, "The kingdom of the Father is like a merchant who had some merchandise, and found a pearl. That merchant was shrewd. He sold the merchandise and bought the pearl alone for himself."

THESE TWO PRONOUNCEMENTS OF Jesus occur as sayings 3 and 76 in the *Gospel of Thomas* (NHC II,2). They enunciate a major theme in that gospel, the search for the self. In the first one, the Kingdom of God is interpreted as something within a person, and something within a person's grasp. In the second one, the Kingdom is likened to a merchant who disposes of all of his merchandise in order to obtain a prized pearl. The pearl in the parable is the human self. Having found oneself, or having come to know oneself, leads to salvation.

The *Gospel of Thomas* is not a Gnostic text, though some scholars argue that it is. But there is no doctrine of pleromatic emanations in it, no Sophia myth, and no ignorant or malevolent Demiurge. What it does share in common with Gnosticism is the emphasis on self-knowledge, but that is not something specific to Gnosticism as we have defined it. There are some additional features in the *Gospel of Thomas* that it has in common with other Christian literature in which Judas Thomas plays a leading role. Reflected in this literature is a variety of Christianity, at home in Mesopotamia, which can be labeled "Thomas Christianity." In the Thomas literature, Judas Thomas is Jesus's twin brother (*t'oma'* in Aramaic and *didumos* in Greek mean "twin"). As such he is paradigmatic of the relationship that pertains between the individual Christian and the living Jesus who can be found within. To know oneself is to know one's own "double," construed as a twin of Christ. A person's double is of heavenly origin and, as a result of self-knowledge, can return again to heaven.

> *Having found oneself, or having come to know oneself, leads to salvation.*

Involved in this notion of the human soul is a doctrine of the soul rooted in Middle Platonism. According to that doctrine, the human soul is of heavenly origin and has descended to the lower part of the universe in a program of education. The soul that achieves virtue and wisdom in this life can return to its heavenly origin. A classic myth that gives expression to this doctrine is the "Myth of Er" found toward the end of Plato's *Republic* in Book 10.

> *The* Gospel of Thomas *is not a Gnostic text, though some scholars argue that it is.*

In Thomas Christianity, this doctrine of the soul is given expression in a specifically Christian myth of the soul that can be seen to lie behind some of the sayings of Jesus in the *Gospel of Thomas* or in pronouncements of Jesus found in another Thomas book, the *Book of Thomas the Contender* (NHC II,7). The myth is given beautiful expression in a hymn embedded in yet another Thomas book, the apocryphal *Acts of Thomas*. It is called the "Hymn (or 'Song') of the Pearl," and tells of a Parthian prince being sent to Egypt in quest of a pearl, where he becomes poisoned by the Egyptians and falls asleep. Finally he is able to find his way back home. In Thomas Christianity this hymn is an allegory of the human soul.

In what follows in this chapter, we will discuss the *Acts of Thomas* and the *Hymn of the Pearl* first, then the *Gospel of Thomas*, and finally the *Book of Thomas the Contender*.

1. The *Acts of Thomas* and the *Hymn of the Pearl* (Foerster 1, 337–64; Layton, 366–75)

Sometime toward the end of the second century, imaginative Christians composed accounts of the travels and adventures of individual apostles, thus expanding on what had been told about various apostles—especially Peter and Paul—in the New Testament Acts of the Apostles. In composing these stories, they adapted the literary genre of the romance novel, widespread by that time in the Greco-Roman world. A major adaptation was the substitution of the ideal of virginity for the erotic themes sounded in the romance novels. The earliest compilations of the acts of individual apostles are those of Peter and Paul. (Which of these came first is a matter of dispute among scholars.)

Sometime in the early third century an unknown member of a church in Mesopotamia, probably Edessa (now the village of Urfa in Eastern Turkey), compiled an account of the adventures of the chief apostolic authority in that region, Judas Thomas, who is the traditional founder of the church in Parthia. In the *Acts of Thomas*, originally composed in Syriac but translated early into Greek, the story is told about how Judas Thomas was commanded to go and preach in India. Thirteen individual episodes are found in that writing, ending with the apostle's martyrdom.

In the *Acts of Thomas,* the apostle Thomas preaches, performs miracles, and is the special recipient and mediator of revelations given to him by Christ. He is miraculously addressed by an ass's colt in the fourth act as "Twin brother of Christ, apostle of the Most High and fellow-initiate into the hidden word of Christ, who receive[s] his secret word, and fellow-worker of the Son of God" (ch. 39). As both an apostle and a brother of Jesus in Syrian Christian tradition, Judas Thomas in the Thomas literature would appear to be an amalgam of three different persons in the New Testament: Jesus's brother Judas (Mark 6:3), "Thomas, one of the twelve, called the Twin" (or Didymus, John 20:24), and "Judas, not Iscariot" (John 14:22), another member of the twelve. The last-named Judas is referred to in the Syriac version of John 14:22 as "Judas Thomas."

> *The* Hymn of the Pearl *is a Christian adaptation of a Parthian folk tale, told in the first person by a Parthian prince.*

Early in the history of the circulation of the *Acts of Thomas,* someone inserted into the ninth act a beautiful hymn, now known as the *Hymn of the Pearl* (*Acts of Thomas* 108–113). The apostle is in a prison in India. Other prisoners ask him to pray for them, and when he is finished he sings the hymn.

The *Hymn of the Pearl* is a Christian adaptation of a Parthian folk tale, told in the first person by a Parthian prince. He tells how, when he was a child, he enjoyed the wealth of his father the King of the East (Parthia). Then his parents took off his royal robe, provided him with provisions, and sent him off to Egypt on a quest for a pearl guarded by a terrible serpent. They told him that, when he returns, he will put on again his splendid robe and inherit the kingdom, together with his brother.

When he came to Egypt he found the serpent and stayed near him, waiting for him to fall asleep. But then the Egyptians fed him some of their food, and he forgot that he was a king's son, forgot about the pearl, and fell asleep. His parents observed this, and resolved to save him. They wrote him a letter, addressed to

259

him by his father, mother, and brother, bidding him to awake from his sleep, to remember that he is a son of kings, and to remember the pearl and his splendid robe. Then he will, with his brother the crown prince, inherit the kingdom.

The letter flew like an eagle and "became all speech." The prince awoke from his sleep, remembered that he was a son of kings, and remembered the pearl. He cast a spell on the terrible serpent, naming over him his father, his brother, and his mother. He took off his dirty garments, and turned to go to his father's house, led by the letter, his "awakener." His splendid robe became for him like a reflection in a mirror, in which he saw himself. Clad in his splendid robe, he was welcomed back to his father's house.

This hymn is an allegory of the human soul, a prince whose home is in heaven. Sent down to the earth, he is bereft of the divine image (the robe). His mission is to deprive Satan (the serpent) of his power and obtain the pearl, his true self. But, as an alien in a world of demons (Egypt), he forgets his commission and falls asleep, until he is awakened by the gospel of Jesus (the letter). He then realizes what his task is, and overpowers the serpent in the name of the Father, the Son, and the Holy Spirit. (The Holy Spirit is feminine in Syrian Christianity, and is depicted in the hymn as the queen mother.) With the pearl in hand, he returns as a king's son to his heavenly homeland, is reunited with Christ, his brother, and receives again the divine image that he had lost. The prince in this hymn can be construed as Adam, whose fall from Paradise and restoration are paradigmatic of the human soul that is awakened to eternal life by the Christian message.

The Holy Spirit is feminine in Syrian Christianity, and is depicted in the hymn as the queen mother.

While some scholars have interpreted the *Hymn of the Pearl* in terms of a Gnostic myth of the "saved savior" (Foerster), such an interpretation must be rejected. The *Hymn of the Pearl* exemplifies the theology of Syrian Christianity as it was lived in Mesopotamia in the second century.

The Parthian details found in the hymn indicate that it was probably composed sometime before 165 in Edessa, the chief city of the nominal kingdom of Osrhoëne in northern Mesopotamia. Until AD 165, Osrhoëne was under Parthian political influence, but then became a dependency of Rome. The religiosity reflected in the hymn matches that of the *Acts of Thomas,* in which it was secondarily embedded. That is to say, it is an exemplar of Thomas Christianity. We know nothing about its author.

2. *Gospel of Thomas* (NHC II,*2*: 32,10–51,28; *NH Library,* 124–38; Layton, 376–99; *NH Scriptures,* 133–56)

Consisting of one hundred fourteen sayings attributed to Jesus, The *Gospel of Thomas* is by far the most studied and the most widely read of the tractates in the Nag Hammadi corpus. It is also the one about which there is the least amount of agreement among scholars on such issues as its relationship to the gospels of the canonical New Testament (dependent or independent?), its date (first century or mid-second century?), its original language (Greek or Syriac?), and its religious context (Gnostic or non-Gnostic?). It is completely extant only in the Coptic version, but papyrus fragments were found at Oxyrhynchus of three separate manuscripts containing the Greek version. These fragments date from the end of the second century (P. Oxy. 1), the mid-third century (P. Oxy. 654), and the early part of the third century (P. Oxy. 655).

The title of the *Gospel of Thomas* is found at the end of the tractate: "The Gospel according to Thomas." The prologue and the first saying read as follows:

> These are the secret sayings which the living Jesus spoke and which Didymus Judas Thomas wrote down. And he said, "Whoever finds the interpretation of these sayings will not experience death."

Most of the sayings in the Gospel of Thomas are introduced with "Jesus says." The living Jesus is speaking now to the community. And right from the beginning the keynote is sounded: Jesus's words are life giving. They are also mysterious; so the effort must be made to "find the interpretation." In so doing, a person will not experience (literally "taste") death. We are reminded of a saying of Jesus in the Gospel of John, "If anyone keeps my word, he will never taste death" (8:52). But in John the emphasis is on "keeping," that is, "observing" Jesus's word, not on finding its meaning. There are a number of similarities between the *Gospel of Thomas* and the Gospel of John, but there are also profound differences as well. We shall have occasion to return to that point later.

One of the mysteries of the *Gospel of Thomas* is that the sayings are strung together with no obvious coherence. Some of the sayings are repeated, but, more importantly, there are basic contradictions to be observed in the collection as a whole. The most plausible way of understanding these contradictions is to view the entire collection as an agglutinative work that reflects the development of a particular community, or group of communities. In other words, over time, sayings have been added to a core collection. The added sayings reflect stages in the religious development of the community. Most of the sayings in the core collection have parallels in the Synoptic Gospels of the New Testament (Matthew, Mark, and Luke). The added sayings lack parallels in the canonical New Testament.

> *Right from the beginning the keynote is sounded: Jesus's words are life giving. They are also mysterious; so the effort must be made to "find the interpretation."*

One can identify with a good deal of probability the core sayings just by comparing the New Testament parallels. As is well-known, the Synoptic Gospels present Jesus as preaching the imminent kingdom, or rule, of God. Jesus's ministry begins in Mark's account with a programmatic pronouncement: "The time is fulfilled, and the kingdom of God is at hand; repent, and believe in the gospel" (Mark 1:15). Jesus's aphorisms and parables in the Synoptic Gos-

262

pels relate to the imminent coming of the Kingdom of God. Jesus can boldly say, "there are some standing here who will not taste death before they see that the kingdom of God has come with power" (Mark 9:1). At his last meal Jesus tells his disciples, "I shall not drink again of the fruit of the vine until that day when I drink it new in the kingdom of God." Jesus's teachings in general reflect the apocalyptic worldview of ancient sectarian Judaism.

There are a number of sayings in the *Gospel of Thomas* that treat the imminent coming of the kingdom of God, and the imminent distresses leading up to the end of the world. These are the sayings that we should assign to the earliest level of the gospel's composition, its core tradition. Here are some examples: "This heaven will pass away, and the one above it will pass away" (saying 11). "People think, perhaps, that it is peace which I have come to cast upon the world. They do not know that it is dissension which I have come to cast upon the earth: fire, sword, and war" (saying 16). "Blessed are you when you are hated and persecuted" (saying 68). "He who is near me is near the fire, and he who is far from me is far from the kingdom" (saying 82). "The heavens and the earth will be rolled up in your presence" (saying 111). The *Gospel of Thomas* also contains a number of parables of the kingdom that have parallels in the Synoptic Gospels.

> *There are a number of sayings in the* Gospel of Thomas *that treat the imminent coming of the kingdom of God, and the imminent distresses leading up to the end of the world.*

It has plausibly been argued that the earliest of the sayings in the *Gospel of Thomas* were circulated independently of the Synoptic Gospels, probably at first in Aramaic. It is probable that the earliest missionaries to Syria and Mesopotamia brought with them a collection of sayings of Jesus. This collection would have been at home in the earliest Jerusalem community, led by James the Righteous, Jesus's brother. In saying twelve, the disciples ask Jesus who will lead them after his departure. Jesus replies, "Wherever you are, you are to go to James the Righteous, for whose sake heaven and earth came into being."

As is well-known, one can find within the New Testament a movement away from imminent end expectation and a settling down in the world of ongoing time. The profound differences that are observable between the Gospel of John and the Synoptic Gospels relate to this phenomenon. In John the emphasis is no longer on the near expectation of the end, but on believing in Jesus, who came from heaven and will return again to his Father in heaven, where he is preparing a place for his own. Those who believe already have life within them. Jesus himself is the resurrection and the life. "Whoever believes in me, though he die, yet shall he live, and whoever lives and believes in me shall never die" (John 11: 25-26).

A somewhat similar phenomenon can be seen in the development of the Thomas community, as reflected in sayings in the *Gospel of Thomas* that were added over time to the core collection. For example, saying fifty-one reflects an emphasis similar to what we find in John. When the disciples ask Jesus when the "repose of the dead" will happen and when the "new world" will arrive, Jesus replies, "What you look forward to has already come, but you do not recognize it."

What is of special interest in the *Gospel of Thomas*, however, is that the horizontal end expectation typical of the earlier history of the community has been replaced by another facet of Jewish apocalyptic, that is, the vertical or mystical aspect. An example of this mystical aspect is saying eighty-three: "Jesus says, 'The images are manifest to man, but the light in them remains concealed in the image of the light of the Father. He will become manifest, but his image will remain concealed by his light.'" This saying reflects a background in Jewish mystical traditions involving a vision of God's "glory" (Hebrew *kabod*). God remains hidden in his light, but his light-image can be seen in a mystical vision by a person who is properly prepared. The oldest example of this in Jewish apocalyptic literature is the visionary experience of the seer Enoch in *1 Enoch 14* (probably third century BCE).

Another aspect of the later stages of the development of the *Gospel of Thomas* involves a protological dimension, according to which the goal is now to recover the primeval innocence of Adam before the fall. This dimension is coupled with a notion of human sexuality that attributes the human loss of innocence to the differentiation of the sexes into male and female. Adam was originally created "male and female" (Genesis 1:27), that is, androgynous. In saying twenty-two Jesus uses suckling children as an example of those who enter the kingdom.

> When you make the two one, and when you make the inside like the outside and the outside like the inside, and the above like the below, and when you make the male and the female one and the same, so that the male not be male nor the female female . . . then you will enter the kingdom.

A variant on this theme is the notion of maleness as equivalent to perfection, and femaleness as equivalent to imperfection, an idea that goes back to Plato and is given wide expression in the writings of the first-century Jewish philosopher Philo of Alexandria. An example of this is the last saying in *Thomas*, saying one hundred fourteen. When Simon Peter says to Jesus that Mary (Magdalene) should leave them because "women are not worthy of life," he replies, "I myself shall lead her in order to make her male, so that she too may become a living spirit resembling you males. For every woman who will make herself male will enter the kingdom of heaven." This saying reminds us of Mary's admonition to the other disciples in the *Gospel of Mary*, "He has prepared us and made us into men" (BG 1: 9,19–20; compare discussion in chapter 8).

It would appear that celibacy was a requirement for members of the Thomas community, at least as this community is reflected in the latest stages of the gospel's composition. Sayings forty-nine and seventy-five are examples of this: "Blessed are you solitary and elect, for you will find the kingdom. For you are from it, and to it you will return." "Many are standing at the door, but it is the solitary who will enter the bridal chamber." In the heavenly bridal chamber the solitary soul will reunite with his or her heavenly double. The Greek word translated here as "solitary" is *monachos*, from which is derived the English word "monk."

As noted at the beginning of this chapter self-knowledge is the beginning of salvation in Thomas Christianity. To know oneself is to know one's heavenly origin and destiny. As we have noted before, there are some interesting parallels between the Gospel of John and the *Gospel of Thomas*. But the latter's emphasis on self-knowledge underlines an important difference. In John, Jesus is the heavenly redeemer who descends to earth, dies on the cross for the salvation of the world, and returns to heaven again to prepare a place for those who believe in him. In the *Gospel of Thomas*, every elect soul originates in heaven and returns to heaven again. It is the role of Jesus to provide the message that leads a person to know oneself. In knowing oneself one also knows the living Jesus and is mystically united with him. But in the final analysis, one's salvation is grounded in oneself. "Jesus says, 'That which you have will save you if you bring it forth from yourselves. That which you do not have within you [will] kill you if you do not have it within you'" (saying 70).

For the Thomas community, it was Judas Thomas who best exemplified the person who knows the living Jesus. He is not only credited with writing down Jesus's sayings, but he is credited with knowledge of Jesus that exceeds that of any other of the disciples.

For the Thomas community, it was Judas Thomas who best exemplified the person who knows the living Jesus. He is not only credited with writing down Jesus's sayings, but he is credited with knowledge of Jesus that exceeds that of any other of the disciples. Right after saying twelve, which extols the leadership role of James, comes an interesting exchange in saying thirteen. When Jesus asks his disciples who or what they think he is like, Simon Peter compares him to a "righteous angel" and Matthew to a "wise philosopher." Thomas has the final word:

Thomas said to him, "Master, my mouth is wholly incapable of saying whom you are like." Jesus said, "I am not your master. Because you have drunk, you have become intoxicated from the bubbling spring which I have measured out." And he [Jesus] took

him and withdrew and told him three words. When Thomas
returned to his companions, they asked him, "What did Jesus
say to you?" Thomas said to them, "If I tell you one of the words
which he told me, you will pick up stones and throw them at me;
a fire will come out of the stones and burn you up."

There has been a good deal of speculation about what the three
words are. One plausible suggestion, since in ancient Judaism stoning was the punishment for blasphemy (Leviticus 24:16), is that the
three words Jesus uttered were the Hebrew words *'ehyeh 'asher
'ehyeh* ("I will be who I will be," or, as usually translated, "I am
who I am"; Exodus 3:14). In other words, Thomas heard Jesus
identifying himself with the name of God, revealed to Moses at the
burning bush. Be that as it may, the importance of Judas Thomas
in the estimation of the Thomas community is clearly underscored
in this interchange.

The core sayings in the *Gospel of Thomas* probably come from
a collection of Jesus's sayings dating to as early as the mid-first century, probably assembled in Jerusalem. (Of course, a number of
these go back to the historical Jesus, that is, before AD 30.) This
collection was brought to Edessa in Mesopotamia, perhaps as early
as the late first century. Sayings were added after that to the core collection, reflecting changes in the beliefs and practices of the Edessene
Christian community. The *Gospel of Thomas* as we know it, that is,
as translated from a Greek (or possibly Syriac) original, was probably composed sometime around 140. It was brought early to Egypt
and circulated there in the second half of the second century. It was
probably translated into Coptic sometime in the late third century.

While the *Gospel of Thomas* should not be considered a Gnostic text as a whole, it is possible that the Coptic translator was
a Gnostic Christian, for there are some observable differences
between the Coptic and Greek versions of some of the sayings that
are found in the Greek fragments. It is probable that the scribe of
Codex II understood it to be a Gnostic work, for he placed it just
after the Classic Gnostic tractate, the *Apocryphon of John,* and
just before the Valentinian tractate, the *Gospel of Philip.*

The *Gospel of Thomas* was in use among Syrian Christians for a considerable length of time and especially by Manichaean Christians from the late third century on. It is quoted or alluded to in the *Acts of Thomas* and in the *Book of Thomas the Contender*. It was also in use in other parts of the ancient world, especially in Egypt.

3. *Book of Thomas the Contender*
(NHC II,7: 138,1–145,19; *NH Library*, 199–207; Layton, 400–9; *NH Scriptures*, 235–45)

This tractate presents some interesting problems. There are difficulties in the text arising from scribal mistakes, corruptions introduced into the text in the course of transmission, and misunderstandings of the Greek original on the part of the Coptic translator. In addition there are two major problems, one posed by the title(s) and the incipit (opening passage), and the other posed by the book's structure and literary genre(s).

At the end of the tractate there are three lines that can be read as a single title: "The Book of Thomas the Contender Writing to the Perfect Ones." Or the lines can be read as two titles: "The Book of Thomas" and "The Contender Writes to the Perfect Ones." If a single title is meant, then "the contender" is Thomas, that is, Judas Thomas, who is referred to in the incipit: "The secret words that the savior spoke to Judas Thomas. . . ." But if two titles are meant, then "the contender" need not be identified as Thomas.

The incipit continues in the first person: "which I, even I Matthaias wrote down, while I was walking, listening to them speak with one another." The reference to "secret words" certainly reflects influence from the incipit of the *Gospel of Thomas*. But who is Matthaias? The name could be a corrupt form of Matthew (*Matthaios* in Greek), to whom is attributed the gospel that goes by his name. Or it could be a corrupt form of Matthias, who took Judas Iscariot's place among the Twelve (Acts 1:23-26). Clement of Alexandria quotes three brief passages from a lost book called the *Traditions of Matthias* (*Miscellanies* 2.45; 3.26; and 7.81). But those quotations bear no relationship to anything in the *Book of Thomas*. Matthaias plays no further role in the tractate.

The other main problem is posed by the structure of the tractate and its literary composition. In the tractate as we have it, there are two main parts: A revelation dialogue in which Jesus is depicted in conversation with his "brother," "twin," and "true companion," Judas Thomas (138,5–143,7); and an eschatological sermon made up of various sayings strung together (143,8–145,16). In the revelation dialogue Jesus frequently addresses an audience with the plural form of "you." So he's not only talking to his brother. Christian and Gnostic revelation dialogues usually include more than one disciple, but in the *Book of Thomas* the others are not named. Judas Thomas himself plays no role at all in the second part of the tractate, although this is the part that consists of sayings that could be construed as "secret words."

One scholar (John Turner) has suggested that the tractate is made up of two sources. Source A (the dialogue, which he sees as ending at 142,26) was attached to source B. The incipit originally belonged to the second part, but with the addition of the first part it now applies to the tractate as a whole.

Another scholar (Hans-Martin Schenke) has put forward an even bolder hypothesis. The tractate as we have it is a lightly Christianized version of what was originally a Hellenistic Jewish pseudonymous epistle of the patriarch Jacob. (A similar theory was applied to the Epistle of James in the New Testament by a German scholar in the 1930s.) It is the patriarch Jacob who is referred to in the second title appended at the end of the tractate, "the contender [or "athlete," Greek *athlētēs*] writes to the perfect ones."

> *Schenke finds in the* Book of Thomas *a number of wisdom features that have parallels in Hellenistic Jewish writings, especially Philo.*

In the writings of Philo of Alexandria, Jacob is regularly referred to as the "contender" or "athlete." Philo interprets the story of Jacob's wrestling with the angel (Genesis 32:24-30) as an allegory of the human struggle to attain virtue. (See, for example, *On Sobriety* 65; *On Dreams* 1.129.) Schenke finds in the *Book of Thomas* a number of wisdom features that have parallels in Hellenistic Jewish writings, especially Philo. In his theory the Christian redactor of Jacob's epistle has introduced the dialogue features in which Jesus is speaking with his twin brother Judas Thomas and also a few Christian glosses here and there. Thus Thomas inherits the epithet "the contender" from its original owner, the Patriarch Jacob.

Whatever one might think of these exercises in literary source criticism, the content of the *Book of Thomas* can easily be seen as representative of the Thomas Christianity that was at home in Edessa in Mesopotamia.

The tractate opens with the Savior expounding for his brother Thomas the importance of self-knowledge (138,5–21). Thomas then asks the Savior to give him ("tell me") answers to questions he had put before the Savior's ascension. Jesus's answer is addressed to unnamed others besides Thomas (using the plural form of "you"). If the visible "deeds of truth" are difficult to perform, what will they do with invisible things? Thomas presses Jesus to tell them ("tell us") about the invisible things (138,21–39). But the Savior's answer has to do with "visible bodies" that perish. Such bodies derive from bestial intercourse (138,39–139,12).

In the interchanges that follow the Savior persists in discussing visible things, such as the "visible light" (the sun). It is incumbent upon the elect to "abandon bestiality," that is, sexual intercourse, and quench the fire of lust. By fleeing lust the wise will make themselves wings with which to flee all visible spirits. The intelligent person is "perfect in all wisdom," but the fool is imprisoned in the darkness of physical lust. The wise person who has sought for the truth and found it will "rest upon it" forever (139,12–141,2).

Thomas then asks the Savior if it is beneficial "to rest among our own," that is, stay within one's own community. The Savior affirms that it is, for "things visible among men will dissolve." When Thomas asks if there is anything useful to be said to "blind men," the Savior replies that such people should be regarded as "beasts" who will be burnt by the fire. He then expands on this with further elaboration of the punishment to come upon such people (141,2–142,18).

In Thomas's last contribution to the dialogue, he tells the Savior that he has persuaded them ("us") of the sufficiency of his words. But since such words are ridiculous to the world, "how can we go preach them, since we are [not] esteemed [in] the world?" (142,18–26). The Savior replies that those who sneer at such things will be handed over to a punishing being who will cast them down to Tartarus, where they will be punished by "the angel Tartarouchos," and subjected to the "seething fire" (142,18–143,7). In Greek mythology, Tartarus was the lowest part of Hades, where the worst of sinners were punished.

The rest of the tractate is introduced with the words, "Then the Savior continued, saying" (143,8), and what follows is an eschatological sermon beginning with a series of "woe" pronouncements.

The "woes" are addressed to "godless ones, who have no hope," people who "hope in the flesh" and "love intimacy with womankind." They are challenged with the question, "Who is it who will cause the sun to shine upon you to disperse the darkness in you?" (143,9–144,19).

A parable follows, in which it is asserted that the grapevine requires the sun to shine upon it in order for it to grow. Weeds also grow in the same environment, but if the grapevine prevails the weeds will be shaded and die (144,19–36). A short woe pronouncement then follows, but much of the text is lost owing to damage to the manuscript (144,36–145,1).

Three beatitudes then follow, pronouncing blessings on those with prior knowledge, those who are reviled because they are loved by their lord, and those who are oppressed (145,1–7).

The concluding passage contains exhortations to "watch and pray" and a promise that when the Savior's followers have "come forth from the sufferings and passions of the body" they will receive rest and "reign with the King" forever (145,7–16).

The *Book of Thomas the Contender* has as its main theme the necessity to shun the fires of bodily passion, and to abstain from sexual intercourse and other passions of the flesh. Since it knows and uses the *Gospel of Thomas,* it is later than that gospel. The Greek original from which the Coptic version we now have was translated can plausibly be assigned to late second- or early third-century Edessa.

10. Hermes Trismegistus and Hermetic Gnosis

Let the person who has mind recognize himself as immortal, that love (erōs) is the cause of death, and let him recognize all things that exist.

The person who recognizes himself has attained the essential good, but the one who loves the body from the seduction of love remains in the darkness, wandering about, sensibly suffering what belongs to death.

THESE TWO SENTENCES COME FROM a revelation received in a visionary experience by Hermes Trismegistus, Thrice-Greatest Hermes, from God, Mind of the Absolute Sovereignty. The revelation is given in the first tractate of the *Corpus Hermeticum,* a collection of works written in Greek and assembled by Byzantine scholars. The first tractate is entitled *Poimandres,* and is the most important work of the Hermetic collection. The sentences quoted above (from chapters 18 and 19) set forth a central theme of Hermetic religious philosophy, that self-knowledge is the beginning of salvation.

Who was Hermes Trismegistus? The answer to that question takes us to ancient Egypt, to a prominent member of the Egyptian pantheon, the ibis-headed moon god Thoth. His name probably means messenger, but this important deity had many duties besides that of a messenger. As scribe of the sun god Re, he was also protector of the moon, the chief measurer of time, the lord of divine words, the inventor of language and sciences, a psychopomp who brought the dead to the other world, and the scribe who recorded the results of the weighing of the soul in the judgment of the dead.

From the time of Herodotus on (fifth century BCE), Thoth was identified by the Greeks with their deity Hermes, messenger of the gods and psychopomp. His Roman equivalent is Mercury (Latin *Mercurius*). The epithet "thrice greatest" in the Hermetic tradition is of Egyptian origin. The Greek word *trismegistos* renders an Egyptian epithet of Thoth, three times great, first attested in a Demotic ostracon from the second century BCE. (An ostracon is a piece of broken pottery; Demotic is one of the later forms of the Egyptian language.)

In the Greco-Roman world Hermes Trismegistus was viewed as an Egyptian sage of remote antiquity to whom were credited magical, astrological, alchemical, and philosophical writings. St. Augustine credits Hermes Trismegistus with teaching philosophy in Egypt long before the Greek philosophers (*City of God* 18.39). In the Middle Ages the idea became current that Hermes Trismegistus was a contemporary of Moses.

Numerous alchemical, magical, and astrological writings attributed to Hermes Trismegistus, in Demotic and in Greek, were produced in Hellenistic and early Roman Egypt. From the turn of the era on, Hermetic writings were composed in Greek in Greco-Roman Egypt (Alexandria) that reflected profound influences from Greek philosophy, especially Platonism and Stoicism. In most of these treatises, Hermes Trismegistus engages in dialogue with a pupil or an initiate, usually his son Tat or Asclepius. Tat is obviously named for Thoth, and Asclepius for the Greek god of healing. In Hellenistic Egypt Asclepius was identified with Imhotep, the famous vizier of the Third Dynasty pharaoh Zoser, a physician and architect of the Step Pyramid at Saqqara (twenty-seventh century BCE).

Scholars have tended to make a sharp distinction between the technical Hermetic texts and the philosophic ones, but it has become clear that both kinds of texts derive from a common cultural and religious milieu, that of Greco-Roman Egypt in the centuries around the turn of our era.

Corpus Hermeticum is the usual designation given to a Byzantine collection of seventeen Hermetic philosophical texts that were brought to Italy in the fifteenth century and translated into Latin. The fifth-century anthologist Stobaeus included in his collection of texts parts of three of the treatises, plus twenty-nine fragments of other Hermetic writings now lost. A lengthy Hermetic treatise called the *Asclepius* circulated in a Latin translation from the fifth century on. Its Greek original is lost, except for a few fragments. Additional Hermetic fragments in Greek have come to light, and a work called the *Definitions* that has been preserved in Armenian. Nag Hammadi Codex VI contains Coptic translations of two passages from the *Asclepius* and a Hermetic treatise previously unknown (see below).

These so-called philosophical texts, distinguished from the technical ones, are really more religious than they are philosophical. The religiosity reflected in them has aptly been referred to as Hermetism, as distinguished from the Hermeticism that is displayed in adaptations of the Hermetic tradition that developed in western esoteric forms of religion from the Renaissance up to the present day.

Since Hermetic texts are often subsumed under the larger category, Gnosticism, the question arises as to whether or not Hermetism is distinguishable from Gnosticism. The Hermetic texts do, in fact, display a good deal in common with the Gnostic ones. Gnosticism and Hermetism both stress the importance of revelation, and the idea that self-knowledge involves knowledge of God. In both forms of religion, salvation is grounded in the knowledge of oneself. In both, the higher soul is of divine origin, and its destiny involves putting off the physical body and ascending back to heaven.

On the other hand, a distinction can be made between Gnosticism and Hermetism in their respective views of God, the world, and humanity. Whereas in Gnosticism the transcendent God is unknowable, in Hermetism it is asserted that the supreme God is accessible to the human mind. In Hermetism there is no elaborate doctrine of pleromatic emanations and no Sophia myth. While a second Mind functions as Demiurge or Creator, as in Middle Platonism, he is not an evil or ignorant being. The Hermetic doctrine of God remains closer to that of the Greek philosophers, whose influence in Hermetic texts is clear.

There is in Hermetism, as in Gnosticism, the idea that bodily existence is something to be transcended, and that one should not succumb to physical passions, or surrender to "drunkenness" and ignorance of God. But in Hermetism the Gnostic idea that human beings are strangers in a hostile world is not to be found.

In terms of cosmology, there is in Hermetism no idea that the cosmos is bad, or that it has been created by an evil demiurge. Indeed, in some Hermetic texts one can find a kind of cosmic religiosity, the possibility of a mystical experience involving a feeling of oneness with the universe.

While there is the usual body-soul dualism in Hermetism that we find in Gnosticism, that of the Hermetics resembles much more the original philosophical doctrine rooted in the Platonic tradition. There is in Hermetism, as in Gnosticism, the idea that bodily existence is something to be transcended, and that one should not succumb to physical passions, or surrender to "drunkenness" and ignorance of God. But in Hermetism the Gnostic idea that human beings are strangers in a hostile world is not to be found.

In what follows we shall discuss five Hermetic texts. Two of them are from the Greek *Corpus Hermeticum*, number 1: *Poimandres*, and number 7. The other three are Coptic texts found in Nag Hammadi Codex VI, the *Discourse on the Eighth and Ninth*, *Asclepius 21–29*, and the *Prayer of Thanksgiving*.

1. *Corpus Hermeticum* 1: *Poimandres*
(Foerster 1:326–35; Layton, 449–59)

The *Poimandres* is an anonymous autobiographical account of a seer's vision of God and a revelation discourse in which God reveals to the seer the origins of the world and of humankind, and the way of salvation. There is no doubt who the anonymous seer is. He is identified in the title that appears at the beginning of the tractate in the Greek manuscripts: "Of Hermes Trismegistus: Poimandres." And references in other Hermetic texts make clear that the recipient of the revelation is Hermes Trismegistus.

Hermes begins his account by reporting an experience of ecstasy, and the appearance of a gigantic being who introduces himself: "I am Poimandres, the Mind of the Absolute Sovereignty." This being is none other than the transcendent God himself. That he is Mind or Intellect (*nous*) accords with a Middle Platonist doctrine that goes back to Aristotle. The mysterious name Poimandres is Egyptian: *p.eime nte re,* "the knowledge of Re" (the Egyptian sun god standing for the transcendent deity of philosophy). The name is clearly related to his Greek identity, "the Mind (or Knowledge) of the Absolute." Poimandres promises to reveal to Hermes what is essential to know about reality and God (chs. 1–3). The revelation that follows consists of a cosmogonic myth (4–11), an anthropogony (12–19), anthropology and ethics (20–23), and eschatology (24–26).

The cosmogony begins with Hermes seeing a bright light, and then a frightful darkness. From the light a "holy Logos" (Word) came upon Nature. Fire and air shot up to the height; earth and water remained below, stirred by the "spiritual Logos" (compare Genesis 1:2). Poimandres identifies the light as "Nous (Mind), your God," and the Logos as the Son of God. When Hermes wants to know how the elements of Nature came to be, Poimandres says that they came "from the Will of God, which took the Logos and saw the beautiful world and copied it." Mind, being "bisexual and life and light," brought forth through the Word "another Mind, the Demiurge," who created seven Administrators. They encompass the world in circles and their administration is called Fate or Destiny (4–9). In Greco-Roman astrology the motions of the seven planets were thought to be involved in the "fate" (*heimarmenē*) of the world and of the human race. The myth continues with the Logos of God uniting with the Creator-Mind, and their activity results in the production of birds, fish, and animals of all kinds (10–11). One can see in this passage allusions to the first creation story in the Book of Genesis (Genesis 1: 9-23).

> *Nature grasped Man in her embrace, "for they were in love." This explains why human beings on earth are "twofold: mortal because of the body, immortal because of the essential Man" (12–15).*

The anthropogonic myth begins with "the Father of all, the Nous (Mind), who is life and light" bringing forth a Man (*anthrōpos*) who "wore his father's image" (compare Genesis 1:27). Man stooped down and "showed to Nature below the beautiful form of God." Nature grasped Man in her embrace, "for they were in love." This explains why human beings on earth are "twofold: mortal because of the body, immortal because of the essential Man" (12–15). Nature then gave birth to seven men, "bisexual and sublime." Their bodies were made up of the four elements, their souls from life, and their minds from light. For a time they remained bisexual, but then they became divided into male and female, and were commanded to "increase and multiply" (16–18, compare Genesis 1:28).

> *Those who have mind are pious, good, and pure, but God is far away from the foolish, bad, and wicked (22–23).*

A hortatory pronouncement then follows: "Let man who has mind (*nous*) recognize himself as immortal, and the love (*erōs*) which is the cause of death, and everything that is." Not everyone possesses mind. The one who does recognizes himself, but the one who "loves the body from the seduction of love remains in the darkness." This is clarified in an exchange that follows. Since the Father of all consists of light and life, and from him comes the Man, "if you learn that you consist of life and light and that you come from these, you will go back to life" (18–21). Those who have mind are pious, good, and pure, but God is far away from the foolish, bad, and wicked (22–23).

In the eschatological section that follows, Poimandres teaches Hermes about the "dissolution of the material body." In the ascent of the disembodied soul all passions and vices are given back to the various spheres from which they were derived in the soul's original descent. The "essential man" proceeds to the Ogdoad (Eighth) where he praises the Father with those who are there. There he hears powers above the Ogdoad, that is, in the ninth sphere, praising God, who is presumably located in the tenth sphere. He and they ascend to the Father, "change themselves into powers, and having become powers they come to be in God. This is the good end of those who have obtained knowledge, to become God." Poimandres then bids Hermes to "become a guide to the worthy, so that the human race may by means of you be saved by God" (24–26).

Hermes then reports that he accepted this commission and began preaching to "earth-born men" to sober up from their drunkenness, and rise up from their sleep. Some of them heard and separated themselves from the darkness and begged Hermes for further instruction. Others went away to the "way of death." Hermes "sowed" in his converts "words of wisdom,"

This is the good end of those who have obtained knowledge, to become God.

and they were nourished by ambrosial water. At evening time, "I exhorted them to thank God; and when they had completed their thanksgiving they went each to his bed" (27–29).

Hermes then reports that he wrote down what he had learned from Poimandres. The utterance of the word brought new growth. "I have come, filled with truth by God's Spirit. Therefore with all my soul and strength I give praise to God the Father" (30).

The praise that Hermes offers consists of three *trishagia*, that is, threefold attributions of holiness. In the first set of three, God is praised in the third person: "Holy is God, the Father of the universe. Holy is God, whose will is performed by his powers. Holy is

God, who wishes to be known and is known by his own." In the second and third sets of three, God is addressed directly: "Holy are you, who. . . ." Hermes then prays that his "rational offerings" will be accepted, and that he will receive grace to "enlighten those who are in ignorance of their origin, my brothers, your children." The text concludes, "I go to life and into light. Blessed are you, Father. Your man wishes together with you to sanctify, as you have granted him all authority" (31).

The Hermetic tractate *Poimandres* functions as the fundamental basis for Hermetic doctrine, and is presupposed in all other Hermetic philosophical texts. In a sense, one can say that it plays a role in Hermetism similar to that played by the basic myth in the *Apocryphon of John* in the development of Sethian or Classic Gnosticism. Like the *Apocryphon of John* it contains a basic myth involving cosmogony, anthropogony, and eschatology, and posits self-knowledge as the basis for salvation. And, like that of the *Apocryphon of John*, the Hermetic myth is indebted to the two great creation texts of the Greco-Roman world, Plato's *Timaeus* and the two creation stories in the book of Genesis. The Anthropos myth may also have been based on an Alexandrian Jewish Gnostic myth of Anthropos (Man). But unlike the *Apocryphon of John*, the *Poimandres* is not critical of the Genesis story and raises no objection at all to what Moses said.

What is of special interest is the profound influence of Alexandrian Judaism that can be seen in the *Poimandres*. Its structure, and some of its contents, reflect influence from a first-century Alexandrian Jewish apocalypse, *2 Enoch* (now preserved only in Slavonic). Several parallels have been noted between elements in the text and the Hellenistic Jewish philosophy represented by Philo of Alexandria. The worship life of Hermes' converts as depicted in chapters twenty-nine and thirty-two certainly reflect influence from Jewish worship in the synagogue. For example, they are depicted as offering "thanksgiving" (*eucharistia*) and "blessing" (*eulogia*) to God. Hermes' praise of God "with all my soul and strength" in chapter 30 is reminiscent of the *Shema'* ("Hear, O Israel"), the command to love God with one's whole soul and strength (Deu-

280

teronomy 6:5 in the Greek version). The hymn in chapter 31, the ninefold ascription of holiness to God, harks back to the *Kedusha*, the hymn of praise of the Seraphim in Isaiah 6:3. The benediction, "Holy are you," is ubiquitous in Jewish prayer, for example in the weekday *Shemoneh 'esrei* (Eighteen Benedictions).

These and a number of other examples that could be cited indicate that the *Poimandres* was composed by someone thoroughly at home in the worship life of the Jewish synagogue. Yet, this person was a Hermetist, a disciple of Hermes Trismegistus, to whom the entire tractate is attributed.

The familiarity with Jewish worship life exhibited by the author of the *Poimandres* could only have been gotten before the annihilation of the Alexandrian Jewish community that took place as a result of the Jewish revolt against the Roman emperor Trajan in 115–117. An early second-century date can, therefore, be assigned to the *Poimandres*. Its author may have been a proselyte or "God fearer" loosely associated with an Alexandrian synagogue before the revolt. In his dissemination of the religion of Thrice Greatest Hermes, he borrowed a good deal from that Jewish affiliation.

2. Corpus Hermeticum 7
(Foerster 1:335–36; Layton, 460–62)

This short tractate has a rather long title in the Greek manuscripts: "That the greatest evil among humans is ignorance of God." It is in the form of a short sermon given by an unnamed preacher, identifiable as Hermes Trismegistus.

He begins his sermon, "You people, where are you rushing in your drunkenness, you who have drained the undiluted doctrine of ignorance?" (ch. 1). He appeals to those who can to sober up from their drunkenness,

Hermes makes it clear that the cause of ignorance is "the grave you carry around with you," that is, the body (ch. 2).

and "seek a guide who will lead (them) to the gates of knowledge." Hermes makes it clear that the cause of ignorance is "the grave you carry around with you," that is, the body (ch. 2). The body is the enemy that people have put on as a garment. It is the body that fills people with "filthy desire" so that they are not able to see or hear what they ought to see or hear (ch. 3).

This brief sermon expands on the exhortations addressed by Hermes in the *Poimandres* to earthborn men, urging them to repent, forsake corruption, and partake of immortality (ch. 27). It has been suggested that the author of this sermon is the same person as the one who composed the *Poimandres*. It can plausibly be assigned to second-century Alexandria.

3. *Discourse on the Eighth and Ninth*
(NHC VI,6: 52,1–63,32; *NH Library,* 321–27; *NH Scriptures,* 409–18)

This tractate is a dialogue between Hermes Trismegistus and an unnamed initiate. Since the initiate is repeatedly referred to as Hermes' son, we can assume that Tat is meant. Hermes is named three times in the text (58,28; 59,11; 63,24) and Trismegistus twice (59,15.24). Formally, the tractate is an initiation dialogue in which the mystagogue (Hermes) takes the initiate (Tat) through the steps of an initiation that leads to a vision of God and incorporation into a mystery community.

There are indications that a short title of this tractate was represented by line one of page fifty-two, but it is now lost owing to damage to the top parts of several pages in this part of Codex VI. The title now in use comes from a request by Tat for Hermes to lead him "through the discourse on the eighth and the ninth" (53,24–26). The discourse that follows represents the main part of the tractate; so its title has been applied by modern editors to the tractate as a whole. "The eighth" refers to the cosmic sphere of the fixed stars and the Zodiac, above the seven planetary

The brothers referred to are members of the Hermetic mystery fraternity into which Tat is being initiated.

spheres. "The ninth" refers to the sphere above that, where angels and souls sing hymns in praise to God. God himself is located in the tenth sphere, as he is, for example, in the Alexandrian Jewish apocalypse *2 Enoch*, the Gnostic *Apocalypse of Paul* (discussed in chapter 8), and the *Poimandres* (ch. 26).

The tractate begins with an introductory discussion between Hermes and Tat. Tat reminds Hermes that he has promised to bring his mind into the eighth and ninth. Hermes reminds Tat of the steps that he must take, and that he must honor his brothers, who are immortal. Tat then makes his formal request for the "discourse on the eighth and the ninth," so that he might be included with his brothers (52,2–53,27). The brothers referred to are members of the Hermetic mystery fraternity into which Tat is being initiated.

Hermes then bids Tat to pray with him to the Father of the universe. Tat is reminded of the progress that he has made in the study of "the books." Hermes tells Tat that it is fitting to pray to God "with all our mind and all our heart and our soul." Tat will be able to understand, and Hermes will be able "to deliver the discourse from the fountain that flows to me" (53,28–55,22). The books referred to here are to be understood as manuals designed to prepare a would-be initiate for the initiation proper. Prayer with mind, heart, and soul reflects the language used by Hermes in the *Poimandres* (ch. 31), which (as noted above) reflects Jewish liturgical language.

The main prayer then begins, in which God is praised for his words, his gift of life, and his providence (53,23–56,17). The prayer includes magical names, Zoxathazo and Zozazoth, and incantations of groups of the seven vowels of the Greek alphabet, from *alpha* to *omega* (56,17–22). A connection between the seven vowels and the seven planetary spheres is probably to be understood here. In the prayer Tat says that they have advanced to the seventh and have fulfilled God's will. Praying that the spiritual sacrifices that they have offered with their heart, soul, and strength are acceptable, he concludes the prayer with a petition for the immortal wisdom that will come with the vision of the eighth and the ninth (56,23–57,25).

Hermes and Tat then embrace, and Hermes announces that the light is coming to them. Hermes sees himself united with Mind, and he sees the angels singing a hymn in silence. Hermes bids Tat to continue his praise of God and sing in silence (57,26–59,23). Tat then exclaims, "I myself see this same vision in you. And I see the eighth and the souls that are in it and the angels singing a hymn to the ninth and its powers. And I see him who has the power of them all" (59,24–60,1). "He who has the power of them all" is God, located in the tenth sphere, as in the *Poimandres* (ch. 26).

Hermes then exhorts Tat not to speak about the vision, but to continue singing hymns to the Father. He is to sing to God that his praises "might be written in this imperishable book" (60,1–17). Tat then offers up a final prayer to God, giving thanks for the power and love that he has experienced. His prayer includes another series of groups of vowels of the alphabet (60,17–61,17).

Hermes then commands Tat to "write this book for his temple at Diospolis in hieroglyphic characters, titling it 'The Eighth Reveals the Ninth.'" The book is to be written on steles of turquoise. The steles are to be guarded by eight guardians, frog-faced and cat-faced statues on the left and the right. Tat is to do this "when I am in Virgo, and the sun is in the first half of the day, and fifteen degrees have passed by me" (61,18–62,20). The temple at Diospolis would have been located either in Diospolis Major, ancient Thebes (Luxor), or in Diospolis Minor (Hou, not far from Nag Hammadi). The sacred animals referred to may be understood as relating to the famous Ogdoad (group of eight primeval gods) at Hermopolis and the equally famous Ennead (group of nine primeval gods) at Heliopolis. In Greco-Egyptian tradition Thoth-Hermes was the local god of Hermopolis. The astrological instructions specify that Tat is to carry them out when Hermes, that is, the planet Mercury, is in the Zodiacal constellation Virgo.

Tat says that he will eagerly carry out Hermes' instructions. Hermes then says that Tat should inscribe an oath in the book that its readers submit to the law of God. The book should not be read by anyone until they have familiarized themselves with the "general" and "guiding" discourses, for one enters the way of immortality in stages (62,22–63,14). Tat agrees, and then the text of the oath is given. Readers are to swear by various divine beings that they will "guard the things that Hermes has said" (63,14–31). The tractate concludes with Hermes saying to Tat, "This is the perfect <discourse>, O my son" (63,31–32).

The *Discourse on the Eighth and Ninth* has been referred to as a reading mystery, designed to initiate readers into a mystery community by leading them through the various stages of an ascent of the soul culminating in a beatific vision. As such, it resembles very much another Hermetic tractate (not treated in this book), number thirteen in the *Corpus Hermeticum*, whose full title is, "A secret dialogue of Hermes Trismegistus on the mountain to his son Tat: On being born again, and on the promise to be silent." One can also find in the *Discourse on the Eighth and Ninth* a number of allusions to the *Poimandres*.

> The *Discourse on the Eighth and Ninth has been referred to as a reading mystery, designed to initiate readers into a mystery community by leading them through the various stages of an ascent of the soul culminating in a beatific vision.*

It is possible that the author was influenced at some points by Gnostic terminology or Gnostic conceptions. For example, the highest God is referred to in a prayer as unbegotten, from whom comes the "self-begotten one" and all "begotten things" (57,13–17). This language reminds us of the three principles of the Peratic system described by Hippolytus (discussed in chapter 7). The unbegotten god is equivalent to the Mind of the Absolute Sovereignty in *Poimandres*, the begotten god to the second Mind, the Demiurge (ch. 9).

Especially noticeable is the profound influence of Egyptian traditions in our tractate, something that one does not find in the Greek tractates of the *Corpus Hermeticum*. (It is possible, of course, that such pagan features would have been edited out of the tractates assembled by the Byzantine scholars responsible for the *Corpus Hermeticum* as we know it.)

The author of the *Discourse on the Eighth and Ninth* was probably a leader of a Hermetic fraternity in Alexandria. The tractate was probably composed sometime in the late second or early third century.

4. *Asclepius* (*Perfect Discourse*) 21–29 (NHC VI:8: 65,15–78,43; *NH Library*, 330–38; *NH Scriptures*, 425–36)

The tractate *Asclepius* is completely extant only in a Latin version, first attested in the fifth century. Some fragments of the Greek original are preserved. Its original title, in the Greek version, was "Perfect Discourse" (*logos teleios*). The earliest reference to the Greek version of the *Perfect Discourse* is dated to the beginning of the fourth century (Lactantius). This lengthy work is really a compendium of Hermetic discourses having to do with the place of humankind in the universe (*Asclepius* 2–18), on nature and the cult of the gods (19–29), and principles of the cosmic order (29–40). It is presented as a series of discourses given by Hermes Trismegistus to Asclepius, and concludes with a prayer (ch. 41).

At the beginning of the tractate Hermes Trismegistus invites Asclepius to join in a divine discourse, and tells Asclepius to call Tat to join them. Asclepius suggests that Ammon also join them, and Hermes agrees. (Ammon is named for the Egyptian god Amun.) Asclepius is usually addressed throughout the discourse, with Tat and Ammon as bystanders. The three are addressed together at one point in what remains of the Coptic version (72,30–31).

> *Evil is present in the world, but God has provided humans with consciousness and other means of overcoming it (14–16).*

Hermes begins his discourse with a discussion of the nature of the human soul, and the makeup of human beings in general (chs. 2–14). The universe is made up of matter and spirit. Evil is present in the world, but God has provided humans with consciousness and other means of overcoming it (14–16). Beside the supreme God, there are many kinds of gods, with different natures and duties (16–19). As for God, Father and Master of all, he is bisexual. All things, whether possessing a soul or soulless, come in both sexes. It is God who devised for all the mystery of procreation (19–21). It is at this point in the tractate that our Coptic excerpt begins.

The Coptic version is thought to be closer to the Greek version than is the Latin, but at points in the text there are some evidences of mistranslation. And there is some damage to the manuscript, resulting in loss of text in some places.

Our excerpt begins with Hermes discussing sexual intercourse between males and females. Sexual intercourse involves holy mysteries that are conducted in secret, lest they be subjected to the scorn of impious people (65,15–38). The discussion then turns to the distinction between people who are impious and atheistic, who are many, and the few people who are pious. The latter are the way they are because they have the gnosis that enables them to control their passions. Gods, since they came into

> As for the gods, they are creations of God; that is, the highest God "creates gods." But man, too, creates gods.

being from the purest element, do not need learning and knowledge. But man, who is twofold, mortal and immortal, needs to attain learning and knowledge (65,38–68,20). As for the gods, they are creations of God; that is, the highest God "creates gods." But man, too, creates gods. As God willed to create the inner man in his own image, so does man on earth create gods "according to his likeness" (68,20–70,2).

An extended apocalypse then follows in which the fate of Egypt is prophesied. Egypt, "the image of heaven" and "the temple of the world," will be abandoned by the gods. Foreigners will come into Egypt and rule it. Egypt, once "more pious than all countries," will become impious, and full of corpses. Egypt will be made a desert, and the River will turn to blood. The pious "will be counted as insane," and the impious "honored as wise." A new law will be established, and wicked angels will teach people things contrary to nature. "Such is the senility of the world: atheism, dishonor, and the disregard of noble words" (70,2–73,22).

But that's not the end of the story. "The Lord, the Father and god from the only first God, God the creator (*dēmiourgos*)," has established his design against disor-der. He who has submerged evil in a flood, or consumed it in fire, will restore the world to what it was. "This is the birth of the world" and the "restoration of nature" according to God's will. It is God's

> *Death comes with the dis-solution of the body and its sensations.*

will that the good world be an image of the Good (73,23–75,8). God (that is, the highest God) controls the heights of heaven; the Demiurge, called Zeus, controls the space between earth and heaven; Plutonius Zeus is lord over the earth and sea; and Kore (Persephone) controls the bearing of fruit for the nourishment of all creatures (75,9–25). The apocalypse concludes with a prophecy that "the lords of the earth" will establish themselves in a great city "on the Libyan mountain" (75,26–76,2).

Hermes' discourse continues with a discussion of individual eschatology. Death comes with the dissolution of the body and its sensations. When the soul leaves the body it comes to a heavenly being (*daimōn*) whom God has appointed as judge. The judge ex-amines the soul, and if it is found to be worthy it is allowed to proceed upward. Souls that are found to be stained by evil deeds are thrown downward. Suspended between heaven and earth, they are subjected to punishment. Severe pains are inflicted on them by punishing demons, the various punishments appropriate to their crimes (76,2–78,43). The Coptic text breaks off just before Hermes turns the discussion to the reward that comes to the souls of those who are pious and upright (*Asclepius* 29).

This excerpt is enough to illustrate the variety of beliefs that occur within the Hermetic literature. In contrast to some of the other tractates, *Asclepius* is considerably more world affirming. The affirmation of human sexuality that occurs at the beginning of the excerpt stands in stark contrast to the doctrine found in the *Poimandres*, that *erōs* leads to death. (One wonders, too, what might have motivated a monastic scribe to include this excerpt in the codex on which he was working.)

The extended apocalypse on the fate of Egypt is of special interest. It has been argued that the foreigners referred to, who establish a new law, are the Christians, who have overturned the native beliefs of the Egyptians. That is unlikely, for the *Perfect Discourse* is attested already in the early fourth century, before the legalization of Christianity and before its establishment in the Empire by Constantine. The apocalypse shows some influence from Stoic notions of cosmic cycles. The world's destruction in a conflagration is followed by a new cycle in which the world is restored and given a new beginning. But more to the point is the influence reflected in it of apocalypses composed in Upper Egypt in which the establishment of the city of Alexandria and Greek rule by the Macedonian Ptolemies are vigorously attacked. Those Egyptian apocalypses contain prophecies of the evils that will come to Egypt with foreign rule, and the eventual restoration of native kingship. The *Oracle of the Potter,* composed in Greek in the second century BCE, is the best-known example.

Asclepius, the "Perfect Discourse," was probably composed in Upper Egypt in the late third century. The excerpt in Codex VI was probably translated into Coptic sometime in the fourth century.

5. Prayer of Thanksgiving
(NHC VI,7: 63,33–65,7; NH Library, 328–29; NH Scriptures, 419–23)

At the end of the Latin *Asclepius,* as Hermes and his three pupils leave the sanctuary, they begin praying. Asclepius suggests that frankincense and spices should accompany their prayer. Trismegistus demurs, saying that all God wants is a prayer of thanksgiving. They begin their prayer, "We thank you, supreme and most high God, by whose grace alone we have attained the light of your knowledge." The prayer forms the conclusion to the tractate (*Asclepius* 41).

Essentially the same prayer is tacked on to a spell intended to establish a relationship with the god Helios that is part of a fourth-century Greek magical papyrus (Papyrus Mimaut, Paris, Louvre no. 2396). The spell occupies lines 494 through 611, the prayer lines 591 through 611.

A Coptic version of the same prayer is the seventh tractate of Nag Hammadi Codex VI. The Coptic version is closer to the Greek than it is to the Latin. Immediately following the conclusion of the *Discourse on the Eighth and Ninth* on page sixty-three, line thirty-three reads, "This is the prayer that they spoke." That line is decorated in the manner used to set off a title, but it is really an incipit and not a title. The title now used has been editorially assigned by modern editors. The prayer begins on the next line, "We give thanks to you! Every soul and heart is lifted up to you."

The names of those uttering the prayer are not given, but we can assume that Hermes and at least one pupil are the petitioners. Thanksgiving is offered to God the Father for giving them mind, speech, and knowledge. They rejoice because, while they were still in the body, God has made them "divine through your knowledge." The prayer is also addressed to a feminine divine being whom they have come to know, the "Womb of every creature," "Womb pregnant with the nature of the Father." It is not clear in the text itself who this is. Perhaps the Womb refers to Nature, who plays a role in the creation story in the *Poimandres*.

Trismegistus demurs, saying that all God wants is a prayer of thanksgiving.

The prayer concludes with a petition that they be preserved in knowledge and not stumble (64,30–65,2). In the Latin version, this petition is followed by a concluding sentence, which reads, "With such hopes we turn to a pure meal that includes no animal flesh." The Greek version has a lacuna in the manuscript, so we don't have the final two-and-a-half lines. The Coptic version has a narrative conclusion in the third person: "When they had said these things in prayer they embraced each other, and they went to eat their holy food, which has no blood in it" (65,2–7). This conclusion certainly reflects an active cult praxis, involving not only prayer but also ritual actions and a vegetarian common meal.

While some scholars think that the prayer was originally the concluding part of the *Asclepius*, it is more likely that it constituted a Hermetic prayer that circulated independently. It was editorially tacked on to the end of the *Asclepius* to give concrete expression to the closing prayers with which that tractate ends. It was also tacked on to the end of the aforementioned magical spell in the Papyrus Mimaut, for reasons that are not at all clear. The scribe of Codex VI thought it appropriate to add it as a closing prayer to the *Discourse on the Eighth and Ninth*.

The original Greek version of the prayer was probably composed sometime in the third century, somewhere in Egypt. It may have been composed by a leader of a Hermetic fraternity.

11 : Mani and Manichaeism

[Previous apostles] established churches that they chose in the places where they were. The apostle who chose his church in the west, his church did not reach to the east. The one who chose his church in the east, his elect did not come to the west. Thus, there are some here, others there. It is my hope and expectation that my church will go to the west and also to the east; and in every language they hear the voice of its proclamation, and it is proclaimed in all cities. Whereas the first churches were chosen according to place and city, it is provided for my church to go out from all cities, and its good news attain to every country.

IN THIS PASSAGE FROM THE *Kephalaia* ("Chapters," this one number 151) *of the Teacher*, a lengthy work preserved in Coptic, the prophet Mani is explaining to his disciples why his religion is superior to all of the preceding ones. His religion's universality is the first reason Mani cites for its superiority over other religions. Another reason is that his religion is set down in his writings and pictures, whereas many previous prophets never wrote anything. Yet another reason is that his religion incorporates the wisdom given in previous religions while at the same time it provides the final revelation that surpasses all others.

In the form of Manichaeism, Gnosticism became a world religion. A native of Babylonia, Mani (216–277) grew up in a Jewish Christian baptismal sect. In obedience to a revelation he received at the age of twenty-four, he founded a new religion and began propagating it in missionary journeys as far as India. Already before his death disciples of his founded the religion in parts of the Roman Empire. In the East, Manichaeism became firmly established in eastern Iran by the end of the fourth century. From there it was brought further eastward along the Silk Road to Bactria and onward as far as China. In the eighth century it became the state religion of the Uighur Turks, and under their patronage the religion became widely diffused in China. In China it survived as a secret religion into the seventeenth century.

> *A native of Babylonia, Mani (216–277) grew up in a Jewish Christian baptismal sect.*

In the West, Manichaeism was eventually established virtually everywhere in the Roman Empire, despite the fact that it was attacked by Roman authorities as a subversive foreign religion. It was largely wiped out in the West by severe persecution in the fifth and sixth centuries, but it continued to be hated and feared by medieval churchmen in the Latin West and the Greek East. The term *Manichaean* was used by church leaders to stigmatize the teachings of various Christian heretics who taught that the human body is intrinsically evil and cannot be the creation of a good God. Even Martin Luther, in the sixteenth century, was attacked by some zealous churchmen as a Manichaean.

The term *Manichaean* is derived from the Greek version of the Syriac name given to Mani by his followers, *Mānī ḥayyā,* "Living Mani" (*Manichaios* in Greek). The name Mani was also equated by his detractors with the Greek word *manēs,* "madman."

Before the twentieth century, the sources for our knowledge of the Manichaean religion consisted in reports found in writings of its opponents, who included such Christian writers as Epiphanius, Hegemonius, Cyril of Jerusalem, Ephraem the Syrian, Serapion of Thmuis, Didymus the Blind, Titus of Bostra, Augustine, Theodor bar Koni, Severus of Antioch, and others. Extensive reports, with varying degrees of reliability, were provided by these writers. The evidence provided by St. Augustine is particularly valuable because he had been a Manichaean for a number of years prior to his conversion to ecclesiastical Christianity. Some Muslim writers also provide extensive accounts of Manichaean teachings and practices. The *Fihrist* ("catalogue") of the tenth-century encyclopedist Ibn an-Nadim is an especially important source, for he relied on genuine Manichaean sources available to him in Arabic.

Early in the twentieth century archaeological expeditions at Turfan in Sinkiang (China) turned up several thousand fragments of Manichaean texts. These texts were written in some seventeen languages and dialects, such as Tokharian, Middle Persian, Parthian, Sogdian, Uighur, New Persian, Chinese, and others. Additional texts were discovered in Tun-huang in Chinese Central Asia. In the West, leaves of a Manichaean codex in Latin were found in 1918 near Tebessa in Algeria. Around the same time Syriac

Fig. 11.1 Manichean temple banner. 10th century. From Chotsko. Painting on ramie, 75.5 cm x 17 cm. Inventory No. MIK III 6283, Museum für Indische Kunst, Staatliche Museen zu Berlin. Photo by Iris Papadopoulos, © Bildarchiv Preussischer Kulturbesitz / Art Resource, N.Y.

fragments were found in Egypt. In November 1929 a large number of Coptic Manichaean texts were found, translations of texts originally written in Syriac. Now accessible are most of the *Kephalaia*, a psalm book, and a collection of homilies. Unfortunately, two codices were lost in the aftermath of the Second World War, one of them a canonical work, a collection of Mani's letters.

One of the most important manuscripts found in Egypt was first published in 1970, a miniature parchment codex of the late fourth or early fifth century inscribed in Greek, now known as the Cologne Mani Codex. It was found somewhere in Upper Egypt. It contains a valuable biography of Mani, including an account of his youth and his first missionary journeys, based on eyewitness accounts of his closest disciples. Since 1991 other Manichaean texts have been discovered in the Dakhleh Oasis in Egypt at the site of ancient Kellis (Ismant el-Kharab). These include some three thousand Greek and Coptic papyrus fragments from the fourth century. They are now in the process of being edited and published.

In what follows we shall discuss the life of Mani, Mani's writings, the Manichaean mythological system, Manichaean community life and worship, and the spread of Manichaeism in the Roman Empire.

1. The life of Mani
(Gardner-Lieu, 46–108; 265–68)

Mani was born in Seleucia-Ctesiphon (on the Tigris River in Babylonia) on April 14, 216 CE. His father's name was Pattig, and his mother's name was (probably) Maryam. Both are said to have been of Parthian royal blood. Pattig had come to Seleucia-Ctesiphon from Ecbatana (Hamadan), the ancient capital of the Parthian kingdom. One day when Pattig was worshipping in a temple he heard a voice commanding him not to eat meat or drink wine, and to abstain from sexual intercourse. Pattig joined a community belonging to an ascetic Jewish Christian sect founded a century earlier by a Jewish Christian prophet named Elchasai. When Pattig joined the group, presumably in obedience to the voice in the temple, his wife Maryam was pregnant with Mani. When Mani was four years old

Pattig brought him to the Elchasaite community, where he remained until the age of twenty-four. The members of the sect practiced daily water ablutions of their bodies and the vegetables they ate for food. They referred to their religion as the Law, and observed the Sabbath. They also honored Jesus as the True Prophet.

At the age of twelve Mani is reported to have experienced a series of revelations given to him by his heavenly twin or *Syzygos* ("yokefellow" or "companion" in Greek). Mani regarded this heavenly double of himself as the "Paraclete" promised by Jesus in the Gospel of John (John 14:16). As a result of the revelations he received, Mani came to reject the practices of the group in which he was living. He rejected the ablutions practiced by his co-religionists, opposed their ritual use of non-wheaten bread, and refused to work any longer in the sect's gardens. Indeed, he tried to reform the group in accordance with his new vision of the truth. Over time his actions caused dissension in the group, and a good deal of hostility. Some members, however, regarded him as some sort of prophet.

At the age of twenty-four Mani experienced a new set of revelations from his heavenly twin. He was commanded to leave the group and to go out on a mission to found a new religion based on the revelations he had received.

Much of what we know of Mani's early life is derived from the Greek Cologne Mani Codex. Unfortunately, nothing is said in that or any other source about Mani's education. By the time that he left the Elchasaite sect Mani was obviously a very learned and well-read man, with a thorough knowledge of most of the New Testament scriptures and other early Christian writings. The writings of the apostle Paul were especially important to him, something that would run counter to the teachings of the Jewish Christians among whom he lived. Mani's veneration of Paul was undoubtedly influenced by Marcionite Christianity, for which

The writings of the apostle Paul were especially important to him, something that would run counter to the teachings of the Jewish Christians among whom he lived.

Paul was the sole apostolic authority. Other early Christian writings known to him would have included the *Gospel of Thomas* and the *Hymn of the Pearl,* and probably the Syriac gospel harmony produced by Tatian (the *Diatessaron*). Indeed, his idea of his heavenly twin probably owes something to the Thomas tradition. His knowledge of astrology seems to have been based on the writings of a Syrian Christian named Bardaisan. He was also familiar with Jewish apocalyptic writings, especially the Enochic literature (*1 Enoch, Book of the Giants*). In the Cologne Mani Codex there are quotations from apocalypses (revelations) attributed to Adam, Sethel (Seth), Enosh, Shem, and Enoch. He had also probably read some of the Sethian Gnostic writings.

> *Mani was not only an intellectual and a mystic, but he was also an artist of note.*

Mani was not only an intellectual and a mystic, but he was also an artist of note. He produced a book of paintings illustrating aspects of his religious system (the *Ardahang,* unfortunately lost). The religion that he founded encouraged the production of works of art, such as illuminated manuscripts. Above all, he emphasized the importance of writing down his revelations and his version of the truth. All this would indicate that Mani must have had access to a library of some sort.

When he left the sect in which he was reared, he was accompanied by his father Pattig, and two other members of the sect. In 241 Mani sailed by boat to India and then traveled up the Indus valley to Turan, where he won over the local king to his religion. Soon after the succession of Shapur I (242–273) as sole King of Kings of the newly resurgent Iranian empire, Mani returned to Babylonia. He probably delivered personally to the king the only writing that he composed in Middle Persian, the *Shabuhragan* ("dedicated to Shapur"). Shapur welcomed Mani into his entourage and gave him permission to propagate his new religion in the realm. Mani also made missionary journeys to Media, Parthia, and the Caucasus.

Mani's experiences in India exposed him to Buddhism, and a number of Buddhist concepts were incorporated into the Manichaean religion as it developed in the East. Since Zoroastrianism had long been the official religion in Iran, Mani incorporated a number of Zoroastrian features into his religion. Of course, the earliest influences on him were Jewish and Christian, and those elements pre-dominate in the spread of Manichaeism in the West.

After Shapur's death, Mani enjoyed a positive relationship with the new king, Hormizd, but this situation did not last long. Hormizd soon died, and his successor, Bahram I (274–77) adopted an attitude of hostility toward Mani. The head of the Zoroastrian magi, Karder, persuaded Bahram to take action against the Babylonian prophet. Mani's religion, after all, contradicted the essentials of Zoroastrian faith and practice. Mani was summoned to appear before the king, accused by Magian officials, and was sent in chains to a prison. After twenty-six days in prison he died, probably on February 26, 277.

His death is described in Manichaean sources as a crucifixion, and was observed annually in a festival called the Bema. In that festival an effigy of Mani was placed on a platform with five steps (the *bema*). The *Manichaean Psalm Book* contains a number of psalms composed for the festival.

Mani considered himself to be the last of the apostles commissioned by God the Father. The line of apostles begins with Seth, son of Adam (regularly referred to in Manichaean sources as Sethel), and includes Enosh, Enoch, Shem, Buddha, Zarathustra (Zoroaster), Jesus, Paul, and an unnamed "righteous man of truth" (probably Marcion) just before Mani himself (*Kephalaia*, ch. 1). As noted at the beginning of this chapter, Mani placed great emphasis on writing down the revealed truth, so it is not surprising that he devised a canon of scripture.

2. Mani's Writings (Gardner-Lieu, 151–75)

There are several canon lists in various languages of Mani's scriptures, which he wrote in the Aramaic dialect of southern Mesopotamia (Syriac). There are minor variations among the lists, reflecting different times and places, but the earliest one, preserved in the

Kephalaia (ch. 1), lists the following seven works: (1) the *Living Gospel*; (2) the *Treasure of Life*; (3) the *Pragmateia*, sometimes called the *Treatise*; (4) the *Book of Mysteries*; (5) the *Book of the Giants*; (6) the *Letters*; and (7) *Psalms and Prayers*. The *Shabuhragan*, a summary of his doctrine written in Zoroastrian guise, is the only work Mani wrote in Middle Persian, the language of the Iranian Empire. It was dedicated to his patron, Shapur I. In addition he produced the *Picture Book* (*Ardahang*, *Eikōn* in Greek), with paintings illustrating aspects of his teachings. All of Mani's canonical works are lost, as is the *Picture Book*. There are a few fragments of some of them preserved in other sources, but there is not enough left to get a good picture of the extent and content of Mani's canonical works.

> There are a few fragments of some of Mani's canonical works preserved in other sources, but there is not enough left to get a good picture of the extent and content of Mani's canonical works.

A subcanonical work of great importance, preserved in Coptic, is the *Kephalaia of the Teacher*. It originally consisted of over 500 pages consisting of teachings of Mani recorded by disciples of the first generation (end of the third century). Most of the second half of the codex is lost.

The prologue of the *Living Gospel* is preserved in the Cologne Mani Codex. The opening passage reads, "I Mannichaeus, apostle of Jesus Christ, through the will of God, the Father of Truth, from whom I also came into being. He lives and abides for all eternity." Mani goes on to say, "I declared the truth to my companions; I preached peace to the children of peace" (Cologne Mani Codex, pp. 66–68). One can notice the influence of the apostle Paul's letters in Mani's opening lines. According to Arabic sources, the *Living Gospel* comprised twenty-two chapters, each beginning with a different letter of the Aramaic alphabet.

There are two extant quotations of a Latin translation of the *Treasure of Life*. In the longer of these, Mani expounds on a well-known episode in the Manichaean myth, featuring the "seduction of the archons." (See discussion of the myth below.)

The Patriarch Severus of Antioch (512–538) quotes a lengthy passage from an unnamed work, probably the *Pragmateia*. In it Mani expounds on the two principles of Light and Darkness, and the time of the "mixture," and teaches that matter will finally be destroyed.

We have nothing from the *Book of Mysteries*, but an-Nadim, writing in Arabic in the tenth century, reports that it began with Mani's discussion of the teachings of the followers of Bardaisan.

Mani's *Book of the Giants* was an adaptation of the *Book of the Giants* attributed to the biblical patriarch Enoch. Fragments of the original Aramaic version of that pseudepigraphic Enochic work were found among the Dead Sea Scrolls in the Judean desert. It was an apocalyptic work that expanded on the story of the fallen angels ("sons of God") in Genesis 6:1-4. Their progeny were the *nephilim* ("giants"). It can safely be assumed that the original *Book of the Giants* was in use in the Elchasaite community in which Mani grew up.

A large number of titles of Mani's *Letters* are provided by an-Nadim. The titles usually relate either to the subject matter, or give the names of individuals or communities addressed. Among the Manichaean manuscripts found at Medinet Madi in the Egyptian Fayum were a codex containing Mani's *Letters*, and a historical work. Unfortunately both of these were lost in the aftermath of the Second World War before they could be edited and published. Papyrus fragments have been found at Ismant el-Kharab in Egypt of a Coptic codex that probably contained at least some of the *Letters*. The fragments are now in the process of being studied in preparation for publication.

A lengthy epistle in Latin translation is found in the works of St. Augustine, the *Fundamental Epistle*. It deals with the two primary substances, Light and Darkness. A quotation from Mani's *Letter to Edessa* is found in the Cologne Mani Codex (p. 64).

As for Mani's *Psalms and Prayers*, we have no certainly identifiable quotations or testimonies. It is possible that some of them are preserved in the *Manichaean Psalm Book*, one of the Coptic codices discovered at Medinet Madi.

3. The Manichaean Mythological System
(Gardner-Lieu, 176–230)

As has already been noted, Mani drew from many sources in devising his own deliberately syncretistic religion. While the complicated myth that he created clearly drew upon previously existing Gnostic sources, his own system drew on other religious traditions as well. The central core, however, is the offer of salvation based upon a revealed knowledge (gnosis) of the nature of God and the world, and the divine nature of the human soul. While we can use the term "myth" to describe his system, the very concept of myth was foreign to Mani, for he considered his religious system to be literally true, almost in a scientific sense.

Mani's system can be epitomized in the expression "two principles and three times." The two principles are Light (good) and Darkness (evil, matter). The three times are "beginning," "middle," and "end." In the beginning Light and Darkness are completely separate one from the other; in the middle time (the present) they are mixed together; in the end they will be eternally separated. Mani's radical dualism of two absolute principles differs from those forms of Gnosticism that feature a tragic

> *As has already been noted, Mani drew from many sources in devising his own deliberately syncretistic religion.*

fall within the Godhead from which evil derives. Of the Gnostic mythological systems encountered thus far in this book, that of the *Paraphrase of Shem* (NHC VII,1), with Light and Darkness and Spirit (mixture) between them, comes closest to that of Mani. While there is no single source that provides us with the Manichaean myth as a whole, its essentials can be summarized on the basis of details drawn from various Manichaean or anti-Manichaean sources.

Mani's system features a considerable number of active divine beings, good and evil. The Kingdom of Light is ruled by the Father of Greatness, and his kingdom is an extension of himself. It has four divine attributes: purity, light, power, and wisdom. The Father resides in five intellectual powers: mind, thought, insight, counsel, and consideration. These five are also depicted as five elements of living air, light, wind, water, and fire. Twelve aeons surround the Father, distributed in threes toward the four directions of heaven. From these aeons come 144 "aeons of the aeons."

Opposed to, and originally completely separate from, the Kingdom of Light is the realm of the King of Darkness, the domain of evil matter. The realm of darkness also has dark elements of smoke, darkness, fire, water, and wind, ruled over by five evil archons. Countless demons populate this realm, constantly fighting and devouring one another.

The Prince of Darkness, reaching the upper limit of his territory, catches a glimpse of the light, and, desiring to possess its life, goes on the attack. In the struggle that follows the Father of Light calls forth the Great Spirit, the Mother of Life, who evokes the First Man. (Avoiding any hint of sexual activity, various emanations in the Manichaean system are not generated, but are "called forth"). The First Man, armed with the five powers of light, goes out into battle and is defeated. His fivefold armor, constituting the "living Soul," is devoured by the powers of evil. The divine soul therefore becomes mixed with the dark elements of matter. The defeated First Man lies unconscious in the depths. This triad of divine beings (Father of Light, Mother of Life, and First

This differentiation of five planets from the sun and the moon is distinctly Manichaean, for other Gnostic systems include the sun and the moon with the five planets as a group of seven.

Man) is somewhat reminiscent of the Sethian divine triad of Father, Mother, and Son. The divine Soul is also called the "Cross of Light," which is also personified as the "suffering Jesus."

In order to save First Man, the Father of Light calls forth Beloved of the Lights, from whom comes the Great Builder. The latter produces the Living Spirit, who has five sons: King of Splendor, King of Honor, Adamas of Light, King of Glory, and Atlas. The Living Spirit sends his Call from the lowest part of the realm of light to the First Man lying below. The First Man is aroused by the Call from his sleep and utters an Answer. The Living Spirit, together with his five sons, descends to the First Man and leads him up to the realm of Light.

But there is still light mixed with evil matter that needs to be redeemed. The Living Spirit creates with the help of his sons ten heavens and eight earths. He thus assumes the role of the Demiurge, who in other Gnostic systems is an ignorant or malicious being. In order to create the cosmos, the Living Spirit has to use material of a mixed compound of light and darkness. While the sun and the moon are vessels of pure light, the five planets and the stars are evil rulers, having been created from material mixed with darkness. This differentiation of five planets from the sun and the moon is distinctly Manichaean, for other Gnostic systems include the sun and the moon with the five planets as a group of seven. The notion of seven planetary spheres (including sun and moon) is part of the standard cosmology of the Greco-Roman world since the fourth century BCE.

With the cosmos in place as a prison for the forces of darkness, the process of saving the divine soul captured in it begins with a third series of emanations. The Father of Greatness calls forth the Third Messenger, whose duty it is to extract from the powers of darkness the light they still contain. The Third Messenger, who dwells in the ship of the sun, has a female counterpart called the Virgin of Light (sometimes depicted as twelve maidens). The Virgin of Light dwells in the ship of the moon. When the male powers of darkness see her as a beautiful naked woman, they are consumed by lust, and eject the light in their semen. Similarly, the female powers of darkness, lusting after the naked form of the Third Messenger, eject their fetuses as abortions. The light thus comes down to the earth, where it is bound up in plant and animal life. The Manichaean Virgin of Light, who elicits the lust of the powers of darkness, reminds us of Norea, whose adventures with the archons are depicted in Sethian or Classic Gnostic texts already discussed (see chapters 3 and 4).

The myth continues with the Third Messenger calling forth the Column of Glory (the "perfect man" of Ephesians 4:13), and equipping the "ships of light" (sun and moon) for the transport of the light to the New Paradise built by the Great Builder. Saved light particles are brought up to the moon in its waxing stage, and with its waning they are sent on to the sun, and from there to Paradise.

In an attempt to retain control of the captive particles of light, the powers of darkness create Adam and Eve, brought forth by the demons Saklas and Nabroel. The Sethian Gnostic Demiurge Saklas (fool) has thus been demoted in the Manichaean system. Adam was created according to the image of the Third Messenger that the demons had seen on high. Human beings are thus of a dual nature, consisting of a material body and a soul created according to the divine image. Jesus the Splendor descends to Adam to arouse him from sleep and provide him with saving gnosis. Adam's salvation is paradigmatic of all human redemption in the Manichaean system. In the subsequent course of history Jesus evokes the Light Mind (Nous), who calls forth the Apostle of Light. The Apostle of Light is incarnated in the various prophets, beginning with Sethel, and including Buddha, Zoroaster, and Jesus the Messiah. The culmination of this process is the commissioning of Mani himself.

The culmination of world history in Manichaean eschatology is the Great War between the forces of good and evil. In the practice of true religion, light is liberated. And with the final liberation of all the particles of light, every soul will be judged. The role of judge will be played by Jesus, who will return for that purpose. The elect will rise to heaven, and the world will be purified in a conflagration that will

> *A striking feature of the Manichaean system is the manifold role played in it by Jesus.*

last for 1468 years. Evil matter and the damned souls will be forever imprisoned in a "lump" (Greek *bōlos*) inside a gigantic pit covered with a stone. The separation of light from darkness thus attained will last forever.

The conflagration that lasts for 1468 years is found in one of the Gnostic texts from Nag Hammadi, the *Concept of our Great*

Power (NHC VI,*4*: 46,27–28; discussed in chapter 8). The lump in which evil matter and damned souls are imprisoned at the end is found in another Nag Hammadi tractate, the *Paraphrase of Shem* (NHC VII,*1*: 45,18; discussed in chapter 7).

A striking feature of the Manichaean system is the manifold role played in it by Jesus. As "Jesus the Splendor" he is one of the gods of the Manichaean pantheon. Jesus the Splendor plays a central role in redemption, awakening Adam from his sleep and providing him with the saving gnosis. As the "suffering Jesus" he is the personification of the "living Soul's" light particles trapped in the material cosmos. As Jesus the Christ he appeared in history as an avatar of the "true prophet." Manichaeism's Christology is docetic: Jesus the Christ only appeared to have a real body, and only appeared to suffer and die. At the end Jesus will preside over the last judgment.

4. Manichaean Community Life and Worship (Gardner-Lieu, 231–81)

Manichaean communities consisted of two interdependent groups, the "Elect" and the "Hearers" or "Catechumens." Manichaean church leadership, drawn from the Elect, was organized along strict hierarchical lines. Its head was the prime Leader (Greek *archegos*, Latin *princeps*), successor to the prophet Mani. Next came twelve Apostles or Teachers, seventy-two Bishops, and three hundred sixty Presbyters (Elders). The number of bishops is based on the story of the sending out of the Seventy in the Gospel of Luke, that is, the variant reading "seventy-two" in Luke 10:1, instead of the majority reading "seventy." The number of presbyters is evidently based on astrological lore. The successor to Mani maintained his residence in the twin cities Seleucia-Ctesiphon in Babylonia until the tenth century, when it was moved to Samarkand.

While the elaborate Manichaean myth was probably not given much prominence in the daily lives of Manichaeans, one detail from the myth was of central importance, that is, the imprisonment of light particles in matter, especially in plant life. It was the duty of those illuminated by the Mind (Nous), that is, Mani's message, to be instruments in the liberation of the divine light imprisoned in the cosmos. Central to this liberation was a dietary regimen that involved a symbiotic relationship between the Elect and the Hearers.

The Manichaean Elect were enjoined to observe the five commandments: (1) truthfulness, (2) non-injury, (3) chastity, (4) purity of the mouth, and (5) poverty. These could be summarized as the "three seals": (1) the seal of the mouth, (2) the seal of the hands, and (3) the seal of the breast. Obeying these precepts involved abstinence from marriage and procreation, abstinence from manual labor, especially that involved in the gathering and preparation of food, and dependence on the Hearers for daily sustenance. By refraining from harvesting or preparing food, they would not do injury to the Cross of Light bound up in fruit and vegetable life. Bathing in water was also forbidden. By their pious lives and prayers, the Elect would liberate the light particles that they had eaten in the fruits and vegetables given to them by the Hearers. This, too, would lead to their salvation after death.

As for the Hearers, they were allowed to marry and carry out normal daily activities. They were enjoined to observe a set of commandments that involved the prohibition of killing, lying, false testimony, unchastity, stealing, and black magic. Their main obligation was to provide for the sustenance of the Elect, and this was the condition of their salvation. Acquisition of wealth was also encouraged for the Hearers. An especially pious act for Hearers would be the giving of a child to the community so that the child could eventually become part of the Elect. Direct salvation after death was usually not possible for the Hearers, except in cases of extraordinary piety. What a Hearer could hope for was reincarnation as a member of the Elect.

The Elect received the offerings of the Hearers, especially bread and fruit, and ate them at their sacred meal, observed once a day except on fast days. The meal was preceded by an apology for the bread, in which the Elect exempted themselves from the guilt involved in injury to the particles of light resulting from the preparation of the food. Weekly fast days were Sunday for the Hearers, and Sundays and Mondays for the Elect. Fasting was also observed on other occasions, and a month of fasting preceded the great annual festival of the Bema. Ritual prayers, hymns and psalms, readings from scripture, and sermons were part of the fasting services. Other ritual actions introduced by Mani were understood as reenactments of divine archetypes, five of them associated with the "mystery of the First Man": "peace," "right hand," "kiss," "salutation," and "laying on of hands."

Especially important in the worship life of the Manichaean church was the annual festival of the Bema, at which the crucifixion of Mani was observed.

Especially important in the worship life of the Manichaean church was the annual festival of the Bema, at which the crucifixion of Mani was observed. The Bema was construed as the "Judgment Seat (*bēma*) of Christ" before which all must finally appear (2 Corinthians 5:10). The actual Bema in the ceremony was a five-tiered platform covered with cloth on which an effigy of Mani was placed. Mani occupies the Bema until Jesus comes as end-time judge. Special psalms were composed for the festival.

The Bema festival seems to have replaced the observance of Easter in the Manichaean church. According to Augustine (*Fundamental Epistle* 8) this is because Mani really did suffer whereas Christ, who only appeared to be a man of flesh, did not really suffer.

5. Manichaeism in the Roman Empire
(Gardner-Lieu, 109–50)

As already noted, Manichaeism was very successful in its march eastward along the Silk Road, even becoming a state religion among the Uigur Turks in the eighth century. The farther east it spread, the more it adapted itself to Buddhist culture and religion. Among Manichaeans in China, Mani came to be known as the

"Buddha of Light." Manichaeism survived in the East a thousand years longer than it did in the West.

In what follows, we shall concentrate our discussion of Manichaean expansion on its dissemination in the Roman Empire, where the opposition to Manichaeism and Gnostic heresies in general was much stronger.

Manichaean missions to various regions in the Roman Empire began during Mani's lifetime. These missions were carried out by able and devoted disciples of Mani. Especially prominent in the sources are the names of Adda, Pattig the teacher (not Mani's father of the same name), Gabryab, Pappos, Thomas, and Akouas. Adda and Pattig are especially prominent in the sources, and Adda composed a number of Manichaean writings. Adda is reported to have reached Alexandria in Egypt by around 270 or a little before. Pappos is also mentioned as a missionary to Egypt, presumably to Upper Egypt. Pappos was a close friend of Mani and a recipient of one of Mani's letters. Gabryab is associated with the mission to Armenia. Among Mani's letters is one addressed to Armenia.

The travels of the missionaries would have followed the trade routes that were well established by that time, both by land and by sea. The missionaries, members of the Elect, would also have been accompanied by scribes and other assistants from the ranks of the Hearers. The Manichaean missionaries, while they are sometimes reported to have gone door to door in various places in quest of converts, certainly must have adopted a conscious missionary strategy. They would aim to convince Christians whom they encountered that their religion was a pure and unadulterated form of Christianity, whereas ecclesiastical (catholic) Christianity was rife with errors.

Indeed, the Manichaean Hearers as a group were not very familiar with the details of the canonical teachings, and the Elect were usually not in a hurry to divulge them.

Many of the Manichaean missionaries were skilled debaters, and were eager to engage members of Christian churches in theological debates. The Manichaean missionaries were eager to point out such errors in catholic Christianity as the retention of the Jewish Bible as the Christian Old Testament, and the doctrine of the true humanity of Christ. In the course of these debates, they did not reveal much of the mythological teachings found in the canonical Manichaean scriptures. Indeed, the Manichaean Hearers as a group were not very familiar with the details of the canonical teachings, and the Elect were usually not in a hurry to divulge them.

Manichaeans also enjoyed some success among non-Christians. In approaching pagans they could draw on supposed links between their religion and aspects of Greco-Roman philosophy and religion. While Christians would argue that the Old Testament contained prophecies of Christ, Manichaeans could argue that Hermes Trismegistus, Plato, and others taught things that Mani found useful in the propagation of his religion.

The spread of Manichaeism into Egypt in the early period of Manichaean expansion is reasonably well-known, thanks to the manuscript discoveries of the last century. Manichaeism probably came into Upper Egypt sometime in the 260s, first by sea from Mesopotamia to the Red Sea coastal seaport Berenice, and from there overland to Hypsele, near Lycopolis. Manichaeism became well established in Lycopolis (Assiut) and the surrounding area, as can be inferred from the Lycopolitan dialect of Coptic that is the language of the Medinet Madi manuscripts. While Medinet Madi is located in the Fayum, the manuscripts would have come from Lycopolis. From Lycopolis, too, came some of the manuscripts recently discovered in the Dakhleh Oasis of Egypt. There is good reason to believe that at least some of the Manichaean Coptic texts found in Egypt were translated directly from Syriac originals, rather than from Greek translations of the Syriac.

The Manichaeans organized themselves into small cells, which met in private homes. The strong emphasis on asceticism found in Manichaeism, especially as practiced by the Elect, would probably have influenced later ascetic movements in Egypt such as the "coenobitic" monasticism (monks living in communities) founded in the early fourth century by St. Pachomius. And we have already noted some possible Manichaean influences in some of the Gnostic texts from Nag Hammadi.

Before the end of the third century, Manichaean teachings were the subject of refutations from the side of ecclesiastical Christianity in Egypt and from the side of pagan philosophy. Theonas, bishop of Alexandria (282–300), wrote a letter against Manichaean teachings partially preserved on a papyrus fragment (P. Rylands 469). Alexander of Lycopolis, a pagan Platonist philosopher, wrote an extensive refutation of Manichaeism.

On the basis of the African proconsul's report the emperor Diocletian issued the first public edict against Manichaeism in the year 302.

From Egypt Manichaeism spread along the northern coast of Africa to Roman North Africa. The proconsul of Africa wrote a detailed account of the sect's activities in that area, and on the basis of that report the emperor Diocletian issued the first public edict against Manichaeism in the year 302. This and other state measures taken against the Manichaeans will be discussed below.

From bases on the eastern frontier of the Empire, Manichaean missionaries brought their religion into Syria and Asia Minor, and from there into Greece, the Balkans, and Italy. A fourth-century inscription on a tombstone of a Manichaean Elect virgin named Bassa was found in 1906 on the Dalmatian coast. Manichaeism is also attested in Sparta in Greece in the early fourth century.

The most well-known Manichaean of the fourth century was St. Augustine.

The first Manichaean missionary to arrive in Rome was called Bundos, and he arrived during the reign of Diocletian. Manichaeans in Rome were put under an episcopal ban by Pope Miltiades (311–314). Also in the fourth century Manichaeans spread their religion in Spain and Gaul.

The most well-known Manichaean of the fourth century was St. Augustine. Born in Thagaste (in what is now Algeria) in 354, he became a Manichaean Hearer in the last year of his studies in Carthage at the age of nineteen. His writings are certainly the most important source of information on the history of Manichaeism during his lifetime. Augustine was a Manichaean Hearer for several years. After teaching in Rome for some time, his Manichaean friends arranged for him to apply for the chair of rhetoric at Milan. It was there that he began to break away from his Manichaean connections. His conversion to catholic Christianity took place in 386, and he was baptized by Bishop Ambrose on Easter 387.

From Augustine's writings we can gain a good idea of what might have attracted people to the Manichaean religion.

As already noted, the Manichaeans found a ready target among ecclesiastical Christians in their acceptance of the Old Testament. Manichaeans were eager to point out the sexual sins of many of the patriarchs recorded in the Old Testament, and the peculiarities they found in many of the Old Testament laws. Since by that time the church was made up mostly of Gentiles, Manichaean rejection of the Old Testament found a ready audience.

Another attraction of Manichaeism was its community life, fostered in the small cells that made up the sect. Close friendships could be established in Manichaean communities, and this is something that Augustine himself experienced.

There was even an aesthetic appeal to be found in Manichaeism. As already noted, Mani himself was an accomplished artist, and he illustrated his teachings with the paintings in his *Picture Book*. Art and calligraphy played a large role in the dissemination of Manichaeism. A good example of the scribal skills among the Manichaeans is the Cologne Mani Codex. That miniature codex has twenty-three lines to a page, copied into a text area measuring only 3.5 by 2.5 centimeters.

The asceticism practiced by the Manichaeans attracted many converts as well. This may sound strange, but it is a fact that asceticism and the taming of bodily passions was widely admired, if not widely practiced, in Late Antiquity.

Finally, Manichaean dualism made sense to a lot of people vexed by the problem of evil in the world. The problem of theodicy—how a good God could permit evil to exist in his created order—was a live issue in postexilic Judaism, and then in Christianity as well. The Manichaean solution was that evil had an independent existence, originally co-eternal with the Father of Light. In this time of mixture, there is an ongoing conflict of light and darkness in the cosmos, and this is experienced in the lives of individuals. In the end, evil will be eternally separated from good.

The expansion of the Manichaean religion in the Roman Empire is truly astonishing. Nevertheless, it seems that wherever the Manichaeans went they experienced opposition and hostility. Emperor Diocletian's edict against the Manichaeans was promulgated a year before the outbreak of the Great Persecution against the Christians in 303. Diocletian portrayed Manichaeism as a Persian threat to

The houses in which Man-ichaeans gathered were to be appropriated by the state, and their teachers were to be severely punished.

the Empire. In due course, he said, the Manichaeans will infect the empire "with the damnable customs and perverse laws of the Persians as with the poison of a malignant serpent." He ordered that their books were to be burnt, and, if they refused to recant, the people among them of low social standing were to be put to death, and those of higher status sent to the quarry at Phaeno or the mines at Proconnesus. Their property was to be confiscated.

After the end of the Great Persecution, and the establishment of Christianity by Constantine, the Arian heresy condemned at the Council of Nicea in 325 was at first seen by the ecclesiastical establishment to be a greater threat to the church than Manichaeism. (Arius taught that Christ was of a "similar being" [*homoiousios*] with God the Father, whereas the Nicene Creed taught that he was of the "same being" [*homoousios*]). But it did not take long for Christian leaders to take measures against the Manichaeans. Around 340 a counter-biography of Mani was composed (the *Acts of Archelaus*) that achieved wide circulation, and bishops and presbyters warned their catechumens of the dangers of the Manichaean heresy.

The first edict directed against the Manichaeans by a Christian emperor was promulgated in 372 by the Emperor Valentinian. The houses in which Manichaeans gathered were to be appropriated by the state, and their teachers were to be severely punished. Emperor Theodosius issued an edict in 381 that denied the Manichaeans the right to bequeath their property, or to live under the protection of Roman law. This was followed by other measures taken by state and ecclesiastical authorities against the Manichaeans. Imperial edicts issued by Byzantine emperors in the sixth century provided for the death penalty for Manichaeans who refused to abjure their heresy.

By the end of the sixth century the Manichaean religion was virtually extinct, both in the Latin West and in the Greek East. After that heretics of various stripes could still be attacked or denounced as Manichaeans, but the term had been emptied of its meaning. Real Manichaeans no longer existed.

12. The Mandaeans

A Surviving Relic of Ancient Gnosis

On Sunday the first of days,
who saw what I have seen?
Who saw the alien
who went and settled in the house of
 his friends?
I am the one who saw the alien,
my eyes were filled with light.
With light my eyes were filled,
and in my knowledge, knowledge
 [manda] settled.
Knowledge settled in my heart,
and my mouth was filled with praise,
Filled was my mouth with praise,
and I arose and praised my Father.
I arose and praised my Father,
from morning until evening I praised
 the exalted radiance.

THESE VERSES ARE FROM A Sunday hymn in the *Canonical Prayerbook* of the Mandaeans. An anonymous Mandaean worshipper tells of a vision of the Savior, Manda dHiia ("Knowledge of Life"), the "alien" or "stranger" who descends from the world of Light to bring the saving knowledge to his chosen ones. Like Seth-Allogenes in Sethian Gnosticism, the heavenly savior is a "stranger" to the world below. The vision takes place on a Sunday, the weekly day of worship observed by the Mandaeans. The vision and the saving knowledge elicit from the worshipper praise of the eternal Father of Light.

The Mandaean community is the sole surviving remnant of ancient Gnosticism. The term *Mandaean* is derived from one of the Mandaic words for "knowledge," *manda* (*gnōsis* in Greek). "Mandaean" is, therefore, the exact equivalent of "Gnostic." Nowadays the term *Mandaeans* (*mandayi*) refers to the lay people of the religion, as distinguished from the "priests" (*tarmidi*) and "initiates" (*nasoraiyi*). The latter group includes mostly priests, but also includes learned lay people.

The Mandaic language is a dialect of Eastern Aramaic, but it includes key terms from Western Aramaic. While the Mandaeans claim that their religion has existed from the time of Adam, their real history can be traced back to the Jordan Valley of first-century Palestine. Their religion features repeated baptisms in running water (called "Jordan"), and seems to derive from a group of Jewish sectarians who practiced repeated ablutions in water. The Essenes of Qumran practiced similar ritual ablutions, and there were other baptizing groups as well at the turn of our era.

Mandaean writings refer to a migration of Mandaeans out of Palestine after the destruction of Jerusalem in 70 CE, up to Haran in northern Mesopotamia, and from there down to the southern marshes of the Euphrates and Tigris rivers. Mandaeans have lived in areas of southern Iraq and Iran for many centuries, but in recent times there has been a very substantial dispersion of Mandaeans into Europe, Australia, and North America.

In what follows, we shall discuss the principal writings of the Mandaeans, Mandaean mythology, Mandaean rituals and

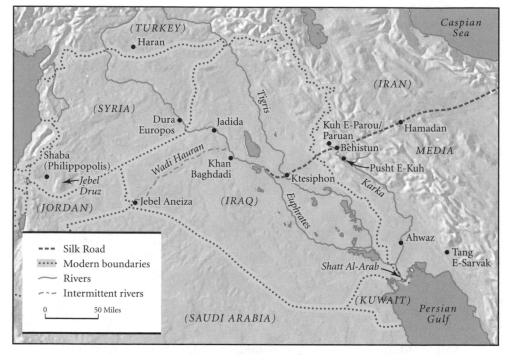

Fig. 12.1 Map of the Mandaean world. © Lucidity Information Design.

ethics, and Mandaean history from the first century up to the present time.

1. Mandaean Literature

Over the centuries, numerous writings have been produced by Mandaeans, many of them still unpublished or unknown to Western scholars. These include ritual writings such as liturgies, hymns, and prayers; mythological and theological tractates; legends related to Mandaean history; illustrated scrolls; and magical texts inscribed on lead tablets and "incantation bowls." Until 1998, when the first printed version of the most important Mandaean book, the *Ginza,* was produced in Australia using Mandaic fonts developed for the Mandaean community, all books were copied by hand. Many of these books include lengthy colophons at the end, in which the scribe, adding to the previous colophons he has copied, gives his name and other particulars. It has recently been determined that the earliest scribe mentioned in Mandaean book colophons was a woman named Shlama, who copied an early version of the *Left Ginza*. She did her work around the end of the second century or the beginning of the third.

Mandaean writings began to be studied by Western scholars in the nineteenth century, when the first editions and translations (into German) were produced. From 1921 to 1947 an English woman named Ethel S. Stevens, better known as Lady Drower, studied the Mandaeans and produced English translations of a number of Mandaean books. She was the wife of a British diplomat based in Iraq. She continued her translating work upon her return to

In discussing Mandaean writings it is useful to distinguish between exoteric writings, meant for the entire community, and esoteric ones reserved for the priests.

England. More recently, Jorunn Jacobsen Buckley, a Norwegian American, has translated other Mandaean writings into English.

In discussing Mandaean writings it is useful to distinguish between exoteric writings, meant for the entire community, and esoteric ones reserved for the priests. The most important of the exoteric works are the *Ginza*, the *Canonical Prayerbook*, the *Book of John*, and the *Haran Gawaita*.

The *Ginza* (Treasure), also known as *Sidra Rba* (Great Book), is divided into two parts, "Right" and "Left." A German translation was published by Mark Lidzbarski in 1925; no English translation exists. The *Right Ginza* consists of eighteen tractates containing creation stories and other mythological traditions, moral exhortations, theological polemics, and revelations concerning history and the end of the world. These tractates are a conglomerate of texts of varying dates, but it is thought that the *Ginza* reached its present form around the mid-seventh century. The *Left Ginza* is the more ancient part, and deals with death and the ascent of the soul to the realm of light.

The *Canonical Prayerbook*, translated by Lady Drower, is a collection of liturgical texts, a composite work containing hymns, prayers, baptismal liturgies, and so forth. There are also mythological references and cosmological teachings. The oldest extant manuscript dates to 1529, but the texts are much older. Some of the hymns were used by the disciple of Mani who composed the "Thomas Psalms" in the *Manichaean Psalmbook*.

The *Book of John*, socalled because it contains stories relating to the life of John the Baptist and his conflict with Jesus, is also a composite work containing traditions of various ages. It was published in a German translation by Mark Lidzarski in 1915; no English translation exists. It contains some interesting material on Miriai, Jesus's mother.

The *Haran Gawaita* ("Inner Haran"), translated by Lady Drower, is a kind of history of the Mandaeans, from their flight from Palestine to the coming of Islam and to the end of the world. There is considerable debate among scholars as to how much real history the book contains.

Lady Drower was able to gain the confidence of Mandaean priests and leaders in Iraq, and obtained access to their esoteric books. She translated a number of them into English. *Explanatory Commentary on the Marriage of the Great Šišlam* contains the marriage ritual. *Explanation of the Coronation of Šišlam the Great* contains the ritual for the ordination of a *ganzibra*,

Fig. 12.2 Souls of the righteous are ferried to the house of Abatur. Illustration from the Mandaean *Diwan Abatur*, MS Drower 8(R). Photo courtesy of the Oriental Collections of the Bodleian Library, Oxford.

the highest-ranking Mandaean priest. *The Thousand and Twelve Questions* is a question-and-answer exchange among celestial beings wherein various rituals are esoterically interpreted. The *First Great World* and the *First Small World* are esoteric speculations on the relation between macrocosm and microcosm. The *Book of the Baptism of Hibil Ziwa* contains instructions on how a contaminated priest can purify himself. The *Book of Abatur* describes the journey of the soul through the various celestial purgatorial houses. Abatur is the judge of the other world. The *Book of the Zodiac* is meant to assist priests in the casting of horoscopes. Another esoteric text, the *Scroll of Exalted Kingship*, recently translated by Jorunn Buckley, contains a detailed description of part of the initiation rituals for the *tarmida*, the lower ranking Mandaean priest. A large number of other texts remain untranslated and unpublished.

2. Mandaean Doctrines and Mythology
(Foerster 2:148–276)

It is not easy to present a coherent account of Mandaean mythology, for no single authoritative source exists. In the *Ginza*, for example, there are at least seven different accounts of the origin of the cosmos, and these differ from one another to a very considerable extent. While it can clearly be seen that Mandaean cosmology is dualistic, resembling in that respect other Gnostic systems, there is no uniformity in the sources as to the nature of Mandaean dualism. Both of the basic kinds of Gnostic dualism are found in the sources, an emanationist model beginning with a single principle, as for example, in Sethian or Valentinian Gnosticism, and a radical dualism of two principles, Light and Darkness, as in Manichaeism. In what follows, an attempt will be made to present a brief account of what can be

> *While it can clearly be seen that Mandaean cosmology is dualistic, resembling in that respect other Gnostic systems, there is no uniformity in the sources as to the nature of Mandaean dualism.*

319

taken as the earliest forms of Mandaean mythology, based on our available sources.

We begin with the world of Light, ruled by a supreme being who has several names: "Life" (*hiia*), "Great Life," "First Life," "Lord of Greatness," "Great Mind," "King of Light," and others. He is surrounded by countless light beings called *'utria* (*'utra* means "wealth"), who inhabit heavenly "dwellings" (*Šišlam*) or "worlds" (*almia*) and constantly praise the Life. From him emanate second, third, and fourth Life, bearing the names Yoshamin, Abatur, and Ptahil. The latter, situated at the edge of the world of Light, comes into contact with darkness and becomes the creator of the world. (His name is probably based on a Mandaic root *pth*, "to mold," plus the divine suffix *il*, which is Hebrew *'el*.) Other beings in the world of Light are personified entities such as Kushta (truth) and especially Jordan, the water of light in which the celestial beings immerse themselves. Earthly baptism is regarded as an imitation of the heavenly liturgy, and the running water (Jordan) used in Mandaean baptism is connected to the world of Light.

The "World of Darkness" is ruled by the "King of Darkness," who arose from the "dark waters" of chaos. Belonging to the World of Darkness is a dragon named 'Ur (which in Hebrew means "light") and a female being called Ruha ("Spirit"), also called Ruha dQud-sha ("Holy Spirit"). Their offspring are various demonic beings, and from them also come the "Seven," that is, the seven planets, and the "Twelve," that is, the twelve Zodiacal constellations. According to some traditions, Ruha originally belonged to the World of Light. Her counterpart in the human makeup is the *ruha*, or spirit, which vacillates between the soul (*nišimta*) and the body.

In the best-known version of the creation myth, Ptahil, on the orders of his father Abatur, creates the cosmos. However, he botches the job, and turns to Ruha, the Seven, and the Twelve, and with their help he moulds Tibil, the created world. Both Abatur and Ptahil are driven out of the world of Light and dwell in their own worlds. Abatur becomes the judge of the dead.

Ptahil and his helpers then create Adam, but botch that job, too. They create *adam pagria*, that is, physical Adam, but he is virtually a body without life and is unable to stand up. From the world of Light comes the "inner" or "hidden Adam," (*adam kasia* or Adakas). Adam is thus animated, but now the "inner Adam," the soul (*nišimta*) or (*mana*) in humans, is imprisoned in the body and needs to be liberated in order to return to the Light. So Manda dHiia descends as Savior and bestows upon Adam the knowledge of his heavenly nature. The Savior also teaches him baptism, and makes him the first Mandaean. The initial salvation of Adam is paradigmatic of the salvation of all other Mandaeans.

Among the *'utria* in the world of Light are the Adamites Hibil, Shitil, and Anush, heavenly counterparts to biblical Abel, Seth, and Enosh (Genesis 4:2, 25-26). These can stand in for Manda dHiia as revealers or intermediaries between the world of Light and human beings here below. There are a number of stories told about Hibil Ziwa (Splendid Hibil) in Mandaean texts. The Mandaeans do not have a historical savior or revealer, but the mythological ones appear in different ages of history reenacting the original revelation of gnosis to Adam.

Early contacts with Christianity made of Anush a rival to Jesus. He is said to have appeared in Jerusalem performing miracles and exposing Jesus as a liar. He also plays a role in the destruction of Jerusalem. (In another tradition the destruction is attributed to Hibil Ziwa.) Jesus's earthly opponent in Mandaean tradition is John the Baptist. The role played by John the Baptist in Mandaeism is that of a true Mandaean priest and prophet, not in any sense a religious founder. We shall return to John the Baptist's role in Mandaeism below (in section 4).

The Mandaeans have some very interesting traditions about the third of the Adamite *'utria*, Shitil (Seth). When his father Adam was a thousand years old it was time for him to die. But Adam fought death, and suggested to the angel of death that Shitil, only eighty years old, die in his place. Shitil accepts this fate, sheds his body, and puts on a radiant robe and turban, outshining the sun. Shitil asks that the earthly blinders be removed

> *Jesus's earthly opponent in Mandaean tradition is John the Baptist.*

from Adam's eyes so that he can see a vision of his son. This is granted, and Adam then desires immediate death. In this story Shitil becomes the very first soul to ascend to the Light, and his journey is paradigmatic of that of future Mandaeans souls. It is his soul that Abatur places in his scale at the judgment to see if an ascending soul is worthy of entry into Light.

The Mandaeans have a linear doctrine of history, divided into four ages of decreasing duration for a total of 480,000 years, from Adam to the end of the world. The first three ages have already past, and we are now living in the fourth and last. The first age, beginning with Adam and Eve, was destroyed by sword and plague. The second, which began with a surviving couple named Ram and Rud, was destroyed by fire. The third, beginning with Surbai and Sarhab'il, ended with the Flood. The fourth age will end with the destruction of the world by fire. This scheme of four ages is probably of Iranian origin.

While there are no stories told about the progenitors of the second and third ages, there are a number of legends about the flood that ends the third age. The Mandaean hero of the flood is Šum bar Nu (Shem, son of Noah). He is regarded as the ancestor of the Mandaeans, the only legitimate son of Noah and his wife Nuraita. Noah also had three illegitimate sons, who are the ancestors of all other peoples.

The Mandaeans, unlike some (but not all) other Gnostics, do not have a doctrine of reincarnation. For them death is a day of salvation, for then the soul is ready to leave the body. Indeed, mourning for the dead is forbidden in Mandaeism. The soul leaves the body three days after burial, and starts a long journey to the light through the purgatories guarded by demonic powers who attempt to trap the soul. Only the pious are able to reach the light, aided by the rituals performed for them and by the heavenly saviors.

> *The Mandaeans, unlike some (but not all) other Gnostics, do not have a doctrine of reincarnation.*

In our brief account of Mandaean mythology the attentive reader will have encountered some familiar territory. The Mandaean 'utria in the World of Light are reminiscent of the aeons in the Gnostic systems already studied. Heavenly counterparts of Adam, Seth, and others recall similar beings encountered in Sethian Gnosticism. Particularly noteworthy is the role played by Seth (Shitil). The evil Ruha reminds us of fallen Sophia, who in some Gnostic (originally Jewish) traditions is referred to as a "holy spirit." The work of Ptahil and his helpers recall the activity of Yaldabaoth and his archons in the creation and governance of the world. The stories of the creation of Adam, his vivification, and his reception of gnosis, are similar to the myths about Adam encountered in Sethian Gnosticism. The tripartition of human beings into body, soul, and spirit is also familiar to us from Sethian and Valentinian anthropology, except that the roles of soul and spirit are reversed.

In short, it must be concluded that the earliest Mandaean mythology was based on traditions very similar to those utilized by other groups of ancient Gnostics, especially the Sethian Gnostics. This has been shown especially by the comparative studies of Mandaean and Coptic texts carried out by the German scholar Kurt Rudolph, who is the preeminent living authority on the Mandaean religion.

3. Mandaean Rituals and Ethics
(Foerster 2:277–95)

An important concept in the Mandaean religion is *laufa* ("connection"), that is, the connection between the world of Light and the lives of Mandaeans here below. This connection was established originally by beings in the world of Light, and is maintained and reconfirmed by Mandaeans in the performance of their rituals. Rituals and prayers were sent down from above, and are constantly being sent back up from here below.

An important concept in the Mandaean religion is laufa ("connection"), that is, the connection between the world of Light and the lives of Mandaeans here below.

Mandaeism differs from other varieties of ancient Gnosticism in the crucial role played by the priesthood in the ritual life of the people. Priests are representatives of the world of Light here below, and in the course of the rituals over which they preside they move ritually between the world of Light and the world below.

There are two main classes of priests. At the higher level is the *ganzibra* ("treasurer"), and below him is the *tarmida* (originally meaning "disciple"). Elaborate initiation ceremonies are required for each of them. There are far fewer *ganzibria* than there are *tarmidia*. In each Mandaean village or community the *tarmida* is regarded as the highest religious and civil authority, at least in those places where there is no *ganzibra*. The priests are assisted in the conduct of the rituals by a *šualia* (a novice preparing for priesthood) and a *šganda* (a lay acolyte).

The most important ritual in Mandaeism is baptism (*maṣbuta*), a ritual that is not initiatory, as in Christianity, but is repeated during the course of one's life. Running water (Jordan) is the form that the Light-world takes on earth. Repeated immersions in the Jordan are the means by which Mandaeans prepare for their reentry into the world of Light.

Baptisms are performed in a river, or in front of a cult hut that is provided with a channel dug and directed from the river in which "living" water can flow. Baptisms are performed every Sunday and on festival days or special occasions. The baptism must be performed by a priest, dressed in ritual vestments with a white silken crown on his head. The first part of the ceremony consists of a threefold immersion in water, with the participants dressed in special white garments, followed by a threefold "signing" of the forehead with water, a threefold draught of water, a sacred handshake (*kushta*) between priest and participant, "crowning" with a myrtle wreath, and the laying on of hands by the priest. The second part of the ceremony takes place on the riverbank. It consists of an anointing with sesame oil, another *kushta*, consumption of a piece of unleavened bread (*pihta*) and water (*mambuha*), another *kushta*, and the "sealing" of

The constituent features of the Mandaean water ceremonies are thought to derive from baptismal ablutions practiced in early Judaism in pre-Christian times.

the baptized person against evil spirits. A fourth *kushta* concludes the ceremony, and the participants throw their myrtle wreaths into the water. These actions are accompanied by prayers and ritual formulae recited by the priest.

In addition to the *masbuta,* which must be performed by a priest, there are two other water rites, ritual ablutions that can be performed on oneself, but always in running water. These are the morning body lustration, and a simple immersion undertaken by a Mandaean when he or she has committed a sin. The constituent features of the Mandaean water ceremonies are thought to derive from baptismal ablutions practiced in early Judaism in pre-Christian times. The baptismal ceremonies practiced by Sethian Gnostics (discussed in chapter 3) have a similar derivation.

The other main ritual is a kind of death mass, the *masiqta* ("ascent"), performed for the soul of a deceased Mandaean three days after the person's death or burial. That is when the soul is thought to be released from the body to begin its forty-five-day ascent through the various purgatories (*matarata*) in order to reach the world of Light. The *masiqta* is a very elaborate ritual that takes about twelve hours to perform.

In spite of the denigration of the body such as we see in other varieties of Gnosticism, the Mandaeans are not at all ascetically inclined.

Its purpose is to ensure the ascent of the soul and the spirit upward to be incorporated into a body of light (*'ustuna*). The rite also incorporates the newly deceased into the community of Mandaean ancestors in the world of Light. The ceremonies include lustrations with water, anointing with oil, crowning with a myrtle wreath, recitations from the *Left Ginza,* and consumption of special foods. Much of the ritual is performed by four priests inside the *mandi* (cult hut).

In addition, there are special funeral meals observed by the next of kin on the first, third, seventh, and forty-fifth days after death or burial. A special meal, *zidqa brika* ("blessed alms"), takes place on the day of burial with a priest present. The *zidqa brika* is also used at the consecration of a cult place, at the initiation of priests, and at weddings.

The Mandaeans have many more rituals, including very elaborate ones involving the initiation of *ganzibria* and *tarmidia,* the marriage ceremony, a special ceremony for the end of the year, and others. The close connection between myth and ritual is an important feature of the Mandaean religion.

Religion plays an important part, too, in the daily lives of the Mandaeans. They have ethical standards similar to those of Jews and Christians, and a collection of laws is preserved in the first two books of the *Right Ginza.* Spiritual benefits are derived from giving alms, practicing mercy, obeying parents, taking regular part in prayers and other religious ceremonies. Like the Christians, the Mandaeans honor Sunday, "the first day of the week." The religious calendar has twelve months of thirty days each, plus five intercalary days, during which time a major feast takes place.

In spite of the denigration of the body such as we see in other varieties of Gnosticism, the Mandaeans are not at all ascetically inclined. Marriage is regarded as a duty for all Mandaeans, including the priests. Mandaeans do not perform circumcision. Elaborate rules of purity are observed by the Mandaeans, many of them involving ablutions with water. There are special rules for food and meals, and for ritual slaughter of food animals (mainly chicken and sheep).

As can be seen from the foregoing, it's not easy being a Mandaean. The survival of Mandaeism into our own day is truly an amazing phenomenon. Mandaean communities are close-knit, and, as an ethnic group, the Mandaeans are endogamous. Unlike the religion of Mani, Mandaeism is not at all a missionary religion. Indeed, there is no provision in any of its ritual writings for the conversion of a non-Mandaean to the Mandaean religion.

4. The Mandaeans in History
(Foerster 2:296–317)

Mandaean history can arguably be traced back to the first century. I say *arguably* because the earliest history of the Mandaean religion is shrouded in myth and legend. Ironically, the only historical personages from the first century that play a prominent role in Mandaean legends are Jews. That is an irony because Jews are routinely denounced in Mandaean texts as impure people whose prophets and Torah are false. Mandaeans are commanded not to have anything to do with the Jews. The same opprobrium applies to Christians. An even greater irony, given the hostility toward the Jews exhibited in Mandaean texts, is an admission that the Mandaean community emerged out of Judaism.

The aforementioned first-century Jews are two who play a positive role, John the Baptist and Mary (Miriai), and one who plays an altogether negative role, Jesus the Christ, Mary's son. According to the Mandaean texts, John was born of Elizabeth and Zechariah in their old age. When he was three years old, Manda d'Hiia took him up and bap-

The believers were persecuted by the Jews, and as a result, the Jewish city and temple were destroyed.

tized him in the heavenly Jordan of living waters, and instructed him in the true religion. John then lived in Jerusalem for forty-two years, baptizing people, healing, and teaching as a messenger of the King of Light.

Jesus Christ, who is said to be an incarnation of Nbu (the planet Mercury), came to John and requested baptism. At the command of Abatur John baptized Jesus, and Ruha descended upon Jesus in the form of a dove. Jesus then proceeded to pervert the baptism, bring wickedness and falsehood into the world, practice sorcery,

Some Mandaean sources even describe Miriai as a Mandaean priest.

and make false claims for himself. In response Anosh Utra descended to Jerusalem in the form of a man, empowered by the King of Light. He performed miracles and gained believers (Mandaeans) among the Jews. Three hundred sixty prophets (or three hundred sixty-five) went forth and bore witness to the truth. The believers were persecuted by the Jews, and as a result, the Jewish city and temple were destroyed.

As for Miriai, Anosh Utra became a healer for her, baptizing her in the Jordan and signing her with the pure sign. The Jews had given birth to her, and had brought her up in their temple. But Miriai rejected the Jewish law, and expressed her exclusive love for Manda dHiia. Some Mandaean sources even describe her as a Mandaean priest.

What are we to make of these stories? A serious historian would certainly take them with more than a pinch of the proverbial salt. The roles assigned to John, Jesus, and Mary appear to be Mandaean interpretations of early Christian traditions, probably arising from the third century on as a result of contacts between Mandaeans and Christians. The birth story of John the Baptist, featuring the aged Elizabeth and Zechariah, could easily be read out of the first chapter of the Gospel of Luke. The story about Mary's early years in the temple could be read out of a Christian apocryphal gospel, such as the second-century *Protevangelium of James* (7.1–3). The positive roles assigned to John and Mary are based on an extremely hostile attitude toward Jesus Christ, and Christians in general. Jesus is portrayed as the ultimate charlatan, the betrayer of two true (Mandaean) believers: his erstwhile master John, and his own mother Mary.

Especially interesting is the role played by John the Baptist. As a well-known prophet who baptized people in the Jordan River, he would understandably be an attractive figure for Mandaeans looking back upon their own history. In addition, certain Syrian Jewish Christians regarded John as a false prophet, and an opponent of the True Prophet, Jesus Christ. They counted among John's disciples the arch-heretic Simon Magus. Their views are recorded in the Pseudo-Clementine literature (see discussion of Simon Magus in chapter 2). The Mandaeans would, of course, reverse the evaluations made by the Jewish Christians, whom they probably encountered in Mesopotamia.

Could there be a real historical connection between John the Baptist and the earliest Mandaeans? While it is doubtful that the earliest Mandaeans were disciples of John, it is probable that John and the earliest Mandaeans shared the same milieu. A second-century Jewish Christian writer named Hegesippus refers to seven Jewish sects that had once existed among the Jews: "Essenes, Galileans, Hemerobaptists, Masbothei, Samaritans, Sadducees, and Pharisees" (quoted in Eusebius's *Ecclesiastical History* 4.22). At least three of these were groups that practiced regular ritual ablutions in water. We now know about the Essenes and their practices from the Dead Sea Scrolls. All we know of the Hemerobaptists and Masbothei are their names: Hemerobaptists were people who "baptized daily," and Masbothei were obviously "baptists" (compare the Mandaic word for baptism, *maṣbuta*). Could the Masbothei have been early Mandaeans? Perhaps. In any case, it can plausibly be concluded that the Mandaeans were a first-century baptizing group that lived in the same area as John the Baptist, that is, around the Jordan River.

Of course, the earliest Mandaeans were Gnostics. We have already cited the evidence for the Jewish origins of the Sethian Gnostics (who also practiced baptism). Given the similarities we have seen between Mandaean gnosis and that of the Sethians, and given the prominence in Mandaean sources of the waters of the Jordan, it is reasonable to conclude that the Mandaean religion originated

The Mandaeans have suffered times of hardship during the centuries, but also times of prosperity.

among first-century Jews in Palestine. And that's what the Mandaeans' own books tell us. As in the case of Sethian Gnosticism, we have no knowledge of a historical founder of the Mandaean religion.

Mandaean texts refer to a migration out of Palestine into the area around Haran in northern Mesopotamia, territory that was then part of the Parthian Empire. A Parthian king named Ardban is said to have given them protection. If, indeed, a Parthian ruler befriended them, it was probably not Ardban, who can be identified as Artabanus V (circa 213–224). He was the last of the Parthian emperors, for the Parthians were displaced by a resurgent Iranian empire in the mid-220s, under Ardashir, the first of the Sasanian "kings of kings." The *Haran Gawaita* reports that, at the time when the kingdom was taken away from the "sons of king Ardban," there were in Baghdad one hundred seventy *manda* houses. So the Mandaeans were living in southern Mesopotamia by that time (early third century), and have remained there until modern times.

The Mandaeans have suffered times of hardship during the centuries, but also times of prosperity. Some of these are recorded in the colophons added by scribes when copying Mandaean books. The same ruler under whom Mani died in 277, Bahram I, suppressed other non-Zoroastrian religious groups, including the Mandaeans. With the coming of Islam, it is reported that the Mandaean "head of the people" led a delegation of Mandaeans to Muslim authorities. They showed the authorities their holy book, the *Ginza,* and declared their prophet to be John the Baptist, a prophet known

As a result of these conflicts, many Mandaeans emigrated, and now there are diaspora communities of Mandaeans in Europe, North America, and Australia.

to Muslims. So the Mandaeans came to be recognized as legitimate "People of the Book," along with Jews and Christians. Arab Muslims refer to the Mandaeans as *ṣubba,* "baptizers."

The first westerner to encounter the Mandaeans was a Dominican from Tuscany, Ricoldo Pennini, whose travels took him to Baghdad around 1290. He referred to them as "Sabaeans," and described some of their ritual practices, also noting their veneration for John the Baptist. In the mid-sixteenth century Portuguese missionaries came into contact with the Mandaeans, whom they referred to as "Christians of St. John."

Mandaean colophons provide information on a cholera epidemic in 1831 that decimated the Mandaean community. Virtually the entire priesthood was lost to the disease. The priesthood was restored through the efforts of learned Mandaean laymen.

Probably no more than thirteen thousand Mandaeans remain in Iraq, and the lives of those people are in serious jeopardy.

Although the traditional homes of the Mandaeans are the southern marshes of the Euphrates and Tigris rivers in Iraq and Iran, groups of Mandaeans also live in

Fig. 12.3 Mandaeans continue to practice their ancient religion today. A priest in Ahwaz, Iran, reads a wedding liturgy, standing behind the crouching bride-groom; beyond them, the bride is led into the waters of the Karun River to be baptized. April, 1996. Photo © Jorunn Jacobsen Buckley.

the principal cities of the region, especially Baghdad and Tehran. They are noted for their work as gold- and silversmiths, but also engage in building trades and other occupations. The Mandaeans have suffered considerably during recent wars, the Iran-Iraq war of 1980–88, the Gulf War of 1991, and the current war in Iraq. As a result of these conflicts, many Mandaeans emigrated, and now there are diaspora communities of Mandaeans in Europe, North America, and Australia. As a result of the American invasion of Iraq in 2003, things have gotten much worse for Mandaeans in Iraq. Living mostly in Shiite-dominated regions, they have been subjected to horrific persecutions. Probably no more than thirteen thousand Mandaeans remain in Iraq, and the lives of those people are in serious jeopardy.

It is not known how many Mandaeans there are in the world— estimates range from 50,000 to 100,000—but those living outside of their traditional homelands now probably outnumber the ones who have not yet emigrated.

The Mandaean religion has attracted considerable attention in recent years. Educated Mandaeans have taken interest in the study of their religion by Western scholars. In 1999 the first international conference on the Mandaeans was held at Harvard University. Participants included not only scholars from around the world but also Mandaean adherents. One of the events of the conference was a *maṣbuta* in the Charles River.

A serious obstacle to the survival of the Mandaean religion is the paucity of priests. If that problem can be overcome, the last survivors of the ancient Gnostic religion might have a future.

Epilogue. The Persistence of Gnosticism

IN THE PRECEDING CHAPTERS WE HAVE LOOKED at manifestations of ancient Gnosticism from first-century Syria/Palestine and Alexandria (chs. 2–4) to twentieth-century Iran and Iraq (ch. 12). Our forays have covered even a wider sweep, from second-century Gaul in the West (chs. 3, 5) to seventeenth-century China in the East (ch. 11). We encountered the earliest recorded Gnostic prophet-teachers, Simon Magus and Menander, in Samaria and Antioch (ch. 2), and we speculated on the earliest history of Classic or Sethian Gnosticism (ch. 3) and Mandaeism (ch. 12), on whose historical founders we have no information.

We noted the important role played by ancient Platonist philosophy and ancient Jewish writings in the formation of the earliest Gnostic systems (ch. 1). We could then conclude that Gnosticism did not start out as a Christian heresy. No, the earliest Gnostics, according to the definition of Gnosticism we established (ch. 1), were sectarian Jews. We could find evidence of Jewish influence even in the earliest religious writings of the pagan devotees of "thrice-greatest" Hermes in late first- or early second-century Alexandria (ch. 10).

Even if the earliest Gnostics were not Christians, we found that many Gnostics embraced the figure of Jesus Christ as their revealer of gnosis. A number of important Christian teachers adapted the mythological system of Classic Gnosticism in their creation of new forms of Christian doctrine and practice, such as Basilides in Alexandria (ch. 5) and the most important Gnostic Christian teacher of all, Valentinus in Alexandria and Rome (ch. 6). Even the third-century prophet Mani, founder of Manichaeism, regarded himself as an "apostle of Jesus Christ" (ch. 11).

In our study of the various Gnostic systems we encountered two basic types of Gnostic dualism. There is, first, the monistic type in which everything begins with a primary transcendent first principle that is entirely good, from which a series of emanations leads to a devolution of the divine and the introduction of evil in the cosmos. This is the type of dualism found in Classic or Sethian Gnosticism (ch. 3), in Basilidian and Valentinian gnosis (chs. 5–6), in a great number of Coptic Gnostic texts whose sectarian affiliation has not been established (ch. 8), and in some Mandaean texts (ch. 12). The other, more radical, type of dualism involves two eternal opposing principles of light and darkness. When darkness encounters light, the resultant mixture accounts for the creation of the world and the evil found in it. This is the dualism we encounter in Manichaeism (ch. 11), in certain three-principle systems (ch. 7), and in some Mandaean texts (ch. 12). All Gnostic systems include an eschatology in which the problem of evil in the world is resolved.

In applying our definition of Gnosticism to the relevant texts, we encountered a problem posed by the *Gospel of Thomas* and other Thomas texts (ch. 9). The problem here is that some scholars regard the *Gospel of Thomas* and related texts as Gnostic, especially because of the emphasis found in these texts on self-knowledge. We have excluded the Thomas texts from our category of Gnosticism because they lack the cosmic dualism found in Gnostic literature, according to which the creator of the world is distinguished from the transcendent God. The Gnostic Demiurge (world-creator) is typically regarded as an ignorant or foolish god, if not downright malevolent.

Even so, the *Gospel of Thomas* and related Christian literature is similar in an important respect to what we find in the Gnostic literature and in the Hermetic literature as well (ch. 10)—that is, the emphasis on self-knowledge. In all of the texts surveyed in this book, the importance of self-knowledge is underscored. The Gnostic, or the Thomas Christian, or the Hermetist, is enabled to come to God through knowledge of the divine self within. In other words, Gnosticism in general can be defined as a religion of self-realization. The same holds true for pagan Hermetism or Thomas Christianity.

Having surveyed the various Gnostic texts and systems that proliferated in antiquity from the first century on, it might be useful to step back and ask some general questions. How does one account historically for the proliferation of Gnostic texts and systems? What was it about Gnosticism that attracted the adherents who embraced it? Why did some Gnostic groups survive longer than others?

Around the turn of the era the Greco-Roman world was in a social and cultural ferment. From the early third century BCE on, there was a great deal of movement of groups and individuals, from east to west and from west to east. Large numbers of people no longer felt tied to their original cultures, or if they did, they created new varieties of their ancient cultures in their new homelands.

The Jewish Diaspora is a classic example of this phenomenon. Jews moving out of their homeland in Palestine established themselves in the Greek-speaking areas of the Mediterranean world, and those who retained their Jewish religion created new Greek-speaking varieties of Judaism, translating their traditions not only into a new language but also into new thought-forms. In that process, they would take on cultural and religious ideas and forms from the pagan environment in which they lived. With the spread of early Christianity in the first century CE the same phenomenon could be observed in the Christian religion.

From the first century BCE on, Greco-Roman culture developed in new ways. Historians of ancient Greco-Roman culture and religion have observed some interesting trends, involving the growth of individualism and a greater interest in new forms of religion. The history of Greek philosophy exemplifies this, for in all of the philosophical schools from the first century BCE on (except Epicureanism), there developed a greater interest in metaphysics, and a quest for individual salvation.

The history of Platonism is an important example of this trend. In the time after Plato, his school, the Academy, took on a generally skeptical stance in matters of philosophy, with an emphasis on ethics. But then, in the first century BCE, there emerged a greater emphasis on metaphysics. Eudorus of Alexandria was a first-century BCE philosopher who exemplifies this trend, and his variety of Platonist philosophy was undoubtedly very influential in learned Alexandrian Jewish circles.

The first-century Jewish philosopher Philo is the most important Jewish example of a variety of Platonism that grounds the salvation of individual souls in the quest for wisdom. For Philo, this involved an individualistic reinterpretation of the biblical scriptures, especially the Torah, in terms of Platonist philosophy.

Another feature of the development of Greek philosophy is eclecticism, that is, members of a particular school taking on teachings of another school. Posidonius of Apamea (first century BCE) was a very influential Stoic philosopher who embraced a good deal of Platonist metaphysics in the elaboration of his Stoic teaching. He was the teacher of the famous philosopher-orator Cicero. Many other examples could be cited.

An interesting example of the growth of individualism in Greco-Roman culture was the widespread reinterpretation of the famous Delphic maxim, *gnōthi s'auton*, "Know thyself." Originally, it meant, "know that you are mortal" but from the first century BCE on, the meaning of the maxim was completely changed.

This change of meaning can be illustrated by a passage from the "Dream of Scipio," with which the Roman philosopher Cicero concludes his *Republic* (6.9–29, mid-first century BCE). In his dream Scipio Africanus the Younger (second century BCE) is counseled by his famous grandfather, Scipio Africanus the Elder, on how to conduct his life. The elder Scipio assures his grandson that it is not he who is mortal, but only his body. "Your spirit is your true self, not that bodily form which can be pointed to with the finger. Know yourself, therefore, to be a god."

Given this cultural environment, it is not difficult to see how it is that Jews could set about to create innovative reinterpretations of their scriptures and traditions. It is precisely such innovative reinterpretations that form the building blocks of the earliest Gnostic mythological systems.

What did people find attractive in Gnosticism? At least a partial answer to that question involves the ages-old problem that has vexed thinking people for millennia. Whence comes evil in the world? How could a good God create a flawed world?

In ancient times some people could look around them and see a flawed world, a world that seemed to be dominated by malevolent powers beyond human control. If one feels alienated from one's social or political environment, as many people did in ancient times (and still do now), and if that same person is eager to embrace a transcendent world where there is no evil, it is not difficult to envision the world in which we live as the flawed product of a foolish or malicious creator, a world controlled by malevolent powers. Such a person might be inclined to look within oneself, to seek the "divine within," and thus to come in contact with a God who is "beyond God." Knowledge of that transcendent God is what the ancient Gnostics offered. Salvation was to be found in coming to the knowledge of that God by coming to the knowledge of the divine self within.

Why did some Gnostic groups survive longer than others? Most of the Gnostic groups surveyed in the previous chapters had died out by the end of the fourth century. Repressed by both the church and the Christian state, they presumably allowed themselves to be integrated into the catholic church. The Manichaeans managed to survive in the Roman Empire until the end of the sixth century, and in China until the seventeenth century. The Mandaeans still exist.

What is it about Manichaeism and Mandaeism that accounts for their relative staying power? I would suggest that this has to do, at least partially, with their respective social and institutional structures. The Manichaeans had a highly organized structure involving a hierarchical leadership, and a symbiotic relationship between the "elect" and the "hearers." The Mandaeans developed a hierarchical priesthood, and a system of rituals that required a highly organized institutional system involving priests and lay people acting in consort.

No such social structures existed among the various Gnostic Christian groups in the Roman Empire, who regarded organizational structures as a matter of indifference. Indeed, many Gnostics looked upon ecclesiastical offices with a good deal of hostility. We recall the sneering dismissal by the author of *The Apocalypse of Peter* of those "outside our number who name themselves bishop and deacons, as if they have received their authority from God" (NHC VII,3:79,23–27, discussed in chapter 8, above).

The non-survival of Gnostic groups is, of course, mainly the result of systematic persecution on the part of the ruling powers. In the Roman Empire the ruling powers were Christians. The Mandaeans were fortunate in living where they did, for their Muslim rulers largely tolerated them as "People of the Book." And so they survived.

In what sense can we talk about a persistence of Gnosticism? There are, in fact, groups of Gnostics even today, and a search of the Web will turn up many interesting varieties of Gnostic churches and societies. Does that mean that underground groups of Gnostics actually survived the persecutions mounted against them and other heretics?

To be sure, various Gnostic-looking dualist groups of heretics appeared during the Middle Ages: Paulicians (ninth century), Bogomils (tenth–twelfth centuries), and Cathars (eleventh–thirteenth centuries). The Cathars ("pure ones") were also called Albigensians, and Pope Innocent III mounted the Albigensian Crusade against them in 1209. Thousands were slaughtered or burned at the stake. Under the French king Louis IX ("the Pious") the last

Cathar fortress, Montségur, was captured in 1244. Most of the Cathar writings were destroyed, and the rest were preserved for the use of officers of the Inquisition. The Cathar movement has been revived in modern times in France, Canada, and the United States.

When we talk about the persistence of Gnosticism, we do not mean to imply that underground groups of Gnostics continued to elude the authorities and persisted into our own time. We can, however, speak of the persistence of Gnosticism in the sense that ideas put forward by ancient Gnostics still have a resonance with certain groups of people even today. These groups include people who refer to themselves as Gnostics.

Our day and age is not all that dissimilar from the Greco-Roman world of the first century in the way in which people look at religion. A lot of people today have grown suspicious of traditional religions. Self-abnegation and a sense of one's own sinfulness is not a prominent part of the world in which we live, and certainly not an attractive attitude to adopt. And it is easy for people to become completely alienated from the power structures that have made such a mess of things in our world. So religions of self-realization have a certain appeal to people interested in spiritual things. Gnosticism is such a religion, but there are others besides, part of a larger scene in our "new age."

What I find interesting is that the Coptic Gnostic texts from Egypt, to which the bulk of this book has been devoted, have elicited an enormous amount of interest among people today, both here and abroad. Of course, most of the people who read the Gnostic texts are not Gnostics themselves. They are people (like myself) who have an interest in seeing the other side of early Christian history, or take a general interest in the religious history of antiquity.

On the other hand, the Coptic Gnostic texts have been put to religious use as well, in that some of them are nowadays routinely used in religious services of recently founded Gnostic groups. The Valentinian texts are regarded as particularly suitable for such purposes.

Of the Gnostic churches or societies that now exist here and abroad, I mention here, in closing, two in California, about which

I have some knowledge. The Ecclesia Gnostica in Los Angeles is led by Bishop Stephan Hoeller. Every Sunday morning people gather in the small church for the celebration of the Gnostic Holy Eucharist. The service resembles in many ways an old-fashioned Roman Catholic liturgy, complete with elaborate vestments, burning candles, incense, and bells.

Hoeller, a native of Hungary, came to this country in 1952. He came to Los Angeles two years later at the age of twenty-three, and joined a group called the Gnostic Society, founded in 1939 by a Theosophist named James Morgan Pryse. The Ecclesia Gnostica is an offshoot of that society. Hoeller had been reared as a Roman Catholic, and had a great love for the rituals of the church. He was also a member of the Theosophical Society, and had an interest in esoterica. In addition, he had developed an interest in the depth psychology of Carl Gustav Jung. It is from a Jungian perspective that he interprets ancient Gnostic and other religious texts.

Something of a scholar, Hoeller lectures widely and has written a number of books, published by the Theosophical Publishing House. When I taught a Gnosticism course at the University of California, Santa Barbara, in the eighties and early nineties, I would invite Hoeller to come to Santa Barbara and give a lecture in my class.

The Web site for the Gnostic Society and the Ecclesia Gnostica is www.gnosis.org.

The Church of Gnosis (Ecclesia Gnostica Mysteriorum) is located in Palo Alto. It was founded by Rosamonde Miller, a bishop/hierophant of an esoteric group called the Mary Magdalene Order, based in Paris, France. She was ordained a priest in 1974 by Stephan Hoeller of the Ecclesia Gnostica in Los Angeles. In 1978 she began holding Eucharistic services in Palo Alto and incorporated under the name Ecclesia Gnostica Mysteriorum ("Gnostic Church of the Mysteries") in 1983. By that time she had already been consecrated a bishop in her Palo Alto church by Hoeller. The rituals of her church are more innovative, and differ in that respect from the rituals of the Ecclesia Gnostica. For Miller and her group, there can be no such thing as Gnostic doctrines. "Gnosis is a matter of experience, not belief," she says.

The Web site for the Church of Gnosis is www.gnosticsanctuary. org.

The two Gnostic churches mentioned here can, in one sense, be seen as examples of the persistence of Gnosticism. However, it must also be stressed that these and other groups like them are in no sense revivals of ancient Gnosticism. They have no particular Gnostic system of belief, are quite eclectic in their use of Christian and non-Christian religious traditions, and do not embrace the kind of dualism that we saw in ancient Gnosticism. But what they do have in common with the ancient Gnostics is their emphasis on intuitive knowledge of the divine that resides in the human soul.

Suggestions for Further Reading

In what follows, the suggestions for further reading—listed under the various chapters—are limited to a few English language items only, since this book is meant for a general readership. To be sure, much important scholarship on Gnosticism is published in other languages, principally German, French, Italian, and Spanish. For a complete bibliography on works published in all languages on Gnosticism and the Coptic Gnostic codices, see David M. Scholer, *Nag Hammadi Bibliography 1948–1969* (Nag Hammadi Studies 1; Leiden: E. J. Brill, 1971), and *Nag Hammadi Bibliography 1970–1994* (Nag Hammadi and Manichaean Studies 32; Leiden: E. J. Brill, 1997). Annual supplements are published in the journal *Novum Testamentum*. For information on critical editions and translations of, and studies on, the Coptic texts, readers are referred to this resource.

For an excellent up-to-date reference work on all aspects of Gnosticism, Hermetism, and Western esoteric groups, containing special articles, with bibliography, on primary literature, persons, and movements, see Wouter J. Hanegraaff, et al., eds., *Dictionary of Gnosis and Western Esotericism* (2 vols., Leiden: E. J. Brill, 2005).

Some of the material in this book is based on more detailed research published by me elsewhere, much of it in the following books: Birger A. Pearson, *Gnosticism, Judaism, and Egyptian Christianity* (Minneapolis: Fortress Press, 1990; reprint 2006); *The Emergence of the Christian Religion* (chapters 5–8, Harrisburg PA: Trinity Press International, 1997); and *Gnosticism and Christianity in Roman and Coptic Egypt* (chapters 7–10, New York/London: T&T Clark International, 2004).

Chapter 1

On problems of definition, see Michael A. Williams, *Rethinking "Gnosticism": An Argument for Dismantling a Dubious Category* (Princeton, NJ: Princeton University Press, 1996); Antti Marjanen, *Was There a Gnostic Religion?* (Publications of the Finnish Exegetical Society 87; Göttingen: Vandenhoeck & Ruprecht, 2005; essays by Marjanen, Michael Williams, Birger Pearson, Karen King, and Gerd Lüdemann); Bentley Layton, "Prolegomena to the Study of Ancient Gnosticism," in L. Michael White and O. Larry Yarborough, eds., *The Social World of the First Christians: Essays in Honor of Wayne A. Meeks* (Minneapolis: Fortress Press, 1995), pp. 334–50; Pearson, "Gnosticism as a Religion," chapter 7 in *Gnosticism and Christianity*, pp. 201–23. For full-length treatments of Gnosticism by noted historians of religions, see Kurt Rudolph, *Gnosis: The Nature and History of Gnosticism,* trans. R. McL. Wilson (San Francisco: Harper & Row, 1983); Giovanni Filoramo, *A History of Gnosticism,* trans. A. Alcock (Oxford: Basil Blackwell, 1990). Still valuable is Hans Jonas, *The Gnostic Religion: The Message of the Alien God and the Beginnings of Christianity,* 2d. rev. ed. (Boston: Beacon Press, 1963).

Chapter 2

On Simon Magus, see Stephen Haar, *Simon Magus: The First Gnostic?* (Beihefte zur Zeitschrift für die neutestamentliche Wissenschaft 119; Berlin/New York: Walter de Gruyter, 2003); Jarl E. Fossum,

The Name of God and the Angel of the Lord: Samaritan and Jewish Concepts of Intermediation and the Origin of Gnosticism (Wissenschaftliche Untersuchungen zum Neuen Testament 36; Tübingen: Mohr-Siebeck, 1985). On Cainites, see Pearson, "Cain and the Cainites," chapter 6 in *Gnosticism, Judaism*, pp. 95–107. On the other groups see Scholer, *Nag Hammadi Bibliography*, and Hauegraaff, *Dictionary of Gnosis.*

Chapter 3

On Sethian Gnosticism see John D. Turner, *Sethian Gnosticism and the Platonic Tradition* (Bibliothèque copte de Nag Hammadi, "Etudes" 6; Québec: Les Presses de l'Université Laval, Louvain/ Paris: Peeters, 2001). On the *Gospel of Judas* see Rodolphe Kasser, Marvin Meyer, and Gregor Wurst, *The Gospel of Judas from Codex Tchacos* (Washington, D.C.: National Geographic Society, 2006). On the individual Coptic tractates see the introductions in *NH Scriptures.*

Chapter 4

On Sophia see George W. MacRae, "The Jewish Background of the Gnostic Sophia Myth," *Novum Testamentum* 12 (1970), 86–101. On the Gnostic anthropogony see Pearson, "Biblical Exegesis in Gnostic Literature," chapter 2 in *Gnosticism, Judaism*, pp. 29–38. On the serpent see Pearson, "Jewish Haggadic Traditions in *The Testimony of Truth* from Nag Hammadi (CG IX,3)," chapter 3 in *Gnosticism, Judaism*, pp. 39–51. On Cain see Pearson, "Cain and the Cainites," chapter 6 in *Gnosticism, Judaism*, pp. 95–107. On Seth see Pearson, "The Figure of Seth in Gnostic Literature," chapter 4 in *Gnosticism, Judaism*, pp. 52–83. On Norea see Pearson, "The Figure of Norea in Gnostic Literature," chapter 5 in *Gnosticism, Judaism*, pp. 84–93. On the varieties of Gnostic biblical interpretation see Pearson, "Old Testament Interpretation in Gnostic Literature," chapter 6 in *Emergence*, pp. 99–121.

Chapter 5

On Basilides see Pearson, "Basilides the Gnostic," in Antti Marjanen and Petri Luomanen, eds., *A Companion to Second-Century Christian "Heretics"* (Supplements to Vigiliae Christianae 76; Leiden; E. J. Brill, 2005).

Chapter 6

On Valentinus and Valentinian Gnosticism see Einar Thomassen, *The Spiritual Seed: The Church of the "Valentinians"* (Nag Hammadi and Manichaean Studies 60; Leiden: E. J. Brill, 2006). On the individual Coptic tractates see the introductions in *NH Scriptures*.

Chapter 7

On the Naassene Psalm see Miroslav Marcovich, "The Naassene Psalm in Hippolytus," in Marcovich, *Studies in Graeco-Roman Religions and Gnosticism* (Studies in Greek and Roman Religion 4: Leiden: E. J. Brill, 1988), 80–88. On the Naassenes and the other groups discussed in this chapter, see Scholer, *Nag Hammadi Bibliography*.

Chapter 8

See Scholer, *Nag Hammadi Bibliography,* and the introductions in *NH Scriptures*.

Chapter 9

On the *Gospel of Thomas* and Thomas Christianity see April D. DeConick, *Recovering the Original Gospel of Thomas: A History of the Gospel and its Growth* (Library of New Testament Studies 286; London/New York: T&T Clark International, 2005).

Chapter 10

For the latest English translation of the Greek *Corpus Hermeticum* and the Latin *Asclepius* see Brian P. Copenhaver, *Hermetica* (Cambridge: Cambridge University Press, 1992). On the *Poimandres* see Pearson, "Jewish Elements in *Corpus Hermeticum* I (*Poimandres*)," chapter 9 in Pearson, *Gnosticism, Judaism,* pp. 136–47. On Hermetism and its history see Garth Fowden, *The Egyptian Hermes: A Historical Approach to the Late Pagan Mind* (Princeton, NJ: Princeton University Press, 1986); Roelof van den Broek and Cis van Heertum, eds., *From Poimandres to Jacob Böhme: Gnosis, Hermetism and the Christian Tradition* (Amsterdam: Bibliotheca Philosophica Hermetica, 2000).

Chapter 11

For a complete bibliography on Mani and Manichaeism see Gunner B. Mikkelsen, *Biliographia Manichaica: A Comprehensive Bibliography of Manichaeism through 1996* (Corpus Fontium Manichaeorum, Subsidia 1; Turnhout, Belgium: Brepols, 1997). On the history of Manichaeism see Samuel N. C. Lieu, *Manichaeism in the Later Roman Empire and Medieval China,* 2nd rev. ed. (Wissenschaftliche Untersuchungen zum Neuen Testament 63; Tübingen: Mohr-Siebeck, 1992). For English translations of Eastern Manichaean texts see Hans-Joachim Klimkeit, *Gnosis on the Silk Road: Gnostic Texts from Central Asia* (San Francisco: HarperSanFrancisco, 1993). On Seth and Sethian traditions in Manichaeism see Pearson, "The Figure of Seth in Manichaean Literature," chapter 10 in *Gnosticism and Christianity,* pp. 268–82.

Chapter 12

On the Mandaeans see Jorunn Jacobsen Buckley, *The Mandaeans: Ancient Texts and Modern People* (Oxford: Oxford University

Press, 2002); Edmondo Lupieri, *The Mandaeans: The Last Gnostics*, trans. Charles Hindley (Grand Rapids, MI: William B. Eerdmanns, 2002.

Epilogue

On the "persistence" of Gnosticism see Robert A. Segal, ed., *The Allure of Gnosticism: The Gnostic Experience in Jungian Psychology and Contemporary Culture* (Chicago: Open Court, 1995).

Indexes

Names and Subjects

as punishers, 228–29
See also specific angels
anthropogony, 14
Antonius Pius, 143–44
Anush, 321
See also Enush
Apocalypse of Adam, 69–74, 79,
108, 131
Apocalypse of James, 172, 230–34
Apocalypse of Moses, 70, 121
Apocalypse of Paul, 228–29, 283
Apocalypse of Peter, 242–44
Apocryphon of James, 218–21
Apocryphon (Secret Book) of John,
10–11, 35, 55, 61–69, 101, 104–
5, 107, 111–12, 116–17, 130,
149, 267, 280
apostles. *See* specific apostles
Archon, 138–43, 185–86, 198
archons, 48, 58, 117, 185–86
as creators, 40, 52–53, 66, 107,
140, 223
as demons, 16
as evil, 224–25, 238, 240–41, 253,
302–3
as God, 138, 198
as rapists, 128–29, 224
as rulers, 47, 65–67, 75–78, 107
as seducers, 123, 128–29, 130, 299
See also Hypostasis of the Archons
Archontics, 53–54, 89–92
Ariael, 223. *See also* Samael;
Yaldabaoth
Aristotle, 103, 213
'Asa'el, 130
Ascension of Paul, 49
Asclepius. *See* Tat
Asclepius (text), 286–89
Askew Codex, 2, 4, 22, 24, 252–53.
See also Pistis Sophia
Athanasius, 24
Attis, 191–93

Augustine, St.
on heretics, 21
on Manichaeism, 294, 300, 307,
310–11
on Thoth, 274
Autogenes, 60, 63, 65, 80, 90, 96,
192. *See also* Adamas
Aza, 127
Azael, 127

baptism
and Philip's teachings, 26
ritual, 33–34, 54, 60, 68, 73–75,
98, 179, 201, 324
See also ablutions
Barbelo, 51, 55, 57, 68–69, 78, 84,
88–90, 236
as aeon, 90, 93, 96
as Mother of Autogenes, 60
as Sophia, 69
as Thought, 64
as thought, 74, 110
Barbelognostics, 55
Bardaisan, 297, 300
Bartholomew, 217, 229
Baruch (person), 43
Baruch (text), 42–43
Basilides, 3, 34, 134–35, 241, 248, 334
anthropogony, 138–29
cosmogony, 137–38
Epiphanius on, 136, 138, 144
ethical theory, 140–41
Hippolytus on, 135, 143
Irenaeus on, 136–44
life of, 143–44
mythological system, 136–41
soteriology, 140
sources, 135–36
and Valentinus, 149
Basilidian Gnosticism, 134–44, 241,
334. *See also* specific Basilidian
scholars

Biblical Passages